C. Brad Faught is Professor and Chair of the Department of History at Tyndale University College in Toronto. A fellow of the Royal Historical Society and a senior fellow of Massey College at the University of Toronto, he is the author of five previous books. In 2012, he was the recipient of the Queen Elizabeth II Diamond Jubilee Medal.

'Written in a very clear and readable style and based upon thorough and excellent research. The various and often dramatic phases of Kitchener's rapid rise to national and international fame are chronicled with great skill, shrewdness and sensitivity... one of the best biographies of Kitchener to be written so far.'

Denis Judd, author of *Empire: The British Imperial Experience from 1765 to the Present* (I.B.Tauris, 2012)

C. BRAD FAUGHT

KITCHENER

HERO AND ANTI-HERO

I.B.TAURIS

LONDON · NEW YORK

Published in 2016 by
I.B.Tauris & Co. Ltd
London • New York
www.ibtauris.com

Copyright © 2016 C. Brad Faught

ISBN: 978 1 78453 350 2
eISBN: 978 0 85772 960 6

A full CIP record for this book is available from the British Library
A full CIP record is available from the Library of Congress

Library of Congress Catalog Card Number: available

Typeset in Garamond Three by OKS Prepress Services, Chennai, India
Printed and bound in Sweden by ScandBook

To the memory of my grandfather, Gunner John George Faught,
a Canadian soldier of World War I

Also by the Author

Clive: Founder of British India
Into Africa: The Imperial Life of Margery Perham
The New A-Z of Empire: A Concise Handbook of British Imperial History
Gordon: Victorian Hero
The Oxford Movement: A Thematic History of the Tractarians and Their Times

Contents

Preface

W riting a full-scale biography of the British military officer and statesman Horatio Herbert Kitchener, Earl Kitchener of Khartoum (1850–1916), in what is a thoroughly post-colonial and post-British imperial age, begs the question, it seems to me, of why? A century after his death and well-beyond the time in which he was considered to be both heroic and important, what is there about him that might repay close re-examination? The ongoing centenary of World War I, as well as the marking of the one hundredth anniversary of the death of Kitchener himself this year, might provide reason enough for a new biography, and in part I am motivated by these two reasons. But beyond mere chronological convenience, lie the compelling and resonant questions of his contestable historical reputation in Britain, as well as in the colonies and territories of the former British Empire, especially where he was active. It is part of the normal undulations of history that the reputations of great men and women rise and fall in public estimation, and Kitchener's is clearly one of these. From the moment of his shocking death by drowning in June of 1916, Kitchener's life story fell into the hands of biographers and publicists of various kinds, and if nothing else an examination of a hundred years of how he has been assessed and re-assessed makes for a highly revealing exercise in epochal historical reading.

In 1920, four years after Kitchener's death and two years removed from the end of the cataclysmic World War I, Sir George Arthur, who had been his personal private secretary during the first two years of the conflict, published a three-volume official biography, *Life of Lord Kitchener*.[1]

Arthur's biography is long (approximately a thousand pages), apologetic, and traditionally heroic; in other words, it is emblematic of its time and would go on to hold the field as the last word on Kitchener for a generation. That is not to say, however, that in the years between Arthur's work and the publishing of the next full-length biography of him – *Kitchener: Portrait of an Imperialist*, by Philip Magnus in 1958 – other, contrary, words were not spoken. Indeed they were, and principally such words came from Winston Churchill, as well as from the wartime Prime Minister, David Lloyd George. The mutual disaffection of Lloyd George and Kitchener, in particular, was a clear feature of their relationship as fellow Cabinet ministers from 1914 to 1916, and in his *War Memoirs*, published beginning in 1933, Lloyd George gave full vent to his negative feelings about his erstwhile colleague.[2] To him, Kitchener had been a martinet and a bungler and therefore had mismanaged the first two years of the British war effort, prior to his own succeeding in office of the deceased War Secretary, and then later of the Prime Minister himself, H.H. Asquith, in December 1916. Arthur may have still held the field in the 1930s, but Lloyd George's dyspeptic memoirs did much to damage Kitchener's posthumous standing in Britain and elsewhere. Not until Magnus's biography was published 25 years later did a fuller-orbed picture of a highly complex man whose record and reputation had been forged largely through 40 years' service as a pro-consular figure of empire, and not by a brief, though highly pivotal, ministerial career, take hold in the mind of the contemporary public.[3] Magnus was much closer to Lloyd George's critical stance towards Kitchener than he was to Arthur's relative hagiography, but altogether the subject still remained in wait of superior work.

Since Magnus's in 1958 a number of other major biographies of Kitchener have been published: George Cassar's in 1977; Trevor Royle's in 1985; and, most recently, John Pollock's two-volume work in 1998 and 2001, respectively, of which Cassar's is the most perceptive and did much to re-set the balance in how Kitchener was viewed both by scholars and, to a lesser extent, by the wider public.[4] In addition, Kitchener's life and work has been the subject of many shorter biographies and essays. As well, he has been portrayed in the well-known feature films *Khartoum* (1966) and *Breaker Morant* (1980), and his life examined in a television documentary, *Reputations: Kitchener: The Empire's Flawed Hero*, broadcast by the BBC in 1998.

Our own age, while much less interested in and accepting of the traditionally heroic status accorded Kitchener by his contemporaries, reveals its own preoccupations by focusing on, for example, his allegedly ambiguous sexual identity; or more pointedly, his 'minorism', as the term of the time denoted homosexuality. 'Was "K" Gay?', asked a writer in 1999.[5] The field of Kitchener scholarship today, therefore, is contested in ways that have changed but remain linked nonetheless to the foundational 'hero/anti-hero' cleavage that has long defined studies of him and continues – as this book will seek to demonstrate – to repay investigation in light of much recent scholarship concerning the idea of the 'heroic'. Indeed, one recent study has argued persuasively that perhaps it is time to amend the viewing of Kitchener through such a dichotomous lens altogether by suggesting a new category entirely: Kitchener as 'anachronistic' hero.[6]

At any rate, in writing this up-to-date biography my main aspiration has been to comprehend Kitchener as fully as possible within the context of his own time and thereby avoid either overt approbation of him on one hand, or censure by a twenty-first-century readership on the other. Of course all good biography attempts to achieve this kind of balanced end, but the reputations of outsized historical figures such as Kitchener make the task more difficult than it is with lesser or little known subjects. Accordingly, and with the benefit of much antecedent scholarship and full access to the rich Kitchener archive, it is hoped that his life as portrayed here may be as complete as the form allows. Biography, like any other historico-literary pursuit is partial; indeed, its very nature makes it to be such. But to the degree that exhaustiveness can be achieved within the arc of some 120,000 words this book attempts to capture Kitchener the man in all stages and places of his life, ranging as it did from his childhood in Ireland through a number of significant military, governmental, and pro-consular appointments in Sudan, Egypt, South Africa, India, and, of course, finally, in England itself. In the end, it will be suggested that the original impulse of biographers to designate him as heroic was correct, although requiring of significant caveats.

Acknowledgements

History-book writing is a collaborative exercise and cannot be undertaken successfully without the help and support of a number of people and institutions. To that end, firstly, I should like to thank the staff at the National Archives (NA) in London. The NA holds the main collection of Kitchener Papers and writing his biography would simply be impossible without access to this finely-housed collection. Similarly, the Kitchener letters that form part of the larger India Office archive kept at the British Library (BL) in London are an invaluable source for a biographer. I thank the staff of the BL's Asian & African Studies Reading Room for their excellent service, as well as those in the Western Manuscripts Reading Room. I should like to thank also the Bodleian Library, Oxford, for its related manuscript sources, especially the Asquith Papers. The National Portrait Gallery in London is a treasure-trove of photos for a subject like Kitchener so my thanks go to the staff there for providing many of the images reproduced in this book. My thanks go also to the Broome Park Golf and Country Club in Kent – the site of Kitchener's former country estate – for allowing me to wander round the property at will and to take photographs, one of which is reproduced in the pages that follow.

In the service of writing this book I travelled to India in order to see up-close some of the places where Kitchener lived and worked during the first decade of the twentieth century when he was Commander in Chief of the Army in India. In particular, I would like to thank the administration and staff of the Indira Gandhi Medical College hospital ('Snowdon Hospital'), Wildflower Hall Hotel, and the Indian Institute of Advanced Study (formerly Viceregal Lodge), all of which are located in Shimla, the one-time 'Queen of the Hill Stations' and as such the former summer capital of the Raj, for the privilege of seeing around their premises and grounds. In Ireland, I would like to thank Patrick and Philomena Galvin for showing me around the site of Kitchener's childhood home, Crotta House, near Kilflynn, Co. Kerry.

My sincere thanks go also to Dr Lester Crook and Jo Godfrey, senior history editors at I.B.Tauris, and to Sophie Campbell, production editor, for expertly guiding the commissioning and publication of this book, my third with I.B.Tauris. All three experiences with them have been excellent.

Equally, I would like to thank Tyndale University College in Toronto, where I teach, especially its recently retired dean, Dr Douglas Loney, as well as his successor, Dr Barry Smith. Research funding and a sabbatical were readily forthcoming from Tyndale over the past couple of years and the book could not have been written without such stellar help. Also, best thanks to my outstanding colleagues in the Department of History at Tyndale, Professors Eric Crouse and Ian Gentles; and to my students, past and present, for their intellectual curiosity, and for making the content of the history courses that I have been teaching now for a number of years always seem fresh.

As usual, and happily so, my greatest debt is to my wife, Rhonda, and our two children, Claire and Luke, who sometimes wonder why quite *so many* visits to the UK are required in order to complete my books. But over time they have gotten used to the routine of a British historian in the house whose work requires regular trips across the Atlantic. For this, and much else – including the work Claire did preparing a comprehensive bibliography of works on Kitchener – I am very grateful.

List of Illustrations

Plate 1. Wildflower Hall: Kitchener's verdant retreat located outside Shimla with a view of the Himalayas, as it appears today in winter as a luxury hotel. (Faught)

Plate 2. Viceregal Lodge, Shimla: The centre of summertime Raj life from the 1880s until 1947, as it looks today. (Faught)

Plate 3. Dhalli Tunnel, Shimla: Located on the road to Wildflower Hall, within which Kitchener broke his leg after falling from a skittish horse. (Faught)

Plate 4. Christ Church, Shimla: Even today the Mall is dominated by its tower. Kitchener attended divine service here weekly when in residence at nearby Snowdon. (Faught)

Plate 5. Broome Park, Kent: The refurbished country estate located near Canterbury barely lived in by Kitchener before his death, which is now a golf club. (Faught)

Plate 6. 2 Carlton Gardens, London: Kitchener lived here in 1914–15, located a short walk from the War Office and across the street from his old nemesis, Lord Curzon. (Faught)

Plate 7. Kitchener *c.* 1885: Kitchener sporting a hint of a smile, something that in photographs he almost never did. Taken at the time of the Gordon Relief Expedition. (NPG 136566)

Plate 8. 1903: Kitchener with his circle of close advisers, including Raymond 'Conk' Marker (second from right), at Shimla. (NPG 193210)

Plate 9. 1910: Kitchener laden with medals, between his years in India and those to come in Egypt. (NPG 35370)

Plate 10. 1914: Kitchener with Marshal Joffre of France leaving the War Office after a meeting. Already the strain of being Secretary of State for War is evident. (NPG 194022)

Plate 11. 1884: General Charles Gordon, Kitchener's hero, on the eve of his fateful departure for Khartoum. (NPG 29693)

Plate 12. Early 1900s: As wartime prime minister, H.H. Asquith understood Kitchener's value to the nation. (NPG 82302)

Plate 13. Early 1900s: Lord Curzon, as Kitchener would have known him during their tumultuous days in India. (NPG 136548)

Plate 14. NPG 197714, Early 1900s: As prime minister, Arthur Balfour ultimately backed Kitchener in his dispute with Curzon. (NPG 197714)

Plate 15. 1903: In defence of her husband, Lady Curzon came to loathe Kitchener, but earlier they had been great friends. (NPG 135594)

Plates 16 and 17. Crotta House, Kitchener's Irish childhood home, located near Kilflynn, Co. Kerry, as it appears today. The Great House is gone; only the former stables and servants' quarters remain standing. (Faught)

1

An Irish and Continental Childhood and Youth, 1850–67

By 1850, Ireland was just over the worst of the cataclysmic potato famine which had brought about both depopulation and emigration on a massive scale over the preceding five years. However, the deaths of as many as one million people and the departure of about a million more meant that the country – having endured a decline in its population amounting to about 25 per cent of the total – would suffer for generations, and as a cause of both ongoing strife between England and Ireland and of political upheaval the potato famine was of singular impact. Issues of land tenure, rental, evictions, and dispossession had long stalked Ireland stretching all the way back to the time of Oliver Cromwell and even earlier. Indeed, conflict over land ownership and tenancy was chronic in Ireland and the years of the famine served to exacerbate all such pre-existing tensions.

In that year, and owing to the consequent attractive land market there to anyone possessed of a reasonable amount of capital, Colonel Henry Horatio Kitchener, aged 45 and at long last married, decided to leave active military service – most recently in the 29th Foot (the Worcestershire Regiment) stationed in India – and settle in Ireland. Of a piece with Ireland's cheap and plentiful land was its quick sale facilitated by the British Parliament's recently-passed Encumbered Estates Act.

Colonel Kitchener was a veteran officer, having first purchased a commission in 1829 in the 13th Dragoons. Little active soldiering occurred for him, however, until the spring of 1842 when he sailed to India with the 29th Foot, his new regiment. After returning home to England later to marry, he then took his young wife, Anne Frances (Fanny) Chevallier, with him back to India in 1845, directly following their delayed nuptials. Stationed at the tiny garrison town of Kussowlie, a little south of what would later become the summer capital of British India at Simla (now known as Shimla), Kitchener, his wife, and their first-born child (in 1846) Henry Elliott Chevallier (called 'Chevally') lived a rather desultory – and for Fanny, an unhealthy – life in the Himalayan foothills. After a few years of increasing infirmity for his beleaguered wife Colonel Kitchener decided that staying on in India was impossible and the family therefore returned to England. A second child – Frances Emily, known as 'Millie' was born in 1848 – and after a brief spell in London a second move was then made across to Ireland, to a large property of some 2,000 acres in the west that bestrode the boundary between Counties Kerry and Limerick and was near to the town of Listowel. Called Ballygoghlan, the estate's owner was a bankrupt and happy to sell his down-at-heels property to Kitchener. Though in a 'wretched state', the prospects for the property's rehabilitation were good.[1] The L3,000 deal therefore closed in April 1850. A little over two months later on 24 June, the couple's third child and second son, Horatio Herbert – named in honour of Admiral Nelson as many English baby boys continued to be in those days, but always going by his second name – was born while Fanny stayed temporarily nearby at Gunsborough Villa, as renovations were already underway at Ballygoghlan.

The 1850s in Ireland proved to be good and prosperous years for the Kitchener family. Having sold his commission, Colonel Kitchener (as he would always be known) plunged into the life of a gentleman farmer, and met with ready success.[2] The size of the family grew with the arrival of more children (Arthur in 1852 and Walter in 1858), Ballygoghlan was improved and enlarged, and in 1857 a second estate, Crotta House, was purchased. Crotta, located nearby to the south and of a considerably grander architectural style than the humbler Ballygoghlan, dated from the seventeenth century. Accordingly, it became the main family residence thereafter and gave evidence of the sturdily gentrified nature of Colonel Kitchener's social status in local Anglo-Irish society. These two houses were at the centre of young Herbert's upbringing and that of his four siblings.

The mid-Victorian era provided the shaping contours of Herbert Kitchener's boyhood formation. His early years were ones in which the British abroad would receive their sternest military tests since the Napoleonic Wars: first, at Crimea from 1852 to 1855, and then in India during the Indian Rebellion (or Mutiny) from 1857 until 1859. At home, the Conservatives under a succession of leaders, the most impressive of whom would be Benjamin Disraeli, contested the political field with the newly-formed Liberals, who later would throw up their own titanic leader in the form of William Ewart Gladstone.[3] Kitchener came of age therefore in a world of outsized political leaders presiding over a period of robust imperial expansion when assumptions about national might and right were commonplace in Britain.[4] And for the child-Kitchener, measuring himself in a military manner began at home under the perspicacious eye of his father, the Colonel. All extant accounts of Colonel Kitchener emphasize his military bearing, his precision not to say punctiliousness, a thoroughgoing dedication to order, and an eccentric wont, suggested, for example, by his apparent use of newspapers rather than blankets in order to more closely regulate cold and warmth.[5]

In the manner of private education of the time, only then beginning to give way to the prestigious Victorian public school, and as a cost-saving measure, Herbert was educated at home by tutors; in his case Church of England clergymen and, for a time, by a cousin named Francis (Frank) Kitchener, a fellow of Trinity College, Cambridge on his way to a career as a schoolmaster. The young Kitchener's father insisted on home tuition even though such education was both rather perfunctory and sometimes spotty. However, its method of private delivery suited the son perfectly as it accorded with his generally reticent nature and with his own sense of local social superiority as a young Englishman living amongst the 'outcaste' Irish peasantry. As one of Kitchener's biographers put it, perhaps in hyperbolic but certainly in suggestively racist terms: he and his siblings were raised to 'regard themselves as the members of a master race in a strange land'.[6] In any event, his upbringing in Ireland – like that of Wellington in the late eighteenth century – was never deemed an impediment to career success even if it always remained somewhat declasse in the social circles within which later the adult-Kitchener would move. No one, it seems, no matter how exalted, could escape the reach of English class snobbery, whether it be a top military leader like Kitchener or a victorious political chief such as Gladstone. 'Ah, Oxford on the surface, but Liverpool below', was the cutting remark made by an unnamed Whig grandee about the Eton- and Christ Church-educated but Liverpool-born future prime minister in 1860.[7]

In the late 1850s Kitchener's physical growth continued apace and as he approached his tenth birthday he was tall and slim with brownish blonde hair and sharp blue eyes, the left one of which contained a small but noticeable imperfection in the form of a cast, sometimes regarded as a sign of good luck. He was also about to experience the beginning of the end of this sylvan period of his childhood. The military nature of his father's exertion of familial discipline continued, and indeed was considered normal for the time: for some early infraction Kitchener once was staked out on the ground spread-eagle style and left to endure the elements in the manner stipulated by the British Army's Field Punishment No. 1.[8] But if the Colonel belonged to the school of discipline that a later generation would call tough love, Kitchener's mother, Fanny, was the fount of all contemporary maternal tenderness and devotion. In Herbert's relationship with his mother he was solicitous and venerative and as her health deteriorated markedly after the birth of her last child (Walter) in 1858, that tendency grew to be even stronger.

Fanny Kitchener epitomized well the elevated state in which respectable Victorian womanhood was held.[9] Her goodness and virtue went unquestioned; her love was believed to be unwavering; and her health was considered delicate. It is not too strong to say that this characterization was a trope in Victorian society and any criticism of it or worse, violation of it or of such women themselves, was considered to be amongst the most heinous of contemporary social and sexual transgressions. Hence, for example, the acute moral outrage felt in Britain over the savage treatment accorded the 220 British women (and children) who were initially imprisoned, and then the survivors of which who were violently butchered at Cawnpore by mutineers in 1857 during the Indian Rebellion.[10]

Fanny's obvious decline in health coincided with the hiring in 1858 of a young woman as nanny to the five children. Herbert was eight years old when the future Mrs Sharpe – 'Nanny Sharpe', no first or maiden name was ever recorded – arrived at Crotta House, and to her fell the close care of the children in light of their mother's increasing invalidism. Many years later, and following her former young charge's death after having become the world-famous Earl Kitchener of Khartoum, Mrs Sharpe would leave an interview record of her memories of the years she spent as the Kitchener family's nanny. She remembered all of the children as being 'affectionate' and living a 'very simple country life'. Order and discipline were absolute under the Colonel, as 'I heard him once say to a servant, 8 o'clock is the breakfast hour and now it is nearly one minute past . . . . So no wonder that in after years Lord Kitchener was such a rigid disciplinarian. It was bred in him'.[11] Nanny Sharpe's duties extended naturally to deepening the children's devotional exercises in Bible reading and prayer. 'Little Herbert was not a good reader,' she recalled some 60 years later, 'but he was quick to grasp a truth or an idea, and if he was once told a thing if it was worth remembering he never forgot it'. Increasingly, the children's prayers were centred on the compromised health of their ailing mother, but in Herbert's case at least they also included a suggestion of a growing career aspiration. Upon Nanny Sharpe's relating to the children the story of a devout soldier by the name of Hedley Vicars, who was 'a soldier of the Lord your Christ, as well as a soldier of the Queen . . . Herbert said I mean to be a soldier when I grow up and be like Hedley Vicars'.[12]

The passage of time and Kitchener's resultant fame may have rendered Nanny Sharpe's memories both fuzzy and purple in this regard, but they do nonetheless have the ring of truth about them. And certainly her comment that the young Herbert 'liked a little bit of quiet' is an observation that fits well the private, even repressed, nature of the man to come.[13]

By the early 1860s the Kitchener household was resigned to the sad permanency of Fanny's physical infirmity. She was suffering from tuberculosis, 'consumption' as it was called then, which attacked the young and middle-aged especially and thereby carried with it a particularly sharp pathos for its victims and their loved ones. In the years prior to the late nineteenth-century discovery of antibiotics – penicillin especially – there existed only the hope of 'breathing cures' for consumptives, which meant that those with sufficient means removed themselves to places where the air was thought to be clear and light and therefore restorative to lungs ravaged by the remorseless disease. All kinds of examples abound in Victorian Britain of those suffering from consumption seeking to find relief in some commodious location. Richard Hurrell Froude, for example, an early Tractarian whose fiery denunciation of what he believed were the irredeemable erastian compromises of the Church of England made him the scourge of Anglican Broad Churchmen, took himself off to Barbados for just such a purpose in 1833. He returned to England in 1835, however, no better than when he had left, dying promptly the next year, forever mourned by his ardent friend and Oxford Movement co-religionist, John Henry Newman.[14]

As Fanny's consumption worsened in what was (wrongly) assumed to be the miasma of Irish air she had to breathe as a result of living near the River Shannon, the Colonel decided that to save his wife's life he must sell up and move the family to a more healthful climate. Switzerland was decided upon in this regard, its higher elevation and more frequent sunshine being considered just the thing for consumptives and a number of spa towns there catered exactly to what it was thought Fanny's condition required. Accordingly, the now much improved and markedly profitable Irish properties were sold at a profit and in the summer of 1863 when Herbert was just entering his teens the family packed up and headed across the Irish Sea to the Continent proceeding to Bex, a small Swiss town near the eastern end of Lake Geneva on the banks of the Rhone river. Famous for its salt deposits which had been mined since the sixteenth century, more latterly Bex had also become a destination for those like Fanny who sought relief from consumption through its elevation (1,400 feet) and its fresh mountain air. Bex was to be their home only briefly, however, before the family moved on to nearby Montreux, seen to be an even better place for those suffering from respiratory diseases. Similarly located on Lake Geneva at the foot of the Alps, Montreux with a population then of about 5,000, was just beginning to attract tourists as well as those seeking health cures, a number that would expand steadily as the century wore on. Today, known best as the home of a famed summer jazz festival, in the 1860s Montreux was a key Continental community for British expatriates and the Kitchener family settled well into life there. But, alas, it would not be for long. A year later, in the summer of 1864, Fanny died, not yet having reached 40 years of age. Though her death had been a long time in coming the family was devastated by it all the same, 14-year-old Herbert not the least among them. Fanny Kitchener's funeral and interment took place at the Anglican church in Montreux, Christ Church, Clarens, a beautiful small stone structure with a peaked roof and spire. Entirely reminiscent of what the bereaved family would have known in Ireland, the church itself perhaps provided some minimal comfort at the nadir of their collective grief.

Losing his mother at such a formative age doubtless effected Kitchener's emotional development. Unsurprisingly for a boy of Kitchener's stern, militaristic upbringing, he did not write down what her passing meant to him. Referred to as the 'great sorrow of his life' by one of his biographers, modern psychology would suggest that such a loss might well have yielded a range of reactions in Kitchener, including emotional depression, as well as repression of a sexual nature.[15] His retiring bent probably was reinforced by her now permanent absence, and the mid-Victorian cultural imperative of apotheosizing women would likely have been confirmed for Kitchener by the sense of his mother having had sacrificed her health in the service of husband and children. At any rate, Fanny's death occasioned the break-up of the family unit. In light of the Colonel's close example, a military career for most or all of his sons was natural and expected. Chevally (Henry) duly was sent back to England where he soon enrolled as an officer cadet at the Royal Military College Sandhurst. As for Herbert, Arthur, and Walter, considerable primary and secondary schooling still awaited them in Switzerland at the Chateau du Grand Clos in Rennaz, a small establishment in a tiny village of fewer than 200 people located near Montreux. The school occupied a grand fifteenth-century house and was what a later age would call 'international' in scope, designed for the education of young (English) expatriates. Herbert would spend the next three years of his life at the school, a time that he neither wrote of nor talked about later as an adult. If adolescence for many is a time of adventure and joy, neither of these things seemed to mark Kitchener's life under the supervisory hand of the Reverend John Bennet, chaplain at Christ Church in Montreux and in loco parentis of the three younger Kitchener boys. Bennet's supervision was necessary for the last part of this period in the lives of Herbert and Walter because in January of 1867 the Colonel chose to re-marry and move to New Zealand in order to re-start family life in what promised to be a productive farm near Palmerston on the South Island. Over two years had passed since the death of Fanny, so the marriage and move cannot be seen as peremptory. Still, the Antipodes was a long distance to go and the family was to some extent sundered by the move, at least temporarily. The Colonel's new wife, Emma Green, had been a music teacher to the teenaged Millie, and together the three of them along with Arthur (the only son not destined for a military career) sailed for Down Under that winter. Later in 1867 a daughter, named Kawaru, in honour of an eponymous river in their new home, was born, a step-sister for the five older Kitchener siblings.

All through this time of family upheaval Herbert and his brothers had not been experiencing a happy time of it at the Chateau. But they persevered, among other things becoming fluent in French and passable in German. The Victorian English were as class conscious abroad as they were at home – perhaps even moreso – and in a way that E. M. Forster might later have captured in one of his novels, the Kitchener boys with their Irish accent and unsophisticated manner were not of the school's usual type and therefore did not fit in very successfully with the mostly English student population. Still, Herbert was hardly the first boy who would survive a less than satisfactory school experience to go on to prosper greatly elsewhere: Winston Churchill and his apparent sufferings at Harrow come immediately to mind. But that would require a return to England. So as a 16-year-old early in 1867 Kitchener did exactly that, removing permanently to England for the first time in his young life.

2

The Making of a Surveyor-Soldier, 1868–82

The immediate impetus for Kitchener's returning to England in the spring of 1867 was an undisclosed breakdown in his health. The nature of this malady is unrecoverable today from the available sources, but by that summer and the passing of his 17th birthday Kitchener had returned to physical fitness and was well into a period of intensive cramming in anticipation of sitting the entrance examination for admission to the Royal Military Academy Woolwich. Initially after returning from Switzerland, Kitchener had stayed with his cousin Frank in the latter's rooms at Trinity College, Cambridge, and at Rugby School where he then went to take up a teaching post. But once recovered from illness and ready to prepare for Woolwich, Kitchener moved down to London for a few months hard of work under the careful eye of the results-proven crammer, the Reverend George Frost. The genial Anglican clergyman was a good tutor, and while in residence in his Kensington house Kitchener not only readied himself academically for what the examination required but also struck up a warm and lasting friendship with a fellow crammer, Claude Conder, with whom he would have much to do over the next few years.

The Royal Military Academy Woolwich was the place of preparation for those seeking a commission either in the Royal Engineers or in the Royal Artillery. Known as 'The Shop' – a nickname having come from the fact that it had grown out of the old royal arsenal workshop at Woolwich – it was less glamorous than the Royal Military Academy

Sandhurst, which specialized in the cavalry and infantry, but its history stretching back to 1741 and establishment under the reign of King George II was no less storied. The same could also be said of its alumni, the most recently famous of whom included Colonel Charles 'Chinese' Gordon, the hero of the just-fought Taiping Rebellion in China, who had received his commission in the Royal Engineers in 1852 and whose life, as we shall see, would intersect in a vitally important way with Kitchener's own. But that was some distance in the future. For now, Kitchener was following the path that seemed almost inevitable for him as a son of the Colonel.[1] Whether or not the father preferred Herbert for Woolwich or Sandhurst is unclear, but the son himself was committed to the former and in January of 1868 he successfully sat the examination, his score coming exactly in the middle of those taking the test, ranking 28th out of 56 candidates.[2] The next month he began what would be almost three years as a gentleman-cadet. Herbert Kitchener's military career now was underway.

Not much is or can be known of Kitchener's years at Woolwich, however. A fire in 1873 destroyed just about the whole of the Shop's archives and records, including those that pertained to Kitchener's time there. He was not, and never had been, an academic high-flyer; but nor was he a mere 'plodder', as one of his early biographers would have it.[3] The general view held by the staff was that he was unremarkable, except for his height (he had now reached his maximum of 6' 2", very tall when the average height of a mid-Victorian male was about 5' 8"), and that he was a keen horseman. But existing beneath the parapet is no bad thing in the highly competitive atmosphere that prevails in any college or school and the naturally reticent Kitchener simply got on with his business. Photographs of the period show him to be notably handsome and well-proportioned with his hair parted quite precisely down the middle of his head. Undoubtedly, like just about any young man in the company of his peers, there was fun to be had, (small) acts of rebellion or hi-jinks. During his cadet years he may have emerged from a kind of self-imposed social retirement and become more inclined to fraternize, but altogether he remained reserved and even awkward in most social settings. What we do know more clearly about Kitchener the cadet is that his most important friendship at Woolwich was with Claude Conder, his former colleague at the crammer Frost's.

Conder was a little older than Kitchener, but they had similar interests and aspirations as 'sappers' (engineers) and perhaps as future surveyors. Conder was interested in languages, particularly those of the Middle East. Kitchener's own linguistic cosmopolitanism may have been a further bond. Whatever the impetus, they began to study Hebrew together with a view to a closer reading of the Old Testament. Engaging in such a pursuit during his personal time suggests a seriousness of mind beyond that typical of a budding military officer. Indeed, in their own amateur way the two young men were participating in a keenly-practiced Victorian pastime: that of pursuit of the ancient languages. Whether it was studying the classics of undergraduate 'Greats' fame at Oxbridge, or the necessarily more rarified learning of the Biblical languages that had grown out of German scholarship's move into Old and New Testament higher criticism earlier in the nineteenth century, studying languages as the key to unlocking Biblical textual meaning was little short of a rage in certain Victorian circles. In this way the young Kitchener was very much a man of his time and soon enough his antiquarian interests would coincide more clearly with both his abiding Christian religiosity and his first real professional military service.

In the meantime, Kitchener carried on with the required work of an engineer cadet and when out of term holidayed with family and friends in the south of England and then, beginning, after the New Year 1869, in France where the Colonel had finally settled permanently after a peripatetic couple of years going back and forth between England and New Zealand. The antipodean farming experiment had not gone as planned, and the Colonel decided that life could be lived best and certainly in those days more economically just across the Channel in Brittany, in a chateau near the beautiful riverside town of Dinan. Like a lot of other Englishmen – for example, Sir John Everett Millais, the celebrated painter and member of the Pre-Raphaelite Brotherhood, whose father had moved the family to Dinan for a few years when Millais was a child – the Colonel saw no incongruity and considerable convenience in taking up residence in northern France. For Kitchener himself, Dinan, then with a population of about 8,000 and built mostly high on the banks of the Rance river, became a favourite vacation destination and with his fluent French learned as a schoolboy in Switzerland an easy place to socialize and relax. His brothers would visit also, as would his sister Millie in the run-up to her impending marriage.

Altogether, after the disjointed years following the death of wife and mother Fanny, the complete family was able to reconvene and thereby re-establish their filial bond.

There is little doubt that Kitchener worked hard at the Shop, ploughing through a curriculum heavy with mathematics, geometry, chemistry, surveying, and drill. His time there would be punctuated by periods of vacation and even by an enforced brief leave of absence owing to another undisclosed illness, perhaps brought on by dint of the pressure of academic work as had likely been the case in 1867 in Switzerland. Beyond the lecture hall, library, and parade ground sport and recreation did not seem to matter very much to the young Kitchener. He would later point to eye trouble as being responsible for his routine avoidance of games. Perhaps relevant too was the fact that his formative private education had provided him with no opportunity for participating in team sports, something that had become greatly popular at the Victorian public school, as epitomized by the Arnoldian 'revolution' at Rugby in which schoolmaster cousin Frank Kitchener was just then participating.[4] Still, given his love of riding he raced steeplechase from time to time, attended dances, and in June of 1869 met the heroic Colonel Gordon at a celebratory Royal Engineers luncheon, a singular highlight of Kitchener's time as a cadet.[5]

In December of 1870, aged 20 years, Kitchener completed his training at Woolwich and successfully passed out of an institution that would go on producing generations of engineers and artillerymen for the British Army until the eve of World War II in 1939, when it was closed and its functions transferred eventually to Sandhurst where they have remained ever since. In military terms, Kitchener was an embryonic sapper awaiting his commission. He did not have long to wait, though. On 4 January 1871, he was gazetted as Lieutenant H.H. Kitchener, R.E. The date of his commission would shortly become problematic for him, however, because after spending the Christmas holidays with his father and family at Dinan he decided that since he was not yet commissioned and therefore technically a free agent, he would seek temporary action with the French, just then engaged in the Franco-Prussian War. At that moment in their brief but highly consequential war the Prussians were about to win a decisive victory from which would flow a declaration of German unity and proclamation of empire under the stentorian leadership of Chancellor Otto von Bismarck.

From his domestic perch high above Dinan old Colonel Kitchener was much engaged by the ongoing war between the up-thrusting Prussians and the overmatched French. The Battle of Sedan in September 1870 had produced an overwhelming Prussian victory, including the capture of France's emperor, Napoleon III, an ignominy that seemed defining of the course of the war.[6] A similar victory at Metz would follow in October and with Paris now under a brutal siege, the French were wholly desperate and on the verge of a general surrender. The Colonel may have become a late-in-life relative francophile, but fatherly advice to his son to join the French army in its hour of need was surely needlessly patriotic, even reckless. But such is what the young Kitchener followed and endeavoured to do. Together with a similarly inclined friend, Harry Dawson, Kitchener was put in touch with General Alfred Chanzy, who just then was attempting to withstand sustained Prussian might with an army comprised increasingly of conscripts. It is unclear whether or not Kitchener and Dawson themselves were ever admitted formally to French service.[7] They did manage to reach Chanzy's headquarters at Laval, however, although their arrival did not come until almost three weeks after what proved to be France's final defeat at Le Mans on 12 January 1871. France's fall now was inevitable. The Prussians, even though outmanned by a ratio of 3:1 (150,000 to 50,000), were battle-hardened professional soldiers opposed by a ragtag, even cowardly it was thought by some, French force. As if to prove the critics right, the French were duly routed, suffering some 25,000 casualties as compared to 9,400 for the Prussians. Altogether, Le Mans was an unmitigated disaster for the French, although Chanzy himself was regarded as both brave and sound in his generalship but hobbled irredeemably by inferior troops. By the time Kitchener got to the front the war therefore was essentially over and on 28 January with Paris in enemy hands the French government declared for an armistice formally ending the conflict.[8]

The tail-end of the Franco-Prussian War, accordingly, did not offer Kitchener any real soldiering, but it did serve up for him a first glimpse of the sights and sounds of semi-modern warfare. As it happened, some of these came from the vantage point of several hundred feet up in the air as Kitchener was offered and accepted a view of the front lines from a hot-air balloon. The episode has the feel of a stunt about it as ever since the Montgolfier brothers had launched the first hotter than air balloon in France in 1783 'balloonomania' had taken hold of both the military and of the popular mind in Europe. Kitchener never wrote about the experience, but presumably he thought it a quick way to gain a clear sense of the battlefield having missed out on the fighting, so up he went. Inappropriately dressed for the cold winter air, however, he got thoroughly chilled during his time aloft and soon enough went down with pneumonia. Recumbent and despairing in a rundown local inn Kitchener asked Dawson to contact the Colonel who came quickly to fetch his sick son. Kitchener would take some time to recover from this adventure. But it was not his physical health that was in peril so much as what his apparent violation of British neutrality might mean for his putative military career.

The timing and nature of Kitchener's actions in France were such that they became known rather swiftly at Horse Guards in London, to which he was duly summoned in March in order to stand under the judgement of the Commander in Chief of the British Army, Prince George, Duke of Cambridge. An overbearing authoritarian whose tenure at the head of the army would last some 40 years, the Duke was notorious for his sharp tongue and his intolerance of either change or challenge. In the Duke's overawing presence the jejeune Kitchener was wisely silent, but believing himself to have acted properly in that he was unaware of his 4 January British commission and therefore free to act in France as he chose, thought the whole business an exercise in tiresome military bureaucracy. At the interview the Duke acted true to form. In his usual forceful way and employing colourful language he dressed down the young lieutenant. As Kitchener recounted long afterwards, 'He called me every name he could lay his tongue to; and said I was a deserter, and that I had disgraced the British Army. I never said a word; and then at the end the Duke, with a funny sort of twinkle, added, 'Well, anyhow, boy, go away, and don't do it again'.[9]

In April 1871, following on his wryly dyspeptic encounter with the Duke of Cambridge, Kitchener was sent to Chatham, to the School of Military Engineering. Chatham was and is the depot for the Corps of Royal Engineers. It looks down over the Medway and across to the spire of Rochester Cathedral in whose shadow Charles Dickens had long lived at nearby Gad's Hill until his unexpectedly early death just the year before. For Kitchener, the next two years would prove to be professionally formative. He took surveying out of the classroom and applied it to the local topography. He rode out constantly and became even more comfortable in the saddle. Eventually, he sat the exams which marked his formal passage on the road to becoming a skilled military engineer. Socially during these years Kitchener's life was typically quiet and, for a time, intensely religious. His best friend at Chatham was a young officer named Captain R.H. Williams, whose introduction to Kitchener came as a result of a brief dust-up over contested room occupancy. Once settled, however, the two men became close friends – 'inseparable' is the way Williams described it – bound together by a shared professionalism and an even more seriously held Christian faith.[10]

The 1870s in Britain was a time in which the theological and liturgical controversies initiated by the Oxford Movement some 40 years earlier were still causing a roil within the Church of England, as well as in society more broadly. Beginning publicly in 1833 the men of the Oxford Movement had called for a sustained recovery of the independent Catholic heritage of the national church which, they maintained, had been compromised by the prevailing erastianism of the first third of the nineteenth century. Over the succeeding two generations, years marked by discord and departure (namely John Henry Newman's decision to leave the Church of England for Roman Catholicism in 1845), an intense brand of Anglo-Catholic churchmanship had developed whose spiritual leader was one of the founding Tractarians, Edward Bouverie Pusey. From his base at Christ Church, Oxford as Regius Professor of Hebrew, Pusey gave shape and meaning to the rituals and practices of Victorian Anglo-Catholicism. These, he believed, were reviving of a church that had grown both increasingly liberal and overly Protestant and therefore needed to be recalled to its ancient Catholic formularies. Within the context of the day where British freedom and prosperity were seen as being very closely allied with the country's manifest Protestantism, and where any brand of Catholicism was seen as implicitly Irish or suspiciously Continental and therefore to be feared, Anglo-Catholic ritualism was believed by many to be religiously suspect at best, and highly disruptive of the national fabric at worst.[11]

R.H. Williams was a devout Anglo-Catholic nonetheless and Kitchener's somewhat dormant Christian faith was revivified by the bracing, disciplined approach to Anglican Christianity taken by his new friend. Consequently, he too began to engage in a highly structured apprehension of religious life. Attendance at service or 'mass' became daily. The Eucharist was made much more central to his liturgical life. Fasting was occasionally practiced. In the mess hall, Kitchener told Williams that fasting would be easier if they were able to 'find something unpleasant' to eat, and the pair of them acted accordingly.[12] Altogether, Kitchener became a devotional Anglo-Catholic, and in an age when church party politics were pronounced, declared his allegiance to Anglo-Catholicism in the last years prior to the government's passing of the Public Worship Regulation Act in 1874. Designed to curb what some believed were the ritualistic excesses of the Anglo-Catholics, the Act was brought in by the Disraeli Conservatives at the behest of the Archbishop of Canterbury, Archibald Tait, in a spasm of governmental overzealousness in defence of Protestant Anglicanism. In response to what was seen by Anglo-Catholics as a blatant attack on religious freedom and tolerance, likeminded partisans had already formed the Church of England Protection Society, later called the English Church Union. Kitchener and Williams were two such partisans and readily took out membership in the Society. These years left a permanent mark on Kitchener's churchmanship as he would remain decidedly Anglo-Catholic – although never personally adopting ritualistic practices – for the remainder of his life.

In 1873, after two years at Chatham, Kitchener was selected by Brigadier General George Greaves to be his aide de camp. His selection in this regard was a singular mark of favour, perhaps prompted by the fact that Kitchener's height, good looks and military bearing were always impressive, and it got him assigned shortly to the manoevres of the Austro-Hungarian army and to the dining table of the emperor, Franz Josef. Exposure at this level of the European politico-military hierarchy was a heady experience for the young Kitchener. In the process his rudimentary German language skills served him well, as did his familiarity generally with Continental life.

The following year, 1874, Kitchener would spend largely at Aldershot Camp. Destined later to become central to British army life, Aldershot then was newly-acquired by the military and rudimentarily basic in its facilities and services. Except for his friend Williams' presence there also, Kitchener did not much like the place – perhaps his recent rather exalted European experience made him less than tolerant of the rough camp atmosphere – but whatever the content of his private thoughts on this latest posting he once again managed to favourably impress his superiors. Described by one of them as 'a most zealous and promising officer', Kitchener regularly displayed high skill in the emerging military field of telegraphy, the long-distance transmission of textual or symbolic messages, as well as in his horsemanship.

As with most young officers in peacetime, Kitchener had to wait on events in order to commence a real career, however. One possibility in this regard which had emerged in 1873 was joining the Ashanti Expedition in Africa under the command of Garnet Wolseley. Designed to exert British control over West Africa's Gold Coast, the expedition would make Wolseley's reputation as a soldier of empire and resulted ultimately in 1877 in his promotion to major general.[13] Kitchener volunteered to go to Africa – 'the next thing you may hear will be my slaying niggers by the dozen' – he wrote to his sister Millie, employing a term of the time that was not yet recognized by most contemporaries as constituting a racist epithet; but he was not called upon to serve.[14]

His work at Aldershot essentially completed by mid-1874 but not yet sure of what his next move would be, Kitchener took a short leave and went across the Channel to Dinan to think about his future. The family remained based there, although his father and stepmother were not getting on well together and would soon separate, but never divorce. Much of the rest of the year Kitchener divided between England and Germany where he had decided to go in order to work on his facility in the German language, and to await future prospects. And indeed, while studying in Hanover that summer he received a letter from his old friend at the Shop, Claude Conder, containing a request that was exactly what the increasingly bored Kitchener needed to hear.

Since receiving his commission in the Royal Engineers in 1870 Conder had spent considerable time in what Europeans were just then beginning to call the Middle East attached to the new London-based Palestine Exploration Fund (PEF). Founded a few years earlier in 1865 by a group of archaeologists and clergymen – most notably, Arthur Stanley, Dean of Westminster – the PEF was rapidly gaining a reputation for first rate survey work in the Holy Land.[15] The question of the Bible's historical veracity was a lively and controversial one in those years, marked as they were by the publication of Charles Darwin's *On the Origin of Species* in 1859, as well as by Benjamin Jowett's *Essays and Reviews* of 1860. Devout Christians felt it their duty to defend the traditional interpretation of the Bible's chronology, while at the same time discovering physical evidence for its chronicled sites and events. The collateral impact – and this is where someone like Conder made his mark – came in the political and intelligence gathering possibilities for the government of having the PEF active in Ottoman-controlled Palestine. Though an out of the way province of the Turkish Empire, Palestine's 6,000 square miles nonetheless had an obvious importance to Western Christian culture, which the PEF had been founded to recognize and elaborate. But Palestine also sat at the crossroads of competing empires, a position that would only heighten in the latter part of the nineteenth century and well into the twentieth, which is why the War Office was willing to make available to the PEF (on secondment) members of the Royal Engineers such as Conder and, soon enough, Kitchener too.

Conder's letter to Kitchener was occasioned by the death of his field assistant, Charles Tyrwhitt-Drake, from malaria in Jerusalem in June. To Conder, his old friend Kitchener was exactly the man to replace his unlucky former assistant who had been with him for the preceding two years. For his part, at rather loose ends in Germany and very glad to be considered for the appointment, Kitchener thought the prospect a sterling one, duly applied, and set out immediately for London and the PEF's headquarters.[16] Upon arrival Kitchener attended an interview, was offered the job – 'the very man' the PEF wanted it seems – enrolled in an Arabic language course and otherwise prepared to leave for Palestine, which he then did early in November.[17] Travelling by way of Vienna, Trieste, and Alexandria Kitchener steamed into the port of Jaffa on 15 November 1874, after having 'got up early to see the sun rise over the Holy Land. It was glorious more from association than anything else, seeing for the first time that land which must be the most interesting for any Christian'.[18] Palestine would be Kitchener's professional home for the next four years and the scene of his first real work as a commissioned engineer, albeit on special service. In many ways Palestine would be the making of him in this initial stage of his professional military life.

Upon Kitchener's arrival in mid-November Conder and his small team were working in the south of the country, in the serrated topography of the Judean hills. Conder met his new assistant at Jerusalem the next day and together they rode out to the survey's camp at El Dhoheriyeh. The landscape was desolate, the camp rough, and the survey party a mere handful of men, together with a few servants, horses, and mules. But the location of the work was storied in Biblical terms – Jericho was not far away – and the task exactly suited to a green and eager sapper like Kitchener. Accordingly, he got down to work immediately, and revelled in it. The daily routine demanded both physical heartiness and attention to detail. A comprehensive ordnance survey – which was the PEF party's assignment – required the full range of engineering and map-making skills. Kitchener therefore was in his element, surveying and sketching, deepening his facility in Arabic which he had begun to acquire in London, and enjoying being back in the ever-convivial company of Conder.[19] The New Year 1875 saw the group move closer to the territory abutting Judea's Dead Sea. Lying at about 1,400 feet below sea level, the lowest surface point on earth, and with a high degree of salinity, the Dead Sea generated an immediate attraction to the dusty survey crew: 'the water looked so blue and nice we were soon stripped and in it. The sensation is extraordinary'.[20] (Kitchener makes no mention, surprisingly, of the nearby ancient mountain-top fortress of Masada, reinforced by Herod the Great around the time of Christ, and the site of a siege in 73–4 AD about which Josephus the Jewish-Roman historian recorded the mass suicide of some 960 Jewish resisters to Roman rule.)

A short time later, however, disaster struck when Kitchener became ill with what was probably malaria. Fearing the same end as the unfortunate Tyrwhitt-Drake a year earlier, he was sick for weeks. But by the end of February Kitchener had passed through the worst of it, and helped by the apparent medicinal effect of consuming considerable amounts of 'small' beer was convalescing and enjoying the sights and sounds of Old Jerusalem including the Western Wall of the ancient temple, the tomb of King David, and the Church of the Holy Sepulchre. The veracity of the latter as the site of the tomb of Jesus would be called into question later in 1883 when during a sabbatical year spent in Palestine Charles Gordon became convinced that a site outside the old city walls constituted both Calvary, as well as the location of Christ's tomb.[21] Meanwhile, at last well and fit, Kitchener readied himself to rejoin the survey, which he did in mid-March.

During Kitchener's absence the work of the survey had continued apace. The demands were many, but being out on the land, riding, hiking, measuring, photographing and, for recreation, swimming, meant that he was living a full and invigorating life. Once having returned, Kitchener fell back into the survey's rhythm immediately and none too soon for at the beginning of April while the group was taking its daily plunge in the Mediterranean, Conder – evidently a rather weak swimmer – got caught in an undertow just off the legendary port of Ascalon, site of the last battle of the first crusade, fought in 1099, and was pulled out into the deep water only to be 'rescued by Lieutenant Kitchener'.[22] Not for the only time would Kitchener play the hero, for later in April while the survey was encamped at Safeh in the hills above Lake Galilee they were attacked by a group of angry locals. Safeh was a small Arab Muslim village whose inhabitants viewed with suspicion the incursion of the obvious 'infidel' in the form of the survey's members. Initially, the local people denounced them verbally and lobbed a few rocks in their direction. But the atmosphere soon became more hostile and a scuffle ensued between Conder and the putative Arab leader, a vituperative village tough named Ali Agha Alan. After Alan made an attack on the survey party he was knocked down in response and restrained with a rope. Conder and Kitchener then thought the unfortunate incident to be over. However, just at that moment one of Alan's allies jumped forward and clubbed Conder on the head, knocking him down, opening up a deep wound in his scalp, and rendering him almost senseless. Unsurprisingly, a melee ensued with Kitchener caught in the middle of it. Outnumbered, the survey members wisely retreated as bullets and stones began to punctuate the air. Dragging Conder along with them, they made it to safety but might just as easily been cut down. Kitchener did his part in the dust-up, in the process suffering a sharp blow to the leg, but soon enough a small detachment of Turkish troops rode in to apprehend Alan and his men, who were later tried, convicted, and imprisoned for their unprovoked assault on the survey party. For Kitchener, the incident at Safeh was his first real 'battlefield' experience and in the subsequent view of Conder his colleague's 'cool and prompt assistance' had made all the difference in their escaping the violent situation with their lives.[23]

In the aftermath of the Safeh incident Conder's physical incapacity, along with the presence of simmering local hostility and the ever present danger of fever, both malarial and choleric, resulted in a suspension of the survey's operations. Kitchener and Conder therefore returned to London in October. At Christmas, Kitchener crossed the Channel to Dinan to spend time with his family, and then returned to London where he would spend the whole of the following year, 1876, working with Conder on map-making and writing up their survey notes.[24] He also put considerable work into preparing and then having published privately a book which he called *Lieutenant Kitchener's Guinea Book of Photographs of Biblical Sites*. Seeking a 'fresh view of many of the most interesting Biblical sites' was Kitchener's stated aim in giving an outlet for his growing hobbyist photography, and while the book did not sell well it was not for lack of authorial and editorial keenness.[25]

This year-long London interregnum also allowed Kitchener to pursue other enthusiasms, principally his continuing religious devotion which he demonstrated by joining the recently-founded Guild of the Holy Standard. 'Brothers' of the guild were military men committed to an overt (Anglo-Catholic) religiosity by way of attendance at Holy Communion, engaging in good works and clean living, and other such practices that spoke of personal sobriety and self-discipline. Apparently, in this way Kitchener, young and at large in mid-Victorian London, posed no danger to the virginal virtue of any of the women he might encounter, and his correspondence on the topic of the opposite sex accordingly is non-existent.

By the end of the year Kitchener, now in excellent health but bored in London, was keen to return to Palestine. Conder, however, was not deemed fit to do so and so the PEF chose to give command of the survey to the 26-year-old Kitchener, a move that did not sit well with the ailing former chief but was inevitable given the circumstances.[26] The PEF also enlarged the size of the survey, which meant that upon landing in Beirut at the beginning of February 1877 Kitchener at the head of almost 20 men: 'quite a little army to feed', he remarked with evident pride.[27] For the next nine months Kitchener and the survey went about their business in a comprehensive and mostly harassment-free manner. On his own and in charge, Kitchener grew quickly into the habit of command. While map-making remained his main focus, the parallel track of politico-intelligence work would soon come into sharper relief because in April war broke out between Russia and the Ottoman Empire.

Conflict between these two powers had simmered for some time and in the context of Balkan nationalism, one of the legacies of the mid-century Crimean War, and complaints about the ongoing ill-treatment of Christian minorities within the Ottoman Empire, the two sides plunged into a war that would rage for ten months and take the lives through both battle and disease of over 300,000 people. For Britain, long supportive of the Ottomans' stance in the Eastern Mediterranean of holding Russia at bay, there was much at stake geo-politically. And Disraeli's Conservative government knew exactly which side it was on, notwithstanding Liberal leader William Gladstone's impassioned defence of Bulgarian Christians in the pages of his bestselling pamphlet, *The Bulgarian Horrors and the Question of the East*, published before the outbreak of war in the autumn of 1876.[28]

Britain's official endorsement of the Ottomans in the war meant that the PEF would receive continuing protection and nothing like that which had happened at Safeh was repeated. And Kitchener, it seems, could not have been happier during these months. 'Every day', he rhapsodized in a letter to sister Millie, 'from morning to night, I enjoy life'.[29] And such would prevail until the survey's work was completed in November, with the whole of Palestine having been surveyed and, eventually, mapped. The PEF's achievement was great, and its success in this regard would have a significant impact on generations of archaeologists and cartographers in the Middle East, notably T.E. Lawrence some 40 years later. The work now complete, Kitchener sent his colleagues home. But rather than go with them, and with his interest piqued by the deepening Russo-Turkish War, he decided to seek a taste of the fighting in Bulgaria. Departing Palestine on 26 November, therefore, he headed for Constantinople and from there travelled to the frontline at Kamerleh. Once arrived he was distinctly unimpressed with what he saw of the Bulgarian Christians for whom so much ink had been spilt by Gladstone, who, in any case to Kitchener, was a political sentimentalist. His visit was brief, but long enough to assure himself that the Disraeli government was right in backing the Ottomans. But the brevity of his time at the front did not preclude his being introduced to Valentine Baker, one-half of the intrepid Baker Brothers of mid- to late-Victorian fame. Just then Valentine was serving as a Turkish officer having been drummed out of the British Army and then spending time in prison for sexually assaulted a young woman in a railway carriage in 1875.[30] As such, Baker was disreputable in the extreme, but his life was exotic nonetheless, and unknown to Kitchener at the time, he was the father of a young daughter, Hermione, with whom Kitchener would fall in love a few years later in Cairo.

The Bulgarian episode over, by the end of 1877 Kitchener had returned to London where he would take up residence with his recently separated father who had relocated there, having left both Dinan and his second wife forever.[31] The New Year 1878 began with Kitchener continuing to work on completing the Palestine map. From his small flat in South Kensington he would walk the brief distance to Kensington Gore, the site of the headquarters of the Royal Geographical Society, in order to complete the work. As a recently-made fellow of the society, he was entitled to use its map room and throughout the first part of the year he, along with a now-recovered Conder, occupied themselves with finishing off the project for the PEF. Early in March while Kitchener laboured over the map, the Russo-Turkish War came to an end with a Russian victory and the resultant signing of the Treaty of San Stefano that would briefly settle the dispute. The British were not well-pleased by all of the treaty's provisions, however, especially the creation of an independent Bulgaria which, it was assumed by Whitehall, would become a satellite state of Russia. Britain's Turkish policy continued to divide political opinion, although for some the issue was never less than crystal clear. As Queen Victoria put it in a note to her prized prime minister, Disraeli: 'Oh if the Queen were a man, she would like to go and give those horrid Russians whose word one cannot trust such a beating'.[32]

Prime minister since 1874 and always much concerned with the vagaries of the interminable Eastern Question, Disraeli saw that in order for British interests to be properly served the Treaty of San Stefano simply could not be allowed to be the final word on the outcome of the war. Great Power interest naturally included Imperial Germany under the direction of its chancellor, Otto von Bismarck, whose own view of the unsatisfactory nature of the San Stefano settlement mirrored that of Disraeli's. Accordingly, within a few months and with Bismarck acting as host and 'honest broker', the Congress of Berlin opened with the express intention of revising San Stefano in order to achieve a settlement in southern Europe acceptable to the Great Powers whose job it was — they believed — to maintain the Continental balance of power.

During the spring of 1878 the chancelleries of Europe therefore were abuzz in the run-up to the Congress, which was slated to begin in mid-June. Pre-Berlin intensive negotiations between Britain and Russia took place apace resulting in the Anglo-Russian Conventions signed at the end of May. Disraeli and his newly-appointed Foreign Secretary, Lord Salisbury, were of the same view in these negotiations; that being, first, Russia needed to trim the territorial size of Bulgaria, and second, be thwarted in extending her reach in the eastern Mediterranean.[33] Both British objectives were achieved, the latter doubly guaranteed by a separate negotiation with the Sultan of Turkey to allow the British use of the island of Cyprus as a military staging base. Located strategically just some 240 miles from the entrance to the Suez Canal, Disraeli and Salisbury − both of whom regarded the route to India to be at the centre of British imperial policy − saw it as an ideal point from which to balance any Russian incursions southward. The Anglo-Turkish agreement, known formally as the 'Cyprus Convention', was signed therefore just ahead of the Anglo-Russian agreement − the order of which Gladstone would shortly complain smacked of Disraelian duplicity − and the British delegation arrived in Berlin full of confidence that what the war had not been able to achieve, diplomacy had and would.

Over the month of negotiations that followed such an assumption was proved correct. By the time the Congress ended on 13 July with the signing of the Treaty of Berlin and its supersession of San Stefano, Disraeli had become the best-known political leader in Europe, every bit Bismarck's match as a negotiator, and in concert with Salisbury the bringer of 'peace with honour'.[34]

The acquisition by Britain of Cyprus as a base for military operations (sovereignty over it remained with the Turks) meant that in order to apply proper administration to the island a map of it must be created. The eastern Mediterranean had long been of strategic interest to the British. Ever since the days of Nelson and the victorious Battle of the Nile in 1798, the region had occupied an important place in official thinking. Nearby to the north, for example, lay the seven major members of the Ionian Islands, which had come under British sovereignty as part of the post-Napoleonic settlement of 1815 and had remained so until just a few years earlier in 1864.[35] Now it would be Cyprus's turn.[36] And who better to undertake the job of conducting its first survey and producing a map than the proven and impressive young subaltern, Lieutenant Kitchener? At least that was the view of Thomas Cobbold, former charge d'affaires at Baden Baden, Rio de Janeiro, and Lisbon, turned (since 1876) Conservative Member of Parliament for

Ipswich (and also Kitchener's distant cousin). Cobbald's access to Salisbury at the Foreign Office meant that his recommendation carried considerable weight. Quickly, therefore, the post was offered to Kitchener, who was more than pleased to accept: 'It is exactly what I like' Kitchener wrote in gratitude to Cobbald, 'and will be a great advance to me professionally'.[37] Accordingly, Kitchener left England immediately and arrived at the Cypriot capital of Nicosia on 15 September 1878, then a small city of some 11,000 people contained wholly within its old Venetian-built walls.

Kitchener's immediate superior in Cyprus was its recently appointed high commissioner, Major General Garnet Wolseley, who had arrived in Cyprus a few months earlier at the end of July. His service in the Crimea, India, Canada, and the Gold Coast had made Wolseley famous, and now here he was surrounded by members of his so-called 'Ring' of subordinate officers encamped at a temporary headquarters in the garden of one of Nicosia's many monasteries.[38] Even though Wolseley and Kitchener shared in common both an Irish birthplace and a surveyor's vocation, they did not get on together especially well. Kitchener's Palestine experience pre-disposed him to believing that surveying and map-making were skills he had mastered. And while he was probably right in this estimation, his high-minded view of what the Foreign Office expected from his Cyprus survey was rejected immediately by the eminently pragmatic Wolseley. Where Kitchener proposed a full survey that would include the island's many archaeological sites in the manner of what had been done in Palestine, Wolseley countered with the view that all the British state required in Cyprus was a simple, short, and inexpensive charting of the island enabling basic distances to be known and taxes collected. In the near term Wolseley was probably right about this view, but doubtless his dogmatic insistence upon it annoyed Kitchener and even, perhaps, damaged his youthful pride. Was he a trained surveyor in charge of a significant task, he may have asked himself, or a mere map-making cypher for Wolseley? In any event, Kitchener's supporting sappers and equipment arrived in mid-October and together they got on with the job, however understood. Owing to the fact that in Kitchener's considered opinion, 'Cyprus was handed over to Great Britain by Turkey in a thoroughly exhausted and ruined condition', the job at hand was a big one, even if its complete scope remained unclear.[39] By early in the New Year 1879, however, Wolseley had grown tired of Kitchener's many imprecations on the point and, in his view, the constant insubordination that accompanied them, and a short while later therefore the high commissioner had the survey suspended. In doing so Wolseley cited the financial cost, but if so it was only because such cost was on account of Lieutenant Kitchener's aggrandized view of the nature of the survey, he maintained.

'I don't like his manner much', had been Kitchener's first impression of Wolseley, and nothing that had happened between meeting him in September and the suspension of the survey during the following May disavowed him of it.[40] Naturally he was bitterly disappointed at this turn of events. He wrote to Lord Salisbury, imploring him to allow the survey to continue. Such overtures from a junior officer were bound to be in vain, however, and indeed they were rejected. As a consequence, shortly thereafter and with the task left incomplete Kitchener returned to London while Wolseley himself left Cyprus for South Africa where he took command of the British forces there just then on the cusp of the Anglo-Zulu War.[41] And with that Kitchener's unfulfilling Cyprus interregnum appeared to be over.

Back in London under less than ideal circumstances, however, Kitchener did not have much time to bemoan the apparent end of the Cyprus survey for almost immediately he was made a British military vice-consul in Anatolia charged with overseeing Turkey's implementation of certain articles of the previous year's Treaty of Berlin. Articles 61 and 62 of the treaty were essentially humanitarian provisions requiring the Ottoman Empire to respect the rights of its Armenian Christian minority living in the region. Kitchener was one of four such vice-consuls named under the supervision of Lieutenant Colonel Charles Wilson, who had been appointed Consul General in April. Kitchener and Wilson were well-acquainted through their mutual service to the PEF. Wilson was a Royal Engineer, having preceded Kitchener at Woolwich by 15 years. He was also an accomplished surveyor through work in Sinai, Jerusalem, Scotland, and Ireland. Later he would be part of the Gordon Relief Expedition where events would result in his taking command of the two-steamer advance party that arrived at Khartoum just 48 hours after its fall and Gordon's death.[42] Later still from 1901 until his own death in 1905, Wilson would be chairman of the PEF. He quite liked Kitchener from the start, admiring his pluck in the recent contretemps with Wolseley. And now that Kitchener was a free agent Wilson thought him perfect for the job of vice-consul. Accordingly, at the end of June he posted Kitchener to Kastamonu in Anatolia for what would turn out to be a brief eight-month diplomatic passage.

Subsequently, Kitchener's time amongst the Armenians, Circassians, Turks and others was usually interesting, occasionally eye-opening, and often enraging. The Anatolian autumn and winter of 1879-80 were especially cold, his house drafty, and the cuisine basic. Corruption and brutality were ubiquitous in the Turkish administration, as far as Kitchener could discern, and human suffering everywhere rampant. On the other hand, the Anatolian natural landscape was beautiful and the local people friendly. Kitchener was in a position to do some social good, and in the limited ways at his disposal he attempted to do so. But, as it turned out, his time in Anatolia would be brief. Back in Cyprus, the departed Wolseley's former deputy, Major General Sir Robert Biddulph, following a brief residency in Constantinople, had succeeded as high commissioner and was keen to see the survey revived and completed. He also was of the opinion that Kitchener's fulsome approach to it had been the correct one and therefore was the right way now to proceed, and that the erstwhile surveyor turned vice-consul was just the man to lead it. By the end of 1879, therefore, Biddulph had convinced Lord Salisbury to renew the survey and in so doing offered Kitchener the position of its director. In Kastamonu, Kitchener was temporarily reticent at the prospect, wondering about the possibilities of life as a British diplomat and also whether or not a second stint in Cyprus would really yield the kind of survey that he believed was right for optimal British administration of the island. In this brief moment of contemplation when, as he wrote to Millie, he had become used to 'being the biggest swell in the country', the cartographer in him won out. 'I shall get used to being an ordinary mortal again before long', he continued.[43] And so by March of 1880 he had left his stint in diplomacy behind and was back on survey in Nicosia.[44]

His return to Cyprus, as expected, was done in a much more confident manner than had prevailed back in 1878. He had the full support of Biddulph, the high commissioner, a good staff to carry out the hard work of surveying, comfortable accommodation, and an increasingly convivial social life. For the next two years – save a three-month home leave in the summer of 1881 – Kitchener enjoyed some of the most halcyon days of his fast retreating youth. During these years he participated in a kind of 'band of brothers' lifestyle: working hard and occasionally being shot at by suspicious locals; riding to hounds and steeplechase racing; and attending dances and balls. He made two lasting friendships during his Cyprus years, one with Pandeli Ralli, an Anglo-Greek merchant trader and scion of the London-based Ralli Brothers firm, who was a sometime MP and to whose fashionable Belgravia townhouse Kitchener would later often retreat; and Sir Samuel Baker, peripatetic man of empire, explorer, just then author of the book, *Cyprus as I saw it in 1879*, and the disreputable Valentine's older brother. Kitchener developed a more cultured side in Cyprus also, taking a keen interest in, for example, ceramics as well as in porcelain collecting, which would continue for the rest of his life. Amusingly, a Black bear cub had been sent to him from Anatolia proving, in the manner of the time, to be a good pet. Physically, Kitchener remained lean, which because of his height made him appear almost thin. A constant outdoor life meant that his complexion had darkened and been made swarthy by steady exposure to the sun. The prominent moustache that would later become his most marked physical feature, had grown out, although it was not yet as bushy as it would be in the future. Altogether, now in his early 30s, Kitchener was having a great time of it, even if occasionally he fretted about the fact that anything that could be called real military service had not yet come his way. But in Egypt, not far to the south of Cyprus, events there were about to change that abiding concern decisively and forever.

3

In Egypt and Sudan, 1882–92

By mid-1882, the Cyprus survey was winding down. Kitchener had given it yeoman service but could see that his time on the island was coming to an end, and without a clear direction as to what he might do next. In those years, events in the British Empire could be counted upon to offer men such as Kitchener steady opportunities, and so it was in June of 1882 that somewhat bored and suffering from a recurrence of fever he decided to take a leave-of-absence from the survey. Rather than relaxing in Nicosia, however, he used his leave to travel the short distance from Cyprus to Egypt. Just then, Ottoman-controlled Egypt was roiling in anti-European feeling. The nominally ruling Khediviate, first under Ismail and now headed by his son and heir, Tewfik, was effectively bankrupt and the country had erupted in a proto-nationalist backlash.

All the way back to the 1820s under the first Khedive, Muhammad Ali, Egypt had been on a halting course toward economic (and to some extent political) modernization. The building of the Suez Canal between 1844 and 1869 symbolized this process, if also that of Egypt's increasing financial control by Europeans. The construction of other significant pieces of modern economic infrastructure such as railways and ship-building, as well as the expansion of cotton production, meant material progress, but it also produced soaring government debt. Indeed, by 1880 approximately two-thirds of Egypt's annual governmental revenues were given over to debt service, a debt held largely by British and French investors.[1] As a key part of the Eastern Question for successive nineteenth-century British governments, Egypt was recognized by the

Conservatives under Disraeli as the cornerstone of its imperial policy and in 1875 the government made this position abundantly clear by purchasing 44 per cent of the Canal's shares. The resulting injection of L4 million into the Treasury of the Khedive gave his embattled regime a financial respite, but only briefly. By the following year an international commission headed by Britain's Controller General in Egypt, Sir Evelyn Baring (Lord Cromer from 1892), had imposed on the country a strict financial regime complete with a tight stringency on expenditures.[2] Some in government – such as Major General Charles Gordon, then the Governor General of Egyptian-controlled Sudan – thought that the debt commission's demands were both unfair and potentially dangerously counter-productive, and argued that some form of debt forgiveness be enacted.[3] Baring, however, had other ideas and insisted on maintaining a financial hardline in order to appease the demands of the always tetchy Anglo-French investors. In light of these strictures it is unsurprising that Egyptian Khedivial independence, such as it was, became severely curtailed and proved to be the tinder from which a nationalist revolt sparked into flame.

The key actor in this Egyptian uprising was an army colonel by the name of Ahmed Arabi Pasha. Educated, affluent, and a long-time nationalist, Pasha was incensed by the political and financial machinations of both the Ottomans and the Europeans, and in February of 1881 led a large and loud street demonstration against them in Alexandria. This provocative action led to others of a similar nature and soon a coup was carried out successfully in which the army was wrested from direct Khedivial control and put under Arabi's supervision as newly-named Minister for War. Unsurprisingly, tensions now rose precipitously. The embattled Khedive was keenly desirous of British help in reasserting control over the deteriorating situation, but only after a simple argument between an Egyptian donkey boy and a belligerent Maltese trader in Alexandria in June of 1882 had escalated into a street riot in which 50 Europeans were killed, was the British government convinced to intervene militarily.

William Gladstone, now two years into his second prime ministerial administration, abhorred this descent into public violence in Egypt but was prepared to send British warships and troops to intervene if doing so was the only way to prevent the escalation of social and political disorder.[4] Even though during his Midlothian Campaign of 1879 that had led up to the general election of the following year Gladstone had articulated a clearly-defined internationalism, he was certainly no pacifist. 'Egypt for the Egyptians' as he put it, may have been the preferred outcome of the situation, but such an achievement could only be expected to come after the various interest-holders in Egyptian government, society, and the economy had been satisfied. As for the latter, this meant essentially those European bondholders whose investments were tied tightly to the stability of the Khedivial regime. One of those bondholders was Gladstone himself, a fiscal reality provoking of some discomfort, yes, but certainly of no incompatibility with holding public office at the time. To Gladstone, public order counted above all else in society. Even though he was routinely unconvinced by strategic arguments about the centrality of the Canal and India to British imperial and foreign policy, by mid-1882 events in Egypt were closing in on him in such a way as to make his voice almost the only one in Cabinet wanting to avoid military intervention. While Gladstone was prepared to intervene in this way, he did not advocate for it. But the rebellious and murderous events of July tipped the Egyptian situation into one of serial disorder and with it the naval bombardment of Alexandria was undertaken and the British occupation of the country ensued. General Wolseley, late of South Africa, was drafted to lead the invasion, and the instructions given to him by Gladstone's Cabinet were pointed and uncompromising: 'Put down Arabi & establish Khedive's power'.[5] By mid-September and the successful battle of Tel-el-Kebir in which the rebellious Egyptian forces were routed and Arabi captured, the instructions had been fulfilled. 'No more blood I hope', wrote Gladstone in his diary two days later on 15 September. And then an encomium typical of the man: 'Wolseley in Cairo: Arabi a prisoner: God be praised'.[6] A mere two months had yielded a thoroughgoing military success, a stunning exhibition of British power, and the beginning of what would stretch into 40 years of British control over Egypt.

Herbert Kitchener's military career would be shaped by the cockpit of Anglo-Egyptian affairs in 1882 for the next 20 years, so it is appropriate that on 11 July as Britain's big naval guns opened up on the Alexandrian ramparts from the roads just offshore, that he was aboard the flagship HMS *Invincible* observing it all. Back on board ship after a dangerous and exhilarating week of onshore reconnaissance dressed in civilian clothes and disguised as a 'Levantine', Kitchener for the first time ever was enjoying the heightened atmosphere of war and his own tiny part in it. If his one-week leave of absence from Cyprus had been occasioned by a bout of boredom mixed with malarial fever, he now desired to extend his leave in order to stay near the centre of the action. To that end, he asked Admiral Sir Beauchamp Seymour, in command of the Royal Navy's operations at Alexandria, to contact Major General Sir Robert Biddulph in Cyprus for an extension of his leave. Seymour, impressed by the young Kitchener, was happy to oblige. His request was met, however, with a flat refusal by Biddulph. Even more off-putting than Biddulph's refusal, however, was his anger at what he saw to be Kitchener's insubordination in using his leave to depart Cyprus for service elsewhere. Kitchener was flabbergasted to think that Biddulph considered him to be both duplicitous and, pointedly, absent without leave. Facing, therefore, the possibility of a court-martial a chagrined Kitchener returned to Cyprus immediately where he sought to appease the enraged Biddulph. His superior was not easily mollified, however, but Kitchener did his best: 'I have been very much pained ever since my return', he wrote to Biddulph on 2 August, 'at the view you took of my absence in Alexandria'. At length he sought to explain himself:

> I think it my duty to let you know how extremely anxious I am to see service in Egypt .... I cannot help feeling that my remaining here in a civil capacity while military service was offered me might be used against me in my future career .... I feel sure that you will agree with me that a soldier's first duty is to serve his country in the field when an opportunity is offered him .... Of course I would gladly relinquish all my pay to those doing my work and I would leave my resignation in your hands'.[7]

Biddulph was not moved, however, by Kitchener's imprecations and so unhappily but stoically, therefore, Kitchener carried on with the survey for the rest of that summer and autumn oblivious to the fact that as he did so the Gladstone government was deciding to re-constitute the shattered Egyptian army and put it under British command. The officer chosen to head it as 'Sirdar' (leader) was Major General Sir Evelyn Wood, selected over the transplanted and now (partially) rehabilitated Valentine Baker. A seasoned, decorated officer (he had been awarded the Victoria Cross during the Indian Mutiny) and a member of

Wolseley's Ring, he was appointed in December and instructed to select 25 commanding officers to serve under him.[8] Both Wood and Kitchener were recommended by Charles Gordon. Kitchener, biding his time completing the Cyprus survey, did not take much convincing, although he was afraid of once again running afoul of Biddulph. 'Will you join me for soldier's duty,' queried Wood of Kitchener on 28 December. '... no allowances except forage two years engagement.'[9] While Kitchener's initial response was negative: 'Very sorry present work will not permit me to leave Cyprus for one year', this opportunity was not one to be missed.[10] Wood persisted in his recruitment attempt, and in the face of an equally persistent Kitchener Biddulph finally relented. Accordingly, by late February 1883 Kitchener was in Cairo, having left behind for good both Cyprus and the 'noble' survey. From the rank of captain Kitchener had been raised to the equivalent of major ('bimbashi') in the Egyptian army.[11] Indeed, he was 'pretty well satisfied' with the course of these latest events as he explained to Millie, and ready at last 'to do some soldiering'.[12]

Once in Egypt, Kitchener was posted to the army's sole cavalry regiment, the 19th Hussars. As second in command, Kitchener was required to ensure that fresh recruits to the regiment were turned as quickly as possible into competent fighting horsemen. Like many people who have mastered a skill with which others remain unfamiliar, Kitchener was less than patient in forging quality horsemanship in his Hussars. But he was doggedly persistent and by July the new Egyptian cavalrymen were riding successfully on parade. During this period he worked closely with fellow officer Andrew Haggard, the elder brother of the yet-to-be famous novelist of empire, Rider Haggard.[13] The two young men got on well together and shared numerous regimental and off-duty meals at Shepheard's Hotel in Cairo, the social heart of British military and administrative life in Egypt from the middle of the nineteenth century until eventually burning down in 1952. In 1895, by then a lieutenant colonel, Andrew Haggard published a memoir of his time in Egypt called *Under Crescent and Star*, in which Kitchener receives ready reference. The prose is often purple, and the memories recorded have much to do with young officer indulgence: 'we [Haggard and Kitchener] had a match with each other, like a couple of schoolboys, to see who could eat the most'; but a portrait of an entirely sociable Kitchener is made clear nonetheless.[14] While reticence and taciturnity were marked features of his character, (the young) Kitchener was always able to relax and enjoy himself, particularly in the company of his fellow officers.

Those early days in Cairo also brought Kitchener his first (and probably only) full-blown love affair. Valentine Baker had come to Cairo in 1882 in the service of the Khedive and remained doing so, though rather desultorily, it seems, as head of what he called the 'rubbishy' Egyptian police, a distinctly second-order appointment in his view once Wood had been named Sirdar.[15] Baker and his family lived in residence at Shepheard's and as a frequent guest and visitor to the hotel Kitchener easily reacquainted himself with them.[16] Being much admired by Baker (as well as by his famous brother Samuel[17]) Kitchener spent considerable time dining and socializing with the family, drawn especially by Hermione, the beautiful teenaged elder daughter of Valentine and his wife, Fanny. Of delicate health – or at least treated that way in the prevailing Victorian fashion – Hermione had fast elicited Kitchener's devotion and throughout the balance of 1883 and into the next year whenever he was in Cairo he paid court to her. Though characteristically silent on the subject others within the small British social circle that centred on Shepheard's assumed that the two young people (Kitchener, at 33, was 15 years older than Hermione) were fated to marry.

One such observer, just then living with her parents beside the hotel in the British Consulate, was the ten-year-old daughter of a judge in the Egyptian native courts, Bonte Amos. In later years Bonte Sheldon Elgood, as she became, practiced as a physician in Egypt, living her entire life there until being expelled in 1956 during the aftermath of the Suez Crisis. She is one of the only – and certainly the best – sources of information on Kitchener and Hermione's (almost certainly chaste) brief love affair. In 1959, retired and living in England, she remembered one particular incident between them from sometime in 1884, near to what proved to be the end of their courtship. Firm in her recollection – 'I knew it as fact' – Elgood recounted it this way:

> Hermione, whom I greatly admired (as little girls of 10 do admire young ladies of 18), was seriously ill in their rooms there [Shepheard's], and my mother (in the absence of any sort of hospital), living next door, frequently went there with specially-cooked diet. On one of these occasions I was with her, and I well

remember that as my mother had just opened the bedroom door to enter, a tall young officer came up and hurriedly spoke to my mother. My mother drew me back and we waited on a nearby couch while he went in alone. I remember clearly saying, 'But why? Doesn't she want the beef-tea?' And my mother said, 'Yes, but Major Kitchener is going to marry her, and wants to see her quietly'. She died, I think, not so long after, and we were all very sad.[18]

On 21 January 1885, not very long after this episode had occurred and just before Gordon's death and the fall of Khartoum during which Kitchener was at Korti as part of the relief mission, Hermione Baker died in Cairo of typhoid fever. A month later her mother Fanny died also, and two years after that and still in Egypt Valentine did likewise, of a heart attack. Altogether, the sad demise of a family. In the interim, however, Valentine had given Kitchener one of Hermione's lockets as a keepsake of their sadly abbreviated relationship, which he kept for the rest of his life.

After the serial frivolities of British social life at Shepheard's, Kitchener's personal heartbreak over Hermione Baker's illness (and later death) was more in line with what was taking place to the south. The year 1883 was a momentous one in Egyptian affairs because of the steady descent into Islamic-inspired warfare in its contiguous dependency of Sudan. The preceding 62 years of Turco-Egyptian rule (the 'Turkiyya') in Sudan had produced a well-spring of resentment in the Sudanese towards their overlords. Heavy taxation, recurring warfare, compromises with 'infidel' Turks, Egyptians, and Europeans were a potent cocktail in the hands of anyone who might seek to conjure a revolt, and by the 1870s such a backlash was brewing under the leadership of Muhammad Ahmad, a young mystic from the Nilotic town of Dongola. Claiming for himself the title of 'al-Mahdi', the Prophet Muhammad's successor as the 'expected one' or 'guide' in the tradition or *hadith* of Sunni Muslims, Ahmad claimed that under him the advent of the 'Mahdiyya' was to prepare the way for Allah's final Day of Judgement. Little of this Islamic theology (and teleology) was understood by the contemporary British or anyone else for that matter in Western society at the time, but the threat to order and stability in the vast one million square mile Sudan was real enough. From Ahmad's announcement of the commencement of the

Mahdiyya in June of 1881 he had gone on the offensive against the 'infidel Turks ...', commanding his followers thusly: 'let everyone who finds a Turk kill him, for the Turks are infidels'.[19]

In response to the threats being uttered by Ahmad and the increasing fervour of his followers, known as the 'Ansar' (helpers), Egyptian authorities moved to have him arrested in December. The attempt failed, however. Emboldened by this failure, Ahmad continued to build strength and with his following now numbering in the thousands he laid siege to a 4,000-man Egyptian force sent from Khartoum to engage him in June 1883 at El Obeid in the province of Kordofan. By now, the situation had become dire in the view of both Cairo and Khartoum. In the latter city throughout that summer a force of some 8,000 troops congregated and was placed under the command of Colonel William Hicks. A 53-year-old veteran of the Indian Army, Hicks had entered the Khedive's service in 1882 and early the next year was sent to Khartoum as military chief of staff. His troops were poor and dispirited, however, most of them having recently fought for the defeated Arabi, and were hardly enthusiastic about a posting to Khartoum, or the prospect of fighting the increasingly fearsome Mahdi. Hicks himself was equally unenthusiastic about their quality. Ordered to attack the Mahdi at El Obeid, Hicks marched his bedraggled force out of Khartoum on 9 September. Some weeks later at Shaykan Hicks's disoriented troops, severely weakened by thirst as well as by a critical lack of provisions, were set upon by the Mahdi's army. A fanatical force of some 40,000 Ansar, they made short work of Hicks's men, almost all of whom were killed. The annihilation was overwhelming, with Hicks's severed head being the ultimate trophy of Islamic war taken to the Mahdi's encampment at El Obeid to be put on display.[20]

News of the Hicks debacle was met with equal dismay in Khartoum, Cairo, and London. To most observers it had become clear that Sudan was slipping into jihadist anarchy. Not only had the western side of the country become almost ungovernable, in the east along the Red Sea one of the Mahdi's lieutenants, Osman Digna, would soon achieve victories against Egyptian troops sent to put down the allied Hadendoa people (the 'Fuzzy Wuzzys', as British soldiers called them, on account of their high-mounted and wildly-matted hair). Led by Valentine Baker who had come south from Cairo specifically for the purpose, the Egyptians nonetheless were quickly defeated at El Teb. A revived

Egyptian force drew a measure of revenge against Digna a short while later, however, only to suffer a reverse again at Tamai.[21]

Throughout the increasing tumult in Sudan Kitchener had continued to acclimate himself to an officer's life in Egypt. His staff responsibilities did not (yet) mean service to the south in Sudan. Indeed, after a busy regimental summer he was able to go on leave and in November 1883 renewed his still close association with the Palestine Exploration Fund by joining its expedition to the Arabah Valley, which runs south for about 110 miles from the Dead Sea to the head of the Gulf of Aqaba. On the expedition Kitchener was accompanied by George Armstrong, later to become secretary of the PEF. Being back on survey was highly enjoyable for Kitchener, and trekking again through Biblical lands, this time in the 'wilderness of Zin' as recounted in the Old Testament book of Numbers, was the perfect way to spend his leave. The enjoyable archaeological and map-making reverie was interrupted, however, at the end of the year when he was informed by General Wood of the Hicks disaster in Sudan. At once, Kitchener resolved to return to Cairo and did so by cross-country passage through the unforgiving Sinai Desert, a 200 mile journey by camel (made again in disguise, only this time not as a Levantine but rather as an Egyptian official). Safely back in Cairo at the beginning of 1884, by March of that year Wood had Kitchener hard at work as an intelligence officer. Fluent in Arabic and well-versed in the geography and politics of the Near and Middle East, Kitchener was ideal for the job.

Kitchener's Arabah and Sinai peregrinations had taken place almost exactly at the same time that the Gladstone government, in the face of the Hicks disaster and the Mahdi's ongoing jihad, decided to enact the evacuation of Sudan.[22] Initially, Gladstone's predisposition against regarding Suez and the route to India as central to British imperial policy had made him downplay the importance of the Sudan crisis, as well as view it through the lens of his developing advocacy of the rights of small states and powerless peoples. Indeed, in the spirit of Midlothian he would later declaim (in)famously in Parliament that the Mahdists were 'struggling to be free; and they are struggling rightly to be free'.[23] But before Gladstone did that, however, decisions about the nature and scope of the evacuation simply had to be made. For certain members of the Liberal Cabinet, the choice of General Gordon to lead the exodus from Sudan became irresistible in the early days of January. Gordon had spent all of 1883 in Palestine on a self-imposed study leave before agreeing to become King Leopold of Belgium's personal emissary to the Congo in an effort to limit the slave trade there as he had done in southern Sudan as Anglo-Egyptian governor general a few years earlier. To do so, Gordon had returned to England on 7 January 1884 intending to resign his British commission and prepare to depart for Africa in the service of the Belgian king. But events intervened. Just a few days earlier, Garnet Wolseley, now Adjutant General of the British Army, had written to Gordon in an effort to dissuade him from taking up Leopold's offer, and instead consider closely the deteriorating situation in Sudan.[24] Others too had Gordon's name on their lips as the right person for Sudan. Cabinet ministers such as Lord Granville at the Foreign Office and Lord Hartington at the War Office were plumping for Gordon to be sent to Khartoum. The popular press was pushing for Gordon too, especially W.T. Stead of the *Pall Mall Gazette* whose liberal sympathies lay clearly with the government and who managed to obtain an interview with Gordon himself the morning of his recent arrival back in England. In the emergent modern 'ambush' journalistic style, Stead appeared unannounced at Gordon's sister's home in Southhampton where he was staying and proceeded to elicit from him the bullish opinion that evacuating Sudan was the wrong policy. 'Even if we were bound to do so', Gordon remarked, 'the moment that it is known that we have given up the game, every man will go over to the Mahdi. All men worship the rising sun'.[25]

The next 11 days proved frantic, as Gordon was drafted for service in Sudan, agreed to go, and left hurriedly on 18 January 1885. His instructions as to *precisely* what he was being sent to achieve in Sudan – report on the situation, or evacuate all British troops, administrators, and civilians? – were unclear. Gladstone was fearful that a man of Gordon's known independence of mind might very easily disregard the instructions of a far-away government. 'Must we not be very careful ...', he wrote to Granville on 16 January, 'that he does not shift the centre of gravity as to political and military responsibility for that country'.[26] In Cairo, Baring, now British Consul General, though sharing with Gordon a background at the Royal Military Academy Woolwich (Baring was an artilleryman, however), never liked or trusted him and was equally uneasy about sending him back to Sudan.[27] But in the heat of the ongoing crisis such misgivings were shunted aside and after meeting with Wolseley, and then a few days later with four members of the Cabinet (which did not include Gladstone who was away at Hawarden, his country estate in North Wales), Gordon set out for Sudan on the 18th. Exactly one month later, on 18 February, he arrived at Khartoum. Once there of course, he would never leave.

The saga of the 11 months that followed until Gordon's death at the hands of the Mahdi's Ansar on 26 January 1885 is one of the defining epics of the late-Victorian British Empire and has been told often and well.[28] A full reprise of it need not be included here, therefore. But what is salient, of course, is the place in it of Kitchener, and to that we shall now turn.

During the handful of months over which Gordon had accepted his assignment, travelled to Sudan, and settled into his executive role in the Governor's Palace on the banks of the Blue Nile at Khartoum, Kitchener had been relishing his life as a peripatetic intelligence officer under the director of military intelligence, Major Reginald Wingate, who later would command the Egyptian Army as Sirdar and become a pivotal figure in the military history of the Middle East.[29] The jihadist uprising in Sudan, the first of its kind in modern Africa and one of the main precursors to what has become readily evident in today's world, convinced the Egyptian government of the necessity of creating a dedicated staff in order to both understand and resist the revolt. The obvious charisma of the Mahdi, the devotion of the Ansar, the ceaseless emotive rhetoric, and the apparent carelessness towards death and destruction that characterized the rebellion produced in the British on the ground an earnest desire for the revolt's defeat. As one of those men on the spot Kitchener therefore threw himself into the task of trying to solicit Arab collaborators whose loyalty to the Anglo-Egyptian regime could be counted upon against the relentless emotional and religious onslaught of the Mahdi. Much of Kitchener's early work in this regard was centred on Berber, located about 200 miles north of Khartoum and invested by the Ansar, or 'Dervishes' as they now had been dubbed by British soldiers in a nod to the 'whirling' Dervishes of Sufi Muslim fame.[30] To the east along the old caravan route about 280 miles away lay the Red Sea port of Suakin, vital to any future British military operation that did not involve ascending the Nile from Cairo. Kitchener's main job at this point in the revolt was to form an irregular fighting force of Arabs who could be used to dislodge the Ansar from Berber and open the way to Suakin.

The spare, elemental, soldierly life Kitchener now lived was one that he had very quickly come to relish. 'Just got back from 17 days desert ride and rather exciting hunt of one of the Mahdi's emirs', he wrote breathlessly in June to a former PEF colleague.[31] On these and other dangerous forays he was accompanied by a small group of Arabs who pledged to him their unquestioning loyalty, and together they hurtled across the undulating desert in an attempt to outwit the Mahdi and achieve whatever end either the British government, or Gordon, was attempting to achieve. Determining what both these parties wanted was of course extremely difficult, and Kitchener dressed in Arab robes, conversant in the language, and caught up in the unfolding drama emanating from Khartoum can hardly have been expected to be anything but a strong supporter of the increasingly heroic Gordon. Kitchener's pre-existing dislike of Gladstone prejudiced him against the Prime Minister of course, but what seemed to be the interminable prevarication of the Liberal Cabinet over the correct next steps in Sudan in the face of what was a rising chorus of loud voices demanding action sealed his contempt for the Grand Old Man of British political life.

Throughout the spring and summer of 1884 Gordon had made it clear through reports, messages (until the telegraph line was cut in mid-March), and letters from Khartoum that he was not about to simply pack up and go home, leaving the field open for the Mahdi to do as he pleased. Logistically, with over 20,000 troops and some 11,000 civilians in Sudan, any sort of evacuation would have been extraordinarily difficult. But even if Gordon had been inclined towards evacuation (which he was not), the actions of the Mahdi militated against any outcome other than a climactic showdown between the two men. 'I have asked Gov't. to give me categorical orders what to do', Gordon wrote to his sister Augusta in Southampton, in an undated (probably March 1884) note.[32] If Gordon remained of the mind that the Gladstone Cabinet was unclear in its purpose, at home pressure was building within both Parliament and public alike that Gordon was fast becoming a hostage to the Mahdi and the only proper course of action that remained was for the government to send a fully-equipped relief mission to save both him and the honour of the nation. Queen Victoria was equally vexed about Gordon's fate, although earlier she had praised Gladstone for sending him out: 'I am glad that my Government are prepared to act with energy'.[33] As the weeks passed, however, the Queen grew increasingly frustrated with what she took to be government muddle and timidity in the face of what was believed to be Gordon's own unfolding and potentially tragic heroism.

By the end of March the Mahdi had moved his Ansar into proximate distance from Khartoum and began to lay siege to the city. 'They will not fight us directly but will starve us out', Gordon reported to Augusta.[34] And that is exactly what transpired. But still the government resisted action on account of its anger at Gordon's apparent insubordination, as well as to a serious misreading of the national mood. As the political temperature rose in London about whether or not Gordon would be 'relieved', and if so by land or water, the man himself continued to hold out doggedly against the Mahdi. In early August, Gladstone finally succumbed to intense political pressure – the Secretary of State for War, Lord Hartington, threatened to resign if a relief force was not sent – and authorized the sending of an expedition under the command of Wolseley. By September therefore, the relief force was staging in Egypt for its chosen route up the Nile, which then commenced on the 27th.

The four autumn months that followed were rife with tension, a knife's edge existence shared by all who participated in this desert drama, including Kitchener. He was assigned as intelligence officer to the relief force, an acknowledgement of the good work he had done already over the preceding months, much of which was encapsulated in a newly written report for the Sirdar, General Wood.[35] Kitchener was under the command of Sir Charles Wilson, his old diplomatic patron who earlier had drafted him to serve as military vice-consul in Anatolia. Wolseley, still harbouring a degree of animus toward Kitchener resulting from their former disagreement in Cyprus, objected both to the appointment and to his being promoted brevet major in the British Army. But as far as Wood was concerned, Kitchener was manifestly the right man for the job. Kitchener duly was grateful both for the appointment and for the promotion: evidence, as he wrote in a note to the Sirdar at the end of August, that 'you approve of my work'.[36] And from his base at ed-Debba Kitchener plunged into such work afresh.

By the autumn of 1884 Gordon's only means of communication with the outside world from Khartoum was via secret messenger. Chosen runners were sent out and if they got through the city's outskirts their messages would be relayed further along the 200-mile route to

Kitchener's headquarters at ed-Debba where successful runners would be paid and then sent back, the cycle repeating itself. Early in the process Gordon thought that Kitchener's own intelligence operatives, his 'outsiders', were a 'feeble lot' and perhaps the only way to improve them was to increase their pay.[37] 'I always pay the messengers well,' Kitchener reassured Gordon in early November, and the quality of them did seem to improve.[38] But on top of the inherent perilousness of communicating in this way was the fact that the messages were sometimes designed intentionally to confuse with dis-information any of the Mahdi's men who might intercept one of Gordon's runners. The result was confusion all-around, however, which made it extremely difficult for Kitchener to know with any degree of certainty the exact nature of the prevailing situation in Khartoum. During these months of direct if uneven contact Kitchener and Gordon developed a certain rapport, which, from the younger man's point of view, would come to elicit near-veneration. Gordon, for his part, was quick to send Kitchener his 'kind regards' too, and the close feeling was to some degree mutual.[39]

Like most men of arms Kitchener deplored the inexcusable slowness of any military operation when it was curtailed by political considerations. He was convinced that a proper demonstration of force against the Mahdi would break through the ring of Ansar encamped around Khartoum and give Gordon the relief he required. As he had stated forcefully to Baring as far back as August: 'Send up your troops. There is no difficulty, and one good fight close to Khartoum will see the matter through'.[40] Almost exactly 14 years later, Kitchener himself would engage in 'one good fight close to Khartoum' at Omdurman, which shattered the Mahdiyya and paved the way for the British re-conquest of Sudan. But in the autumn of 1884 no such readily available expedient existed and as Wolseley's force gradually ascended the Nile it remained unclear to Kitchener and hence to Gordon just what form the final plan of relief would take.

As the Mahdi's noose tightened around Khartoum, Gordon sent a steamer downriver with a handful of men, including his second in command, Colonel J.D.H. Stewart, hoping that they would be able to establish a clearer communication network than the one afforded by runners, possibly making it all the way to Cairo. Departing Khartoum on 12 September, within days, however, the *Abbas* had run aground on rocks not far north of Berber. Disembarking from the stricken steamer the men warily accepted an offer of traditional Arab hospitality, which indeed proved to be a trick and they were all killed almost immediately by Ansar. Meanwhile, in ed-Debba Kitchener's messenger network had informed him that the steamer had been seen approaching Berber and he asked Wolseley if an armed vessel therefore might be dispatched to escort Stewart's party downriver. Wolseley, short on river-craft and not fully trusting of Kitchener's information, replied no. In response, Kitchener had then sent one of his runners across the full 200-mile expanse of the Bayuda Desert from ed-Debba to Berber in an attempt to intercept Stewart and tell him to leave the steamer and cross over to his headquarters by land, thus avoiding the long loop taken by the Nile and the steady presence of hostile Ansar along its banks. The message, alas, never got through and the next thing Kitchener heard was that Stewart and his colleagues were dead. Understandably, he was furious about this 'murder by Red Tape', as he called the sad episode.[41]

In Khartoum, the Stewart debacle confirmed for Gordon that without the soon arrival of the relief expedition he would have to take on the Mahdi alone. In a letter from his nemesis at the end of October Gordon was indeed told to surrender and convert to Islam and therefore all would not be lost. Rejecting the ignominy inherent in the offer, Gordon responded flatly: 'It is impossible for me to have any more words with Mohammad Achmed, only lead'.[42]

The weeks of waiting continued to pass and with them hopes of success dwindled. Wolseley proposed to continue upriver as far as Korti, the place where the Nile begins its long loop, and from there send a column of about 1,100 men across the Bayuda on camelback to Metemma, located about 100 miles north of Khartoum. The balance of his force meanwhile would continue on the river as far as Berber. For the Camel Corps, once having arrived at Metemma an advance on the besieged city could be made, which would then be buttressed by the arrival of the troops on board the boats. Kitchener joined the new column as intelligence officer, accompanying them as far as Jakdul, about mid-way across the desert, before being ordered back to Korti to await further instructions. Chafing at this enforced return to base, Kitchener poured out his frustration to sister Millie: 'My Lord Wolseley has not forgotten or forgiven and has just sent me a gentle reminder .... I fancied I had little claim to get on to Khartoum'.[43]

The Gordon saga was now fast approaching its climacteric. A few days later at Abu Klea, the Camel Corps endured a ferocious attack by Ansar that they were ultimately able to withstand, but at great human cost. Kitchener was well to be back in Korti and away from the fighting, although that was little consolation at the time. At last, a few days later on 28 January 1885, an advance party of 20 men arrived at Khartoum on board a steamer. Under Sir Charles Wilson, to whom command had devolved after some other senior officers had been killed at Abu Klea, the clutch of men on board the steamer stared out at the utter ruin and desolation of the city. Two days earlier the Mahdi had chosen to launch a final attack and early on the morning of the 26th the Ansar had poured into the stricken city and for the next dozen hours had killed, raped, and plundered indiscriminately. Fully one-quarter of Khartoum's population of 40,000 were killed that day by the Mahdi's frenzied jihadists, including of course Gordon, who, Kitchener later reported, likely had been 'killed near the gate of the palace'.[44] Gordon's body was never found, however, but his head was placed on a pike for display in the victorious Mahdi's encampment across the river at Omdurman.[45]

In the aftermath of the failed relief expedition there of course was much recrimination, most of which fell upon the head of Gladstone, now called derisively by some the M.O.G. (Murderer of Gordon) rather than the hitherto affectionate G.O.M. (Grand Old Man). Kitchener's own feelings about the sad situation were angry and raw. He blamed Gladstone, but so too did just about everyone else who shared the British imperial creed, not the least of whom was the Queen. As we know she had long been outraged by the delay at 'rescuing' Gordon and now despaired utterly at his loss.[46] Wolseley, whose view of Kitchener had come to change completely given his stellar work on campaign, was singularly apoplectic about what he regarded as the total disaster of Sudan and of Gordon's loss, and was certain as to Gladstone's culpability for both. His animus towards him in this regard would be long-lasting. In January 1886, a year after the events of Khartoum when Gladstone had again won (brief) re-election, he wrote to Kitchener lamenting the outcome of the vote. 'God must be very angry with England', opined Wolseley, 'when he sends back Mr. Gladstone to us as First Minister, ... an unprincipled man .... Nothing is talked of or cared for at this moment but this appalling calamity that has fallen upon England'.[47]

In the days following the certain news that Khartoum had fallen and that Gordon indeed was dead Kitchener played his part in bolstering the morale of the dispirited British troops. Jubilant Ansar attacked the retreating British and at Abu Klea, site of the signal though costly victory just a few weeks earlier when hopes still ran high of saving Gordon, Kitchener took the lead filling in the wells. Such an action was regarded as contrary to the rules of war and therefore ungentlemanly, but in light of the fact that marauding Ansar continued to harass the British Kitchener felt justified in doing so.

By late-February Kitchener's work potentially was almost done. He was now back at Korti (and then later ed-Debba) and beginning to prepare for a possible return to England, although the prospect of further action in Sudan remained and would not be made firm until the British government's decision on 21 April that no subsequent offensive operations would be undertaken. While at Korti some of Gordon's personal effects salvaged from the destroyed Governor's Palace in Khartoum were brought into camp. Included among them was one of the last of Gordon's letters, dated 26 November 1884, in which he criticized his political masters for almost the last time: 'There will be no peace between me and Gladstone's Government – that is certain'. He then goes to on conclude with a ringing encomium in praise of Kitchener as his natural successor as governor general, stating that his appointment 'would be well for the people, and you would have no difficulty that you could not master'.[48] To be endorsed in this way by the fallen hero who was fast being turned into an 'imperial saint', was the height of validation for Kitchener and he sent the totemic letter to his father for safekeeping.[49] 'It is the best reward that I shall get for a good many months' hard work ...', he wrote about Gordon's endorsement. 'I feel that, now he is dead, the heart and soul of the Expedition is gone. The shock of the news was dreadful, and I can hardly realize it yet'.[50]

Gordon's posthumous praise may have been enjoining for Kitchener, but a similar kind of commendation from the living had served also to raise his reputation in the minds of the popular readership at home. Gordon's saga had been followed very closely in England and in it the role of the trustworthy 'Major Kitchener' was given great play, especially in the pages of *The Times*.[51] Owing to his earlier work in the PEF especially, Kitchener's name had become at least incidental to newspaper readers prior to the Sudan expedition. But with the events in Sudan his name now gained widespread recognition, and the ensuing public acclaim also had an impact on the way his military superiors viewed him.

In his as yet continuing role of intelligence officer Kitchener had drafted a long memorandum for Sir Redvers Buller, who had been given command of the Desert Column as it began its retreat in the aftermath of the failure to advance on Khartoum. A soldier of long experience, winner of the Victoria Cross during the Anglo-Zulu War, and later to take command in South Africa in the Anglo-Boer War, Buller thought highly of Kitchener's abilities, a view reinforced by Kitchener's 15-page summative memo submitted to him on 1 May 1885 detailing his 'Report on the Present Situation & Future Government of the Sudan'. Kitchener's informative memo had followed on a series of linked notes written on 4 February and based on immediate intelligence of events detailing Gordon's final days. In Kitchener's hand the notes comprising 'The Fall of Khartoum' are highly emotional in tone and in that way starkly different from the bureaucratic memo written by him a few months later. In these earlier notes the state of affairs in Khartoum is grimly recounted by Kitchener: dwindling food stocks and desperation leading to the fact that 'all the donkeys, dogs, cats, rats, etc. had been eaten'; betrayals and butchery; and finally, 'sudden assault when the garrison were too exhausted by privations to make proper resistance'. Some of the emotion of his notes naturally crept into his official 'Report', and altogether, Kitchener's 3,000-word document is a tale of woe that tells the story of 'noble resistance' owing to the 'indomitable resolution and resource of one Englishman. Never was a garrison so nearly rescued, never was a Commander so sincerely lamented', he concluded.[52]

On 8 May 1885, a week after Kitchener's Report was submitted, the Gladstone government announced that a full-scale withdrawal from Sudan would be undertaken. Ridiculed by Kitchener and others as a 'Policy of Scuttle', the decision was final (and would be maintained by the Salisbury Conservative government when it won power in July 1886 by defeating the Liberals, who by then were riven by internal dissension over the Irish Home Rule bill).[53] Kitchener's Sudan service therefore was ineluctably winding down. In June, the Mahdi died unexpectedly, probably of typhoid fever, and he was succeeded by Abdullahi Ibn Muhammad, the 'Khalifa', with whom Kitchener later would be indelibly linked. In recognition of Kitchener's excellent intelligence work, he was promoted brevet lieutenant colonel. Shortly thereafter he resigned his commission in the Egyptian Army and on 3 July, having just passed his 35th birthday, he boarded ship in Alexandria and sailed for home.

After the intense strain of the preceding months in Sudan Kitchener's summer in England proved halcyon. He spent it on leave and was feted, even lionized, as the returning hero, basking in the reflected glory of the slain and now-considered-to-be saintly Gordon. Feting of this sort began in mid-July at Osborne House on the Isle of Wight, the Italianate architectural confection purchased and renovated by Queen Victoria and the late Prince Albert 40 years earlier in 1845 and afterwards the royal family's favourite residence. For Kitchener, newly returned from the desert, Osborne was all lush greenery and cool water and he reveled in his visit there, as he did equally in his first meeting with the Queen, as each officer was formally presented to her. The balance of the summer was spent mainly in London and in Leicestershire socializing and visiting old Colonel Kitchener and Millie, who had taken up residence there. Kitchener's London headquarters became the Belgravia home of Pandeli Ralli, while at the same time he began to be exposed to aristocratic country house life when invited to Taplow Court near Maidenhead in Berkshire, the estate of William Henry Grenfell. Athlete, mountain climber, big-game hunter, and MP, Grenfell was the epitome of the Victorian 'hearty' and took an instant liking to the war-hero Kitchener, which prompted the first of many weekend invitations. The feeling was mutual and Grenfell's friendship was an important step in Kitchener's socio-political education in the ways of the late-Victorian elite. His lack of wealth, title, and public school or university education meant that Kitchener's 'outsider' status needed to be compensated for by military achievement and helpful friends if the heights of smart society were to be scaled. The Sudan had supplied one, and Grenfell (later Lord Desborough) assisted in showing the right path to the other.

By the autumn of 1885 the thoroughly feted Kitchener was ready for a fresh assignment but when it came it did so in the form of a disappointing posting to Ireland with the Royal Engineers, there to assist in the building of a new barracks in Cork. Hardly the sort of task to set the blood pumping – especially after the serial excitement of Sudan – Kitchener made a vociferous appeal to the War Office to have the order rescinded and something better put in its place. Perhaps Kitchener's gradually developing network of friends in high places helped in the situation, although his correspondence does not reveal anything specific in this regard. In any event, on 7 October he received a letter of appointment from the Prime Minister and Foreign Secretary, Lord Salisbury, that his services were required by the Foreign Office (he was loaned out again by the War Office) as the British representative on the Zanzibar Boundary Commission.[54] Together with his fellow commissioners from Germany and France, Kitchener was charged with evaluating the Sultan Barghash of Zanzibar's claims to a large swathe of East Africa (much of today's Tanzania and Kenya), a pressing diplomatic question in the aftermath of the Berlin West Africa Conference that had ended just a few months earlier and which had set down rules for the European delimitation of Africa. The 'scramble' or 'partition' of Africa was just about to begin in earnest, and Kitchener, much better-pleased about his replacement assignment, was to be engaged in one corner of its execution.[55]

The clove-scented island of Zanzibar, located about 40 miles off the coast of East Africa, had been of considerable British interest as far back as the early part of the nineteenth century when the Royal Navy's anti-slaving squadron had begun to do its work of intercepting slave ships of the Arab trade. By mid-century Zanzibar was host to a series of explorers – most notably David Livingstone – who used it as a staging base for forays inland, and now as the century was drawing to a close the island and its ruling sultan were at the centre of how East Africa would be divided up amongst the three major European powers concerned: Germany, Britain, and France. As it happened, the Germans had the most pressing local claims. Their explorers, missionaries, and agents, such as Johannes Rebmann, Johann Ludwig Krapf, and Karl Peters had arrived in advance of any other Europeans, and – in the case of Peters – had drafted treaties with some of the local tribal groups, which the Germans argued were legal and therefore deserving of international ratification. The British and the French were a little late in taking up the diplomatic game on the African east coast and inland, but in light of the Berlin Conference they too desired a settling of the fluid situation, especially as it bore on access to the Great Lakes in the interior and hence to the Nile watershed with its decisive geo-strategic implications related to India.

Kitchener arrived in Stone Town, Zanzibar's capital, on 29 November 1885, and was met by Dr John Kirk, the British Consul. Kirk, famous for his part in Livingstone's Zambesi Expedition of some 25 years earlier, welcomed Kitchener (with whom he had already corresponded) and gave him a full briefing on the prevailing diplomatic situation.[56] The German and French commissioners were already in residence and for Kitchener the next nine months would prove to be a rather prickly period of argument with his fellow commissioners and diplomatic jockeying for position. As the new Foreign Secretary, Lord Rosebery, appointed by Gladstone following the Liberal defeat of the Tories in the Commons over the Irish land bill at the beginning of 1886, put it to him in a letter in March: 'I think it well to give you a hint that at Berlin they think you lean a little towards the French commissioner'.[57]

Loneliness too was a problem: 'one is dreadfully cut off from the world ...' he wrote to Millie. But a cruise along the east African coastline was rewarding, a foreshadowing of Kitchener's later extensive land purchase in Kenya, which he thought would be ideal for his eventual retirement.[58] In the end the deliberations of the Commission were circumvented by executive action in the three home capitals by which the Sultan was given a 600 mile coastal strip along with the islands of Zanzibar, Pemba, and Mafia; the French were awarded control of the Comoros Islands near Madagascar, the latter of which they gradually succeeded in formally colonizing in 1897; and Germany and Britain had their 'sphere of influence' claims over what would later become German East Africa (Tanganyika) and British East Africa (Kenya) recognized. Altogether, the Berlin Conference mandate had been exercised in a swift and patronizingly effective way: executive imperialism at its most blatant. As for Kitchener, however, the whole episode proved mostly forgettable, except for the fact that to ensure the balance of power in the Indian Ocean he recommended that the British government acquire the then tiny port of Mombasa as a naval base, which, in due course, is exactly what it did.[59]

Happy to have the Zanzibar assignment behind him, Kitchener headed for home in August of 1886. Upon reaching Suez, however, his journey was interrupted by a message apprising him that the new Tory government of Lord Salisbury, which had vaulted back into office after defeating the Liberals on the Home Rule Bill and subsequently winning the general election, had chosen to appoint him 'Governor-General of the Eastern Sudan and Red Sea Littoral' and that he was required to report immediately to Suakin, his new territorial charge's capital. England therefore would have to wait.

Despite the grand-sounding title, Kitchener's appointment at Suakin was largely about maintaining British control over its last Red Sea port and keeping it out of the hands of the irrepressible Osman Digna and the ascendant local Mahdists. 'What curious people these Arabs are', Wolseley wrote incredulously to Kitchener, 'to allow Osman Digna to come back to bully them'.[60] A small, ancient town, Suakin was built originally of coral harvested locally. Conquered by the Ottomans in 1517, it soon fell into decline and eventually in 1865 the town was given to the Khedive Ismail. Stiflingly hot from May until November and without obvious strategic value until the 1880s, Suakin had then emerged as an important port in the ongoing struggle against the imposition of the Mahdiyya. Kitchener's arrival there in the intense heat of summer marked a new chapter in Britain's attempt to contain the ramifications of the fall of Khartoum the year before.

Over the preceding few years the British, as noted earlier, had fought three battles locally: twice at El Teb and once at Tamai, in an attempt to keep open the land route from Suakin to Sudan's interior. Brief success gave way to defeat, however, and in the aftermath of the Khartoum debacle and the government's decision to withdraw from Sudan, Suakin was now a pin-prick outpost pressed down upon by the preponderant power of the Khalifa's regional subordinate, Digna. Despite the less than optimistic situation into which he arrived, Kitchener nonetheless was gratified to have been made a 'Governor-General' and set about immediately to settle in and transform the rather neglected Residency into a home fit for the Queen's representative. There is something earnest, perhaps even grasping, about the Kitchener of Suakin, trying very hard to live up to the perceived grandeur of his gubernatorial appointment, even if it was that of a tiny, dusty Red Sea port town. Still, the job was reasonably important given the geo-politics of the day and together with his aide-de-camp, William Staveley Gordon, he got down to work. Son of the late general's elder brother, Sir Henry William Gordon, the young Gordon was an accomplished artilleryman and went by the nickname of 'Monkey'. Just 23 years old, Monkey Gordon immediately ingratiated himself to Kitchener and proved to be the first of a number of young aides that he would employ for the balance of his career. 'A nice little chap' may not be the highest form of praise, but in first describing him in this way to Millie, it is clear that the young Gordon had begun to make himself indispensable to Kitchener in his early days at Suakin.[61]

The local battles of the preceding three years had left Kitchener with an Anglo-Egyptian force under his command of about 2,500 men. The territory inland from Suakin was almost completely controlled by Digna, however, whose operational design was to squeeze the garrison until it had no choice but to surrender and decamp. Digna, a slave dealer and participant in Arabi's uprising in Alexandria in 1882, was fully committed to the Mahdist cause and his February 1884 defeat of Valentine Baker's force at El Teb made it evident that despite the 'Fuzzy-Wuzzys' unconventional appearance – their hair rose up from their heads in tower-like fashion – they were nonetheless skillful and fierce fighters. Their reputation was burnished again at the Second Battle of El Teb as well as at Tamai, the latter being chosen by Kipling to sing the praises poetically of the properly-named Beja people (more specifically the sub-group Hadendoa) in his famous poem, 'Fuzzy-Wuzzy', in which he acknowledges that they had 'broke a British square!' (which had never happened before, but would happen again within a year at Abu Klea).[62]

Naturally emboldened by Gordon's defeat and the fall of Khartoum, Digna had endeavoured to export the Mahdist cause to Ethiopia later in 1885, but was defeated in September at the Battle of Kufit. Still, his position in eastern Sudan was strong, and as Winston Churchill later put it effusively in his history of the British re-conquest, 'under the leadership of the celebrated, and perhaps immortal, Osman Digna', the Mahdists began to put pressure on Suakin.[63] Kitchener countered by attempting to co-opt local sheikhs into rejecting the warlike position of Digna, stressing to them that long-term stability in the region lay in their acceptance of the Anglo-Egyptian regime. 'Peace to those who enter and who leave this place' was written on the town gate at the behest of Kitchener and during the latter months of 1886 and throughout the following year an attempt was made to live up to the injunction. Kitchener implemented a no-trade policy with the Sudan interior as a means to choke off support for Digna, but it had the unintended effect of annoying resident European traders who claimed that choosing to trade with the Mahdists was their absolute right. Most of Kitchener's time, however, was taken up in ensuring that Suakin was well-fortified. Additionally, he continued to do his best imitation of running a full-fledged Government House, which included hosting formal dinners and welcoming his sister Millie, for example, as a guest during which time she became something of a chatelaine in her brother's service. Meanwhile, Digna tested the outer defences of Suakin, but under Monkey Gordon's direction the town was reasonably well-protected from successful attack.

After a relatively quiet 1887, the contest of wills between Kitchener and Digna heated up again in January of the New Year. Just then Digna was encamped at the village of Handub located a little to the northwest of Suakin, and Kitchener saw his known proximity there as an opportunity to go on the offensive against him. To do so he used no regular Anglo-Egyptian troops – the Sirdar, Francis Grenfell, would not authorize regulars for a raid – but rather a combined force comprised of about 400 Turkish troops, ('bashibazouks'), Egyptian police, and non-Mahdist Sudanese. Early on the morning of 17 January 1888, therefore, before the baking sun had risen, Kitchener struck at the Mahdists' camp and landed an effective surprise blow, nearly capturing Digna in the process. The now aroused Mahdists, however, recovered quickly and the lesser quality of Kitchener's irregulars began to show as many of them broke and ran in the face of withering fire from the enemy. Kitchener himself was shot in the face, the bullet splintering a piece of jawbone and coming to rest awkwardly near his throat. While grisly, the wound was not likely going to kill him, but it was severe nonetheless and bleeding profusely he had to leave the field immediately and return to Government House in Suakin for treatment. Kitchener's second-in-command, T.E. Hickman, therefore took over and conducted a reasonably well-ordered retreat. Initially, the episode had the smell of defeat about it. However, the superior firepower of Kitchener's otherwise undependable force meant that some 200 of the enemy were killed compared to a handful of Kitchener's men. In the pages of *The Times*, therefore, the Handub raid was treated as an example of the sound exercise of government policy by a commander and governor general who knew the country well and understood that 'hostile tribes and predatory bands must, whether 'rebels' or not, be taught to respect the Egyptian flag and the territory and property it covers'.[64]

The aftermath of the successful raid on Handub saw Kitchener sail for Suez and then proceed on to Cairo where he was hospitalized for a month. Buoyed up by letters of concern from Wolseley, among others – 'I hope that by the time this note reaches you, the wound in your face may have made good progress towards healing', he wrote in February, by mid-March Kitchener had recovered sufficiently to return to Suakin, there to reap the rewards of his forward policy against Digna.[65] In April, he was promoted brevet colonel and appointed aide-de-camp to the Queen, all on the same day! Kitchener's star now was rising fast, in large part because of his success in blunting Digna's impact along the Red Sea. He was the leading man-on-the-spot at an important crossroads of the British Empire and it did not matter seem to matter very much that the relatively tiny engagement at Handub had been a marginal affair, and, depending on how one looked at it, more of a defeat than a victory. The fact that the battle had taken place, that Kitchener was in charge of it and had been wounded, and that some kind of 'victory' could be claimed over the interminable Mahdists, was enough to propel him even higher up the ladder of success. Validated in this way he returned home to London for the summer where his facial wound healed fully and equally important, personal adulation prevailed. Highly impressed with the young governor general and commander, the Prime Minister, Lord Salisbury, invited Kitchener to Hatfield, his family's storied country estate in Hertfordshire. Dating from the Elizabethan period, Hatfield's 127 rooms were alive with numerous members of the Cecil family and their steady stream of guests. Altogether – and Kitchener would henceforth get to know them very well – the Cecils were engaging and talkative – 'the family learnt everything by discussion' – and the normally taciturn Kitchener spent an enjoyable and gilded weekend there during which Salisbury told him that he would be returning to the Middle East with the new appointment of adjutant general of the Egyptian army and therefore second in command to the Sirdar.[66] In retrospect, Salisbury's decision to reward Kitchener in this way was the key moment of his early career and would set him up for subsequent swift promotion.

Kitchener duly arrived back in Cairo in September 1888 and was drawn in quickly by impending military action; first at Gemaizeh that autumn, and then later at Toski, where the Khalifa's attempt to export Mahdism across the border between Sudan and Egypt was stoutly resisted. Led by the Sirdar, a small Anglo-Egyptian force annihilated a Mahdist army of 6,000 men, killing some 1,200 of them (including its commander, Emir Wad-el-Nujumi) and capturing 4,000 others while suffering few casualties in return. Such complete battlefield domination was a clear example of Western technological prowess, a foretaste of the even more lopsided Battle of Omdurman in 1898, as we shall see. These were signal battles nonetheless, especially Toski, fought on 3 August 1889, and Kitchener was involved closely in both of them. At Toski under the command of Grenfell – whose own conduct was rewarded with immediate promotion to major general – Kitchener led the cavalry, was mentioned glowingly in despatches, and afterwards was awarded the Companion of the Order of the Bath (CB). Altogether, his rise within the British military now had become inevitable.

Accordingly, shortly thereafter at the beginning of 1890, Baring appointed Kitchener inspector general of the Egyptian police.[67] Viewed initially by Kitchener as potentially a career-stalling move, he protested to Baring who replied with the un-disguised scorn that had made his nickname of 'Over-Baring' apt: 'My dear Colonel, if you do not accept posts that are offered you, you may have *no* career!'[68] Rather than being a drag on Kitchener's upward trajectory, however, the post proved instead to smooth his rise to the position he now coveted more than any other: Sirdar of the Egyptian army. And after a successful year of directing the Egyptian police, on 13 April 1892 such an appointment came to pass, the decision being made by none other than the Duke of Cambridge, 21 years after having reprimanded the young Kitchener for his brief service in the French army in their memorable interview of 1871 and still Commander in Chief of the British Army: 'I am personally very much pleased', he wrote to the equally well-disposed Prime Minister, Salisbury, 'that the choice should fall on Colonel Kitchener, whom I always considered a very good man for the place'.[69] Promoted to the local rank of Major General on the same day as Sirdar, Kitchener was just 41 years old. Among other things, he was now in a position to eventually avenge Gordon's defeat, the preparation for which would be his main task for the rest of the decade and lead to the crowning field operation of his career.

4

Sirdar of the Egyptian Army, 1892–8

Kitchener's appointment as Sirdar came as a welcome surprise to some, and as a disappointment to others. At 41 years of age he was comparatively young, and that was remarked upon disapprovingly. But what seemed more to the point was that Kitchener's friends in high places – namely Baring and Salisbury – had engineered for him a sizable leap up the career ladder and in the process had bypassed other, better-suited candidates for the job, principally Colonel Jocelyn Wodehouse, the popular officer in command of the Egyptian army, just then stationed at the Sudanese border. But despite such criticism and internecine grumbling, Kitchener was manifestly ready for the task, one that would be mainly administrative for the first four years but then conclude with a very sharp sting in the tail beginning in 1896.

As Kitchener's immediate superior Baring – ennobled now as Lord Cromer – oversaw Egyptian financial affairs with a hawk's eye. As far as he was concerned Kitchener indeed was absolutely right for the job of Sirdar; first, precisely because he was in fact 'young, energetic, ardently and exclusively devoted to his profession', but also because he was frugal financially: 'He did not think that extravagance was the handmaid of efficiency', as Cromer remarked pithily.[1] Putting Sudan to rights would be a very long and arduous process, Cromer believed, perhaps taking as many as 20 years. Achieving its re-conquest also would be highly expensive. Initially, at least, neither the meager Egyptian treasury, nor the terminally disinclined British one, were sources to be tapped to avenge lost British honour at Khartoum. If such were to come – and both Cromer and Kitchener believed that it must – then the road to its achievement would have to be paved with serial economy. And for that, Cromer was sure, Kitchener was the sole man for the job.

In July of that year the British general election once again returned the seemingly ageless Liberal leader William Gladstone to No. 10 Downing Street in what would prove to be his final administration. His victory was hardly resounding, however. Indeed, the Liberals were obliged to form a minority government with the help of Irish nationalists. Such assistance had been required in order to defeat the Tories under the leadership of a stubborn Lord Salisbury in a post-election vote of no-confidence in August. Only then did Gladstone assume office, and the advent of a Liberal government was lamented immediately by those, such as Kitchener, who had hoped that re-conquering Sudan by smashing the Khalifa would be undertaken sometime soon. Despite the change of government in London, however, Kitchener was confident in his resolve that the strategic situation in the Middle East demanded an invasion of Sudan in due course. And to that (long-term) end he expended all his considerable energies.

The economy with which Kitchener would now supervise the Egyptian army was evident immediately, and it infused the thinking of those who formed the ring of junior officers selected by the new Sirdar to do his bidding. Principally, this meant the ever-affable Monkey Gordon, who Kitchener had made Director of Stores, along with Major Reginald Wingate, who was appointed Director of Intelligence. Wingate would prove a pivotal figure in Sudan. He was highly experienced in the region and already had organized a network of informants; was fluent in Arabic; had published a book, *Mahdiism and the Egyptian Sudan*; and had even shown pluck in helping a Roman Catholic missionary priest, Father Ohrwalder, escape from imprisonment in Khartoum.[2] Wingate was devoted to Kitchener and they would be closely allied right through until 1899 when he succeeded him as Governor General of Sudan.[3]

To these two men were added a number of others, as we shall see, giving Kitchener a kind of Wolseley-like reputation for gathering acolytes from which to forge an incorruptible cordon of subordinate staffers. He insisted that they be unmarried, but that is no more remarkable for the time than what had been demanded of Oxford dons

until just a few years earlier or, a little later, of Rhodes Scholars.[4] The
apparent predilection to surround himself with young, unattached men
produced in the mid-twentieth century a pronounced degree of interest
in the nature of Kitchener's sexuality, the premise of this interest being
that such a circle of subordinate men was highly suggestive of (repressed)
homosexuality. During Kitchener's lifetime no one thought of him in
this way save for a muckraking journalist at *The Times* whose accusations
of sexual misconduct were plainly scurrilous. But while the point is
admittedly interesting it makes no material difference to his historical
accomplishments, nor should it. Today, when many scholars and others
(in the West at least) speak of having entered a 'post-gay society', seeking
to determine the form and nuances of Kitchener's sexuality seems
somewhat obscurantist.[5]

Still, Kitchener's supposed homosexuality resonates in our society
because of a kind of contemporary cultural demand that forces
biographers to unearth facts (or innuendos at least) that will reveal the
essential sexual self of their subjects, even though such revelations
usually have little or no bearing on either the professional achievements
or, indeed, on the failures of the person in question. Were, for example,
William Gladstone's nocturnal 'rescue' missions of prostitutes through
the streets and laneways of mid- and late-Victorian Piccadilly, and their
apparent psycho-sexual motivations, of any consequence to British state
business? Almost certainly not. For someone like Kitchener, indeed, the
point becomes faintly ludicrous. Just what, for example, does a vestigial
femininity, perhaps suggestive of homosexuality – as we have seen he
grew to like collecting porcelain and, especially later when Commander
in Chief in India, hosting dinner parties – have to do with the outcome
of Omdurman or the South African War, or later still the establishment
of the New Armies?

One of Kitchener's biographers, John Pollock, included a substantial
appendix – 'Kitchener and Sex' – on the issue in his work in an attempt
to rebut the accusations of his subject's alleged homosexuality.[6] And
while his rebuttal might be considered either laudable, or indeed risible,
depending on where one stands today on homosexuality, or on the issue
of gay rights and same-sex marriage more specifically, it is clear that in
Kitchener's capacity as both military leader and imperial pro-consul the
impact of an assumed homosexuality would have been by turns both
negligible and unimportant. To point out that there is absolutely no

evidence that Kitchener engaged in any sexual activity with men (or women, for that matter) is both unsurprising and utterly in line with both his professional dignity and with his personal religious beliefs. Can we say in the modern way, therefore, that Kitchener remained firmly 'in the closet', repressing his homosexuality in a tortuous hidden life? We can say it, as Jad Adams does in a measured way and others such as A.N. Wilson do more forcefully, but again the credible evidence for him having done so is non-existent and in any event, how much does it really matter?[7]

Kitchener probably would have married Hermione Baker, as we have seen, in the mid-1880s, but sadly she died. Were there other opportunities for marriage? Relatively late in life, when he was 52 years old, Kitchener briefly pursued Helen Mary Theresa, daughter of Lord Londonderry, the future Lady Ilchester. He proposed marriage and she refused him, which, apparently, had no discernible impact on their friendship and frequent mutual letter-writing. All in all, Kitchener was emotionally repressed – just like many others of his time – but made even moreso by the early death of his mother, as suggested earlier. Accordingly, he seems to have been 'morbidly afraid of showing any feeling', as described by his aide de camp and Lord Salisbury's son, David Cecil. He was also highly unlucky in love.[8] Is that evidence for suppressed homosexuality? Probably not. If Kitchener had lived in a later age such as our own an attempt to 'out' him likely would have been made. Successfully so? Almost certainly not. Perhaps erotic thoughts about his circle of junior officers passed through his mind, although there is no evidentiary reason to think so. Moreover, unlike his (in)famous contemporary Oscar Wilde, there simply was no action. Nor were there words. Neither his, nor really anyone else's. Ultimately, we are left with an issue about which historians can say almost nothing useful. Consequently, it may be argued that the wisest thing to do with the so-called 'debate' about Kitchener's sexuality is to consign it to the margins, which henceforth shall be the course of action taken in this book.

In his first months as Sirdar Kitchener set a tone that would last throughout his tenure of seven years. Hard work, efficiency, emotionless service, perhaps even brutality in inter-personal relations, marked the manner of the man. Kitchener's asceticism, developed largely during the privations of his surveying days, was given full rein in an attempt to speed up the ultimate realization of Sudan's re-conquest. 'Comfort, affections, personalities', to Kitchener, observed Cecil, 'all were quite inferior considerations'.[9] Of course, more than ever Kitchener looked the part too. Taller than just about everyone else he encountered, sinewy and taciturn, his face was weathered and permanently tanned by constant exposure to the wind and sun of the desert. The eyes, sharply blue and withering, and the now full bushy moustache completed the picture of a commanding officer who had reached his personal teleological end. There was no doubt in his mind, and little in the minds of those around him, that his appointment as Sirdar had become a kind of military ordination, the proper goal of which was to achieve General Gordon's vindication. 'He felt', continues Cecil in this vein, 'he was defrauding the Almighty if he did not carry out his task'.[10]

In the meantime, for Kitchener, as well as for everyone else in the small British circle in Cairo, social requirements were many. He participated, often grudgingly, in the round of receptions and parties put on at the British Agency by Cromer, and at the nearby Abdin Palace by the Khedive. By virtue of long exposure to such events Kitchener was now much more at ease when attending, but he never grew to like them. Classist assumptions ruled these social encounters, and in that regard Kitchener would never be able to overcome the social snobbery of those whose self-validation depended entirely on the level of their birth. To wit: 'A little underbred', is how Margot Tennant, shortly to marry the future Conservative prime minister, H.H. Asquith, described Kitchener tartly during a visit to Cairo in 1892.[11]

If enduring the pointed, if veiled, social offence of a society woman like Tennant was part of the job, so too was the much more congenial atmosphere of strictly military life, as well as that of fraternal societies such as the Freemasons, which Kitchener joined shortly after settling in Cairo and would remain a keen member of for the rest of his life.

Professionally in Egypt, Kitchener's most important relationships were with Cromer and the Khedive. Kitchener and Cromer did not much like one another on a personal level, however. Part of this dislike was based on Cromer's social elitism, a la Tennant, and part grew out of his own reluctance to give up too much control over Egyptian affairs to Kitchener and the military. Still, both men realized the other's ultimate value and as in most effective professional partnerships, pragmatism ruled.[12] But adding a new point of pressure to their relationship was the

unexpected death of the Khedive Tewfik in January 1892. He was duly
succeeded by his 17-year-old son, Abbas Hilmi, known as Abbas II
upon his accession as Khedive. Abbas, mainly educated abroad in
Lausanne, Geneva, and Vienna, was still in school when his father died
and he returned to Egypt with a half-formed character and an
understandable degree of animus toward the British occupiers of his
homeland. Once installed in the Abdin Palace, the latter feeling would
only grow and Cromer spent much of 1892 and the following year
managing an immature teen-aged Khedive who persisted in
impertinently questioning – at least as far as Cromer was concerned
– received British authority. For Egyptian nationalists, then as well as
later, however, the young Khedive's robust assertiveness in the face of
Cromer's paternalistic control was admirable and inspiring, and spoke
of a desire to modernize his country. But the British, blind to anything
redeeming in his character and with Arabi's revolt still fresh in their
minds along with the uncertainties of the ongoing Mahdiiya in Sudan,
found the Khedive's insubordination unacceptable and strove to check
it. Abbas needed to be squared, in their view, and when the young ruler
decided to unilaterally dismiss the Egyptian prime minister, Mustafa
Fahmi, in January 1893, Cromer made clear his intentions. As far as
the Khedive was concerned Fahmi, old and ailing, was a British puppet
and needed to be replaced by someone whose Egyptian nationalism was
clearly in evidence. Upon dismissing Fahmi, Abbas called upon such a
person in the form of Hussain Fahkri Pasha, a former minister of justice
who disliked the British intensely and openly questioned the idea that
their occupation was 'temporary'. Naming him prime minister came
in defiance of Cromer's unsolicited and unwanted advice on the point
and a crisis quickly blew up over the nature and extent of Britain's
authority in Egypt.

Cromer's position in the crisis never wavered, but the triangular
nature of affairs of state: London – the Agency – and the Abdin Palace –
meant that for over a week at the beginning of 1893 he was in the midst
of a whirlwind of personal and cable-based diplomacy. At home in
London, Gladstone's Liberal cabinet debated over how, and the extent to
which, the recalcitrant Khedive could be brought to heel. Cromer was
quick to suggest the use of military force if a diplomatic settlement
could not be reached. Gladstone and his Foreign Secretary, Lord
Rosebery – leader of the imperialist wing of the party – were at odds

over this heightened and potentially violent stance which revealed that competing visions of re-visiting the summer of 1882 were afoot in Cabinet.[13] Ultimately, Cromer was able to convince the Khedive that dismissing the prime minister without consulting (and obeying) the British was going to damage the Anglo-Egyptian relationship beyond repair and that he must 'willingly adopt the advice of Her Majesty's Government on all questions of importance in the future'.[14]

By late-January 1893, and to this end, the immediate crisis had passed, but the damage had been done. Abbas felt supremely cowed and continued to be deeply resentful about the British occupation, which would shortly reappear in a new and different way. Cromer's own position was renewed in strength but to Egyptian nationalists the episode smacked hard of the remorseless nature of British imperial power, the shadow of which would be cast long. Wilfrid Scawen Blunt, the writer and journalist and a permanent thorn in the flesh of British imperial pretensions in Egypt, heaped scorn on this exhibition of naked British coercive power dressed up, in his view, as a virtuous temporary trusteeship.[15] Meanwhile, at the opposite end of the rhetorical scale, Alfred Milner's recently published book, *England in Egypt*, provided a political and historical framework that could be used to justify such high-handed British action, and indeed it was employed by many in just this sort of way.[16]

Throughout this diplomatic dust-up, Kitchener had remained largely an interested, though highly vexed and mostly quiet, bystander. But the continued disaffection of Abbas for his British overlords would touch Kitchener directly in January 1894 when the Khedive travelled to the always-restless Sudan frontier in order to inspect some units of the Egyptian army stationed there. Throughout the previous year, but especially in the summer and autumn, Cromer had come to believe rightly that the Khedive was highly sensitive about what he considered to be British control of 'his' Egyptian army.[17] Tensions over the issue therefore simmered, marked by Abbas's provocative appointment of the nationalist Muhammad Mahir as under-secretary of war in September. The appointment was designed to demonstrate to all concerned that the Khedive retained some freedom of action, even if the diplomatic contretemps the year before had seen him emerge from it as the partially chastened loser. Ever since the bloody and protracted Indian Mutiny of 1857 army loyalty of course was an issue of supreme importance to the

British everywhere in the empire and the continuing attitude of defiance demonstrated by the Khedive, and what it might mean for potentially restive Egyptian rankers, was highly unsettling to authorities in both Cairo and London.[18]

On 13 January the Khedive accompanied by Under-Secretary Mahir and hosted by Kitchener began his inspection of the frontier troops at Aswan and Wadi Halfa, just north of the border with Sudan. That day, and those which followed, turned into a disaster as the 19-year-old Abbas proceeded to criticize and mock the standard of drill, dress, and comportment of the troops on parade, making racist remarks about black soldiers, and then heaping blame on British officers for this alleged poor state of affairs. The disrespect and impertinence shown by the Khedive, as Kitchener believed them to be, continued until six days into the tour when he could stand it no longer after listening to Abbas exclaim: 'To tell you the truth, Kitchener Pasha, I consider it a disgrace for Egypt to be served by such an army'.[19] Fairly brimming with rage, Kitchener promptly, if not peremptorily, offered the Khedive his resignation. If reports of insufficient deference in the behaviour of Abbas had not been enough to convince Kitchener that a teenaged ingénue was in residence at the Abdin Palace, the Khedive's immature and dyspeptic display at Wadi Halfa confirmed Kitchener's permanent loathing of him.

The Sirdar's on-the-spot offer to resign, however, appeared to have jolted the young Khedive into the realization that he had probably gone too far in his serial criticisms. Immediately, therefore, he began to beg Kitchener to reconsider. The episode has been well-told by other biographers, most often in defence of Kitchener's actions: Roger Owen, Cromer's most recent biographer, on the other hand, takes a more pro-Abbas view. But it is clear from accounts of the episode that Kitchener was entirely serious about resigning, as he made clear in a cable he sent immediately to Cairo.[20] Ultimately, however, Kitchener did not persist in threatening his resignation, in turn demanding that Under-Secretary Mahir be dismissed and that the Khedive's calumnies about the army be withdrawn and an apology issued to the army as an Order of the Day.[21]

Perhaps Kitchener acted too precipitously in his dealings with the Khedive. No doubt he was driven to exasperation by the steady imprecations of Abbas and probably enjoyed the sight of the shocked Khedive trying to squirm out of his self-induced predicament. Certainly, Abbas was the only one (apart from Mahir) to pay a price for the episode at the Sudanese frontier. Once again, just as in the previous January, the Khedive had been brought under control, his wings clipped. Abbas's introductory khedivial year of stretching his nationalist muscles had come to an ignominious end, and Cromer's consolidation of power as the real 'ruler' of Egypt was complete – as the journalist G.W. Steevens later would put it – in part thanks to Kitchener's refusal to be insulted by a callow youth.[22]

In order to emphasize the point of Kitchener's checking of khedivial power, Rosebery – on the verge of becoming prime minister in March in a cabinet power struggle that marked the end of Gladstone's political career – recommended him for the K.C.M.G., his third such honour.[23] He was now Sir Herbert Kitchener, enjoying the new appellation during a home leave that summer during which he visited family and bid a final tearful farewell to his 88-year-old father who died in August. Kitchener himself was now 44 years old, well-honoured and with high position, but in a permanent state of agitation over the potential re-conquest of Sudan. To be able to do enact it, he believed, was essentially the whole point of being the Sirdar at this particular juncture in the history of Anglo-Egyptian Sudan. And with the ascendancy of the British now largely uncontested – the Khedive, nevertheless, would go on quietly engendering nationalist feeling in Egypt – the time had come to act on this aspiration. Accordingly, during his 1894 leave in London Kitchener began to press hard the case for the commencement and execution of a fresh and comprehensive Sudanese campaign, the duration of which – little did he know – would come to last four long years.

Kitchener's insistence that the right way forward for the British in Egypt was to reconquer Sudan as soon as possible was not disputed by any of his colleagues in power, but nor was it held by them with a fervour equaling his own. Salisbury was sympathetic to the idea, but as yet non-committal.[24] Cromer, for his part, saw Sudan as a necessary appendage to the Anglo-Egyptian state, but the trauma of the Gordon experience had been such that now almost ten years later he still was in no hurry to adopt a position on the matter that would necessarily re-join Egypt and Sudan precipitously in a renewed territorial partnership. For Cromer, it was enough that the Mahdiiya had begun to slacken its hold over Sudan and that perhaps the time was approaching when a British campaign under Kitchener might be approved formally. But that time was definitely not the summer of 1894 when, in the midst of his persistent lobbying for just such a campaign, Kitchener was effectively told to cease and desist. 'I have to be quiet for a while', is he how explained the situation to Wingate in light of the fact that Cromer's agenda was topped by the prospect of building a dammed reservoir near Aswan on the Nile and what such a massive construction project might mean as a spur to the troubled Egyptian economy.[25] In this prevailing situation, the idea that the British position in Egypt would best be served by launching an expensive vengeance-seeking campaign into the desolate wastes of Sudan was to Cromer almost pure folly. Kitchener was savvy enough to understand that there was nothing to be gained by hectoring Cromer on this front. Nor was it to his advantage to employ the soft diplomacy of his personal friendships with any of Lord Edward Cecil, Lord Salisbury, or Lady Alice Cranborne (Salisbury's daughter-in-law), the latter of whom had become one of Kitchener's regular correspondents stemming from his now annual summertime visits to Hatfield House.

Throughout both the balance of 1894 and the following year this politico-economic equipoise held firm. But an event upset it early in 1896 and altered the course of British policy in Egypt, the result of which brought Kitchener to his desired course of Sudan's re-conquest. The impact of the 1884–5 Berlin West Africa Conference was now beginning to be felt more overtly and systematically throughout the northern half of the continent, including in the Horn of Africa where the newly unified Kingdom of Italy had made inroads in an attempt to extend its interests against those of the regionally more prominent British and French.[26] To that end, Italy had already claimed Eritrea and Somaliland, both impoverished and with poor prospects and demonstrative of exactly what Ronald Robinson and John Gallagher later would have in mind when stating famously that in going into tropical Africa when they did the Europeans were 'scraping the bottom of the barrel'.[27] Whether in that lowly station or no, King Umberto I of Italy's grand imperial vision was to link the two colonies with Ethiopia thereby forming a contiguously Italian bloc of territory. Ethiopian royalists had other plans, of course, and under Menelik II the country's longstanding and fierce independence was defended.

Earlier, in 1889, Ethiopia and Italy had signed the Treaty of Wuchale, which had ceded a handful of Ethiopian provinces to the Italians in return for support for the Menelik dynastic regime. In the years that followed, however, a dispute between them arose over the interpretation of the treaty, the Italians claiming that they had been granted control over Ethiopian foreign affairs, a claim that the Ethiopians rejected vehemently. The Italian perspective was that the treaty had rendered Ethiopia its protectorate and in 1894 they decided that the only solution to the simmering dispute was to launch a military invasion of Ethiopia. Initially, this first 'Italo-Ethiopian War' (the second would come some 40 years later under Benito Mussolini in 1935) went well for the technologically superior Italians. But that changed decisively on 1 March 1896 when Menelik's forces comprehensively defeated the Italians at the Battle of Adwa (or Adowa) where nearly 12,000 Italian troops were killed, wounded, or captured. Adwa was a signal victory for native troops over a European aggressor – one of just a handful in the African colonial era – and it guaranteed Ethiopia's independence, making it along with Liberia the only two African territories not to be colonized by the European powers in the nineteenth century. In the aftermath of the battle, the Treaty of Wuchale was duly abrogated and replaced by the new Treaty of Abbas Ababa, which solidified both Ethiopia's future and that of Menelik himself. In the context of the time the defeat was crushing to the Italians and naturally it sent shockwaves throughout the capitals of imperial Europe.[28]

In London, Salisbury, having returned to power following the Rosebery Liberal interregnum, acted almost immediately upon the events of Adwa and the Italian request for a show of British force in Sudan's northernmost Dongola province near Italy's now- exposed western Ethiopian outpost of Kassala. The Italians understandably feared that the rapturous response to its defeat at Adwa would inspire a Mahdist uprising there. On 12 March, therefore, after a vigorous discussion in Cabinet Salisbury telegraphed Cromer to this end. By early the next morning Kitchener too had been informed. Indeed, this was the moment that Kitchener had been waiting for: in a sense since 1885, but certainly since becoming Sirdar in 1892. Adwa was a casus belli, a reason for action, a chance to launch the re-conquest of Sudan. Apparently, so pleased was Kitchener to receive the news when it was delivered to him at 3 o'clock in the morning, that standing clad only in his pajamas he danced a celebratory jig.[29] At last, the chance to avenge Gordon, to take back Britain's lost honour, and, as we shall see, to dish the competitor French in the process, had presented themselves in the form of Italy's misfortune. A nocturnal, pajama-wearing jig would be only its beginning.

Immediately, Salisbury put Cromer in charge of the proposed expedition and in order to close tightly the circle of command his instructions, he made plain, would come from the Foreign Secretary alone, which as usual was Salisbury himself, and not from the War Office. Cromer immediately made Kitchener's assumed operational command formal. Accordingly, just a week later, on 16 March, the Sirdar was already almost 90 miles into Sudan, encamped at Akasha on the Nile, having reached this tiny village virtually unopposed. The re-conquest was on, and Kitchener could not have been happier. 'Lord Cromer is a splendid man to serve under', he would write shortly to Sir Edward Barrington, Cromer's private secretary, 'he has done everything one can possibly want and has been most kind'.[30]

As had been the case a dozen years earlier when the Gordon Relief Expedition was launched, logistics would count for much in trying to traverse the same hostile desert terrain as had been encountered then. Kitchener's long experience of surveying, campaigning, and organizing now served him exceptionally well in the biggest military endeavor he had yet faced. Since becoming Sirdar he had also gained an unflattering reputation for pushing frugality over the edge into niggardliness – such as issuing used uniforms to Egyptian troops – but if ever a campaign required eagle-eyed economics it was this one.[31] Both Cromer and Salisbury continued to understand that any sort of desert campaign would be prohibitively expensive, and that the Egyptian treasury was bare. Hence a stringent parsimony was the unbending rule from the beginning of the re-conquest.

Reconquering Sudan was also going to require the re-building and extension of the existing rail line and Kitchener threw himself into this project fully while at the same time ensuring that the flesh and blood ship of the desert, the camel, was in constant supply too. Accordingly, the odorous, bad-tempered beasts immediately were marshalled together by the hundreds. In London, reports of this marshalling caused a moment of uneasy levity where it was thought by some in Cabinet that given Kitchener's desert column experience of 1884–5 he was about to embark upon a reprise of it by marching off 'into the wilderness at the head of a string of camels', as Salisbury put it, not entirely in jest.[32]

Such would not be the case, but Salisbury, initially at least, was not far wrong. Railway-building would take some time to undertake; not so setting out across the desert astride a camel. Nothing about this re-conquest mattered to Kitchener as much as guaranteed and dependable transport and he immediately imported his seasoned brother, Walter, from India to direct its operations. Eight years Kitchener's junior, and a veteran of service in both India and Afghanistan, Walter worked well with his older brother and was enjoying a successful military career in his own right, one that would take him eventually to the rank of lieutenant general, and finally an appointment as a colonial governor.[33]

Having reached Akasha so easily Kitchener was anxious to continue the momentum by pushing deeper into Dongola province. Wingate, as Director of Intelligence, was telling him that the time was ripe, that a number of sheikhs were sympathetic to the re-conquest, and, at this point, Kitchener's purely-Egyptian and -Sudanese force of some 18,000 men would be more than adequate against what he had learned was a force of 'Dervishes' numbering no more than 10,000.[34] The clash duly came soon thereafter on 7 June at Firket, located about 15 miles upriver from Akasha. There the re-conquest received its baptism of fire in a quick engagement between Kitchener's Egypto-Sudanese force and those representing the Khalifa, Abdullahi. In a foreshadowing of the entire campaign that would culminate over two years later at Omdurman, Kitchener's troops scored a rout. Some 800 Dervish lay dead, clad in their signature patchwork *jibbah* (smock) were counted after the battle, as compared to a mere 20 Egyptian and Sudanese killed.[35]

Firket was a small but important victory for Kitchener, a talisman for the future of the campaign. He had proven that administratively and militarily his untested army could achieve its goals, having done 'the whole thing admirably', observed Cromer. 'I always felt that he would do so, as he is a first rate man'.[36] The proper next steps, however, were unclear. The obvious one was to advance on Dongola, the dusty and shambolic provincial capital about 200 miles beyond Firket and the furthest point to which Salisbury had authorized the campaign then to proceed. Wingate along with Sir Archibald Hunter, governor of Dongola province and commandant of the Frontier Field Force, were pressing their commander to continue on to Dongola town, confident that the Khalifa's men were melting away in advance of the increasingly confident Egypto-Sudanese troops.[37] Kitchener demurred, however, not inclined to stretch his force across almost 200 miles of desert. The disastrous fate of Colonel Hicks at Shaykan back in 1883 was never far from the minds of any British officer in Sudan, least of all Kitchener. Instead, the Sirdar ordered that Hunter bring the gunboats upriver, past the treacherous Second Cataract in order to supply a tertiary line of firepower and supply should it be needed. This task done, Kitchener then ruminated on his next move.

Before a definite plan was made, however, epidemic illness intervened on a massive scale. Dysentery and then cholera struck Kitchener's army shortly after the fighting at Firket in mid-June, debilitating the force for a number of weeks and killing nearly a thousand troops (and camp followers), far, far more than would die from battle wounds during the campaign. Kitchener himself escaped sickness, but the furnace that was the Nubian Desert in the summer was severely taxing to the body and mind of everyone on campaign nonetheless. Squinting into harsh daylight, face burnished a deep brown by the relentless sun, Kitchener had encountered this same physical environment before both in Sudan and Palestine. He therefore knew what to expect, and simply endured stoically its daily challenges.

By September, the hellishly hot summer was nearly over. Despite the hardships, illness, deprivation, and disease-induced delay of the preceding two months, Kitchener and his subordinate officers had pushed and pulled the Egyptian army into shape for an assault on Dongola. The gunboats – five of them, along with some supporting steam transports – had arrived at Firket and then moved a little further along to Kosheh, and were ready to continue upstream. The railway had by then come that far too. In London, Salisbury kept a close eye on the campaign through regular telegrams, partly for ongoing financial reasons and partly because of the strategic challenge posed by the French over the Nile Valley about which more will be said later.[38] Whether or not a victorious advance on Dongola would be followed by an eventual culminating assault on Khartoum still remained an open question, at least in the minds of Salisbury and Cromer, if not Kitchener.

On 12 September, after one final frustrating delay of overseeing the repair of a burst cylinder in one of the gunboats, Kitchener and his men (an advance column under brigade commander, Lieutenant Colonel Hector 'Fighting Mac' MacDonald, had departed a few days earlier) set off for distant Dongola. Some marched, some went by boat, but a week later all converged at Karma just above the Third Cataract and within striking distance of Dongola. The Dervish commander, the emir,

Mohammed Bishara, was well dug-in across the Nile at Hafir. He was outnumbered badly in troop strength, about three to one, and had quickly thrown up stout fortifications in an attempt to hold off Kitchener's numerically superior force. Battle was joined early on the morning of 19 September. The cascading firepower of the Egyptian guns made an immediate effect on the enemy's lines. The Dervishes, with much lesser effect, returned fire but the inevitable outcome soon became clear. Wounded, Bishara, left the field in the evening and retired to Dongola, about 30 miles away. Hafir, the penultimate act in the Dongola drama, now belonged to Kitchener.

Two days later on the 22nd, after a hasty ascent the rest of the way, the full force of Kitchener's 18,000-man Egyptian army advanced upon Dongola. The men, the horses, the colours – on both sides – gave the impending action an almost medieval feel. In the event, the encounter proved anti-climactic, however. One of the enemy's battle wings wheeled and left the field, prompting Kitchener and his officers to assume briefly that a tactical withdrawal was occurring.[39] In the end, it was later learned, Bishara had insisted upon a frontal assault, which so appalled his fellow emirs owing to its presumed suicidal outcome, that they had had him arrested and removed from command. The field thus left open in this way, the Egyptians moved forward to win an easy victory, taking along with it the usual spoils of guns, ammunition, food stocks, and conquered men – principally Sudanese – happy, it soon became clear, to serve under a new flag and throw off the *jibbah* of jihad. The first phase of the putative re-conquest of Sudan was now complete.

Kitchener's relatively swift taking of Dongola with minimal loss of life on the Egyptian side gave a kind of logical force to continuing on to Khartoum. Not only that, but the victory was met with high approbation in London as a partial vindication of General Gordon's spectral defeat of 11 years before. A special campaign medal was struck and Kitchener would soon be honoured yet again (Knight Commander of the Bath) and promoted brevet major general. In the aftermath of Dongola he sent his army around the great bend in the Nile to Merowe and then he himself set off for Cairo in order to consult with Cromer. Ever the paragon of fiscal prudence – even more so than Kitchener – Cromer was glad of the campaign's unalloyed successes but was still not at all sure about the cost of proceeding on to Khartoum in an attempt to break fully the Khalifa's power over Sudan. 'I had thought to stop two or three years at Dongola', Cromer wrote hopefully to Salisbury. Accordingly, for Cromer, the question was 'wholly one of finance'.[40] For Kitchener, similarly, it was one of finance too, but it was a problem that he thought could be solved in a different way. Cromer's position as consul-general and his diplomatic strengths gave him the opportunity to squeeze money out of the Debt Commission (Caisse de la Dette Publique) that had acted as a holding treasury for Egypt since the late 1870s. But, unsurprisingly, the French and Russian commissioners objected to Egypt's request for L500,000 to continue the Sudan campaign and ultimately the loan was not approved.[41] That left Kitchener with the military campaign-like task of returning to London in order to lobby directly the Chancellor of the Exchequer, Sir Michael Hicks Beach, for the funds needed to complete what the victory at Dongola had portended.

Kitchener, in travelling to London with Cromer's blessing, embarked upon a lightning strike against the Chancellor. Arriving on 9 November, he spent the next 12 days working various back channels in order to convince Hicks Beach that it was supremely in the British national interest for the Sudan campaign to continue until the task of re-taking Khartoum was complete. There was no advantage in delay and deliberation, only action, Kitchener insisted. In order to secure Egypt against the French in particular, Sudan must be pacified, he argued. There simply was no other acceptable course of action. Kitchener's insistence duly won the day and before leaving to return to Cairo on the 21st he had convinced Hicks Beach to authorize a loan to the Egyptian treasury which, in the end, totalled about L800,000.[42] He had also charmed Queen Victoria at both a dinner and then a luncheon, at which during the latter he was made K.C.B. 'Striking' and 'energetic-looking' is how a clearly impressed Queen described him in her journal.[43] And with that, and with the re-conquest now guaranteed financially, Kitchener returned immediately to Egypt in order to plan the concluding stages of the campaign.

Kitchener arrived back in Cairo at the beginning of December with a firm idea of how the rest of the Sudan campaign should unfold. Key to this presumption was the extension of the railway, but not along the Nile as it had been built thus far, but rather in a daring dart across the Nubian and Bayuda Deserts from Wadi Halfa to Abu Hamed in a manner that would eliminate the long, exposed, and slow curve in the river. The length of the proposed rail line would need to be about 230 miles but if successful would trim the distance to Khartoum by over double that distance and also remove three sets of challenging cataracts from the calculation. All in all, it was an ambitious – perhaps even foolhardy – plan and according to Archibald Hunter, one of his circle of commanders, it was Kitchener's 'idea, and his only'.[44]

The building of what would shortly be called officially the Sudan Military Railway (SMR) was a significant feat in an age full of epic railway construction. From Canada, to the U.S., to Siberia, to India, to east-central Africa, railway building was in the vanguard of late-nineteenth century industrial and economic expansion worldwide.[45] Kitchener's 230 mile stretch of desert railway might pale in length to the recently completed (1885) transcontinental Canadian Pacific (CPR) line, for example, but in overcoming severe obstacles it promised to be almost as daunting. The chief of these obstacles was whether or not water could be found regularly along the proposed route. To do that Kitchener had just the man, he believed, in Edward Cator, a young sapper in his army who was known also to be a superb water diviner. The proposed route map was duly divided into ten stations and Kitchener then marked two of them as possible locations for successful wells. Off went Cator into the desert wastes to practice his divining, and true to form he returned having found water in both! 'K's luck', he said, and so it was to be.[46] Having a dependable water supply for the construction gangs, locomotives, and camels meant that the desert could probably be conquered. The rest of it was up to a professional railway man and for that Kitchener had someone in mind also: a young engineer named Percy Girouard.

Edouard Percy Cranwill Girouard was a lieutenant in the Royal Engineers and had come out to Egypt in April of that year. A Canadian from Montreal who had trained at the Royal Military College in Kingston, Ontario, Girouard had spent a couple of years after graduating in 1886 working for the CPR in Quebec and Maine before taking up the offer of a commission in the Royal Engineers. In 1888, therefore, he left Canada and moved to Chatham, quickly making a name for himself there, and then later at the Royal Arsenal at Woolwich where he first happened to meet and impress Kitchener. A spell of rather desultory service followed but then early in 1896 came 'the greatest day of one's life', as Girouard described it, when he was ordered by the War Office to proceed to Egypt and thence to the railhead at Wadi Halfa and into Kitchener's service.[47] Later, Girouard would enjoy a British gubernatorial career in Nigeria and British East Africa. But beginning on New Year's Day, 1897 when his work in Sudan commenced, his life became all about building Kitchener's railway to victory.

The SMR would be built at speed and with a very high degree of cooperation between Kitchener and Girouard. The latter passed his 30th birthday during the first month of the line's construction, but his relative youth belied superb engineering expertise and a confident personal manner that the Sirdar found immediately to his liking. The first question to be answered was the persistant question of railway guage. Kitchener advocated and won approval for the 3' 6" width as against the Egyptian narrow (3' 4") standard. Cecil Rhodes's 'Cape to Cairo' railway scheme was afoot just then and Kitchener was keen to play a part in this grand caper of linking up British rail lines from the top of Africa to the bottom, Cromer's objections to the wider guage notwithstanding. Securing sufficient rolling stock was another pressing question. And, as if to answer the favour, Girouard was sent by Kitchener to London in February to obtain locomotives and other necessary railcars – 'Don't spend too much, Girouard. We are terribly poor' – which he did from Rhodes who had originally intended the stock to go to South Africa.[48]

These delays and final work on the river railway to Karma meant that intensive work on the desert line did not begin until May, but when it did rails were laid at the impressive rate of a mile per day, the inexorable and inhospitable desert being eaten up thanks to the work of the 2,000 labourers employed and to the water from Cator's wells, located assuredly along the way at Stations 4 and 6. Kitchener, ever the engineer and surveyor, was in his element during these months, supervising every jot and tittle of the operation and strategizing over the impact of its soon-completion. Winston Churchill, in writing later of the achievement of the SMR, was typically unbridled in his praise of all concerned, especially Girouard: 'Sitting in his hut at Wady Halfa, he drew up a comprehensive list. Nothing was forgotten. Every want was provided for; every difficulty was foreseen ... and such was the comprehensive accuracy of the estimate that the working parties were never delayed by the want even of a piece of brass wire'.[49]

Kitchener – with 'a machine-like regularity' – drove himself and everyone else extremely hard. Work began in the cool of the very early morning at 3 o'clock and continued with breaks until late-afternoon.[50] Early-July brought the line to nearly the half-way point. Abu Hamed was now about a hundred miles away but it remained in the grip of the Khalifa's troops and therefore posed a potential threat to the steadily approaching rail camp. Having anticipated this situation, Kitchener ordered Major General Archibald Hamilton to come up the north bank of the Nile with a flying column from his encampment at Merowe, where the Egyptian army had been stationed since the previous September following its victory at Dongola. If Abu Hamed could be taken then the initial terminus of the SMR could be secured. Serving under Hamilton was Hector MacDonald commanding a brigade, along with a troop of cavalry and accompanying guns. Speeding along the riverbank, they remained undetected until having almost reached their destination. Bursting upon the enemy in the dead of night the expedition was a complete success and on 7 August the town was taken easily, clearing the way for the furious completion of the line approaching from the north. Accordingly, by the end of October, Kitchener, Girouard, and the thousands of 'platemen' who had laid the line were standing uncontested in Abu Hamed, only five months after plunging into the job. K's luck, indeed.

The achievement was great. The town of Berber, further south still than Abu Hamed, was soon taken also, but the pressure on everyone involved had been immense. Kitchener himself was near to breaking point. 'You have no idea what continual anxiety, worry, and strain I have through it all', he had written on 6 October to the undersecretary for finance in London, Sir Clinton Dawkins, with whom he had been corresponding regularly about the cost of the railway. 'I do not think I can stand much more, and feel sometimes so completely done up that I can hardly go on and wish I were dead. Before next year's work in the field begins I must get some leave or I shall break down'.[51] Consequently, shortly thereafter on the 18th, so overburdened by work was Kitchener, that he sent a telegram to Cromer tendering his resignation.[52] Cromer did not pay it much mind, however, knowing that the strain of the task at hand had overtaken him temporarily and that when his mind cleared he would be able to re-focus with vigour on the remaining goal of the Khalifa's defeat.

Indeed, in referencing the following year's 'work in the field' in the Dawkins letter Kitchener was making clear his insistence that the re-conquest must be completed in full. 'I hope there will be no question about finishing off the whole thing at Omdurman next year', he noted to Dawkins.[53] Despite the rather soft tone of the statement, Kitchener was in no doubt about the situation. He and his men had not come this far to pull up short, wait upon events, and give time to the Khalifa to consolidate the Ansar in a desperate attempt to resist the inexorable on-rush of the Egyptian army. Exhaustion, worry, and angst over the endless imprecations required to secure funding for the railway and re-conquest may have driven Kitchener close to collapse. But the prize of running the Union Jack up the flagpole on top of what remained of the Governor's Palace at Khartoum where Gordon had scanned the horizon in forlorn hope of seeing the approaching relief mission, was too keenly anticipated for Kitchener to fall permanently into the slough of despond. Omdurman, the Khalifa's main encampment, was now just some 190 miles away, a tantalizing prospect, and the year 1898 would be spent in its single-minded pursuit.

In London, the success of the campaign, both the field victories and the building of the SMR, engendered an increasing amount of bipartisan political support for the re-conquest. Adding impetus too was the geo-political pressure injected into the prevailing situation by the presence of the French in the Upper Nile region. A French expedition from West Africa under the leadership of Captain Jean-Baptiste Marchand would shortly culminate in the tri-colour flag being planted within what the British assumed was their sphere of influence, and the potential re-conquest of Sudan would make such a position inviolable according to the provisions of the Berlin Conference of 1885.[54] Hence, when Chancellor Hicks Beach rose in the House of Commons at the end of November and announced that it was the government's decision that Kitchener's advance should continue on to Omdurman and Khartoum, it was met with a rousing round of huzzahs from both government and opposition benches alike.[55]

By the early months of 1898, therefore, preparations to advance on Omdurman were in full fettle. Kitchener had requested the sending up of additional troops. Using the SMR as far as it would take them and then by marching, the troops arrived en masse so that by February about 14,000 men, almost the full Anglo-Egyptian force, was encamped near Berber. The vortex of culminating war now was close. The Khalifa's troops were under the command of the young emir, Mahmoud Ahmed, and of Kitchener's old nemesis, Osman Digna. Together, they presided over a force of about 15,000 Ansar, but the two commanders differed as to their deployment. Ahmed favoured marching alongside the Nile and hitting the Anglo-Egyptians frontally, while Digna was convinced that a wide flanking movement would yield the best result. As their debate continued, Kitchener pushed them (inadvertently?) towards a decision by bombarding the Dervish lines with shells from his gunboats. In the face of such constant harassment, they opted for Digna's plan and swung away from the river and marched until pitching camp near the confluence of the Atbara, a tributary of the Nile, and the great river itself. Once there, early in March, they dug in by constructing a gigantic mud *zariba* with a width of about a thousand yards complete with a trench-works and firing ramparts.[56] And then they sat back and waited. Confronted by this hurriedly constructed desert fortress and not sure what to do, Kitchener did the same thing. The Dervish encampment was some 40 miles from the Nile, potentially a brutal desert march and once again conjuring of the Hicks debacle at Shaykan. If left alone, the Dervish army could be expected to eventually run out of food (the Ansar were joined by thousands of dependent camp followers) and be forced into debilitating acts of desperation, which might be turned into a victory by attrition. Still, thought Kitchener, what to do?

On the last day of March the vexed Sirdar convened a war council. Hunter, Wingate, and the new British brigade commander, Colonel William Gatacre, met with Kitchener. They all, it seems, although the record is unclear, suggested that they wait and not launch an assault on the fortified Dervish position. Kitchener, however, was cautiously confident that a clear victory at Atbara would open the way to Omdurman, and the sooner it was achieved, the better. Still, he waited, the hesitation continuing for a tortuous week. Telegrams were sent to Cromer in Cairo, who in turn consulted Lord Wolseley, Commander in Chief, in London.[57] No one was sure what to do and Wolseley, rightly, told Kitchener that he was in the best position to decide: 'You must be a better judge than Lord Cromer or me or anyone else can be. You have your thumb upon the pulse of the Army and can best know what it is capable of'.[58] Wolseley's emboldening words had the desired effect, it appears, because on 7 April Kitchener made the decision that the attack would launch the next day, Good Friday. 'The *Sirdar* is absolutely confident that every officer and man will do his duty', he stated in his battle orders in an echo of Nelson's famous injunction at Trafalgar. 'He only wishes to impress upon them two words: "Remember Gordon". The enemy before them are Gordon's murderers'.[59] And with that, the Battle of Atbara commenced.

As dawn broke over the Sudanese desert on 8 April 1898 Kitchener directed his Egyptian, Sudanese, and British troops into a line about 1,500 yards across and just 600 yards or so in front of the Dervish zariba. At just after 6 o'clock in the morning battle was joined as Kitchener gave the order to fire and the great guns opened up on the mud fortress of Mahmoud and Osman.[60] The latter, forecasting defeat and showing a well-developed talent for self-preservation, decided to slip away. Mahmoud, in contrast, fought ferociously beside his men, was captured, and later imprisoned in Egypt. Good Friday – as it would be similarly for the Canadians later at Vimy Ridge in 1917 – proved a highly auspicious day.[61] The rout was on, an exercise in nascent industrial warfare. Within two hours the defending Dervish army had been completely smashed. Three thousand lay dead or wounded while a further 2,000 were captured. Kitchener's army lost just 80 men killed, with a further 500 wounded. The scale of victory for this new kind of warfare was typical and would be seen again with even greater force at Omdurman. Regardless, the day was Kitchener's, the penultimate one on the road to the Khalifa's final destruction. In a very rare show of public emotion tears rolled down Kitchener's cheeks that afternoon during the funeral for the British fallen.[62] The victory was unqualified and was reported as such in London by a number of journalists – the best example of which is G.W. Steevens of the *Daily Mail* – who were a relatively new 'embedded' feature of contemporary war reporting.[63] As Steevens, the most famous war correspondent of his time described it, the victory parade through the streets of Berber on 12 April saw Kitchener at its head, 'tall, straight and masterful in his saddle', the crowds in paroxysms of cheers as they celebrated their liberation from the callous control and serial violence of Mahmoud.[64] Telegraphed congratulations poured into Kitchener's headquarters, such as that from the legendary

Field Marshal, Lord Roberts, just then Commander in Chief in Ireland but soon to be the same in South Africa, who wrote effusively, congratulating Kitchener on 'the very complete blow you dealt the Dervish Army. Nothing could have been better'.[65] The re-conquest was nearly complete. Before him lay Omdurman and Khartoum, the beating heart of the *Mahdiiya*. But unlike in 1885 with Gordon, this time Kitchener and the British would not be arriving 'too late'.[66]

5

Omdurman, Fashoda, and Khartoum, 1898–9

The Anglo-Egyptian victory at Atbara complete, Kitchener spent the summer of 1898 in both Cairo and at the front preparing for the impending march on the Khalifa's army, now holding fast at Omdurman. The chief question debated by the Sirdar and his subordinate generals and staff during those weeks was whether or not Abdullahi would keep his men behind the protective mud walls of the city in anticipation of the advance of the Anglo-Egyptians, or lead them out to wage an open-field battle. Reginald Wingate, based on earlier precedent as well as on information gleaned from his intelligence-gathering network, was sure that a fight on the open plain would be the Khalifa's choice.[1] To that end, a convinced Kitchener ordered additional men and equipment including gunboats be brought up on the almost-finished railway, which had reached Atbara by the beginning of July. By then the enlarged Anglo-Egyptian army encampment was a buzzing hive of activity. Everyone was readying for what was assumed would be the final act in the 15-year British desert drama that had commenced with Colonel Hicks in 1883 and would reach its climax with Kitchener by the end of the year.

Later, in July, and having returned from four restful weeks spent in Cairo, Kitchener led his powerfully reinforced army unopposed to encamp at Wadi Hamed, located 60 miles north of Omdurman. Under Kitchener's command now were some 25,000 men, comprised of about 17,000 Egyptians and Sudanese, and around 8,000 British regulars.

The ordnance in support of these troops was substantial: ten well-armed gunboats, along with some 60 field pieces, including 20 maxim guns – the signature weapon of the age about which Hilaire Belloc would write sardonically that year in recognition of European technical superiority in the age of empire: 'Whatever happens, we have got the Maxim gun, and they have not'.[2] In addition, covering the Sirdar's flanks, was a force of about 2,500 Arab irregulars on one side, and the Egyptian Camel Corps on the other. All told, Kitchener's desert army was a formidable force. Altogether, the assembled army, its stentorian commander, and the prospect of a comprehensive and highly symbolic victory lent the advance on Omdurman a certain celebrity made more pronounced by the continuing presence of journalists. Lamentably, as far as Kitchener was concerned, one such journalist – in the person of the young subaltern Winston Churchill – was exactly the wrong kind of scribe to be on the campaign (G.A. Henty, the novelist of imperial adventure, on the other hand, was also there and was manifestly the right kind, in Kitchener's estimation) and he made no compunction about his dislike of both him and his meddling society mother Jenny, Lady Randolph Churchill, who had done much to ensure her son's unwelcome presence in Sudan.[3]

Churchill, as he himself of course hoped, was fast making a name for himself on campaign. In the spring of 1898 he had published his first book, *The Story of the Malakand Field Force*, chronicling the eponymous Indian North-West Frontier campaign in which, in truth, he had played a very minor role.[4] In Kitchener's view, therefore, Churchill was little more than a glory-hound who had used every possible political connection – including that with Prime Minister Salisbury, who had read the book – to enable a posting of 'convenience' to Sudan.[5] Thoroughly indisposed towards Churchill from the beginning, Kitchener was pestered unremittingly by Lady Randolph and other sympathizers to find a post for the young aspirant, and finally in exasperation he approved his attachment to a cavalry regiment, the 21st Lancers. But on no account did Kitchener actually want to meet him. Churchill duly arrived in Cairo at the beginning of August, cavalry commission in hand, to go with the one he had also with the *Morning Post* to file letters describing the campaign, 'as opportunity served'.[6] By the end of the month Churchill was encamped at Wadi Hamed, writing to his mother that shortly 'there will be a general action, perhaps a very severe one'. As always, supremely confident in his own destiny, Churchill

assured her that he would come out of it all right and that 'nothing . . .
would make me turn back now'.[7]

Churchill certainly was right about timing. The impending great
battle indeed was imminent. The Nile was in full flood meaning that the
array of gunboats and steam transports could be used to their maximum
advantage by Kitchener. Accordingly, on the morning of 26 August the
army started its final march to confront the Khalifa. The sight, as well-
described later by Churchill, was nothing less than breathtaking: a vast
array of khaki-clad, topi-wearing men, accompanied by heavy and
cumbersome equipment and bawling, snorting animals moving along
the western bank of the Nile. 'In the clear air the amazing detail of the
picture was striking', he wrote, almost in awe. 'There were six brigades
of infantry, composed of twenty-four battalions; yet every battalion
showed that it was made up of tiny figures, all perfectly defined on the
plain'.[8] Kitchener rode at the head of this massive agglomeration, sitting
astride his white Arab charger, like a vision of Alexander himself. The
front stretched almost three miles wide, the troops in ready formation in
case they were called upon to fight immediately. Wingate had reported
that a Dervish force of at least 50,000 men, potentially more, lay in wait
at Omdurman; but they might be expected to move at any minute out of
the mud-walled fortress to advance onto the open Kerreri Plain just a few
miles north of the city. In command under Kitchener were the trusted
Brigadier General William Gatacre, of the British Division, and his
counterpart commanding the Egyptians, Major General Archibald
Hunter. Meanwhile, the 15-boat flotilla continued to churn through the
high-water of the Nile. All was in readiness. Kitchener himself was
poised for action, 'very cheery and in great fettle', as his brother Walter,
in charge of the expedition's 2,500 camels, described him.[9]

On the morning of 1 September the entire force – 'the grand army of
the Nile', as Churchill called it – was encamped at El Egeiga, a village
on the west bank of the river.[10] A zariba was hurriedly constructed, the
expectation being that they were at the place from which battle would
most probably be joined. From a nearby 300-foot-high elevated
viewpoint called Jebel Surgham Kitchener looked out across the Kerreri
Plain to Omdurman in the middle distance, about three miles away, its
cityscape punctuated only by the gleaming 85-foot-high tower of the
Mahdi's tomb. Beyond that a little further southeast and across the Nile,
lay the still-ruined city of Khartoum. On the plain in the foreground

could be seen a gigantic, dark moving mass. The Ansar in their thousands had indeed left their Omdurman base and were advancing toward Kitchener's position. When, just before noon, an official report was brought to him about the advance by none other than Second Lieutenant Winston Churchill, Kitchener – without betraying whether or not he recognized the messenger (he did) – ruminated for a few minutes, and then said: 'How long do you think I've got?' Churchill replied that he figured about an hour or so.[11] Kitchener took in the estimate calmly and then dismissed him. Shortly thereafter he ordered the Anglo-Egyptian brigades to advance about 500 yards beyond the zariba in anticipation of impending action. Having done so they waited, wilting in the intense 40-degrees Celsius heat of the mid-afternoon desert sun. The tension of the atmosphere was soon broken, but not by rifle-fire; rather it came from the throaty, piercing call of *Allahu akbar* ('God is great') emanating from the mouths of more than 50,000 Islamic warriors. The war cry was strange and chilling to most of the (new) British troops, but when it ended the desert, apart from the sound of Kitchener's Arab irregulars successfully putting down intermittent resistance on the east side of the Nile, lapsed again into silence. For the time being, the enigmatic Ansar had ceased their advance and remained unmoving in position. In the early-afternoon, British artillery fire commenced and shells began to rain down upon Omdurman, especially upon the dome of the Mahdi's tomb, inflicting serious (and symbolic) damage to the city.[12] A cataclysmic fight was coming, but it would not come that day, however. Kitchener instructed that the gunboats should keep their searchlights on as evening fell, sweeping brightly across the plain and as far as the Dervish lines. Both sides then settled into a long and fitful evening and night.

The next morning, 2 September 1898, the bugles and fife & drums of reveille awakened the Anglo-Egyptian-Sudanese camp at 4 o'clock. Dawn was still an hour away. The nighttime rain – August and September is the wettest time of the year in Sudan – had only just ceased so the troops were soaked through, as well as hungry and jumpily nervous. The British ate their usual breakfast of porridge and bully-beef rations, cleaned and oiled their weapons – principally the Lee-Metford bold action magazine rifle (the Egyptians and Sudanese carried the lesser-quality Martini-Henry single shot lever action rifle) – and waited for the word. Based on past practice the expectation was that a Dervish attack would come about the same time as sunrise, which was expected around 5 o'clock.

By 5:30, however, no movement amongst the Khalifa's forces could be detected. Kitchener decided that he could wait no longer and ordered that the lines should begin to form up in front of the semi-circular zariba. In the near distance, less than two miles away, the Ansar were also forming up along a broad front spread across four to five miles of desert. Kitchener's men were outnumbered over 2:1, but far exceeded their enemy in firepower. The Ansar were mainly foot soldiers armed with sword and spear. Some had Remington rifles, and a handful of field artillery pieces (mainly captured at Khartoum in 1885, and before that in 1883 at Shaykan) bolstered the Khalifa's killing power. He also had some 2,000 cavalry. In the main, however, the only hope for success lay in an onrush of thousands of enraged Ansar whose determination and sense of ordained fanaticism – the Khalifa claimed that in a vision both the Mahdi and the Prophet Mohammad had assured him of victory and all who died would be ushered straightway into paradise – would prove overwhelming to the well-ordered and well-armed British, Egyptian, and Sudanese forces.[13]

Shortly after 6:30 a.m. with the sun well-up and fully bathing the Kerreri Plain in bright morning light, the first of the Ansar crested the low hill of Jebel Surgham to the southwest of the zariba. Churchill – always, it seems, in the optimal spot – reported breathlessly that indeed they were on the move, and what a sight it was! 'All the pride and might of the Dervish Empire', he wrote later in admiration, 'were massed on this last great day of its existence'.[14] The onrush was underway, which is exactly what Kitchener had expected would happen. As about 8,000 Ansar under the command of one of the Khalifa's generals, Osman Azraq, began their automaton-like approach in wave after wave, giving voice to their war cry of *La Ilaha illa Ilah wa Mohammad rasul Allah* ('There is one God and Mohammad is the messenger of God'), Kitchener ordered his main (32nd) field battery to open up at a range of about 2,700 yards. The effect on the enemy was immediate and devastating. As the incoming shells burst metal tore with ease through their flimsy patchwork *jibbah* and the Ansar began to fall in droves. In a foretaste of mechanized modern warfare (seen first during the US Civil War of some 35 years earlier) the bravely advancing Ansar, fighting in medieval formation, were cut down en masse in great numbers and in horrific style.

As the sky rained hot metal for what would be almost an hour on the centre of the Khalifa's army, his divisions to the north (fighting under the Green Standard), to the south (under the White Standard, from which Azraq had detached his troops), and the rear (under the Black Standard) began to move more deliberately into position. Together, these three divisions comprised some 40,000 men, about 17,000 of which were under the Khalifa's own Black Standard and were purposely being held in reserve. As the British barrage continued dead and mangled bodies lay everywhere, covering the battlefield in a shockingly bloody palimpsest of human detritus. Artillery, the gunboats, the Maxim gun, the Lee-Metford rifle – 'pound, pound, pound', remembered one of Kitchener's officers, all had produced an enormous butcher's bill of dead Ansar.[15] By 7:30 a.m., barely an hour into the battle and even with the assistance of Kitchener's old enemy Osman Digna, Azraq's onrush had petered out in the face of the endless withering fire emanating from behind the trenches and the Mimosa hedge that demarcated the British zariba. The courage of the enemy in facing down this remorseless fusillade was clear to ordinary British soldiers, with one of them, Sergeant Edward Fraley, for example, remembering it this way: 'The Dervishes are very brave – to stick it like they did was wonderful . . . . First one dropped, then the fellow carrying the flag, another picked it up and still came on, when the two left almost dropped together, they marched straight to death right enough'.[16] Their blind fortitude stands as a rebuke, as it were, of the Khalifa's old-style, head-on strategy and its clear lack of any understanding of the killing power of modern weaponry. But of course, there would be many in the early part of the twentieth century, especially of course during World War I, who likewise could not comprehend what to do in the face of the immutable stopping power of mechanized weapons. In the event, having never gotten closer to the British lines than about 300 yards, at least 2,000 Ansar lay dead in the dust, with thousands more wounded. Azraq himself mounted a final charge, a forlorn hope, and was duly annihilated by a wall of British metal. The face of ultra-modern warfare had had its baptism here on the Kerreri Plain, a terrible introduction to what would soon define a whole generation in Britain after 20,000 of the nation's soldiers were killed in a not dissimilar fashion just 18 years later on the first day of the Battle of the Somme on 1 July 1916.

At just the moment that Azraq met his grisly end, Kitchener was observing the slaughter from a position behind the trusted Cameron Highlanders as they fired pell-mell onto the enemy from the safety of the zariba. Anglo-Egyptian casualties over that first hour of the battle totalled fewer than a hundred and the enormous disproportion in the numbers of killed and wounded boded exceedingly well that the day would soon belong to the Sirdar. Kitchener, impassive and observant throughout the early morning's action, 'sat stolidly upon his horse', wrote a junior officer later, 'and at this period of the day no expression upon his face gave evidence of any emotion. The only evidence of what he must really have felt was in the many short questions which he shot incessantly at the various members of his staff'.[17] Around 8 o'clock he called for an end to the firing: 'Cease fire . . .', he called out, 'What a dreadful waste of ammunition!'[18] The cacophony duly died away briefly, at least within Kitchener's direct line of sight. But to the right in the near distance, 250 feet up in the Kerreri hills, the next significant chapter in the day's battle was forming. The Anglo-Egyptian cavalry and the Camel Corps under the command of Lieutenant Colonel R.G. Broadwood were massed there and looking down upon about 15,000 Ansar as they marshalled under the Green Standard of Osman Din. For them, the possibility of being cut off from the safety of the zariba was real. What to do?

Broadwood's options for action were limited. If he were to fall back on the zariba, as shortly Kitchener would instruct him to do, he might easily bring with him the full brunt of Din's men in hot pursuit.[19] Having made rather short work of the first frontal Dervish attack on their entrenched position the British may have been equal to such a challenge, but the prospect of 15,000 Ansar smashing into the centre-north face of the zariba – believed to be the weakest part of the redoubt since it was being held by the Egyptians and Sudanese only – was to Broadwood a risk not worth taking. Instead, he decided to try and draw Din's force away from the zariba in a fighting retreat that would take both him and them farther into the hills. In part, he was successful. The trouble with the plan, however, was that the ponderously slow Camel Corps was in no position to escape the onrush of the swiftly pursuing Ansar. But in a frantic attempt to reach the zariba it had begun a race that it had no chance of winning. The Camel Corps galloped hard, but the Ansar on horseback galloped faster. The moment it were to be overtaken a fearful massacre would surely ensue, of this the now helpless Broadwood was in no doubt. Recognizing early the perilous situation in which the Camel Corps now found itself, Kitchener had instructed the gunboats to move down the Nile so as to bring them into optimal position to rain shells down upon the heads of the fast moving Ansar.[20] Major Monkey Gordon, the Sirdar's long-time trusted protégé, was in command of the gunboat *Melik* and he was first on the scene, opening up on the unsuspecting Dervishes with a devastating combination of Maxims, various cannon, and Nordenfelt guns, a multiple barrel machine gun of uniquely destructive power. The attacking Ansar staggered immediately under the onslaught, and when another gunboat (the *Abu Klea*) likewise moved into position and began to pour down additional hot fire they broke and retreated, leaving the way clear for the Camel Corps to gain the zariba after having suffered few casualties and avoiding sure catastrophe. Shortly thereafter, a greatly relieved Broadwood – assisted by, among others, Captain Douglas Haig, then at the outset of a military career that would of course culminate in World War I – arrived too with the cavalry.[21]

The excitement of the Camel Corps' near escape had temporarily drawn Kitchener's attention away from what now was expected to be the attack of the Khalifa and his Black Standard troops, in a kind of last-ditch effort reminiscent of a Napoleonic battle in which the French Imperial Guard would be thrown into action to save (or seal) the day. At 8:30, almost two hours into the battle, Kitchener ordered a charge by the 21st Lancers in an attempt to cut off any possibility of the Khalifa's troops angling in retreat towards Omdurman, should the enemy decide to take this moment to re-group and fight another day.[22] If any sole action of the battle spoke of old-style British imperial warfare, this charge (made famous by Churchill as one of its participants) was it. Indeed, the charge of the 21st Lancers would be the last of its kind in the history of British warfare. And even though the charge was immortalized by its enamoured chronicler Churchill, success did not come easily and had it failed might just have given enough hope to the faltering Ansar to rally and save themselves – and the Mahdist state – from what was looking now like their sure destruction.[23]

In advance of the Lancers' expected charge a couple of patrols were sent out to reconnoitre Jebel Surgham hill and to determine the status and movement of the Black Standard troops. Kitchener was duly informed that indeed a long line of Ansar could be seen on the move towards Omdurman, but the Black Standard itself signifying the location of the Khalifa was not apparent. To this intelligence, the Sirdar replied flatly: 'advance and clear the left flank and use every effort to prevent the enemy re-entering Omdurman'.[24] Lieutenant Colonel Rowland Martin, in command of the 21st, took this instruction as a mandate to attack, which he did forthwith at a shallow hollow or *khor* to the left of Jebel Surgham. Lying in wait there was a force of about 2,500 Ansar, a far greater number than was thought by the British and certainly too many to risk a charge. But thinking that the number was considerably smaller (perhaps a thousand) Martin gave the order to attack and into the fray rode some 300 British horsemen. Slamming into the stationary and partially hidden Ansar at full gallop, the impact was immense and it staggered the enemy, sweeping them 'head over heels into the *khor*', wrote Churchill, in typical form overjoyed to be one of the 300 riders.[25] The momentum of the charging Lancers carried most of them right through the shattered Dervish line and at some 200 yards distant they dismounted, turned, and enfiladed the Dervishes with rifle fire. Those British cavalrymen who had not made it through the Dervish line – such as Churchill – were engaged immediately in savage hand to hand combat, the result of which would lead to the awarding of three Victoria Crosses.[26] Dramatic and violent though it was, the whole action was brief, the charge and ensuing melee lasting mere minutes.

In response to the Lancers' successful charge, Kitchener believed a comprehensive victory now was close at hand. At 9:15, therefore, he set off for Jebel Surgham at the head of a substantial force of five brigades, the most important of which was Hector MacDonald's, bringing up the rear. Kitchener trusted MacDonald implicitly, believing that if the Green Standard troops still in the Kerreri hills were to attack from behind MacDonald would be able to fend them off. Indeed, they would attack in just that manner in due course, but more menacing still was the presence of the Black Standard troops, which the desperate Khalifa now chose to unleash. A furious firefight ensued, second only in intensity to the opening Dervish attack of the day. Ultimately, MacDonald's brigade needed to be reinforced in order to withstand it and the oncoming Dervishes got to within 300 yards of the brigade's lines before being beaten off. The Black Standard itself was seen fluttering in the wind and surrounded by a mound of bloodied bodies, was captured. But not before the Khalifa had fled rather ignominiously on a donkey towards the relative safety of Omdurman amidst an artillery bombardment ordered by Wingate when he spotted the Dervish leader stealing away from the battlefield.[27] Thus by about 11:30 a.m., not quite four hours after Asraq's initial assault on the British zariba, the battle of Omdurman was well and truly over and won. Relieved, satisfied, and triumphant, but ever phlegmatic, Kitchener turned to his gathered officers and remarked that the enemy had been given 'a good dusting'.[28] And with that cryptic comment the Sirdar put away his field glasses, signalled for a general advance to begin shortly, and then crossed the last few miles to the gates of the stricken city of Omdurman.

Kitchener's understatement describing the battle belied the fearful slaughter of that blood-soaked morning. All told, around 10,000 Dervishes had been killed with a further 12,000 wounded and some 5,000 taken prisoner. Fully half the Khalifa's army were casualties of battle that September day. In stark contrast, Kitchener's army had suffered a mere scratch, as it were: 48 dead and 382 wounded.[29] There was no mistaking the comprehensive nature of the victory, the completely disproportionate casualty numbers lending the Battle of Omdurman an air not of a fair and honourable fight, but rather of an imperial bully having run rampant over a completely outclassed opponent. 'It was not a battle, but an execution'. So wrote the embedded, and otherwise usually admiring, journalist G.W. Steevens.[30] More of this will be said later, but of course, the same charge of an unfair fight could be (and had been) made against the Mahdi's descent upon Khartoum when in his final attack against General Gordon in January 1885 some 10,000 defenders and inhabitants of the city – as we have seen, one-quarter of its long besieged and starved population – were without mercy put to the sword by a force of some 50,000 Ansar.[31] However calculated, Kitchener's victory that September day signified the imminent end of a 15-year theocratically retrograde regime in Sudan. As Fergus Nicoll points out in his probing book on the period, few people could rightly lament the passing of the Mahdi-Khalifa governing axis, even if the human cost of ending it was high.[32]

Kitchener, in advance of his culminating entry into Omdurman and after the exertions of the morning, rested briefly. Then at 2:00 p.m., he mounted his white horse and riding alongside Major John G. Maxwell and his brigade cantered an hour later into what was a supremely cowed city. The Khalifa's capital was a shambles of destroyed mud buildings and houses. Human and animal corpses lay everywhere, the stench almost unbearable in the hot afternoon sun, which caused some of the

British troops to vomit.[33] No resistance to the arriving British was given apart from the occasional pocket of loyal Ansar determined to fight on in what was manifestly a lost cause. A lone elderly emir approached Kitchener and after being told that the surviving women and children of the city would not be massacred – as they would have been in internecine jihadist warfare – he presented the Sirdar with the key to the city. Kitchener was then roundly cheered by the relieved populace. On rode the triumphant British along the sole unobstructed avenue in Omdurman, which cut through the abundant destruction and squalor all around, towards the Khalifa's citadel located at its centre. Enclosed within its 14-foot high mud walls was what had served as the headquarters of Mahdist rule for the preceding 13 years. The armoury and treasury; the prison; the mosque; the battered Mahdi's tomb, where the Khalifa had come after earlier fleeing the battlefield and from which he had not long since departed once hearing that Kitchener had entered the city; the palace. The prize, such as it was, had been won, but the Khalifa himself had escaped and Kitchener soon tasked Lieutenant Colonel Broadwood with tracking him down in what would prove to be a vain attempt at his capture.

In the meantime, Kitchener and his retinue approached the Mahdi's tomb amidst the dangerous incongruity of friendly shellfire ordered in the belief that the Khalifa might still be present. Having spied the Khalifa's standard waving near the tomb (as he was escaping) the gunners of the 32nd Field Battery opened up as instructed and in the process inadvertently killed a newspaper correspondent (Hubert Howard of *The Times*), and very nearly hit Kitchener himself. Unperturbed in the face of the continuing fire, however, Kitchener remarked flatly that 'I don't see how we can stop it, and it would be a pity to lose our ticket when the day is won. I am afraid we must give them the honour'.[34] He then proceeded on to the prison, where about 30 Europeans remained languishing in what Churchill described as a 'foul and gloomy den'.[35] Just a few years earlier in 1895, one of the then-prisoners, Rudolf von Slatin, had escaped. An Austrian, Slatin had served as a provincial governor in Sudan under Gordon until taken prisoner by the Mahdi. At the time of the fall of Khartoum he had identified Gordon's decapitated head in the Mahdi's camp and as a colleague of the slain governor general was subsequently jailed for a decade in Omdurman.[36] After breaking out of prison with Wingate's help early in 1895, as noted earlier, Slatin had made it safely to Aswan and then eventually was seconded to service in the Egyptian army for the re-conquest.[37] Now, at the moment of supreme vindication, he was determined to capture the Khalifa in repayment for his brutal ten-year incarceration, but ultimately would be disappointed in the event. At the prison, Kitchener freed the captives, which included some Roman Catholic nuns – 'Out you go!' – before eventually composing and dispatching telegrams to London telling of the nature and success of the battle. Exhausted after a supremely momentous day, the victorious Sirdar then retired for the night.[38]

The next day, 3 September, Kitchener inspected the heavily damaged tomb of the Mahdi and decided that to prevent it from becoming a place of future fanatical pilgrimage it should be razed to the ground. The job would be given to Monkey Gordon, who happily obliged a few days later. Before that, Kitchener had had the bones of the dead Mahdi disinterred and in a controversial move that was seen by some – including Queen Victoria – as both dishonourable and distasteful, had them cast into the Nile. Later, after writing to Kitchener that what had been done with the Mahdi's remains was suggestive of the 'Middle Ages', the Queen reminded him that 'the graves of our people have been respected and those of our foes should, in her opinion, also be'.[39] Amazingly, the Mahdi's skull was retained briefly by Kitchener for possible use as an inkpot, but then he felt better of it and eventually had it buried secretly in a Muslim cemetery at Wadi Halfa. The jocular consideration of the Mahdi's skull and the callous disposal of his remains rightly did Kitchener no credit, either then or later. Indeed, in Churchill's private letters of the time he was scathing in his view of Kitchener's actions in this regard, although as we have seen earlier, he had his own agenda when it came to criticizing the Sirdar.[40] A short while later, in the first edition of *The River War*, Churchill's chronicle of the campaign which came out in 1899, he continued to criticize Kitchener, accusing him of 'vandalism' in razing the Mahdi's tomb. Doing so had been nothing less than a 'wicked act' in Churchill's estimation, along with dumping the Mahdi's bones in the Nile. Moreover, he also accused Kitchener of treating the Dervish wounded abominably and of allowing the shooting of prisoners, a charge, however, which was untrue.[41] For his part, Cromer expressed to the Prime Minister, Lord Salisbury, that he was sure that toppling the tomb was 'necessary' and 'justifiable'.[42] Still, Salisbury thought that the way in

which the Mahdi's bones were dealt with was questionable at best, and if
they had simply been re-buried immediately in a Muslim cemetery, 'no
one would have said a word'.[43] For Kitchener, his actions after the taking
of Omdurman certainly removed some of the shine from the victory and
did nothing except reinforce his public reputation as a harsh and
unbending military man, something that was played up in the press and
periodicals, especially by Ernest Bennett in the *Contemporary Review*.[44]
Nevertheless, Kitchener insisted to Cromer that his actions were only
'taken after due deliberation, and prompted solely by political
considerations'.[45] Such a position certainly was explanation enough for
both the Egyptian and British governments, the latter of which would
honour him in the highest manner, as we shall see.

Immediately, however, it was honouring the memory of the slain
General Gordon that was of utmost importance to Kitchener and this he
did at Khartoum on 4 September. Appropriately, for the Christian
service presided over by an ecumenical group of army chaplains, the 4th
was a Sunday. That morning, two gunboats were loaded with hundreds
of men representing all the various corps and regiments of the Anglo-
Egyptian and Sudanese force, and ferried the short distance across the
Nile from Omdurman to Khartoum. There they disembarked directly in
front of the ruins of the Governor's Palace where Gordon had held out
against the Mahdi and his Ansar before finally succumbing to their
terrifying onslaught on 26 January 1885. Now, almost 14 years later,
and in numbers Gordon could only have dreamed of as he waited in vain
for the promised relief, the troops assembled in front of the crumbling
wall of the palace near the steps where it was thought he had been
speared to death before his body too – like his nemesis, the Mahdi – had
been severed from its head and thrown into the Nile.

The memorial service, which Kitchener had drawn up himself, was a
set-piece of British imperial memorialization. Flags were unfurled, first
the Union Jack and then that of Egypt. Bands played 'God Save the
Queen' and the 'Dead March' from Handel's oratorio, *Saul*. Then came
'huzzahs', gun salutes with live ammunition, Bible readings, the mournful
braying of the bagpipes, the hymn, 'Abide with Me' – believed to have
been Gordon's favourite – and finally, a stirring benediction. By this
culminating point in the service all present, it seems, were in tears,
including the usually emotionless Kitchener. Awash in memories of the
planning, hard work, battles fought, and men killed that had led to this

moment, Kitchener's trademark impassivity could not be maintained and tears rolled down his sunburned cheeks.[46] Finding himself too emotionally distraught to dismiss the troops he motioned for it to be done by Major General Hunter. Altogether, the scene reads cathartically for all involved, particularly Kitchener. And when it was over he and the assembled men wandered round the ruined palace taking in the atmosphere and one supposes trying to imagine the nature of Gordon's predicament in the course of his final days before the Mahdi's attack. For the only time in his military career, it would seem, Kitchener was completely at peace, one of his junior officers remembering the scene in the following way: 'The sternness and the harshness had dropped from him for the moment, and he was gentle as a woman . . . . His manner had become easy and unconstrained. He was very happy'.[47] If a later writer chose to describe Kitchener as always looking 'faintly absurd' owing to his humourless visage and overlarge moustache, there was nothing remotely absurd about either him or the service on the banks of the Nile that morning.[48] The Queen noted in her diary that she had received from Kitchener 'a most touching account, and most dramatic, of his entry into Khartoum and of a memorial service held to the memory of poor Gordon on the spot where he was killed! Surely he is avenged!'[49] And in holding this view the aged Queen, the victorious Sirdar, and the triumphant British people on that memorial day in Khartoum were of one accord.

As moved emotionally by the events of 4 September as he had been, Kitchener, however, had very little time to savour their afterglow because almost immediately following the Gordon memorial service he was required to embark on a diplomatic exercise further up the Nile. The mission would prove fraught with danger and the potential for a major rupture in Anglo-French relations was close at hand. As it so happened, throughout the latter stages of the Sudan campaign, Kitchener had carried with him sealed orders from Prime Minister Salisbury to be opened only after Khartoum had been re-taken. Upon duly reading them in the few days following the victory at Omdurman he discovered that they ordered him to lead an expedition up the Nile from Khartoum deep into equatorial Sudan. Over a decade's worth of Anglo-French diplomatic jockeying over the Nile Valley was just then reaching a climax, and Kitchener was the chosen conduit to prevent an attempt by France to claim the Nile basin in the service of its growing West African empire. That claim had come in the form of a French expedition under the command of Captain

Jean-Baptiste Marchand, a 34-year-old career military officer who had
participated in the conquest of Senegal by France in 1889 and since then
had been engaged principally in West African exploration. Recently, he
had led a 150-man French force east to the upper-Nile, and since July had
been encamped at the remote village of Fashoda, where they had re-built
the fort and run the French tri-colour up the flagpole.

The 'Fashoda Incident', as this diplomatic moment in late-nineteenth
century Anglo-French relations came to be called, had its genesis in the
growth of parallel national interests in the Nile Valley. These interests
had their roots in the anti-slavery measures of the 1870s, which then
continued through the British occupation of Egypt in 1882, the French
desire to expand into West Africa, the Berlin Conference of 1884-5, and
subsequent British and French moves in East-Central and West Africa,
respectively. By 1898, all told, Britain and France found themselves on a
collision course in Africa and the point at which they came together
would turn out to be the squalid village of Fashoda, located some 400
miles south of Khartoum, about as remote an African location as can be
imagined, both then and now. Barely more than a run-down anti-slaving
fort, but situated almost exactly at the geographic intersection of the
British 'Cape to Cairo' imperial dream and its French analogue, 'Dakar
to Djibouti', Fashoda bore the full weight of competing Anglo-French
imperial aspirations in the climactic phase of the partition of Africa.[50]

In order to ward off this impending dispute the Salisbury
government's intention for Kitchener was to complete the consolidation
of Britain's position in the Nile Valley that the occupation of Egypt and
the recent victory at Omdurman portended. Fashoda, Salisbury believed,
was the all-important coda that would seal Britain's regional
paramountcy by right of conquest; and 'of this the Union Jack would
be the symbol'.[51] (A secondary prong of the strategy was to keep at bay
the Abyssinians should they threaten to move westward. Accordingly,
Major General Hunter was assigned that task, which he carried out
successfully at the same time along the Blue Nile.) On the morning of
10 September therefore, barely a week after his victory at Omdurman,
Kitchener, accompanied by Wingate, a few other officers, and about
1,500 men steamed out of Khartoum in a small flotilla of five boats.
By this point in time they had been apprised that Fashoda was to be their
destination and that the small number of French and Senegalese troops
there were under the command of Marchand. Upriver they went, beyond

contact with London as the telegraph wires were down, to the lip of the *Sudd*, the vast swamp that extends far in to the southern regions of Sudan. In advance of landing at Fashoda, Kitchener drafted a letter announcing his imminent arrival. In practiced French, he praised Marchand for the achievement of marching his expedition (it had taken 14 months) to the Nile from West Africa, told him about his fresh victory over the Khalifa at Omdurman, and about how he would be coming as an emissary of the Khedive in order to re-affirm Egypt's authority over Sudan and the Nile Valley. Any mention of Britain's role, per se, in these matters was purposely omitted so as to emphasize the Egyptian nature of the exercise.

Two days later on 19 September, Kitchener's small flotilla approached Fashoda. Standing on the upper deck of the steamer *Dal*, the Sirdar could see the French flag flying above the makeshift government buildings on the riverbank. Affronted by the fluttering tri-colour's presence, about which he would shortly lodge an official protest, Kitchener then noticed coming towards his gunboat a small craft. Manned by a detachment of smartly red-uniformed Senegalese, the boat flew two French flags, a small one in the bow and a substantially larger one in the stern. Presently handed a letter from Marchand by one of the Senegalese – 'I hear with the greatest pleasure of ... the final death of Mahdism in the Nile valley' – Kitchener proceeded to lead his flotilla into dock where he was met by his French counterpart, sporting smart dress whites for the occasion.[52] Accompanied by a junior officer, Marchand then came on board the *Dal* and for the next two hours a delicate negotiation took place in which the potential of a local (diplomatic) conflict escalating into a wider Anglo-French military one lay in the balance. The whole undertaking was highly gentlemanly in the Victorian manner, with occasional bows and bon mots. But it was backed up nonetheless on the British side by the proximate presence of three gunboats and 1,500 battle-hardened men as opposed to Marchand's seven French officers and perhaps as many as 200 lightly-armed Senegalese.

As discussed by Marchand and Kitchener, the essential French diplomatic position since the fall of Khartoum in 1885 was that Sudan had been made *res nullius*; that is, territory belonging to no one.[53] Certainly, the French had never recognized any form of British sovereignty over the country, and only grudgingly that of Egypt itself. On legal grounds the French stood strong, but the *realpolitik* of the situation was what really mattered and in that world Britain and its

Egyptian client were paramount. In this light, therefore, Kitchener insisted that the Anglo-Egyptian position was a sound one in international law and that it trumped that of the French. Accordingly, he maintained, Marchand should respect it without reservation. To that end, Kitchener said that he was willing to supply Marchand and his party with a gunboat to take them down the Nile to Egypt and with that all the fuss over Fashoda would come to an end. Unsurprisingly, the Frenchman refused, however, suggesting provocatively that only the use of force by Kitchener would budge him from the 'glob of mud' that he claimed belonged to France.[54] At this point in their talks the situation understandably became extremely sticky as the prospect of a devolution into violence had become clear.

Kitchener, without question, was no natural diplomat. But his French language skills were good, and after all he was dealing soldier to soldier. Given his recent exertions at Omdurman he also did not want to unleash the dogs of war if doing so was avoidable, especially against the ultimately formidable French. Altogether, Kitchener desired a compromise and indeed would find one by suggesting that the Egyptian flag (not the British one) be raised in accordance with his orders, and possession of the area taken in lockstep with the French. Once these local actions had been undertaken jointly, he suggested that the matter should then be turned over to London and Paris for a final diplomatic determination. After a tension-filled wait for Marchand's response, Kitchener's halting diplomacy seemed to have won the perfect compromise. While showing his Gallic pride and admitting to a 'terrible desire' to refuse the offer and let events run their natural (and therefore probably martial) course, Marchand nonetheless agreed with the British proposal. Kitchener, dressed in his Egyptian uniform to further appease the terminal anti-British sensitivities of the French, the agreement was struck and the Egyptian flag was duly hoisted accompanied by a 21-gun salute. Kitchener then at last came ashore to drink champagne at Fashoda's Fort St-Louis. 'Nothing could have exceeded the politeness and courtesy of the French officers', remarked Kitchener afterwards.[55] Having achieved all that was possible, the next day the flotilla (save for one boat, left behind as a slightly menacing guarantor) turned around and steamed northward for Khartoum. As a fillip, copies of some London newspapers were left behind at Fashoda containing coverage of the breaking 'Dreyfus Affair' that would roil the

French government for years to come, effectively removing its eye from any issues in far-away Sudan. In reference to the unfolding Dreyfus scandal Kitchener earlier had startled his French hosts by saying that in what had just taken place between Marchand and himself 'the French government will not back you up'.[56] Isolated for months from the outside world, neither Marchand nor any of his men were aware of the scandalous catastrophe that the Dreyfus case was visiting upon French government and society, especially following the January 1898 publication of Emile Zola's *'J'accuse'*, in which he had charged the French Army and the War Ministry with committing perjury in their anti-semitic treatment of the scorned putative spy, Captain Alfred Dreyfus. In the event, Kitchener was right. Even then in Paris, French Foreign Minister Theophile Delcasse was part of a tottering government and a week later when he had been informed about the events at Fashoda, Delcasse stated with accurate ruefulness: 'We have nothing but arguments and they have got troops'.[57]

Throughout the early autumn the Fashoda 'Crisis', as the chancelleries had quickly come to style it, would rumble on in Paris and London. But its outcome was never really in doubt. Salisbury was supremely confident in the British position and simply waited for the French to quit blustering and face the inevitable outcome. Right of conquest made all of Sudan fall under British paramountcy, he maintained, and there was no way around that reality. Indeed, Marchand himself had rather simplified matters by peremptorily decamping from Fashoda five weeks after his meeting with Kitchener. After that, only the diplomatic niceties remained, which would be duly contained in the Anglo-French Declaration of March 1899. As Salisbury then happily told the Queen simply and in person: 'it keeps the French entirely out of the Nile Valley'.[58] France thus excluded, the meaning of Fashoda for the British had now been clarified: their strategy had connected ineluctably the Mediterranean, the Nile and Suez, and India, and therefore, in London's view at least, the world had been made a much more secure place for British interests.[59]

His work at Fashoda completed successfully, Kitchener and the flotilla returned to Khartoum five days later on 24 September, the downstream flow of the Nile speeding their progress. En route he was brought a telegram from the Sudanese capital sent by the Queen informing him that the re-conquest and its signal victory at Omdurman had merited him a peerage, which would soon be bestowed. Buoyed by such adulatory royal news, and by the receipt of a number of laudatory letters from others – 'I had such good men under me that it would have been difficult to go wrong' – he wrote to Lord Wolseley in response to his former colleague's congratulatory missive, Kitchener nevertheless was exhausted by the preceding many months of intense work.[60] A return to England for a rest therefore was both imminent and required. And by the end of October, after settling some last details in Khartoum, Kitchener very happily had arrived home.

In returning to England for a well-deserved rest Kitchener was to find that in fact he did not have much time to do so. A celebratory and tumultuous arrival at Dover on 27 October, where he was hailed as the conquering hero, foretold a similar reception when his special train pulled into Victoria Station later that same day. 'Popular feeling' for Kitchener, reported *The Times*, was as high as it had ever been.[61] Here was Kitchener, the hero of Omdurman, restorer of Khartoum, avenger of Gordon, and even the diplomatic winner (as would be shortly confirmed) over France at Fashoda! Indeed, he really was the 'Sudan machine', as George Steevens had admiringly dubbed him in his book of the re-conquest that had just been published hurriedly.[62]

Everyone, it seemed, wanted a piece of England's newest hero. Of course that included the prime minister, with whom he had already spent the weekend at Hatfield discussing his plans for the rebuilding of Khartoum and Sudan, post-re-conquest. Then it was on to Balmoral Castle in Scotland and an audience of the similarly enamoured Queen on 31 October, still relishing the previous year's Diamond Jubilee of her reign and now able to celebrate its appropriate encomium in the presence of Gordon's triumphant legatee. It is little wonder that she had insisted upon a peerage for Kitchener and that the honour came the next day when he was created 'Baron Kitchener of Khartoum' (which came with a substantial parliamentary grant of thanks in the amount of L30,000).

Back in London on 2 November and staying at the Belgrave Square townhouse of his enduring friend, Pandeli Ralli, the newly ennobled Lord Kitchener lent polish to the words of a speech he would give that evening at a celebratory dinner held in his honour by the Lord Mayor at Mansion House. Then it was off to Cambridge for an honourary degree. The whirl of serial feting was not exactly enjoyable for a man of Kitchener's retiring nature, but it did give him the opportunity to act on some features of his plan to re-generate Khartoum and Sudan; especially and in the first instance was his hope of establishing a college of higher education in the capital named in honour of Gordon. He went public with this idea in *The Times* on 30 November, accompanied by an appeal for L100,000, a significant sum (approximately L5-million in today's values).[63] The money flowed in quickly and Gordon Memorial College (the foundation of the University of Khartoum) would be launched shortly after Kitchener's return to Africa at the end of the year. His return there as governor general, about which he was voluble in his correspondence with a number of people, including a deeply sympathetic and encouraging Salisbury, was keenly anticipated.[64]

Even though Kitchener had been away from Sudan for only two months prior to his return in December 1898 a considerable amount of work had been done already in Khartoum clearing up the rubble of the ruinous 14 years of Mahdist rule. Having left his brother Walter in charge of the city while he was England, Kitchener returned to the first stirrings of his plan for Khartoum's renewal along the lines of grid-like town planning and new government and public buildings, the initial centerpiece of which was to be Gordon College. Lord Cromer – newly bereaved, his wife had died in October but he was keen nonetheless to tour the battlefield at Omdurman – came for a visit shortly after Kitchener's return. They discussed plans for revivifying Sudan's civil governance as an Anglo-Egyptian condominium with Kitchener as governor general and Wingate as head of the army. Directly, on 4 January 1899, Cromer laid the cornerstone of the new college with much pomp and ceremony. Kitchener contributed to the festivities also, though in the sardonic view of a junior administrator named Harry Boyle, at least, just a bit too grandly in 'helmet, khaki riding breeches, and coat with insignia and ribbons of the Bath across it'.[65]

Two weeks later on 19 January the Anglo-Egyptian convention establishing the condominium was signed into law. As Cromer explained to Kitchener, he would 'control the big questions', while 'detail' would be left to Kitchener as governor general and therefore 'managed locally'.[66] There is no surviving record of what Kitchener may have thought of this directive, but its likely effect was to confirm Cromer's usual patronizing impact on most of those with whom he worked. In any event, Kitchener got on with the job at hand, but as a civilian administrator, at least, Cromer thought Kitchener to be lacking in understanding and finesse. The charge was mostly groundless, however, and making it betrays more about Cromer's own difficulties in selling the condominium structure to a skeptical Khedive and a similarly ill-disposed Egyptian government than it does with anything Kitchener might have been doing to assist in the development of a devastated country. If anything, the real problem was the perennially stingy Egyptian treasury and the lengths to which Kitchener had to go in order to wheedle out of it the funds necessary for Sudanese reconstruction.

During the early weeks of his governor-generalship one of the most pressing questions with which Kitchener had to deal was the status and whereabouts of the escaped Khalifa. After hurriedly departing Omdurman, as noted above, and eluding initial attempts at capture afterwards, he had gone to ground and simply disappeared. In February, however, Wingate's intelligence operatives reported that the Khalifa now had emerged from hiding and was advancing on Khartoum.[67] In fact, nothing came of this particular report but the new Sirdar and former intelligence chief spent most of his time following up leads pertaining to the Khalifa and would, as we shall see, eventually preside over his death in battle.

As the months passed Kitchener, unsurprisingly, found the work of an administrator to be increasingly wearisome. In some ways, as a stickler for detail with a wont to economize to the last penny – he had, after all, managed well the Sudan campaign that all-told had cost about L2.3 million, an enormous sum – he was ideally suited for the job.[68] But the endless back and forth correspondence with Cromer, as well as with Eldon Gorst, the Khedive's officious – at least in Kitchener's view – new financial adviser – 'the meanest little brute I ever met', he remarked – left him yearning for the hard clarity of being on campaign. 'I am very sick and low', he had opined to Wingate in February, 'so I will not bother you. I can quite see there is no confidence in my work'.[69]

Throughout this period widespread famine was one of the main problems with which Kitchener was wrestling. It had first struck south of Khartoum during the early Mahdist years and then was exacerbated under the brutal rule of the Khalifa. To stem its remorseless impact Kitchener negotiated with local merchants and contractors to try and rebuild their broken crop growth and importation systems, but it was a thankless task for which, in his view, the authorities in Cairo had no nuanced understanding. Miserable local conditions, and the fact that with the elusive Khalifa still at large southern Sudan remained almost a war zone, precluded an effective economic and marketing strategy that would have alleviated some of the obvious suffering of the destitute and starving Sudanese. Altogether, by mid-1899, though sympathetic to the plight of the local populace, Kitchener was fed up with the situation, as well as with the constant carping of Cromer – all former good feeling having dissipated – and the similarly inclined Gorst. Cromer, by now in a not unexpected manner, had even chosen to lecture Kitchener face to face that as a 'Christian ruler' he needed to remember that the Sudanese were 'human beings, not blocks of wood'.[70] In the event, an angry Kitchener went home to England that summer ready for a long break from both Cromer and Gorst, and declaring altogether that he had had 'about enough of the Sudan'.[71]

Kitchener's anger did not last, however. That summer in England proved a balm to his frazzled mind and upon returning to Khartoum in the autumn he plunged anew into the interminable problems of governing the country. Kitchener was the first, as it turned out, of a series of British governors who would stretch all the way down to Sudanese independence in 1956. And beginning under him the Sudan Political Service developed its key governing role as it carved out a sterling reputation both at home and on the ground in Sudan as a thoroughly just and efficient body of district administrattive officers.[72] But before any of these positive developments could take place Kitchener believed that all vestiges of the Khalifa's baleful influence in Sudan must be extinguished. The Khalifa's capture was therefore imperative as the scope for recidivist action by him and his remaining loyalist followers was great, and Kitchener enjoined Wingate to redouble his efforts to either capture him or defeat him in battle.[73]

Accordingly, by late-November Wingate had been able to do exactly that, tracking the Khalifa to Umm Dibkayarat in the province of Kordofan and there, when capture was unsurprisingly resisted, defeating him in a very much smaller reprise of Omdurman.[74] The Khalifa died in the bloody encounter, his body discovered lying prominently amongst the corpses of the last of the thoroughly defeated Ansar. Unknown to Kitchener, just then he was about to be called away from Sudan to the war the British had undertaken recently in South Africa. The Khalifa's defeat and his 'grand and fine' death on 24 November – as the greatly impressed Queen put it in a letter to Kitchener — marked the true end of the Sudan campaign. His presence at Gordon's re-built Governor's Palace in Khartoum to hear the news of the Khalifa's demise therefore offered a poetic end to that, and as it turned out just a few days later, to his governor-generalship of Sudan altogether. If the South African War would come to mark in many respects the end of the old British Empire, its heightened prelude came in the overwhelming power of Britain's re-conquest of Sudan. In the exultation experienced in England at Kitchener's triumphant return home as the conquering hero in the autumn of 1898, and in his subsequent ennoblement as 'Lord K of K', one of the many news magazines covering the spectacle had enthused that he came overwhelmingly from 'a fighting race'.[75] Never again, however, would fighting and winning come so easily for Kitchener and the British as it had just done in Sudan. The war in South Africa, for which he departed on 18 December 1899, would make sure of that.

6

The South African War, 1900–2

In departing for South Africa in the unexpected manner in which he did, Kitchener was saying goodbye to Egypt and Sudan after nearly 17 years of military and pro-consular service there. 'I was surprised by a wire to say I had to go to South Africa', he wrote to another of his many female correspondents, Lady Ilchester, with whom he would develop an unrequited romantic attachment. But despite Kitchener's peremptory departure from Sudan he was determined to 'get things square' in South Africa and 'to show the Boers a somewhat different war game to that they have been having lately', he continued.[1] In what had become a wholly imperial life, Kitchener's task in South Africa as Chief of Staff to the newly appointed Field Marshal Lord Roberts, Commander in Chief, would see him continue to serve at the centre of British imperial and military affairs. But unlike the campaign that Kitchener had just waged so successfully in Sudan whose victorious outcome was essentially a foregone conclusion, the war against the Boers had begun badly for the British and showed no (early) sign of changing for the better. In the manner of the time for the British the war had commenced with the same spirit of invincibility as seen in Sudan, but very quickly any assumption that they would have an easy stroll across the *veldt* disappeared in a hail of bullets from the enemy's superior Mauser rifles. From the moment that the Afrikaners' ('Boers', Dutch for farmer, as the British called them) had declared war on Britain on 11 October 1899, rather surprisingly they had been able to maintain the upper hand.

Three signal and successive victories by the Boers in mid-December ('Black Week') had a devastating impact on British morale both in the field and back in Britain, imperiling the war altogether as far as the Salisbury government was concerned. Hence the call went out to Roberts of Kandahar – 'the pocket Wellington' – and to Kitchener of Khartoum – 'the Sudan machine' – the twin luminaries of late-Victorian British imperial arms. The prevailing belief was that in their perennially victorious and capable hands the recent British losses could be reversed and the war would move toward the inevitability of a triumphant conclusion.[2] To this end, having reached Alexandria on 21 December, Kitchener boarded ship for Gibraltar where he met up with Roberts who had just arrived from his former post as Commander in Chief in Ireland. Together they made a physically incongruous pair: Kitchener standing tall as we know at 6'2" beside the diminutive 5'4" Roberts. But in every other way except for height they were perfectly compatible and complementary. Their two-week passage to Cape Town beginning on the 27th was a time of much earnest conversation and strategizing about the state of the war, which included everything from leadership, to weaponry, to supply. Broken only by a New Year's 1900 toast on board the *Dunottar Castle* (on which Kitchener's bete noire, Winston Churchill, had also sailed to Cape Town just two months earlier), and dampened by Roberts's grief over the death of his only son, Freddie, at the Battle of Colenso just a few weeks earlier, they arrived in South Africa ready to turn around British fortunes.[3] The cheers for their appointment and assumed success both there and in Britain were deafening.

In reaching Cape Town on 10 January, Kitchener was sailing into some 300 years of direct British engagement with South Africa. The Cape had long been of interest to the British because in the years prior to the opening of the Suez Canal in 1869 the journey to India meant an obligatory re-provisioning stop there en route. The ruling East India Company had foundered on the sharp crisis entailed by the Indian Mutiny of 1857, but the years of using Cape Town as its main port on the slow passage to the sub-continent meant that Britain's connection to South Africa was strong, especially so from 1806 when it had come under Crown control in the midst of the Napoleonic Wars.

By that year the descendants of the region's first European settlers, the Dutch, who along with a smaller group of Germans and Huguenots from France, had arrived in 1652, saw South Africa as their home and were disinclined to share any measure of it with the British. They called themselves Afrikaners and clung fiercely to a Calvinistic sense of their own destiny as participants in a land-based covenant with God, and certainly in superiority to the pre-existing native peoples.[4] At first, after 1806, these old verities continued to be operative. The British were not yet very interested in colonization and Cape Town continued largely to be a trading and provisioning entrepot and therefore of no threat, as such, to the exceptional way in which the Afrikaners regarded their own burgeoning settlement in the Cape. Similarly, the nearby naval base at Simonstown was of strategic use only to the British and therefore of no day to day concern to the Afrikaners. But the British and allied victory at Waterloo in 1815 and the final end of the long period of war with French Revolutionary and Napoleonic France changed how Britain regarded South Africa. Consequently, the view from London progressively became more expansive and expressly colonizing and the die was cast for a much keener intra-European competition than had hitherto prevailed at the Cape.

Meanwhile, for generations, the Afrikaners had been gradually pushing north and east from Table Bay, moves that long pre-dated the British arrival. Indeed, this migration continued but with greater urgency after 1806 and it meant both interminable clashes with the native Xhosa and Zulu populations, as well as an unfolding problem for the extension of competitive British rule. In essence, the Boers' trekking away from the Cape was an expression of their desire to avoid the inevitable anglicisation of the region by the paramount British. But it also had geo-strategic consequences because it spread the Boer population even more thinly than it already was, therefore obliging the British to either follow and potentially supervise and govern these remote settlements, or leave them be as quasi-independent and largely beyond their effective reach.[5]

Until the mid-1830s, leaving the Boers *in situ* was the prevailing British policy, but during that decade two sets of events altered significantly the approach the British at Cape Town took to their putative South African hinterland. The first was the Zulu uprising under their great chief, Shaka. The *mfecane* (crushing) that he unleashed resulted in the consolidation of a powerful nation of some 250,000 people, 20 per cent of whom comprised a celibate warrior elite. His creation of Zululand was both unifying and displacing, in that those who were not brought into the newly consolidated kingdom found themselves exiled beyond its traditional boundaries, which meant essentially north of the Orange river. This (forced) migration potentially extended the British zone of responsibility in ways that few in Cape Town saw as a good or manageable development. Second, and partly in response to the robust, military nature of Shaka's nation-building success, and partly as a result of the abolition of slavery within the British Empire in 1834, thousands of Boers decided that in order to escape beyond the reaches of both the ensconced British and the expanding Zulu they would migrate even further to the northeast and there found a new Boer homeland, which they did, calling it the Natal 'republic'. The Great Trek, as this event became known, saw some 15,000 *voortrekkers* leave the Cape and set out on a hard and warlike journey to establish a new and remote home. This passage, especially, the decisive Boer victory over the Zulu at the Battle of Blood River in 1838, consolidated the necessary elements of land and covenant in their minds and contributed mightily to their self-understanding as a myth-driven people chosen of God.[6]

Faced with the political and geographic reality of Natal the British decided that the only way to prevent Afrikaner competition on the frontier was to formally annex the embryo colony, which it did in 1843. Annexation, in turn, led the outraged Boers to repeat the process of the Great Trek, though in a less dramatic but ultimately longer-lasting fashion, by founding two new republics, calling them the Transvaal and the Orange Free State. For the next generation there matters stood, the British at the Cape (and in Natal) looking on in considerable discomfort as the Afrikaners gradually consolidated their 'covenant' society in the South African interior. Later, and spurred by the attempts of Sir Theophilus Shepstone, an unofficial imperial agent based in Natal, to conjure British federal control over the South African interior, the Transvaal was annexed in 1877. For a short time it seemed that British imperial power locally-exerted might just be strong enough to contain the proto-nationalism of the Boers (as well as that of the Zulu). But that assumption was given a sharp rebuttal through the signal defeat of the British by the Zulu at Isandlwana in January 1879; although that defeat was reversed a few months later when a decisive revenge was achieved by the British at the Battle of Ulundi.[7] But the victory had a short-lived impact on Anglo-Boer relations because the crushing of the Zulu by the imperial fist worked as much in the Boers favour as it did in the British by allowing the Boers to consolidate their own strength in light of the destruction of that of the competing Zulu. By 1880 therefore, and under the defiant religio-political leadership of Paul Kruger, the Transvaal was in open revolt against the annexationist claims of the British. The next year a trio of surprising British military defeats culminating at the Battle of Majuba Hill put an exclamation point on the Boers' refusal to live under outside rule.[8] Faced thereby with an intractable enemy, the Gladstone government in London decided that there simply was no effective way of exerting British control over the Afrikaners of the South African interior so they negotiated the Convention of Pretoria and with it, in the words of John Darwin, 'scrapped the Transvaal's annexation and threw away the federal plan'.[9]

Constitutionally and politically, the re-emergence of 'stalemate' in Anglo-Boer relations in South Africa might have continued uninterrupted except for the impact, first of the discovery of diamonds in 1867, and then of gold in 1886.[10] Mineral wealth had already altered and would continue to change just about everything in imperial equation making in the region and it pushed the British to (re-)assert their regional suzerainty, a provision preserved for themselves in the Pretoria convention. Naturally disliked by Kruger, upon becoming Transvaal's president in 1883 he succeeded in having the suzerainty principle eliminated from the succeeding 1884 Anglo-Boer convention. But two years later, the Witwatersrand gold rush began and with it the so-called European 'gold bugs' – led by Cecil Rhodes – were determined not to let Kruger block their path to both riches and preponderant British control over the Transvaal, and indeed all of South Africa. For the balance of the 1880s and into the next decade the Transvaal thus became the fulcrum of the Anglo-Boer struggle for the interior of South Africa. Moreover, for Rhodes in particular, as a member of Cape Colony's legislative assembly and later its prime minister, he was determined to actualize his 'big idea', the dream of a constitutionally unified South Africa in which Anglo-Boer cooperation transcended old animosities and together (using the Cape as a model) the two peoples would create a society in which the whites were in the ascendant politically over the blacks and London was the paramount power of all.[11]

By 1890, Rhodes had combined political power in the Cape with a persuasive imperial dream in London to yield a British government charter allowing for settler expansion north of the Limpopo river into what would become Rhodesia (modern-day Zimbabwe). Indeed, Rhodes's plan for imperial aggrandisement knew no bounds; he would later lash out at Sir William Harcourt, the Liberal party leader and a vocal critic of his expansive plans, by saying haughtily: 'Nobody is going to name a country after you'.[12] But these serial provocations – which included an enormous expansion in the non-Boer *uitlander* ('foreigner') population attracted by mineral-rich Transvaal – prompted Kruger to do everything possible to resist what to Rhodes at least was Britain's imperial manifest destiny. This resistance ultimately would prove unanswerable to Rhodes, and feeling the frustration that always arose when he was not able to 'square' a problem, he decided to hit Kruger hard because he more than anyone else stood in the way of his grand dream for South Africa.[13] The desperate result was the so-called Jameson Raid carried out at the end of 1895. Launched peremptorily by Rhodes and financed with L200,000 supplied by one of the other leading gold bugs, Alfred Beit, the raid was an attempt to provoke an *uitlander* uprising against the Kruger government over its civil restrictions affecting what had become the Transvaal's majority non-Boer population.[14] Ill-conceived and badly executed, the 500-man raid was under the direction of one of Rhodes's loyal associates, Dr Leander Starr Jameson, and ended as a fiasco. The outcome of the failed raid was three-fold: first, it consolidated Kruger's position both as President of the Transvaal and as the moral leader of the Boers throughout South Africa; second, it blackened but (owing to political chicanery in London) did not destroy Rhodes's public reputation; and third, it laid bare the likelihood of a future war between Boer and Briton in South Africa.

For the next three years, most close participants in or observers of the situation in the Transvaal and throughout South Africa generally assumed that it was now merely a matter of time before the two sides resorted to violence in order to firmly and finally impress upon the other what would be the victorious identity of the regional paramount power. 'It is our country you want', Kruger stated bluntly in mid-1899 to Sir Alfred (later Lord) Milner, the British High Commissioner to the Cape.[15] The burly Boer was absolutely right. Coarsely, Milner admitted privately that he was out to 'screw' the Boers.[16] And indeed, to most Boers such appeared to be the case. In London, Colonial Secretary Joseph

Chamberlain, a strong supporter of Rhodes's and Milner's view of the situation – 'I believe in the British Empire, and I believe in the British race. I believe that the British race is the greatest of governing races that the world has ever seen' – plumped for war and in the event he got what he wanted when an exasperated Kruger finally issued a war ultimatum in the autumn of 1899.[17] Chamberlain duly used it as a necessary *casus belli* to convince Prime Minister Salisbury and the Cabinet that given the circumstances going to war against the Boers was their only option.[18] Accordingly, on 11 October 1899, the British having let the ultimatum expire, a column of Boers crossed the border from the Transvaal into Natal and the long percolating war boiled over into reality.

For the properly militarily confident British the first few months of the war would prove to be a sharp shock, however. Most assumed that the war would be a quick and decisive engagement against an obviously inferior enemy; 'another Omdurman picnic' as a young and cocksure British infantryman put it.[19] Very soon into the war, however, the fierceness and unconventional fighting style of the Boer enemy, together with the as yet unrecognized mastery of their use of a superior weapon in the form of the German Mauser assault rifle, left the British reeling. Especially was this true after a triumvirate of defeats (at Stormberg, Magersfontein, and Colenso) in December that collectively constituted Black Week to the British. 'The feeling here,' wrote Major General Hector MacDonald – like Kitchener having transferred from Sudan to South Africa – 'though not openly expressed, is one of profound helplessness'.[20] Stunned, demoralized, and embarrassed by these losses, immediately following upon the Black Week disaster the call went out for fresh British military leadership to take control in South Africa and reverse the so-far disastrous course of the war. And so it was that Field Marshal Roberts – nursing the 'terrible trial' of the death of his 27-year-old son – and General Kitchener, directly from Sudan, steamed into Cape Town on 10 January 1900 ready to reverse the failed trajectory of the war in ways that would restore equipoise in the face of the incongruous reality that the greatest military power in the world was so far being bested in battle, as one newspaper had earlier derided the Transvaal, by a 'trumpery little state' led by its 'impudent burghers'.[21] No one was saying that any longer, however.

During the first four weeks following their arrival at the Cape Kitchener and Roberts mapped out the specifics of a new strategy aimed at winning a complete victory, plans that included importing the newly honoured Sir Percy Girouard of Sudan fame to direct railway expansion and transport. The preceding defeats were thought to be the fault of erroneous strategy, failed execution, and inferior supply, and the two generals worked immediately to rectify them all. The difficulties faced by the new British military brain-trust were made plain again, however, within a fortnight. On 24 January under the command of the hapless and recently-demoted-but-still-in-the-field General Redvers Buller the British had suffered yet another humiliating defeat, this time at Spion Kop in northern Natal. Over 1,700 British troops were killed there (compared to just 300 Boers) and any hope of relieving the nearby besieged town of Ladysmith evaporated with the comprehensive defeat.[22] This setback was hardly what the new duo of commanders would have wished for, but it did reinforce the urgency with which they needed to act in order to turn the tide of the war in Britain's favour. To do so, their new strategy initially meant establishing a single thrust north in order to push back the hitherto successful Boer incursion of the northern Cape made under General 'Piet' Cronje. Accordingly, early in February, their plans now operative, Kitchener and Roberts secretly stole out of Cape Town by train and steamed north about 600 miles to the Modder river where almost 40,000 British troops were now encamped in accordance with their most recently issued orders.[23] Not very far away from them a surprised Cronje lay bivouacked with his troops. In the ensuing fight, as we shall see, he made it clear however that it would take more than famous generals and the element of surprise to best him and his tight and fierce band of Afrikaner men hunkered down in their protective *laager*.

The Battle of Paardeberg, as the Modder river engagement would be called, and fought from 18–27 February 1900, turned into a partial disaster for the British that threatened to make almost normative the narrative of their serial defeat which had so far defined the Anglo-Boer War. Paardeberg would prove also to be a highly frustrating experience for Kitchener and do nothing to burnish his reputation for victory so recently consolidated at Omdurman. Still, despite Paardeberg's uneven impact on both sides of the conflict, its outcome signalled the renewal of British fortunes in the war by beginning the steady march toward victories in the field, the relief of a number of besieged towns, and hence to a halting form of peace later that year.

In light of Black Week the uncomprehending British public were baying for a victory of any sort in South Africa. Kimberley's state of siege (along with that of Ladysmith and Mafeking) was well-reported in the press, and the inability of British commanders and troops to relieve its suffering inhabitants was a constant source of outrage to both journalists and readers well-used to the jingo model of British success rather than to the impotence of protracted besiegement. Leading the demand for relief was Cecil Rhodes himself, trapped in Kimberley and vociferous (even theatrical) in his calls for action. 'In the interests of humanity', he wrote in the local *Diamond Fields Advertiser* on 10 February, 'the relief of this beleaguered city can no longer be delayed'.[24] In fairness to Rhodes, Kimberley had been under siege for some four months by then and the situation was indeed grim. Still, the state of affairs there was no worse than anywhere else in Boer-held territory, and Roberts was certainly moving at speed towards breaking the enemy's hold over the diamond capital of South Africa. But relieving Kimberley was only one piece of a larger puzzle that he was trying to solve. And in military terms defeating Cronje (with another strong Boer commander, Christiaan De Wet, also located nearby) was more pressing than acting on Rhodes's impudent demand sent to Roberts and containing the line: 'It is high time you did something'.[25] Still, Rhodes got his wish on 15 February when Kimberley indeed was freed by British forces under the command of Major General Sir John French, who later would join other Boer War veterans like Edmund Allenby and Douglas Haig in going on to serve prominently in World War I.

The relief of Kimberley, though welcomed deliriously by the exhausted and dispirited inhabitants of the town, proved a prelude to the bloody Battle of Paardeberg. On the same day as Kimberley's relief was achieved, Cronje began to move his men from Magersfontein – site of one of the key Boer victories during Black Week in December – to the Modder river. By the evening of the 17th he and his roughly 7,000 troops were dug in along the north side of the river and had formed a defensive *laager*. Observing this typical Boer formation from a hill (*kopje*) on the other side of the river was Kitchener. Given the fact that Kitchener's force was vastly superior in manpower and guns, the battle to come should have been a relatively easy one for the British. But no such ease was found, however, over the ten-days that followed.

From the summit of 'Kitchener's Kopje', as it came to be called, Cronje's embedded troops appeared vulnerable to a sustained bombardment of their position. Such certainly was the view of Lieutenant General Sir Thomas Kelly-Kenny, commander of the British 6th Division, and he was probably right. He was overruled, however, by Kitchener, who, in light of Roberts having just fallen ill with a severe fever, had been given overall command of the fluid situation on the banks of the Modder. Kelly-Kenny was unhappy about this state of affairs, which diminished his role, but he had no choice but to fall in train with Kitchener's decision to try and smash Cronje's position through a series of infantry attacks rather than through long-range bombardment.[26] Kitchener's instinct here was that of the predatory general in search of a decisive victory, not only because of what it would mean in the field, but even more because of its potential to significantly raise morale amongst the British troops in South Africa, as well as of people in England and throughout the Empire. Above all, given the war's prevailing situation, no one on the British side wanted to endure another siege.

'It is now seven o'clock', said Kitchener to one of his aides-de-camp on the morning of 18 February. 'We shall be in the laager by half past ten'.[27] The bravado exhibited by Kitchener here might be understandable given the overwhelming nature of his still fresh-in-mind victories in Sudan. But archaically- and lightly-armed jihadists were a world away from the battle-hardened Boers who lay dug-in across the Modder river, and Kitchener's determination to break them in a direct attack was peremptory, if not reckless. In the event, he ordered the artillery to open up on Cronje's laager, followed directly by an infantry advance. The guns caused havoc, as expected, and he would have been wise to let them continue to do their destructive work. But ordering the subsequent infantry advance meant that British troops began quickly to die in droves, picked off with ease hundreds of yards before reaching the river by Boer sharpshooters using their accurately-sited Mausers. By 10:30, far from being in the laager, the battle was showing signs of a slog cum potential disaster as British casualties mounted in lock-step with the relentless rise in the day's temperature.

At Paardeberg Kitchener had adopted his usual sole-commander mode, partly as we have seen earlier out of habit, but partly too because in the hurried devolution of command from the ailing Roberts he had been left without a proper staff. As the day wore on the pattern of attack therefore continued unchanged. British infantry assaults from the south, east, and west were all parried by the Boers and the harvest of death continued apace. Supplementing the British were a contingent of recently-arrived Canadians, so-called 'Imperial' troops, the vanguard of which had departed Quebec City to tremendous fanfare at the end of October 1899. Thrown into action at Paardeberg, they fought well (34 were killed) in what amounted to the first-ever use of Canadian troops abroad.[28] More than any other single action during the early part of the war, the use of the Royal Canadian Regiment at Paardeberg made the actual fight against the Boers the business of the dominions within the British Empire.[29]

By the evening of the 18th the stout defence that Cronje and his hunkered-down men (and women) were able to mount in their bowed but unbroken laager made it clear to Kitchener that a decisive victory was not going to come his way that day. In an earlier bid for a breakthrough Kitchener had ordered a mounted charge – 'the laager must be rushed at all costs'.[30] Led bravely by Colonel Ormelie Hannay, the full-speed gallop by him and his chosen men put them directly in the line of fire and they suffered an unsurprising fate, even though the Boers themselves were reluctant to shoot such an obviously misguided target.

The day thus ended on a sour note for the British. Kitchener was intensely frustrated at the inability of his men to dislodge Cronje's troops and force them to surrender. Indeed, the day was shaping up as yet another British Boer War folly in the form of 1,270 British and Canadian casualties, including 303 killed, the number outstripping easily that which had been suffered at Omdurman.[31] Indeed, no other single day in the South African War would offer up such dreadful figures, providing hundreds of examples of Thomas Hardy's fictional composite, 'Young Hodge the Drummer', his poetic memorialization of those who fell and were buried on a 'kopje-crest that breaks the veldt around'.[32] If Cronje's beleaguered force had been in such a hopeless position themselves, folly might have been exactly the outcome for Kitchener and the British. But the Boers had suffered too, and had neither the resources nor the manpower to absorb the relentless British pounding. Some 100 of them had been killed by bombardment, with a further 250 wounded. Hundreds of their horses had been killed also, their putrid and bloated bodies floating downriver and carrying disease into the camp of the British and the Canadians, the latter of whom promptly renamed Paardeberg, 'Stinkfontein'. Given the over 2:1 British numerical superiority, their lack of mobility, and the unlikely nature of Boer reinforcements making it through to help them, Cronje and his men were themselves in a hopeless situation. But out of honour and defiance they chose to remain encamped along the Modder for more than a week. Having been informed by Kitchener that the laager had not been breached but that optimistically 'I hope tomorrow we shall be able to do something more definite', a recovering Lord Roberts arrived during the morning of the 19th and quickly surveyed the prevailing scene.[33] Kitchener, insistent that the battle could be won, pressed him hard to keep up the pressure on Cronje in an attempt to win an outright victory. But Roberts demurred. Meanwhile, Cronje asked the British for doctors (he had none) and a truce to bury the Boer dead. Rather inhumanely, Roberts refused. The stalemate thus continued. Nearby and still at large the tough and talented Boer commander De Wet – who later would be immortalized in one of Kipling's poems of the Boer War, 'Ubique', was hopeful that he just might be able to spring his comrades from the British noose.[34] But he was bombarded relentlessly and finally on the 21st De Wet simply gave up and retreated. Cronje now was approaching his wits' end. Outraged that his request for a truce had been rejected, he defied the British to do their worst: 'Do as you please. I shall not surrender alive. Therefore bombard as you please'.[35] But defiance in the face of a superior enemy usually has its limits and Cronje met his a few days later on the 27th. After a couple of final British and Canadian assaults on the Boer laager, he could stand it no longer and reluctantly raised the white flag. After a brutal ten days the Battle of Paardeberg at last was over.

By the time of the Boer surrender Roberts had ordered Kitchener to leave the battlefield in order to start preparations for the planned march on the capital of the Orange Free State, Bloemfontein. Paardeberg had proved to be a necessary stop on the Field Marshal's drive northwards. The battle had been protracted, bloody, costly, not very well commanded, and, to some extent, inhumane. But it was a clear victory, the first significant one of the war for the British and one that in the minds of many had reversed the ignominious defeat at Majuba Hill, the 19th anniversary of which had come exactly that day. This fact was lost on none of the combatants. Criticism of Kitchener's command at

Paardeberg, both then and later, was strong and in part is justified. But in his drive to attain victory in a war that hitherto had spiralled into ignominy he was prescient in understanding that in an age when war existed as a tripartite enterprise amongst the government, the military, and the public, the latter of these especially would welcome victory with little remonstration as to cost. He was exactly right in this assumption, and in both the view of the public and that of the government, the victory at Paardeberg was the catalyst that turned around British fortunes in the war. The sight of over 4,000 Boer soldiers being led away into captivity from the Modder river was graphic evidence that all could be right again for the British in South Africa and victory over those who were considered a lesser people attained.

Naturally, Kitchener shared the renewal of British martial spirit that accompanied the victory at Paardeberg and hoped that it portended more of the same in the immediate future. The overmatched Boers indeed now were reeling and as the British continued to blunt their enemy's offensives and relieve long-held towns such as Ladysmith (on 1 March) the turning-point that was Paardeberg became clearer still. To this end, Roberts and Kitchener continued to work very closely together in the late-winter and early-spring of 1900. The informal nature of Boer military service meant that an increasing number of their fighting men decided that in the face of burgeoning British power (both home and Imperial troops continued to flood into South Africa) returning to their farms and towns to defend their families directly was the right thing to do. Roberts wished to maximize every advantage that the recent victory afforded and within two weeks of Cronje's surrender he was marching with over 30,000 men, intent on taking Bloemfontein, which duly occurred on 13 March. The much-maligned Buller's success at Ladysmith – 'General Buller Gets There At Last', shouted a representative newspaper headline – sent an already heightened British and Empire public into paroxysms of celebration, giving the impression that final victory might now really be at hand.[36]

Of course, such thinking would prove to be significantly premature, but in the glow of victory – and nothing would match the celebrations surrounding the relief of the 217-day siege of Mafeking (17 May) where Colonel Robert Baden-Powell had created an epic of survival, sparking sheer, unadulterated jingo joy across Britain and beyond – the end of the war seemed nigh.[37] In the meantime, Kitchener was tasked by Roberts with putting down rebellion in the Western Cape, which he did with his usual grim ferocity. As the war dragged on Kitchener's regard for the Boers sank ever lower. While admiring of their patriotic spirit, he considered their constant movement and wont to hide and dash about somehow unmanly in warfare and therefore faintly dishonourable. A fair fight meant *mano a mano* to Kitchener – notwithstanding, however, the tremendous mechanized pounding he had just recently inflicted on the Mahdi's Sudanese. But at least they had come on a straight line. Chasing the Boers, on the other hand, who 'are always running away on their little ponies', he complained, had become nothing but aggravating to him.[38]

Despite such complaints the spring of 1900 would belong to the British. Following on Roberts' taking of Bloemfontein in March his next major target was Pretoria, the capital of the Transvaal. By April he was readying to make a direct march on it and in so doing, he believed, win the war. In support of this belief his army kept growing larger and larger. Roberts now commanded 170,000 troops in the field, and he intended to use over half of them to take Pretoria. In defence, the Boers could muster no more than about 30,000 men. Could David beat Goliath, or would this particular version of the story have a different ending?

A distance of 300 miles stood between Roberts and Pretoria. Beginning on 3 May he would traverse it in just 34 days. His passage was not quite an 'Omdurman picnic', but resistance to his passage indeed was limited, the Boers melting into the margins in the face of a swarm of British and Empire troops, well-armed and singing triumphantly: 'We are marching to Pretoria!' as they moved virtually unimpeded across the veldt. En route Roberts announced the annexation of the Orange Free State. Crossing the Vaal river the approach to Johannesburg was made with little resistance and on 31 May the Union Jack was hoisted over the nearly-deserted city. Pretoria was now just 35 miles distant. Within the city panic reigned as the British approached. President Kruger fled east, and would leave the country altogether in October, beginning a peripatetic exile through France, Germany, and the Netherlands before dying eventually in Switzerland in 1904. In the event, Pretoria's defences proved to be almost non-existent, reduced to a pair of battalions, and on 5 June the remaining denizens of the Transvaal capital witnessed the raising of the Union Jack over the central square watched keenly by a triumphant and satisfied Roberts and Kitchener.

The Boers had been duly smote and the war was drawing swiftly to a close, or so it seemed.

As victory prevailed in Pretoria outside it in the Transvaal countryside a new kind of war was developing, however, which would prolong the Anglo-Boer conflict and prove to be a harbinger of many other twentieth-century wars to come. Thousands of Boers – some calling themselves *bittereinders* – were not willing to accept that their cause had come to an end with the fall of their capital cities and therefore they would fight on to the 'bitter end', guerilla-style. As stark as the symbolism of set-piece defeat may have been, the fight could and should go on, they believed, and with the inspirational leadership of a number of commanders remaining in the field – principally De Wet – such is exactly what took place. In light of this emergent development, Kitchener immediately was sent south by Roberts following the rapturous scenes in Pretoria to deal with De Wet's series of successful pin-pricks against British supply- and communications-lines. These raids were proving highly inspirational to those commandos who wished to maintain the fight against the British despite their defeat in otherwise conventional terms. De Wet's success and that of other field commanders such as 'Koos' De la Rey, Marthinus Prinsloo, and Marthinus Steyn, erstwhile president of the OFS, and what they represented, were of serious concern to the British and on 12 June, just prior to his 50th birthday, Kitchener experienced up-close just what daring Boer commandos could do.

On that day, merely a week after Pretoria had been taken, Kitchener was bivouacked not far south of the city at the Heilbron Road rail station after a day spent supervising a series of repairs to railway lines and bridges. As evening fell, De Wet and his men stole silently into the British camp and began to overwhelm and take prisoner a number of soldiers who had been guarding Kitchener and his work company. Alerted to the enemy's presence, Kitchener, his ADC, and a number of other men made immediately for their horses and swiftly set off cross-country to the safety of another British camp. At the outset, at least, it looked like only Kitchener would escape the Boer net.[39] Indeed, De Wet did not realize just how close he had been to snaring Roberts' Chief of Staff and right-hand man, but Kitchener had come as near to being caught by the enemy as he ever would be while in a position of senior command.

The celebration that had resulted from the taking of Pretoria and the accompanying British assumptions about an impending end to the war thus rapidly became short-lived. Indeed, by the middle of June the situation was devolving into a full-scale guerilla war – much to the satisfaction of De Wet who had long advocated that an unconventional war was in fact the only way the Boers could hope to defeat the British – and Roberts responded by enunciating the manner by which support for the commandos could be interdicted and destroyed. Farm-burning thus became British policy (over 600 Boer farms were burned by the end of the year) when it could be shown that Boer commandos were gaining succour from the community in which their acts of sabotage and destruction were taking place. As a necessary corollary to this policy Roberts ordered that women and children resident on such farms were to be placed in 'camps of refuge' until such time as the war came to an end and they could return home. Throughout the summer and autumn of 1900 as some Boer fighters surrendered themselves to the British under a general amnesty, many thousands of others chose to defy the offer and remain in the field starkly refusing to lay down their arms. To have done so would have meant abandoning the hope of maintaining an independent Afrikanerdom. Roberts, now on the cusp of being named Commander in Chief of the British Army by the recently re-elected Salisbury Unionist Government, resigned and sailed for home at the end of November, his almost-full year fighting the Boers complete. Kitchener, likewise looking ahead to what might be in prospect beyond South Africa – 'Am anxious to get India. Can you help?' he wrote to St John Brodrick, Secretary of War – was named to succeed Roberts and wrap up the conflict.[40] Notwithstanding the success the commandos were having against the British Kitchener still considered the war to be 'almost over', as he wrote to the Queen just a few months before her death, and thus planning for the future must be made.[41] But for Kitchener the really hard work of the war in fact was only just beginning and, as it transpired, the war would extend all the way until mid-1902.

The New Year 1901 opened with Kitchener strategizing over how to end the infuriating effectiveness of the Boer commandos. The ever-elusive Christiaan De Wet had acquired folk-hero status in the eyes of many of his sullenly defeated countrymen, one of the few bright lights that existed for patriotic Afrikaners in the aftermath of the annexation of their two erstwhile states by the British. Adding a cruel fillip to their conventional defeat was the fact that one of the chief architects of the war and the arch-enemy of Kruger, Sir Alfred Milner, was now in charge of the civilian administration of both the Transvaal and the re-named Orange River Colony. As suggested earlier, Kitchener's relationship with Milner was both perfunctory and testy. He was happy enough to let Milner go quietly about his work while he himself got on with executing the war, but they distrusted one another implicitly and Milner's 'race patriotism' – as he later called it himself – and insistence that the Boers must offer an unconditional surrender in the service of his imperial zealotry Kitchener found to be both distasteful and unrealistic.[42] For Milner's part, he understood his own position, however, and was 'quite willing to lie low, and let my administratorship [*sic*] be a farce, until the country is pacified, if there is only progress in that direction'.[43]

And progress was exactly what Kitchener was planning to make when he settled upon a plan to break the commandos' ability to harry and sabotage British troops, railways and rolling stock, and supply lines, the very work that would inspire Kipling to pen yet another of his odes to the Boer War, 'Bridge-Guard in the Karroo'.[44] Characteristically, Milner thought Kitchener muddle-headed in his being unable to come up with a plan to combat successfully the commandos.[45] Others shared the criticism and it is one that some biographers and historians have held since.[46] But given the circumstances, Kitchener's ruminations over what to do in order to win a guerilla war, something that (outside of the Spanish-American War of 1898) no modern commander fighting a mechanized war had yet been required to do, is hardly surprising. 'I puzzle my brain to find out some way of finishing but without much result', as he wrote to a friend in the midst of his attempt to work out an answer to the commando question.[47] Indeed, the only surprise is that it took him just a few weeks to come up with the rather ingenious plan that by building a series of linked blockhouses across the veldt Boers riding out on commando could be systematically funnelled into catchment areas and thereby have their raids nullified. By the end of January, and barely into the top-job, he was sure of the plan's potential and therefore implementation of it began. The task of constructing blockhouses was immense, however, but eventually over 8,000 of them were built connecting a network of lines almost 4,000 miles long. Linked initially by barbed wire before being replaced by stronger annealed cables highly resistant to cutting, the blockhouses stood about one and a half miles apart. Later the distance between them was cut in half. Almost immediately the impact of the blockhouse system was felt by the Boers. The 'bag', as Kitchener referred colloquially to apprehended Boer commandos, duly increased steadily: the old sapper now was at work, doing what he did best.

The main target in this new endeavor was De Wet and any of the other prominent commando leaders still at large. He proved, however, too slippery to catch and indeed came to make sport out of eluding his putative captors and their elaborate 'spider's web', as he derided the blockhouse system.[48] There's little doubt, however, that with the introduction of the networked blockhouse Kitchener and the British had increased greatly the territorial pressure that they could bring to bear on De Wet and his commandos. In conjunction with securing as many of the river *drifts* (fords) as possible, and continuing with Roberts' policy of farm-burning, the blockhouse web was having the desired effect. Altogether, the war had turned dirtier than ever, however. Perhaps it is a romantic conceit to see conventional war as being more honourable than what the Anglo-Boer War had turned into, but clearly the conflict had devolved into a highly nasty scrap in which any and all means to defeat the enemy were being used by both sides. Britain's size advantage leant it considerable weight in achieving its military goals through reprehensible practices, but the Boers on a smaller scale re-paid their enemies in kind, including – and with considerable vociferousness – those black Africans who chose to support the British. When captured by the Boers summary execution was their usual fate. 'It is a horrid war. No straight fighting,' wrote Kitchener in April, and indeed that is exactly what it had become.[49] But worse, if there could be such a thing in this war, was yet to be seen.

Roberts' decision in June of 1900 to begin to place Boer women and children (and some men) in camps of refuge had resulted in tragically unexpected ramifications. The impulse to establish camps to house those who were forced to evacuate their farms prior to the buildings being burnt, within the context of war, was a humanitarian one, though the plan became seriously flawed in execution. The burning of farms itself, while harsh, was not out of line as a tactic of war, and certainly given that the Boers had chosen to continue the war in guerilla style they had given to British command every justification for attempting to eradicate their method of sanctuary and supply. Still, to many at the time (and many more later), farm-burning and turning out of doors vulnerable non-combatants was seen as a reprehensible step by the British, especially as it led to the development of a series of so-called 'concentration' camps. (The Nazis' later use of the term prior-to and during World War II has meant that it is almost impossible to examine the camps in an un-emotive way. Still, it was clear from the outset that neither Roberts nor Kitchener, nor anyone else directly involved in the construction and maintenance of the camps, harboured any of the sinister plans for systematic murder or genocide by which the Nazis would later become infamous.)

No one in British command liked doing what was believed to be necessary to speed up the end of the war by breaking the will and ability of the Boer commandos to remain operative in the field. Farms were at the very heart of Afrikaner society and setting them alight seemed an assault on its very essence, which it was. Indeed, many British soldiers tasked with the job of evacuating farm residents prior to putting their properties to the torch did so reluctantly, but accepted that the sooner the resistance could be broken, the sooner the war would end, and the sooner they could all go home. But pitiable sights in the process were unavoidable. 'At another farm', recalled one such British soldier, 'a small girl interrupted her preparation for departure to play indignantly their national anthem at us on an old piano. We were carting the people off ... a miserable, hurried home-leaving ... and this poor little wretch in the midst of it all pulling herself together to strum a final defiance.'[50]

During the latter part of 1900 and into the next year a number of refugee camps were established (some of which Kitchener visited[51]), most of them consisting of tented accommodation for the apprehended Boers with common eating and lavatory facilities. In the main the camps were ramshackle affairs for refugees, not unlike what is seen today under the United Nations flag in various world trouble-spots. Eventually, 45 such camps were built for Boer internees, with a further 64 for blacks. Designed as a temporary measure in response to a fluid battlefield situation they were not very well designed or administered. Meanwhile, those designated as Boer prisoners of war were mostly sent overseas to, among other locations, St Helena, made famous for its six-year service as Napoleon's island prison. Left behind, the families of the POWs were sent to the camps, which came to be scattered mainly across the Orange River Colony and the Transvaal, with a few of them located in Natal and the Cape.

Isolated, miserable, and unhygienic, the camps fast became riven with communicable diseases and the death rate climbed quickly to over 300 per thousand, a rate worse than in British field hospitals during the war but not markedly so.[52] By mid-1901, however, the plight of the internees had become public knowledge nonetheless, mainly because of the visit to some of them by the enterprisingly dogged figure of Emily Hobhouse, secretary of the South African Conciliation Committee, a London-based group committed to ending the war. Forty years old, single, well-connected politically, and a life-long Christian social activist, Hobhouse had stood out against the war at its outset and from the summer of 1900 had become severely exercised by the grim news that hundreds of Boer women were being 'left ragged by our military operations .... The poor women were being driven from pillar to post, [and] needed protection and organized assistance'.[53] Such protection she was determined to provide, and having formed a new society which she called the Distress Fund for South African Women and Children, she sailed for Cape Town, arriving there on 27 December. Immediately, Hobhouse gained an interview with a dyspeptic Milner and in a decision that he would later (partially) regret, she was provided with a couple of railway cars in order to take supplies to the Bloemfontein camp. Upon arrival at the camp Hobhouse was appalled by what she found there. Labelling it and the others she visited subsequently 'a wholesale cruelty', she was especially galled by the impact of malnutrition and disease on the young: 'To keep these Camps going is murder to the children'.[54] After touring the camps for a few months she returned to England in May 1901 (on the same ship as a vacationing Milner) and immediately wrote a damning paper on what she had witnessed in South Africa. Entitled, 'Report of a Visit to the Camps of Women and Children in the Cape and Orange River Colonies', it had an electrifying effect on public opinion, especially that portion of it which was left-leaning. The first politician to publicly respond to it was the Welsh opposition Liberal party member David Lloyd George who accused the Salisbury government of carrying out 'a war of extermination' against the Boers. Then the Liberal leader himself, Sir Henry Campbell-Bannerman, excoriated the same in a speech in London given on 14 June, by asking rhetorically: 'When is a war not a war? When it is carried on by methods of barbarism in South Africa'.[55]

Not everyone, of course, found the shrill critique of Hobhouse and the condemnatory words of Lloyd George and Campbell-Bannerman convincing. Both in South Africa as well as in England she was attacked by some for being disloyal and pro-Boer (which she was to a degree). Unsurprisingly, Kitchener found her dangerously meddlesome and selective in how she presented her findings. Parliament responded to the uproar with a full-blown debate nonetheless, producing a directive that Kitchener file a statistical report about the situation, which he duly did in July. The numbers were undeniably bad: almost 100,000 Boers were then being held in the camps (along with a similar number of blacks), and the death rate remained stubbornly high. To show its seriousness the Government appointed a commission with Millicent Fawcett, Liberal MP and leading suffragette, as its chair, and between August and December the commission carried out its own tour of the camps in South Africa. One of the ironies of the Fawcett Commission was that it finally gave Milner something to do in his capacity as civilian administrator of the former Boer republics because the camps were transferred out of military hands and into administrative ones. Having done so, significant improvements came about immediately, it must be said, but the early months of camp life had done their worst with the final statistics for them showing that about 28,000 Boers had died in the camps (out of a cumulative interned population of 116,000), of which some 24,000 were children. The figures for interned blacks were scarcely better: about 14,000 dead out of some 107,000.[56]

The camps proved a very difficult trial for Kitchener, as did attacks – such as that made by Jan Christiaan Smuts, the Afrikaner general, in January 1902 in a reprise of Campbell-Bannerman's words – in which he referred to the British Commander in Chief as presiding over a campaign against the Boers of 'unbelievable barbarism and gruesomeness'.[57] Kitchener, ever phlegmatic and fixated on ending the war before all else, took such hyperbolic criticisms in stride. Later, Smuts would come to count Kitchener as a friend. As for Hobhouse, 'that bloody woman', Kitchener thought her a cypher for leftist political opposition, which was much too quick to look for evidence of insidious military policy when in fact haste, circumstance, and the exigencies of war were to blame.[58] 'Kitchener no more desired the deaths of women and children in the camps', observes Thomas Pakenham persuasively, 'than of the wounded Dervishes after Omdurman, or of his own soldiers in the typhoid stricken hospitals of Bloemfontein'.[59] Still, a good deal of the blame for the inhumane nature of the camps must fall on him. More could have and should have been done earlier to alleviate their dire condition and, if so, the disease and death rate would have fallen commensurately. Ultimately however, Kitchener was simply relieved to hand the administration of the camps over to Milner's civilian authority, even though ceding any degree of control in South Africa to his nemesis as a general principle he greatly disliked. The camps were Milner's problem now, 'a bad business' yes, he agreed, but no longer his to manage.[60]

During the first half of 1901 the other great issue of concern to Kitchener was the apparent possibility that the Boers might finally be willing to agree to a negotiated peace, in lieu of a complete surrender, which he did not think either likely or even necessarily desirable. Kitchener's columns riding out on the veldt and funneling Boer commandos into the blockhouse net continued to have the desired effect. 'The boers [*sic*] are growing very weak', he wrote to a friend in July. 'The constant drain of killed, wounded and prisoners is telling on them but they won't chuck it hoping for something to turn up'.[61] In fact, Kitchener had assumed this weakness in the adversary for a considerable amount of time and it had spurred him already to seek a peace agreement with the Boer leadership in February. For critics of Kitchener then and later the attempt by him to bring the Boer War to an end as early as the first months of 1901 sits incongruously in the midst of his well-documented martial record. But given his growing understanding of the nature of the war he was fighting and (to him at least) the objectionable way in which the continued course of it would inexorably run, the fact that he extended the olive branch to the enemy should come as no surprise.

Kitchener, therefore, became a key figure in this attempt at brokering a peace. In it he had the clear backing of Joseph Chamberlain at the Colonial Office, who now that the Boer republics had been defeated and partially occupied, was keen to bring the war to an end and put paid to the interminable guerilla attacks of the commandos. In this attempt the Colonial Secretary was supported by Salisbury, although the Prime Minister would remain wary of making concessions to the Boers that would allow them to 'retain any portion of their independence'. The point for all those involved was to end the fighting as soon as possible and then turn to diplomacy in order to find the right way forward politically. But 'we must be the masters' Salisbury told the House of Lords in stentorian fashion in mid-February, because weakness now would simply open the way for the Boers to 'accumulate new forces, new armaments, and prepare once a fitting occasion arises, for the same attack which we had to meet eighteen months ago'.[62]

Kitchener's initial year of dealing with the Boers had taught him that far from their being a monolithic enemy – which Salisbury's words suggest was his own understanding of them – the Boer leadership cadre spanned a spectrum, from vitriolic belligerence to reasoned accommodation. By early 1901, with the blockhouse-and-drive strategy beginning to have a positive impact, thus making the Boers 'more peacefully inclined' than earlier, as he wrote to the Secretary of State for War, St John Brodrick, Kitchener proposed to make a direct overture of peace to the Boers.[63] Indeed, Kitchener believed (rightly) that amongst the Boer leaders there was a great deal of pride at not 'being the first man to give in, as he will be held to be a disgrace to his country ever afterwards'.[64] Kitchener calculated that in this regard his best chance of success lay with Louis Botha. Despite having defeated the Jameson Raiders back in 1895 and being a fierce commando general operating in the Transvaal, Botha was known to take the long view of the future of Anglo-Boer relations in South Africa.[65] Therefore, cannily using Botha's wife as a successful intermediary, the two men set up a secret meeting for the end of February at Middelburg, a town conveniently located for both of them along the rail-line running east towards Delagoa Bay. In so doing, Kitchener was counting on Botha's status amongst his peers and his powers of persuasion to convince men like De Wet, Steyn, and other leading Boers that a negotiated peace was the best way to end the war successfully and with honour.

Accordingly, on the morning of 28 February, and apprised by Brodrick of the British government's parameters for the talks and therefore hoping not to have to insist on 'anything humiliating' to the Boers, Kitchener met Botha at a requisitioned house in Middelburg.[66] The two men of military iron had a straightforward but respectful exchange, breaking for a reasonably sociable lunch and a rather severe-looking group photograph. Still, at the end of the one-day meeting they were mutually satisfied that what they had discussed and agreed upon together was something that both sides could potentially both endorse and enforce. Perhaps, however, the glow of diplomacy indeed was too bright; in Kitchener's case his highly successful foray into diplomatic negotiation with Marchand at Fashoda in 1898 may have made him too optimistic about the meeting, and in the event, the Middelburg overtures for peace ended in failure. Why?

Milner, Kitchener believed, was largely to blame for this failure because his strict ideological approach to the war whereby he resisted anything other than the complete vanquishing of the Boers stood in the way of the kind of accommodation required to produce a mutually acceptable peace. Botha had come to Middelburg with a ten-point list for discussion. Chief on the list was the post-war restoration of Boer independence, which Kitchener rejected out of hand in accordance with his instructions from London. But the other points were negotiable – at least in Kitchener's mind – and so he talked them through in good faith. Amnesty for Boer soldiers upon surrender? Yes. Money for re-building destroyed farms? Yes. A prohibition on voting enfranchisement for black Africans? Here, Kitchener counter-proposed that instead of a prohibition the decision should be deferred until self-government was eventually restored to the former Boer republics. Altogether, both men departed Middelburg on the evening of 28 February 1901 confident in the outcome of the day's work and properly hopeful that they would be able to convince their respective political colleagues that if such terms were accepted then peace might reign.

Following the meeting, at Milner's insistence, Kitchener met him at Bloemfontein to discuss the content of the cable that would shortly need to be sent to London informing the British government of the outcome of the talks. Their meeting was mostly cordial though occasionally testy. Milner's usual ideologically-driven position that the British needed to 'knock the bottom' out of the Boers was ever-present, although the only issue the two men in fact disagreed upon was the proposed amnesty for Boer soldiers. In principle, however, as Milner had always made abundantly clear, he was opposed to peace talks until the Boers had been beaten and forced to surrender. His grand imperial vision, the animating principle of his so-called 'kindergarten' of likeminded thinkers such as Lionel Curtis and John Buchan (afterwards Lord Tweedsmuir), who later would gather around him during South African reconstruction, simply rejected trying to accommodate the 'weak link' Boers in any version of a future South Africa.[67]

The cable was duly sent to Chamberlain and on 6 March he replied. Immediately upon reading it, Kitchener realized that there would be no peace. Milner's 'narrow' attitude combined with Chamberlain's own wariness as to what might be given away to the Boers in such a negotiated peace, had swayed others around the Cabinet table (including Brodrick) to amend Kitchener's provisions in such a way as to render them unacceptable to Botha.[68] Kitchener knew that the revised terms (especially the British government's refusal to offer a full amnesty to Boer soldiers) would be impossible for Botha to finesse through the tangled thicket of Boer leadership. Privately, Kitchener thought the government's position to be 'absurd and wrong'.[69] Accordingly, Botha responded just as Kitchener assumed he would. There would be no deal. Above all, the utter 'destruction' of Afrikanerdom was the message understood by the Boer leadership as salient to the British government's response. That this clearly was not Kitchener's own intention – despite being the government's chief sword-arm – is one of the starker ironies of the Boer War. Even Lloyd George, no admirer of Kitchener's either then or later, made plain his disgust at the government's inability to act on the Commander in Chief's recommendations and broker a binding peace. In Lloyd George's' inimitable oratorical style he made plain to Parliament what Kitchener had offered, compared to what Chamberlain had scuttled: 'There was a soldier who knew what war meant; he strove to make peace. There was another man, who strolled among his orchids 6,000 miles from the deadly bark of the Mauser rifle. He stopped Kitchener's peace!'[70]

By the early-spring of that year the proximate opportunity for peace therefore largely had passed and the cruel but effective impact of the blockhouse network continued to weaken the ability of the Boers to operate in the field. Still, they gamely fought on, but still not in the way Kitchener would have preferred. 'If they would only fight', he complained again, this time to Lady Ilchester in a letter of 22nd March, 'we could soon finish them off but they have quite given up any idea of doing more than cut off any weak party moving alone or blowing up a train by a mine set under the rails'.[71] That summer the war continued, therefore, in its desultory, now even banal way in Kitchener's view. But one event in particular in August would, when ramified, both shock and appall not only the British and Boers, but for different reasons, do the same for Australian troops (as well as for their countrymen back home). They, like the Canadians and other colonial troops, had come in their thousands to South Africa in answer to the Empire's call. In the minds of many the event also (especially to Australians both then and now) confirmed the picture of Kitchener as a hard, remorseless military man for whom mercy could not be expected to be visited upon either foe or friend.

Earlier, as the guerilla war had rolled out in the first weeks of 1901, one of the additional responses to it by Kitchener had been to make routine the so-called work of the 'flying column'. (Something that would be adopted more famously by both sides not very many years later in Ireland during the nationalist struggle.) Charged with apprehending as many of the Boer enemy as possible, certain of these columns had also functioned as irregular forces, indeed as 'special forces' in a way that subsequent generations would come to understand. In February one such force had been raised. Named the Bushveldt Carbineers (BVC), it was a regiment of around 300 men, almost half of whom were Australian. Based in Pietersburg about 160 miles northeast of Pretoria, its field of operations was the Northern Transvaal, a remote and hard-to-control region from the perspective of British command.[72]

Three of the many Australians serving in the BVC were Harry Morant (although English-born), Peter Handcock, and George Witton, all of whom would shortly be charged with shooting Boer prisoners in the course of their service and in so doing spark a controversial court martial, the impact of which is still felt today in Australian popular culture.[73] Although all three of them held the rank of lieutenant, Morant (born in 1864) was senior to the others both in terms of age and experience.[74] He was also relatively sophisticated in a way not shared by his two younger colleagues, as his published poetry suggested. A superb handler of horses (hence his nickname, the 'Breaker'), Morant had migrated from Somerset to Queensland in 1883 and then spent the next 16 years living a 'bush' life in the wilds of the Australian Outback. Upon the outbreak of the Anglo-Boer War in 1899 he enlisted in the South Australian Mounted Rifles and by the spring of 1900 found himself on active service in the Transvaal. In the event, he served well, his cultured manner and outstanding riding ability winning him the admiration of both his peers and superiors. Morant had been part of Lord Roberts' march into Pretoria, and otherwise saw action at Kroonstadt and at Diamond Hill. Later in 1900 he made a brief return to England, his first visit there in 17 years, where he befriended a certain Captain Percy Hunt, likewise home on leave from South Africa. Upon Hunt's signing on with the BVC early in 1901, he convinced Morant to do the same, which he did, obtaining a commission on 1 April. By that summer Morant was serving under Hunt and their BVC column was achieving considerable success in foiling Boer attacks in the violent Strydpoort district of the Transvaal, located not very far south of Pietersburg.

Up until the time of Hunt and Morant the BVC's early operations had been reckless and undisciplined. Looting of food and livestock was common and the men had established backcountry liquor stills for their own enjoyment. The regiment's main base of operations in the north had been established at Fort Edward, which was little more than an occupied farmhouse, located some 90 miles from Pietersburg in what was known as the Spelonken region. The BVC's original commander, Captain James Robertson, had been weak-willed, but a semblance of order had been maintained by Captain Alfred Taylor, a British intelligence officer sent north by an informed and therefore concerned Kitchener to assist Robertson. In July, unbeknownst to Taylor at least, a group of six Boer commandos had approached Fort Edward, intending to surrender. Instead, they were arrested and summarily shot. For being the commanding officer under which this brazen act had been carried out Robertson was forced to resign. His replacement was Captain Hunt. Accompanying him as part of a refreshed column were, among others, Morant, Handcock, and Witton.

Hunt, together with the stellar support of Morant, soon was able to restore considerable discipline to his new BVC column, although some of the longer-serving men were not pleased that their spoils of war now were being curtailed by the new leadership cadre. But these sorts of troubles would pale with what would come their way beginning on the night of 5 August 1901. Riding out of Fort Edward Hunt had taken a small detachment of men (not including Morant) to conduct a raid on the farmhouse of a leading Boer commando leader named Barend Viljoen. In making the raid, Hunt's men were unprepared for the surprise and strength of the Boers' resistance. During the attack Hunt was killed, and allegedly mutilated by Boer commandos. When word reached Fort Edward about the failed raid and Hunt's purported ugly death, Morant became enraged and together with a similarly disposed detachment of men set out immediately for the Viljoen farm. Finding it abandoned they began to track the Boer escapees, coming upon their encampment the next evening, 6 August. Peremptorily opening fire by the itchy trigger-finger of Morant and therefore losing the advantage of surprise, almost all of the hunted Boers escaped. The unlucky one that did not, named Visser, was trussed up and severely questioned by the BVC detachment and the next morning while they were returning to Fort Edward, an angry Morant simply ordered him shot.

Despite the rough justice of Visser's execution Hunt's death continued to effect Morant deeply. During the ensuing days he allowed his grief to work itself into a vengeful lather and a little over two weeks later on 23 August he led a patrol to intercept an apprehended group of eight of Viljoen's commandos being brought into Fort Edward, and had them shot too in a roadside ditch. Regrettably, it did not end there, however. Their grisly deaths became linked to one more. A German-born Lutheran missionary, the Reverend C.A. Daniel Heese, who lived near Pietersburg at Makaanspoort, knew some of the arrested commandos and when he was informed that they had been shot told Captain Taylor that when he passed through Pietersburg he was going to report this outrage to British command. Shortly thereafter, he was found dead too, shot while driving south in his horse and buggy.

In fairly short order this spate of killings was reported to the British authorities and resulted in the arrest of seven men in October, including Morant, Handcock, and Witton. Their court-martial began on 16 January 1902 in Pietersburg with two hearings, one concerned the eight Boer prisoners executed on the side of the road, while the other focused on the death of Visser. Proceedings then moved on to Pretoria where the trial pertaining to the murder of the Reverend Heese was conducted. Ably represented by counsel (Major J.F. Thomas), they were acquitted of the Heese murder. But the case against them for the murders of the other nine men (including Visser) was proved. They were sentenced to death on 26 January, with Witton's sentence immediately being commuted to life in prison on account of his lesser role in the affair. The next morning Morant and Handcock were duly executed outside the fort, their death warrants having been signed by Kitchener, as he shortly informed Brodrick at the War Office.[75] 'Shoot straight, you bastards!' the irrepressible Morant is alleged to have called out to his executioners. 'Don't make a mess of it!'[76]

Morant said more than he knew. In what would prove to be the waning days of the Anglo-Boer War it indeed had become messy, and in addition to its many and sometimes nameless victims now were added those of these two unfortunate Australians. They were perpetrators much more than victims in this sordid case, to be sure, but in the context of the times when shooting Boer prisoners of war was believed by many – both in South Africa and in Britain, and in both civilian and military life – to be British policy, Morant and Handcock come off as considerably less villainous than their trial had painted them to be. Indeed, as far back as the beginning of the guerilla war some people had been questioning the conduct of British soldiers in South Africa under Kitchener. John Dillon, an Irish nationalist MP, for example, stated in Parliament in January 1901 that Kitchener had authorized that 'all [Boer] men are to be shot so that no tales may be told'.[77] There were other reports also, spurring Roberts, now in London and in his new post as Commander in Chief of the British Army, to question Kitchener about their veracity. 'Absolutely untrue', replied Kitchener.[78] And there it was left. But for some the suspicion that an informal policy – as suggested by an unnamed Welsh soldier in a newspaper report, that 'we take no prisoners now .... There happened to be a few wounded Boers left. We put them through the mill. Every one was killed' – prevailed.[79] For such a view, however, no official evidence is extant and Kitchener was absolute in his denial that such a policy, either formal or informal, had ever existed.

In the aftermath of the Morant and Handcock executions the newly federated (in 1901) Australian government made an official request for an explanation from Kitchener, to which he was quick to reply. In a closely-worded telegram to the Australian Governor-General, Lord Hopetoun, Kitchener explained why Morant 'the originator of these crimes', and Handcock, who 'carried [them] out in a cold-blooded manner' were properly sentenced to death. Kitchener's telegram was published in the Australian press, setting off what has become a never-ending public debate about the nature of the 'Morant case'.[80] The transcripts of the court-martial were destroyed by fire in London in 1940 during the Battle of Britain so it is likely that the case will never be resolved to everyone's satisfaction. As folk-heroes in Australia, Morant and Handcock live on, however, inspiring an attempt as recently as 2013 to have them pardoned on the basis that 'Kitchener conspired to get them executed'.[81] But the modern penchant for conspiracy theories will not likely overthrow the fact that alleging a cover-up by the authorities in the case is simply not credible. Morant and Handcock had acted badly and with deadly force. They were not of course the only ones to do so in a war that had become notably dirty – 'a new kind of war for a new century' – but their culpability in the case was proven beyond a reasonable doubt.[82] In the event, they were most certainly not, as Witton later named his memoir of the case, 'Scapegoats of the Empire'.[83]

By April, with the unfortunate Morant case behind him, Kitchener was now keenly hopeful that the war might well indeed be drawing to a close. Exhausted by the unending strain of conducting all facets of the conflict, he was anxious for the end to come, partly because of the interminable nature of the killing and destruction that singularly marked the Anglo-Boer conflict, and partly because he continued to anticipate a move to India in order to become Commander in Chief of the army there. But if Kitchener thought that the war would end with the Boers vanquished and in supplication, he continued to be frustrated that as successful as the blockhouse system had been in parts of the Orange River Colony and the eastern Transvaal, elsewhere Boer commandos continued to range widely and with attendant success. Men like Steyn, De la Rey, and of course De Wet – who jested now that the blockhouse system should really be called the 'blockhead' system – were at large, seemingly impervious to the determined attempt by the British to hunt them down.[84] On 7 March, Lord Methuen, who had been pursuing De la Rey in the western Transvaal, was attacked himself at Tweebosch. His men beaten and scattered, and having been shot in the thigh, the wounded Methuen had no choice but to surrender to the commando leader. It was a moment of deep humiliation for Methuen, as no other British general had yet been captured during the entire South African campaign.

News of the Methuen disaster landed on the already emotionally-rent Kitchener like a thunderclap. In response, for the next two days he created a hermitage for himself out of his bedroom at Melrose House headquarters in Pretoria, refusing to talk to anyone or to eat anything.[85] Finally, hungry and determined, he emerged from this slough of despond saying that regardless of this particular setback the war was inevitably Britain's to win, and victory would commence with an immediate response to De la Rey. He informed Brodrick at the War Office that he was going to hit him 'hard as soon as possible'.[86] Fresh columns were duly sent to the western Transvaal and a ferocious fight began in late-March that would last into May.

Meanwhile, Kitchener could not have guessed given the recent successes of the commandos in the field, that the Boers – including De la Rey – were only steps away from utter exhaustion and consequent defeat. Notwithstanding their ability to resist and even from to time defeat the stronger foe, the relentless power and deep resources that the British were able to bring to bear on the strategic situation made moot ultimately the occasional Boer tactical success. While Kitchener's operatic response to Methuen's defeat and brief captivity might have suggested otherwise, the spent Boers were ready to deal, and by early April such talks were on the cusp of taking place, which they would do in earnest beginning on the 12th at Kitchener's headquarters in Pretoria.

The peace negotiations that would yield the binding Treaty of Vereeniging seven weeks later on 31 May were an exercise in realism, compromise, vision, irony, and for the Boers, the admission of defeat. At their request, a group of Boer leaders, principally Botha, Steyn, De Wet, and De la Rey, met with the British delegation headed by Kitchener (Milner joined later) in the elegant surroundings of Melrose House, a recently constructed Pretoria mansion that Lord Roberts had been offered by its (anxious) businessman owner after the city was taken by the British back in June of 1900.[87] Roberts had used it as his home and headquarters until succeeded by Kitchener in November of that year. Now, in the spring of 1902, Melrose House would serve as the main scene for the move from war to peace in South Africa.

Over the 15 months that had elapsed since the aborted peace talks of March 1901, Kitchener had remained realistic about what was good and desirable in the war's outcome. He, unlike Milner, was not doctrinaire about re-making South Africa into a thorough-going 'British' colony. That is to say, where Milner continued to insist upon the Boers' unconditional surrender as a prelude to South Africa's complete anglicisation, Kitchener rejected the idea that the Boers' language, culture, religion and whole way of life could somehow be done away with through diplomatic negotiation, or that such a drastic development would even be desirable. Without saying so he might have instanced the similar dilemma faced by the British after their victory over the French on the Plains of Abraham at Quebec in 1759. The right way forward then was to see the (early) British Empire as capable of absorption rather than of wholesale elimination, something that allowed for the continued existence and ultimate flowering of French-Canadian society within British North America.

The split over this issue between Kitchener and Milner was plain for all to see, as was a similar split amongst the Boer delegation. Some, such as Orange 'Free Staters' Botha and De la Rey, saw the Boers' military situation as dire and un-winnable and therefore a negotiated peace was their best option; whereas the men from the Transvaal, Steyn and De Wet, were strong on the idea that if they kept fighting they would eventually turn the tide because despite Britain's overwhelming power a guerilla war was an extraordinarily draining style of fight to maintain, with a high political cost not easily borne by the faraway London government.

When the meeting got underway on the morning of 12 April, the sense of déjà vu in the room must have been strong because of the Boers opening gambit that independence was still at the top of their list of priorities. Once again, Kitchener had to emphasize the point that independence was not on the table. Back and forth the two sides went, Kitchener attempting to move the Boers off their insistence on independence while reiterating the point that self-government within the British Empire should be seen as a desirable outcome. Such, he implored them, should in no way be seen as a humiliating concession as they would be sharing it with leading dominions such as Canada and Australia, whose people obviously were 'proud of their nationality.'[88] Kitchener made for a strong but magnanimous presence in the dining room at Melrose House, impressing – perhaps even over-awing – the Boer delegation.[89] Kitchener's strong position on self-government, however, did not ultimately convince them and so the telegram that was sent to London that evening went without much accompanying optimism for success.

Adding to the sense of relative gloom at the resumption of talks two days later on the 14th was the addition to them of Milner. His had been a spectral presence on the first day of the meeting but now here he was in the flesh. Accordingly, the Kitchener-Milner dynamic of mutual distrust permeated the proceedings, which was exacerbated by the ongoing, as Kitchener described it to a friend, 'loathing for Milner' by the Boers.[90] Still, the day went better than expected because the British government's response to the telegram of the 12th was more accommodating (and therefore much less sympathetic to Milner's intransigent position) than had hitherto been the case. Thus encouraged the delegates continued to negotiate for the next few days until on the 17th the meetings came to a successful interim conclusion. On that day it was agreed that the Boer delegates would report back to their constituencies and organize a general conference of 60 representatives (30 from each of the former republics) to discuss and vote on the framework of the treaty thus far discussed. There would be no armistice during this period, Kitchener ruled, so that the impetus to negotiate would not slacken. But all those involved in the prospective Boer conference slated for 15 May at Vereeniging – known to the British then only as the site of one of their discredited refugee camps – would be guaranteed safe passage and no fresh attacks would occur anywhere near the meeting site.[91]

For Kitchener the three weeks that followed were a time of considerable apprehension. As much as he relished the prospect of war's end – 'It is quite exciting to think that by the 20th of next month we may have peace' – he was acutely aware of the toxic effect Milner had had on all the major parties to the talks and he was under no illusion about the civil administrator's back-channel influence in London.[92] Moreover, how would the Boers likewise ameliorate their own internal differences in such a way as to not scupper a peace, even if the British did not do so themselves? All was pins and needles at Melrose House as Kitchener read frequent intelligence reports from Vereeniging and awaited the outcome of the Boer plenary meeting there, news of which reached him on the evening of 16 May. The Boer delegates had met for two days in a park under a huge marquee and after much impassioned discussion and pointed debate the conference agreed to a set of four terms that were to be relayed to Kitchener and the British delegation in Pretoria. To do so, a group of Boer leaders consisting of Botha, De Wet, De la Rey, Smuts – a Cambridge-educated lawyer in addition to being a military man – and J.B.M. Hertzog, a rising 'Free State' judge and later politician, would travel by rail 65 miles north from Vereeniging to the erstwhile Transvaal capital. And there, on Monday, 19 May at 10 o'clock in the morning, the final act of the Anglo-Boer War commenced in the expansive and richly-appointed dining room of Melrose House.

Over the next 12 days the two delegations would work to achieve a binding treaty – modelled on the terms of Kitchener's attempted peace at Middelburg – that would bring an end to an enormously costly war.

But the negotiations were riven by misunderstanding, disagreement, and frustration before yielding finally to a ten-clause document that all present could bring themselves to sign. Throughout the near-fortnight-long event Kitchener chaired the proceedings, clarifying, cajoling, and generally moving the Boer representatives (ten of them altogether) along with Milner to the point of a binding agreement. Kitchener's task was extremely difficult, and success depended upon the diplomatic and conciliatory approach that he had unwittingly rehearsed at Fashoda. On the Boer side, the most difficult member to manage was De Wet. A hard and uncompromising military man – indeed much like Kitchener himself – he was not sure that even yet the time had come to surrender.[93] Most of the rest of the Boer delegation were sure, however, that the Boer people – especially its women and children – had suffered enough and should not be sacrificed further on the altar of Afrikaner nationalism. Still, in remaining obdurate on the point De Wet drove Milner to distraction and the talks themselves seemed in jeopardy until Kitchener intervened with the welcome suggestion that on the finer legal points concerning surrender (Clause 1) the legal members of the conference – namely Smuts – be allowed to do their work exclusive of the representative members. This suggestion was agreed to, and with, the departure of De Wet and Milner from the room the heightened temperature of the talks fell immediately.

Similarly, on the question of self-government (Clause 7) and the rapidity with which it would succeed military administration in the two former Boer republics, Kitchener spoke privately to Smuts suggesting (presciently) that the Liberals under Campbell-Bannerman were likely to win office within two years and, if so, would probably move much more quickly towards its realization than would the Conservatives. So convinced was Smuts by the honest and forthright comments by Kitchener that later he credited him with having 'accomplished the peace'.[94]

Throughout the first week of the peace conference as the various clauses were debated and personal diplomacy reigned, the government in London traded telegrams with Kitchener and Milner.[95] Considering their usual disaffection the two men in Pretoria worked rather well together during this time. However, on the issue of the amount of financial compensation to be used for Boer economic restoration they disagreed sharply. Kitchener advocated for an amount of L3 million, with few encumbrances as to recipient. Milner thought this suggestion was both profligate and dis-honourable as it would make tangible a payment to the Boers for having been engaged in 'fighting us'. Moreover, he believed that not everything need ride on the success of the talks anyway since his assumption was that the Boers now were so weak that 'if the assembly at Vereeniging breaks up without peace they will surrender right and left'.[96] No one, however, could be sure of that, least of all the Cabinet in London. Chamberlain certainly did not want the talks to founder, especially on a money issue, a view made clear to both Milner and Kitchener. Accordingly, they set to work on a revised money provision with which they could agree, the result of which became Clause 10, and then at last the drafting of final terms.

On 27 May, shortly after receiving the Kitchener-Milner revision, the Cabinet cabled Melrose House with its own final terms and the next day they were delivered to the Boer delegates. They were given three days to take the ten-clause treaty to the assembled Boer representatives waiting patiently at Vereeniging for ratification or rejection. A yes or no answer to the terms as stated was all that would be accepted by the British, otherwise the war would continue to be fought. By this point the Vereeniging gathering had become an assembly of defeated people. The weight of almost three years of war lay heavily upon them. The present picture of their predicament was bleak; the prospect of fighting on even bleaker. All talked out by 31 May, Schalk Burgers, with the much-earlier departure of Kruger having now become the Acting President of the Transvaal, shared the sombre mood of the gathering when he stood up Pericles-like and orated emotionally that 'We stand at the graveside of two Republics'.[97] The funereal atmosphere of the Vereeniging gathering meant that the vote could really go only one way. And it did, 54 to six in favour of accepting the treaty as drafted.[98] Late that evening at 11 o'clock, the ten Boer representatives, having returned by rail from Vereeniging, re-convened at Melrose House to sign the treaty. Beginning with Burgers' signature the other nine Boers added theirs, which were then followed by that of Kitchener and, finally though reluctantly, Milner's. All was over. In the immediate aftermath of the dramatic late-night signing the room was awkwardly silent until Kitchener, maintaining his magnanimity to the very end, stepped forward and began shaking the hands of the Boer delegates and saying animatedly: 'We are good friends now!' Kitchener's unrehearsed gesture seemed to break the accumulated tension, for De la Rey then did likewise, adding with a rueful smile: 'We are a bloody cheerful looking lot of British subjects'.[99]

Kitchener could not have been more pleased about anything in his life up to that point than he was on the night of 31 May 1902. At long last the brutal Anglo-Boer War was over and soon he would be free to take up (hopefully) his sought-after post in India. As news of the treaty broke in London and around the Empire an undoubted victory was tempered by knowledge of the human and financial cost of the 32-month long war. Even the animals expended was part of the accounting. The bill in all these regards was exceedingly high. Some 450,000 British and Empire soldiers fought in South Africa with about 22,000 dying in action or from disease, and another 80,000 plus suffering wounds. Astonishingly, over 400,000 horses, donkeys, and mules used by British forces did not survive the conflict, a grim portent of World War I to come. On the Boer side, of the approximately 90,000 men who served some 7,000 had died with another 30,000 wounded. The camp deaths of women and children, as we have seen, were tragically high, perhaps as many as 28,000, while black Africans who died in the war numbered at least 14,000. The financial cost was similarly staggering as the war cost the British Treasury upwards of L200 million.[100] The long-term impact of the war on politics, race, economics, and government in South Africa, as well as that of the Treaty of Vereeniging and the period of reconstruction, is of course a topic which has occupied historians now for over a hundred years.[101] Suffice it to say here that the cost paid by black Africans for the Boers and British to work out their enormously complicated relationship in South Africa well into the twentieth century was incalculably high.

For three weeks after the signing of the treaty Kitchener remained in Pretoria. A service of Thanksgiving was held following the treaty and then a victory parade and later a celebratory banquet. Part-way through this period of serial feting Kitchener was informed that the Salisbury government intended to offer him a viscountcy. This honour, which would make him 'Viscount Kitchener of Khartoum, and of the Vaal in the Colony of the Transvaal, and of Aspall in the County of Suffolk', together with promotion to full general and a Parliamentary grant of L50,000, put an exclamation point on the nation's thanks for the hard-earned victory in South Africa. But pomp and circumstance notwithstanding, the Anglo-Boer War was anything but a sterling victory. Against overwhelming numerical superiority the Boers had fought on long after the British thought that they should have succumbed to defeat. British generalship – at least early in the war – was not up to successfully facing down the Boers, and there was clear discomfort (and, by some, impassioned denunciation) about the methods used to eventually achieve a somewhat pyrrhic victory. Moreover, British military organization and supply were found to be inferior, and despite attempts by Roberts and Kitchener to improve both, at the end of the day most soldiers in the field knew that British might had proven to be anything but invincible. 'We have had no end of a lesson: it will do us no end of good', summed up Kipling critically of his country's military performance in South Africa.[102]

These issues would take time to engender action, but when they did Kitchener would have a hand in some of the (military) reforms initiated by the war in South Africa.[103] Moreover, the war had already induced the crusading journalist John Hobson to dissect its alleged economic underpinnings in his book, *The War in South Africa: Its Causes and Effects* (1900), and from them fashion the first nuanced anti-imperial theory of a century that later would reject virtually every facet of empire as an acceptable basis for world order.[104] Hobson's comprehensive anti-imperial critique, contained in his subsequent book, *Imperialism: A Study* (1902), was not something that Kitchener ever considered directly (at least there is no record of him having done so).[105] On the other hand, it would seem reasonable to assume that he would have been aware of the nature of Hobson's politico-economic argument against (African) empire, although he did not live long enough to see its anti-capitalist features taken up with spectacular impact by Lenin and the Bolsheviks in Russia in 1917.

But all of that could wait. In the short term, an exhausted though elated Kitchener simply wished to return home, and after a triumphant rail journey south to Cape Town he departed for England. Sailing into Southampton on 12 July 1902, he was met in much the same jubilant way as had occurred almost two years earlier upon his return from Sudan. And in a (recorded) first for Kitchener in public, he even smiled.[106]

7

India and Afterwards,
1902–11

Kitchener's first months back in England after returning from South Africa saw him engage in a round of obligatory feting and feasting, none of it, as usual, much to his liking. The protracted victory in South Africa and the Treaty of Vereeniging were being celebrated heartily by the country – perhaps too much so in a self-consciously overdone way in light of the manifest difficulties of winning it – and King Edward capped the celebrations by inaugurating a new royal honour. The Order of Merit as it was named, was to be limited to just 24 recipients, six of whom were to be generals, and Kitchener was delighted to be told by the King himself that he would be the new Order's first invested member.[1] Adding to the festive atmosphere of that summer of 1902 was Kitchener's elevation to viscount and the gift of a Parliamentary victory grant of L50,000, an enormous sum that would effectively confirm his independent wealth for the balance of his life. Throughout the summer too, the prospect of service in India awaited Kitchener. He had long been keen after the appointment of Commander in Chief – 'if you want me I am always ready to come' – Kitchener had written to Lord Curzon, then embarking on his new appointment as Viceroy of India back in December of 1898, and his very public aspiration in this regard was met in kind by the Queen's Viceregal representative.[2] Highly intelligent, aristocratic, superbly educated, and confident of his destiny as a ruler of men (especially of Indians), Curzon had made plain his desire to have Kitchener join him in India as soon as his exertions in Africa were over.

Advised against the appointment, however, by a number of his contemporaries – notably Lord Lansdowne, former Viceroy, on the grounds that Kitchener would be a disaster in India because he had no experience of native (sepoy) troops (which was untrue), Curzon rightly ignored the naysayers, listened to advice from those who heartily endorsed Kitchener, and plumped hard for his eventual appointment.[3] Curzon was almost four years into his own term as Viceroy before the appointment came to pass, but he still wanted the best man for the job. As events would unfold, the presence of two strong, single-minded figures working side by side in the two Raj capitals of Calcutta and Simla, would prove the naysayers right. But not in the way that they expected and certainly not because, as Curzon's most recent biographer would have it, Kitchener was 'artistic, devious, and unscrupulous'.[4] Why in particular an artistic streak should be held against Kitchener when Curzon's own interests ran to preserving the spectacular art and architecture of Moghul India, seems simply churlish, or is 'artistic' merely a code-word for the tired calumny that Kitchener was gay?

In any event, Kitchener's summer and early autumn in London and the Home Counties, of visiting family and friends, of pitching up once again at his favourite Belgravia redoubt of Pandeli Ralli's, and of preparing to embark for India came to an end on 17 October when he quietly departed Victoria Station and crossed the Channel en route first to Cairo and Khartoum, and then on to Bombay. Kitchener's stop-over in Sudan was occasioned by the opening and dedication of Gordon Memorial College in the re-built capital city. His handful of days back in Khartoum were celebratory, and he was greatly pleased with the opening of the college named for his slain abiding hero. At the college's inauguration on 8 November Kitchener spoke at length and with urgency about what Sudan required in order for it to prosper, including how its people were 'anxiously desirous of education for their children'.[5] The ceremony and Kitchener's speech were given widespread newspaper coverage in Europe and North America, the foreign correspondent of the *New York Times*, for example, being especially impressed (and surprised) by Kitchener's 'gracefully worded' remarks, containing as they did 'much good common sense, and describing excellently the purposes for which the college has been founded'.[6]

Departing Khartoum on 11 November, Kitchener returned briefly to Cairo before leaving for Bombay via the Suez Canal and the Indian

Ocean. 'My best salaams to Lady Curzon and His Excellency' he enjoined one of his staffers, Major Raymond 'Conk' Marker, to pass on to the Viceregal couple. 'I am looking forward with great pleasure to serving under him in India'.[7] On 28 November the new Commander in Chief arrived in Bombay where he met briefly with his outgoing and unlamented predecessor, Sir (Arthur) Power Palmer. Shortly thereafter Kitchener headed north for his first meeting with the Viceroy, which took place at Bharatpur in Rajasthan, the site of an embarrassing British loss back in 1805 during the ultimately successful Second Anglo-Maratha War, a conflict that had marked the emergence of Arthur Wellesley (later Duke of Wellington) as a commander of great promise, especially during the signal Battle of Assaye in 1803. Despite the inauspicious location, the meeting between the two men at Bharatpur was warm and constructive. Having met on a few occasions previously in London, this meeting was their first in India under these new and official circumstances and it went exceedingly well. As Curzon described it: 'We had long, confidential and most friendly talks .... I feel at last that I shall have a Commander-in-Chief worthy of the name and position'.[8] The two men were agreed that reform of the Indian Army was absolutely necessary; as to its nature and format, however, more time was needed for Kitchener to acclimate himself to India and to study the configuration and workings of the army as it then stood. Curzon's use of the possessive in describing their initial meeting was perhaps his first mistake in dealing with Kitchener, but regardless all was harmony between them at this very early stage in their Indian relationship, and that included Kitchener's regard for the Viceroy's highly attractive American-born wife, the former Mary Leiter of Chicago. She and Kitchener would quickly forge a close friendship, which would be sustained over the next few years by numerous reciprocal letters until later foundering irrevocably as part of the fall-out over her husband's epic clash with his military chief. In the meantime, Kitchener was the man, as he had written to Curzon back in 1898, who 'means to take her [Lady Curzon] down to dinner some day in India'.[9] That day was now at hand.

The initial two-day meeting with Curzon over, Kitchener departed for Simla, the summer capital of the Raj. Part of his discussions with the Viceroy in Bharatpur had revolved around the fast-approaching Delhi Durbar, which Curzon had been planning meticulously in order to celebrate on Indian soil the recent coronation of King Edward VII.

But before it would commence at the end of December, and Kitchener's part in its spectacular display of British imperial pomp and circumstance, the new *Jangi Lat* (Lord of War) had decided to make 'a run to Simla,' as he wrote to the Vicereine, 'just to look at the place and see what Snowdon will require'.[10] Snowdon, the Commander in Chief's residence there first occupied by Lord Roberts during his term as C in C during the 1880s, would be his part-time home for what would prove to be seven inimitable years in India at the very height of the power of the British Raj.[11]

By the time Kitchener first glimpsed Simla in December of 1902 the British had been ascending regularly to its 7,200-foot perch for almost half-a-century. The first Governor-General to decide that escaping the sultry and debilitating summer heat of Calcutta and moving the operations of the Raj lock, stock and barrel to Simla was John Lawrence, 1st Baron Lawrence.[12] He did so in 1864, not long after the signal rupture of the Indian Rebellion in 1857, and his own part in bringing its murderous violence to an end. Moving the headquarters of the Raj to Simla was an exertion of a different order of course, but once the British decided that the foothills of the mighty snow-capped Himalayas was the right place to locate themselves for six to eight months of the year, then no expense or trouble was spared in ensuring that the move north became an annual rite of passage. Indeed, by the 1880s, the move had become official. Shortly thereafter a railway was built, a narrow-guage winding snake that pushed its way through 103 tunnels before arriving at the picturesque town that stood anchored to a high, mile-long ridge with spectacular views north to the Himalayas and south down across steeply-pitched valleys to the plains below as they stretched away to Delhi some 200 miles distant.

Simla fast developed its own society and mores, as well as its own architecture and social calendar. To it flocked an assortment of government officials and military personnel, of course, capped by the Viceroy and his entourage, but also various other denizens of the Raj, including the young newspaperman and budding fiction writer Rudyard Kipling, whose early prose was much-inspired by what he saw and heard of the Anglo-Indian community at Simla. Kipling's first visit there occurred in the summer of 1883 when he was just 17 years of age, freshly back (home) in India from his English education and on staff at the *Civil and Military Gazette* in Lahore.[13] That first summer in Simla he booked himself into the Tendrils Cottage on the Mall and every summer for the next five years he would make the journey over from Lahore for what in his memory became (mostly) youthful halcyon days amidst the cool breezes and green deodar trees of this stunning British retreat.[14]

The centrality of Simla's position to the Raj was made that much more permanent in the early 1880s too when Lord Lytton fixed upon the idea that a stately home for the Viceroy needed to be constructed in the town. Viceregal Lodge, located at the far western end of the Ridge was duly opened in 1888 under the Viceroyalty of Lord Dufferin, and for the next 60 years until Indian independence in 1947 this Scottish baronial-style castle was the beating-heart of Raj society half the year-round.

The Commander in Chief in India's residence in Simla, on the other hand, was not grand in the way of Viceregal Lodge. Snowdon, as it was called, was located at the opposite end of the Ridge on the slopes of Jakhoo Hill. Not much more than a bungalow, as soon as Kitchener saw Snowdon he determined that it must be altered and enlarged in order for it to serve the rather more august purposes that he saw it fulfilling under his residency. Immediately therefore, he set about making plans to have extensive renovations carried out and within a year after his arrival in India Snowdon had become a showpiece in what had become a crowded local architectural competition.[15] He also, as we shall see, would build a small retreat for himself about five miles outside of Simla, and at an additional elevation gain of about a thousand feet. He called this retreat Wildflower Hall and to it he would go regularly when in Simla, retiring to an alpine, flower-bedecked hideaway, accessible only by horseback (or, for the hearty, a very vigorous hike).[16]

Having reconnoitered Simla thoroughly over the course of a couple of early-winter weeks, Kitchener descended back to the plains in mid-December in anticipation of the Durbar. At Delhi, he presided over the last of the pre-Durbar military manoeuvers engaged in by almost 40,000 members of the Indian Army, and on 29 December he took a leading position in the state procession that wound its way through the city. The Durbar, once underway, was an almost overwhelming mélange of sights and sounds. Painted and be-jewelled elephants, flashing swords and glinting boots, colourful military uniforms and costumed Indian princes, the whole panoply of British imperial rule was on display until it climaxed on 1 January 1903 when the King-Emperor, Edward VII, was proclaimed. Most everyone thought the Durbar was a stunning and magnificent success, which in its time and on its own terms can hardly be disputed. There can be little doubt, however, that Curzon had used the Durbar in part to aggrandize himself, something which fit rather nicely with his well-known reputation for arrogance. Not for nothing had he been mocked long before by his Oxford undergraduate peers for being a 'most superior person'.[17]

As for Kitchener, once the Durbar's festivities were over he departed Delhi directly for the North-West Frontier and what was understood to be the chief geographic vulnerability of that Raj grandeur which had just been celebrated. The mid- to late- nineteenth century was the era of the so-called 'Great Game' in Central Asia. That period during which Britain, Russia, and to a lesser extent Ottoman Turkey, vied with one another in order to gain preponderant control over the strategically important Afghan borderlands.[18] Beginning in 1839 with the disastrous First Afghan War, the British had played the game hard in an attempt to keep at bay the thrusts of Imperial Russia as it pushed down on the historic mountain passes – the most famous of which was the Khyber – through which an invasion of British India might potentially take place. The Great Game was just that: a surpassing exercise in feints, jousts, half-truths, diplomatic insincerity, and occasional violence engaged in by an assortment of official and unofficial frontier characters, one of the most notable of which was the intrepid, if eccentric, British explorer and diplomat Sir Francis Younghusband.[19] Earlier in his life Curzon himself had travelled extensively in the region, in the process becoming an Asia expert, which naturally and justifiably accorded him a strong and persuasive voice in debates about the nature of British policy on the frontier.[20] Kitchener was new to the geographic area (if not to the nature of the issue itself) and during his first traversal through the region travelled rough and hard, accompanied by a handful of staff and led by General Sir Charles Egerton, commander of the Punjab Frontier Force.

By the end of January Kitchener had completed this is his first inspection of the turbulent North-West Frontier and had ensconced himself at Treasury Gate, his residence located within Fort William in British India's capital city of Calcutta. Founded by the East India Company in the Seventeenth Century, Calcutta had grown around Fort William, which itself had had two iterations and now was located permanently a short distance south of Government House along the

banks of the Hooghly river. Calcutta then of course was still a very long
way from the modern conurbation of today with its millions of people
and a well-demonstrated reputation for poverty and human
degradation on a wide scale. In 1903 when Kitchener first saw it,
the city was a great deal smaller. The square-mile core of the city
contained a coterie of Company and Government buildings, most of
which were attractively constructed in an Indo-European style. The
Maidan, an enormous grassy parkland, was bounded by the elegant
Esplanade and the lively avenue called Chowringhee.[21] Everywhere,
architectural evidence of the Raj abounded. Government House,
constructed a century earlier by the Governor-General, the Earl of
Mornington (the Duke of Wellington's elder brother) and modelled – as it
happened – on Curzon's ancestral seat, Kedleston Hall in Derbyshire,
dominated the city. But Dalhousie Square with its Writers' Building and
memorial to the victims of the Black Hole, St John's Church and St Paul's
Cathedral, and the Bengal Club, all contributed to a cityscape indicative of
what some chose to call a 'tropical London'.[22]

Kitchener's first two months in India had been rather a whirlwind, and
beginning in February of 1903 he began to settle into the role of
Commander in Chief, which meant not simply the apprehension of his
physical surroundings, living quarters, and ubiquitous need for transport,
but much more importantly, his relationship with the Viceroy and the
desire that they both held for substantive, if yet not clearly articulated,
reform of the Indian Army. As usual, Kitchener had gathered around him
a trusted coterie of staff officers, principally Colonel Hubert Hamilton,
Major Frank Maxwell, and Major Marker. Almost always they travelled
as a group, and in residence, whether in Calcutta or Simla, formed a
tightly-knit band, all of whom were devoted to Kitchener as their 'Chief'.
He in turn had nicknames for all of them, respectively: Hammy, the Brat,
and, as noted earlier, Conk. They shared the easy camaraderie that is
characteristic of military life and to which Kitchener, without a wife and
family of his own, was especially drawn.

The other emotional lynchpin of Kitchener's early days in India was
Mary Curzon. As Vicereine, she was at the pinnacle of Raj social life
and Kitchener's overtures to her were constant, bordering sometimes
on the unctuous. From the very outset of his appointment: 'It will be
most interesting being in India with your husband who has so covered
himself with glory in his most able administration of India', he gushed

to her in August of 1902, he cultivated a warm and solicitous relationship, which, as we have seen, had become a hallmark of his dealings generally with married aristocratic women.[23] Indeed, there was something of the 'salonniere' about the way in which Kitchener conducted himself initially in India, and clearly Lady Curzon was flattered by his steady attentions. But it is obvious too that the relationship was highly useful politically in navigating the official relationship of the Viceroy and the Commander in Chief, the two most powerful men in British India and through whom everything pertaining to military operations and potential reform had to run.

The first major social occasion attended by Kitchener following the Delhi Durbar occurred at Government House in Calcutta. In commemoration of the hundredth anniversary of its opening, the Viceroy held a state ball at the end of January in which all participants were enjoined to wear period dress. Given Kitchener's diffidence about these kinds of events it is a testament to his regard for Lady Curzon that he had earlier informed her from Delhi that 'I have wired for a dress of a general of the period for your ball at Calcutta, but you must overlook indifferent dancing'.[24] In due course, and having entered into the spirit of the prospective evening, he arrived in a scarlet uniform, of the cut and colour worn by a British full general during the early part of the nineteenth century. As for the quality of the dancing that ensued, the written record is silent.

For the remainder of his first winter in India Kitchener remained in Calcutta. During this time he turned his attention to some minor renovations of Treasury Gate, a reasonably attractive residence fronted by a wide and long terrace supported by columns and offering a commanding view of the Maidan. Meetings with his officers were many, along with regular gatherings of the Viceroy's Council held a short ride away at Government House. To anyone from a northern climate the Calcutta winter was close to balmy with temperatures in the moderate 50 F range. December, January, and February were much this way, but then inexorably the temperature would begin to climb and the debilitating heat and humidity that were (and are) Calcutta's climatic signature would strike. By the end of March, Kitchener was entertaining the prospect of escaping increasingly steamy Calcutta for the north, of enjoying 'cold weather and long rides' and of leaving behind what he would soon come to regard as infernal Council meetings.[25] By now he had been long enough in the country to begin drawing some conclusions about what ailed the Indian Army, and he was determined to ensure that the Viceroy saw the prevailing situation in the same way that he did. But before any of the hard discussions about army reform commenced Kitchener happily departed Calcutta for another tour of the North-West Frontier, culminating with his arrival at Simla in May.[26]

Kitchener's return to Simla coincided with that of much of the rest of the Indian government in its annual May migration north from the scorched plains to the verdant hills. Stations like Simla existed all over British India: Ootacamund, Darjeeling, Mussoorie, the list is a long one. But it is Simla, owing to its designation as the official summer capital, which became the so-called 'Queen of the Hill Stations'. Indeed, by the first decade of the twentieth century, Simla was a well-developed burgh with a hint of sophistication and an accompanying whiff of scandal. 'No one should go up to Simla', warned the authors of a contemporary book on Raj manners, 'who has not a bag of rupees and many pretty frocks'.[27] Army officers abounded, many of them single, and there was no shortage of women – both married and unmarried – so the scope for both romance and adultery was considerable. Scandal, the handmaiden of both, of course was never far behind, and it was this element of Simla life that Kipling had recognized early and chose to chronicle in his writing of the period, if not overtly.[28] Kipling's 'Simla Notes' became a regular part of the pieces he filed for the *Civil and Military Gazette* in the mid-1880s, although the constant round of dances, theatricals and balls ultimately left him bored, complaining that 'the dullest of dull things is to be *chroniquer* of a Gay Season in the hills'.[29] As a chaste, though typically hormonal young man, the frisson of sex that was a part of the Simla scene proved serially vexing to Kipling, especially when it was going on right next to his room, its varied ecstasies easily communicated to him through paper-thin walls: 'Wish they wouldn't put married couple next door to me with one $\frac{1}{2}$ [inch] plank between', he diarized. 'Saps one's morality'.[30]

For the stern figure of Kitchener, Lord of War and living an unattached life however, much of what Kipling had written of Simla a generation earlier was of little consequence to him. Kitchener's experience of it was social and festive, to be sure: 'I have been having a dose of Simla entertainments', he wrote to Lady Curzon. But, he concluded in a style typical of the man, 'the effect is depressing'.[31] Nonetheless, as Commander in Chief, Kitchener certainly enjoyed being

Plate 1 Wildflower Hall: Kitchener's verdant retreat located outside Shimla with a view of the Himalayas, as it appears today in winter as a luxury hotel.

Plate 2 Viceregal Lodge, Shimla: The centre of summertime Raj life from the 1880s until 1947, as it looks today.

Plate 3 Dhalli Tunnel, Shimla: Located on the road to Wildflower Hall, within which Kitchener broke his leg after falling from a skittish horse.

Plate 4   Christ Church, Shimla: Even today the Mall is dominated by its tower. Kitchener attended divine service here weekly when in residence at nearby Snowdon.

Plate 5 Broome Park, Kent: The refurbished country estate located near Canterbury barely lived in by Kitchener before his death, which is now a golf club.

Plate 6 2 Carlton Gardens, London: Kitchener lived here in 1914–15, located a short walk from the War Office and across the street from his old nemesis, Lord Curzon.

Plate 7 *c.* 1885: Kitchener sporting a hint of a smile, something that in photographs he almost never did. Taken at the time of the Gordon Relief Expedition.

Plate 8 1903: Kitchener with his circle of close advisers, including Raymond 'Conk' Marker (second from right), at Shimla.

Plate 9   1910: Kitchener laden with medals, between his years in India and those to come in Egypt.

Plate 10   1914: Kitchener with Marshal Joffre of France leaving the War Office after a meeting. Already the strain of being Secretary of State for War is evident.

Plate 11   1884: General Charles Gordon, Kitchener's hero, on the eve of his fateful departure for Khartoum.

Plate 12   Early 1900s: As wartime prime minister, H.H. Asquith understood Kitchener's value to the nation.

Plate 13   Early 1900s: Lord Curzon, as Kitchener would have known him during their tumultuous days in India.

Plate 14   Early 1900s: As prime minister, Arthur Balfour ultimately backed Kitchener in his dispute with Curzon.

Plate 15   1903: In defence of her husband, Lady Curzon came to loathe Kitchener, but earlier they had been great friends.

Plates 16 and 17 Crotta House, Kitchener's Irish childhood home, located near Kilflynn, Co. Kerry, as it appears today. The Great House is gone; only the former stables and servants' quarters remain standing.

one of the only residents of Simla to be allowed the luxury of conveyance in a carriage along the Mall, and his 90-minute 'charming' rides on horseback out to Wildflower Hall he valued as a highly welcome form of recreation. Moreover, invitations to dine, especially at Viceregal Lodge presided over by Lord Curzon and accompanied by his highly admired chatelaine, appealed greatly to the otherwise socially reticent Kitchener.[32] But he was also keen to return the favour and therefore he began to hold dinner parties at Snowdon regularly. But still, Kitchener's life in Simla was largely a steady round of military meetings together with Sunday morning service attendance at Christ Church located at the top of the Mall, next to the aptly-named-for-Simla Scandal Point. The church had been built in 1857 and its tower dominated the Simla skyline. The Commander in Chief's reserved pew was second on the right, directly behind that of the Viceroy's, and invariably Kitchener and members of his staff could be found there for Matins or Holy Communion every Sunday.[33]

Kitchener's staff, on the other hand, all young(ish) officers were of the very type written of earlier by Kipling and happy to make the most of just those 'Simla entertainments' mostly scorned by their chief. Such was especially true of Conk Marker. Tall and handsome with slicked-back dark hair and a moustache outdone only by that of Kitchener himself, Marker was the alpha-male amongst the Commander in Chief's men. Simla ladies of good breeding were known to almost swoon in his presence, especially when he played the leading man role in one of the many plays put on at the Gaiety Theatre. The centre of Simla's social life, the Gaiety had been built in 1887. Seating about 300, complete with a Viceregal box, a deep-set stage and (eventually) electric heat and light, the Gaiety could be counted on to offer a series of plays and musicals every season, its well-trod boards populated mostly by extravert army officers. One of the regular actors in the troupe was Marker, and Kitchener, not known for his appreciation for the stage, was nonetheless coaxed out to watch his man act and sing with aplomb.[34]

During Kitchener's first year in Simla it was hardly surprising then that Marker became engaged to Lady Curzon's younger sister, Margaret 'Daisy' Leiter. Earlier, Marker had served on the Viceroy's staff and in due course had been introduced to the visiting Miss Leiter in Calcutta. In short order they had fallen in love, before her return to the US. Her presence later at the Delhi Durbar had re-kindled their mutual ardour and now in the spring of 1903 it culminated in a betrothal. Ultimately, however, no wedding would follow. A year later, Marker found himself jilted by Daisy, who went on to marry a peer, the Earl of Suffolk. The charismatic Marker, who had probably never been thrown over in his life, was devastated by this capricious turn of events. 'I have never seen anyone so completely knocked out', commented his officer colleague Hubert Hamilton.[35] But the damage was done. Upon hearing of Marker's fate Kitchener wrote to Lady Curzon that he was 'much astonished ... to hear the sad news of your sister's affections'.[36] Altogether, their story was exactly as Kipling might have scripted it, and in the end, as we shall see, Marker's subsequent posting to England put him in a position to be of great service to Kitchener when eventually the tide broke in his relationship with the Viceroy. In the short term, however, a small squall had disrupted the otherwise rather placid waters of the Viceroy's relationship with the Commander in Chief, or at least that part of it dependent upon concinnity between Kitchener and Lady Curzon.

Throughout that summer of 1903 until the autumn descent to the plains and thence to Calcutta took place Kitchener continued to acclimate himself to all facets of life in Simla. Renovations continued apace at Snowdon, although to Kitchener at least they proceeded in a rather glacial fashion. The residence was having a second storey added, and the whole house was to be wired for electricity, an uncommon occurrence in Simla; indeed electricity had come to the town only 15 years earlier when it was installed in Viceregal Lodge and powered by a generator.[37] By no means common even yet, having electricity at Snowdon would be a significant step forward and a boon to Kitchener in his desire to show off his war banners, china and pottery – including two new 'delightful mustard pots' from Lady Curzon – and flowers with which he had assiduously decorated all of his official residences going all the way back to his first one at Suakin.[38] Better the electric switch than the '50 candles' entertaining usually required, and even then the room is dark, he had complained to the Vicereine.[39]

The winter in Calcutta and his speedy apprehension of life in Simla spurred Kitchener now to turn his undivided attention to what he believed to be the fundamental reforms necessary to enable the Indian Army to withstand any potential threat to British India, emanating principally, as it was thought, from Imperial Russia. Internal threats from nascent (Indian) nationalists, which were beginning to be felt in Bengal especially, were not regarded as potentially imminent in the same way as the broadly geo-strategic threat along the North-West Frontier. But Kitchener's eye was on both as he started to draft a comprehensive plan for reform of the army.[40] To that end, he began to correspond with and speak directly to Curzon about the issue, while at the same time sounding out his old South Africa colleague, Lord Roberts, whose friendship was firm and who brought with him some 40 years' experience soldiering in India, including serving as Commander in Chief from 1885 until 1893, about which he had recently published his memoirs.[41] If the first half-year of Kitchener's time in India had seen a durbar and a series of glittering balls, riding out, and supervising the renovations of three official residences, together with some necessary meetings, tours and inspections, such (mundane) engagements would now swiftly give way to over two years of concerted struggle between the two titans of the contemporary Raj over the nature and extent of army reform. In the end, as we shall see, the outcome of that struggle brought the glittering Curzon Viceroyalty crashing down. For those whose sympathies lay with Curzon in the dispute Kitchener would be cast as the villain of the piece, and by extension the destroyer of that sepia-tinged era when the Raj had reached its apotheosis.

The history of the Indian Army stretched back to the mid-eighteenth century and the era of the expansionary East India Company. Major General Stringer Lawrence, a contemporary of Clive's, was considered the army's father, and after him had come a steady line of successors of which Kitchener numbered 59th. In that long list were counted a series of storied names in the annals of Company and Raj history, including Clive, of course, as well as Sir Eyre Coote, Sir Hector Munro, Earl Cornwallis, Lords Dalhousie and Bentinck, Sir Charles Napier, Sir Colin Campbell, and Sir Hugh Rose.[42] The traditions of the army naturally were strong, therefore, if not perhaps congealed, and the understanding of it as a bulwark set against all enemies both external and internal was a shibboleth of command. Its necessary reorganization in the 1860s following on the severe challenge to its authority made clear by the Indian Mutiny was the last time thoroughgoing reform had been carried out. Kitchener's firm position was that now, almost half-a-century on from the Mutiny, the time had come to re-organize and modernize the Indian Army in such a way as to ready it for twentieth-century duty.

No one, least of all Curzon, was against the army's reform, *per se*. The necessity of army reform as a first principle therefore was shared by the

Viceroy and his expectation in this regard was clearly a part of what Kitchener's appointment as Commander in Chief portended. In their very first discussion at Bharatpur in December of 1902, as we have seen, just after Kitchener's arrival in India, the subject of army reform had been broached. The new Commander in Chief's considered view – and the fount from which would flow his entire argument concerning army reform – was that the presence and reach of the Military Member on the Viceroy's Council compromised irredeemably the ability of the C in C to perform his duties in a maximally effective way, and therefore the position should simply be eliminated. Curzon disagreed, however, arguing that in Constitutional terms the presence of the Military Member on the Council ensured civilian control of the army. Fundamentally therefore, the two men disagreed over first principles and therein lay the nub of the argument, an argument that would fester and grow until becoming unresolvable, leaving a showdown as the only way forward and the subsequent declaration of a winner and a loser.[43]

In mid-May 1903, Kitchener decided that the time was now ripe to push forward the issue. As Commander in Chief, he controlled the Indian Army's operations and training; but supply, transport, ordnance, and general organization were under the purview of the Military Member, a position then-occupied by Major General Sir Edmond Elles, a career military worthy, but in Kitchener's view slavishly devoted to the existing 'dual control' system and therefore beyond convincing that reform was urgently required. Kitchener believed that the main failing of the Indian Army was that its balkanization precluded its ability to mount a coordinated defence against a potential Russian invasion. 'Higgeldy-piggeldy' was the way he described the current disposition of regiments around India, and it was simply beyond debate to him that uniformity in the interests of strategic viability must prevail.[44] In order to achieve uniformity and hence better execution, Kitchener held, complete control over the totality of military supply, disposition, and operations must be in the hands of the Commander in Chief. His view was powerfully rational, spoke to efficiency, and kept the thinly-veiled Russian strategic threat plainly in view. But of course such a view necessarily undercut the role and power of the Military Member, and in the person of Elles opposition to Kitchener's view therefore was nigh unto automatic. Curzon, with evident sympathy for Elles's position, explained the prevailing situation to Kitchener on 20 May: 'I have seen

Elles .... He says frankly that he would feel it his duty to oppose them [Kitchener's proposals] since they amount in his opinion to the abolition of the Military Department and the reduction of the Military Member to being a staff officer of the C. in C.'.[45]

The balance of May was spent in a flurry of missives back and forth between Kitchener and Curzon each of which attempted to state ever more clearly and with increasing force that the position held by the other party was impossible to uphold and therefore should be surrendered. Stymied, Kitchener wished to put his proposals before the Viceroy's Council, a plan rejected by Curzon since it had become his opinion that behind Kitchener's plan for reform lay a grander scheme to 'revolutionise the Constitution'. He therefore advised him 'not to persevere with your plan'.[46] To Kitchener, talk of revolution and the Constitution was little short of nonsense. Curzon may have believed that India's august position within the British Empire had yielded its own 'Constitution' in which the norms pertaining to the office of Commander in Chief were immutable, but in any principled sense this view was a stretch and, at any rate, it was held by no one else.[47] Kitchener was dumbfounded that his eminently reasonable proposals had elicited such a strong response from the Viceroy given that none of what he was saying about the nature and necessity of reform should have come as a surprise to him. Elles's resistance, for his part, was understandable to Kitchener since his stake in the existing system was obvious. But for Curzon as the Viceroy to continue to advocate for the continuation of the present system meant that for Kitchener it appeared 'quite hopeless ... to expect any success', and, as he continued in a letter to Curzon on the 21st, 'under the circumstances I agree with you that it would not be wise for me to now press the matter further'.[48]

Over the following few days after sending this letter Kitchener fretted over what to do about the growing cleavage between his position and that of Curzon. His residence of Snowdon became a kind of forcing house in the service of determining what he believed to be the right way forward in this, as yet, two-person dispute. On 25 May, spurred by other niggling issues with Elles such as control over the issuing of daily orders to the army, Kitchener peremptorily made up his mind to resign: 'I feel there is no course open to me', he opined to the Viceroy, 'but to resign my present command; I need hardly say that I shall greatly regret to leave India, as I was in great hopes of being able to do some good in the

Indian Army'.[49] Shocked, but acting sensibly given the scope for severe upset both in India and in London should Kitchener leave his post after a mere six months, Curzon rejected his resignation immediately.

Kitchener's fit of pique and attempted resignation at this moment in the dispute was rather operatic, to be sure, and Curzon was right to try and marshal the direction of their relationship and send it toward calmer waters. But their division over the issue of dual control was clear and without agreement on the fundamental issue of the normative ambit of the Commander in Chief's powers it would only be a matter of time before the dispute would flare up again. But *status quo ante-bellum* prevailed, for now. Stung sharply by the whole business, Kitchener chose this moment to rely more heavily on Lord Roberts's counsel about how to deal with the widening chasm between himself and the Viceroy. On 28 May, just three days after his attempted resignation, Kitchener packaged up his recent correspondence with Curzon, and together with an explanatory covering letter, sent everything off to Roberts who was then in his final year as Commander in Chief of the British Army before the position was abolished and replaced by a new model of military governance complete with a Chief of the General Staff. Hoping that once having read the correspondence Roberts would think he had taken the 'right line' in his dispute with Curzon, Kitchener enjoined the outgoing Commander in Chief not to show the private correspondence to anyone, especially 'not to Brodrick', the Secretary of State for War who was soon to become the Secretary of State for India, and an odious politician in Kitchener's view.[50]

In drawing Roberts into the dispute Kitchener may have been acting unethically, as some have sinced maintained, although in matters of state amongst Privy Councillors virtually nothing by way of consultation was considered *ultra vires*. Moreover, Roberts was bound by Kitchener's request for confidentiality, which he duly respected. Kitchener, as would befit his close relationship with Roberts, wrote freely about the 'very galling' state of affairs in Simla over the issue of dual control and how 'what would have been a pleasure [has become] a disagreeable duty'. Kitchener saved most of his pointed criticism for Elles rather than for the Viceroy, lamenting to Roberts that if the Military Member had any 'knowledge of what an army ought to be to hold its own in a big war, we might get on, but he is narrow minded and bigoted to a degree'. Elles, as far as Kitchener could tell, simply wished 'to keep things as they are, certainly not to improve, possibly the reverse'. Sadly, he concluded, 'the Viceroy will, of course, support Elles'. This fact, more than any other, kept Kitchener from wanting to engender a public rupture between Curzon and himself; at least not yet, and so his settled conviction was clear: 'I do not want to have a fall over a question of this sort'.[51] Throughout this stressful period Roberts, while in agreement with Kitchener's goal of improving the Indian Army's ability to fight, advised caution. After all, the former Commander in Chief himself had spent eight years in India under the very same system and had made it work.[52] And thus, there the matter stood mid-way through 1903.

Still, even though the situation remained quiet at that moment, enough had been said over the preceding few weeks to render doubtful an amicable future between Kitchener and Curzon. Indeed, as it turned out, mid-1903 comprised only early days in the ultimate course that the disagreement took, but once the initial heat of the moment had passed the two men settled back into the normal run of affairs for the balance of that year's Simla Season. Conversations, dinners, consultations, all were conducted with little or no reference to the unresolved dispute. Later that summer Kitchener went back out on tour once again through the always testy Frontier region, as well as up into the stunning natural beauty of Kashmir, before returning to Simla in late-October for the last weeks of the Season: 'Will there be sufficient dancing people left in Simla at that time. What do you think?'[53] His jaunty question to Lady Curzon was made in a letter inviting the Viceregal couple to dinner on 3 November. They duly came across the mall the short distance from Viceregal Lodge, past Peterhof, the original rather tumbledown informal residence of the Viceroy, to Snowdon. Once there they enjoyed themselves thoroughly as over the years Kitchener had developed into a superb host, sparing nothing in quality of food, wine, plate, and presentation. Both they and Kitchener were preparing shortly to decamp back down to Calcutta for the winter. Indeed, Kitchener had made 16 November his projected departure date. On the 15th, a Sunday, he decided to take one last ride out to Wildflower Hall. Shortly after attending church and eating lunch at Snowdon, his horse was saddled and, unusually, he rode out unaccompanied by a staffer (most of his staff had gone down already to the railhead at Kalka where they planned to meet him on Monday). As always, the ride was pleasant, about five miles over a good, if winding mountain road that if followed to its end would (then as today) terminate at the Tibetan border. The road is steep, but the footing was stable and Kitchener visited his arrestingly beautiful mountain retreat and started his return to town by late-afternoon. The descent brought him back down to the village of Sanjauli located on the other side of Jakhoo Hill. Years earlier in 1870 a tunnel had been bored through a spur at Sanjauli that allowed traffic coming from both Chota (little) Simla and Simla to connect to the mountain road.[54] Upon his descent from Wildflower Kitchener proceeded through the then dimly-lit and narrow tunnel supported only by wooden braces. Halfway through the tunnel his horse was spooked by a passing pedestrian. It reared and then moved sideways jamming Kitchener's left leg between two of the unforgiving braces hard against the side of tunnel. A further turn by the skittish horse put enormous pressure on the leg and the bones above the ankle gave way. Stricken, Kitchener tumbled from the horse. Unable to walk he waited to be rescued, which happened quickly, and by suppertime he was back at Snowdon, but in great pain and in a supremely foul mood. Plans to depart the next day for Calcutta naturally had to be shelved.

In short order an army surgeon was called in to set the broken leg, which he did by elevating it and then encasing it in splints. In the manner of the time only after a few weeks would a plaster cast be applied. Altogether, for Kitchener, the accident was highly unfortunate, vaguely embarrassing, and irritatingly inconvenient. Its impact was also long-lasting as he was left for years with a recurringly painful leg and a slight limp. For the next month he hardly left his bed. The leg was checked regularly, including by the world-famous London surgeon, Sir Frederick Treves – whose fame had been made by his performing the first appendectomy in England in 1888 and around the same time offering treatment (and friendship) to the horribly deformed 'Elephant Man', Joseph Merrick. Treves, who had been Surgeon Extraordinary to the Queen and now was one of King Edward's Honourary Surgeons, made a special trip up from Bombay to Simla in order to examine Kitchener. But there was not much to be done other than to allow the bones to heal, which they did, although too slowly for the terminally impatient Kitchener. 'I am now able to get out of bed', he wrote in exasperation to Lady Curzon, just before finally departing Simla for Calcutta on 17 December, a month later than planned. The Vicereine had written to suggest that once arrived in Calcutta he should come and convalesce at Government House. But he declined the 'extremely kind' offer in favour of staying at Treasury Gate and receiving 'regular treatment of the leg'.[55] By Christmas therefore, and cheered by a note from the Prime Minister, Arthur Balfour, saying 'how thankful I am that we have got you ... as our military adviser and guide on the problems of Indian defence', Kitchener had settled back into his residence at Fort William and was enjoying the relative winter warmth of Calcutta after Simla's seasonal chill.[56] 'A happy Xmas to you and the Viceroy', he wrote to Lady Curzon on 25 December. 'They are tinkering at my leg which is rather unpleasant ... and fear that the leg will take longer [to heal] than was originally supposed'. Indeed, Kitchener was right in his prediction because it took until well into the New Year 1904 until he was fully mobile, and much longer still before he was effectively pain-free.[57]

Throughout this period of enforced convalescence Kitchener complained of having no energy and little desire to accomplish work. Unsurprisingly, he was grateful for the solicitations of Lady Curzon especially and told her so in a letter penned on New Year's Day: 'I can never forget the constant and unfailing kindnesses you have shown me since I have been out here'.[58] Little did either of them know that the year to come would effectively sunder their amity because of the ongoing crisis over Kitchener's determination to re-make the role of the Military Member on the Viceroy's Council in the face of her husband's strenuous objections.

For the second half of 1903, as we have seen, Kitchener had complied dutifully with the Viceroy's request and therefore had desisted in his desire to take the issue of army reform to the whole Council. But his thinking on dual control was firm and unwavering and just as when he had drawn in Lord Roberts to his debating circle, he now began to do likewise with others such as Lady Salisbury, and much more importantly, Arthur Balfour. In office since the summer of 1902 when he had succeeded his uncle, the ailing Lord Salisbury, as prime minister, Balfour's view of India's place in the Empire was similar to that of Kitchener's; that is, India's interests were inseparable from but subordinate to those of the Empire as a whole. The exceptionality that Curzon accorded India as against the wider Empire was not a view shared by Balfour. The Prime Minister's party political Conservatism did not preclude him from sharing at least part of his Liberal predecessor William Gladstone's view, expressed to the then Viceroy, Lord Ripon, back in 1881, that 'I am one of those who think that to the actual, as distinguished from the reported, strength of Empire, India adds nothing'.[59] No late-nineteenth or early-twentieth century Conservative prime minister was going to disavow the centrality of India to Britain's international position even if, as has been suggested by some historians, India had become a strategic burden by then.[60] But Balfour certainly was well-prepared to ensure that Indian strategic and defence policy ran through the Commander in Chief and hence emanated from the British Cabinet, and not solely through the Viceroy's Council. And in his 3 December 1903 response to Kitchener's earlier letter Balfour could not have been clearer on the point: 'My own personal conviction is (at least at present advised) that the existing division of attributes between the Commander-in-Chief and the Military Member of the Council is quite indefensible'.[61] Thus it was that despite Kitchener's leg woes and mental lethargy at the outset of 1904 he was becoming increasingly confident in his position versus that of the Viceroy for the simple reason that his views lined up much more readily with those of the home government than did Curzon's. The Viceroy's, on the other hand, were suggestive of the belief that the Indian government was in some significant measure sovereign from, rather than creaturely of, London. *A priori*, then, Curzon's position on the issue was potentially weak in a way that Kitchener's was not.

By February, Kitchener's leg had healed well enough to allow him to take 'a short ride in the mornings', and with the winter soon over he went back out on tour in April – mostly to South India where in addition to regular army inspections he indulged in an obligatory round of tiger shooting – before going into residence once again at Simla.[62] His correspondent, Lady Curzon, had returned earlier to London in order to give birth near the end of March to the Viceregal couple's third (and final) child, a daughter they named Alexandra. 'I am so sorry it is a daughter as I think you would have preferred a son', wrote Kitchener a little brusquely though accurately since they had two daughters already and had expressed the same opinion themselves.[63] It had been a difficult pregnancy, and in conjunction with her other ills Lady Curzon's health suffered permanently because of it, which would lead two years later to her sadly premature death. In the meantime, the Viceroy – whose own health was not stellar – would shortly join her in England leaving Indian governance in the hands of the acting Viceroy, Lord Ampthill, from the end of April, which came just after Kitchener had moved back into Snowden for the new Season.

Kitchener's summer of 1904 in Simla was much as it had been the previous year. Meetings, dinners, rides out to verdant Wildflower Hall – 'it all looks very nice and when more flowers are out I shall be quite satisfied' – but he found life to be somewhat tedious.[64] 'There is very little going on here', he wrote to the convalescing Lady Curzon in July. 'The rains are on us and it pours steadily. The usual lot of uninteresting bores everyday'.[65] There's little doubt that the recent partial break-up of Kitchener's staff had something to do with his melancholy as Conk Marker had gone back to England in order to attend a course at the army's Camberley Staff College. But Kitchener's ennui also was simply part of the price he paid for the bachelor life. Clearly too, the absence of the genuine pleasure he derived from socializing with the Curzons had put a damper on the Simla Season. While balls of course still took place amidst the Burmese teak-panelled splendour of Viceregal Lodge now under its temporary occupant, Ampthill, without Lady Curzon in residence 'the sun', wrote Kitchener to her effusively, 'has given up shining'.[66]

And so it went for the balance of the Simla summer. Meanwhile, Kitchener's mind was never too far away from the continuing question of dual control. But with Curzon still in England the issue remained unresolved, although Kitchener continued to advocate for its abolition with both Ampthill, and with Arthur Balfour in London. At a meeting of the Committee of Imperial Defence in June Curzon was angered by the fact that Kitchener's earlier memorandum on Indian defence was gaining ground in its singular focus of blaming the Military Member for all of India's alleged troubles in this regard. Curzon would react strongly with a detailed memorandum of his own later in the year in which he made clear his belief that 'Lord K's desire is to centralize the entire military administration of the Government of India in the hands of the C-in-C'.[67] Kitchener's back-channel strategy in this regard was risky to say the least since such communications probably should have gone through Curzon as Viceroy, which Balfour took the trouble to point out to Kitchener. Naturally, therefore, Curzon's reading of Kitchener's full-blown memorandum detailing his abolition plan made him properly indignant that the Commander in Chief would engage in what he saw to be underhanded politics in this way. In the estimation of some historians and biographers, this course of action by Kitchener is enough to brand him conniving and duplicitous. Certainly that is the view of David Gilmour.[68] The more balanced view of the situation, however, and one that steers clear of demonization by arguing that Kitchener was within the bounds of political convention in operating in this way, is that offered by David Dilks.[69]

At any rate, by mid-1904, the dispute over dual control had begun to move from a disagreement largely confined to the principal parties concerned, to one that was pulling into its vortex a range of persons political, military, and civil. Kitchener threatened to resign yet again on 24 June, driven to it by Elles's ordering of a troop movement without consulting him. But throughout all the strain Kitchener kept up his exceedingly friendly correspondence with Lady Curzon herself – 'I am sure you know and realize how deeply we have all felt for you in your terrible illness', he wrote to her in November – just before the erstwhile Viceroy left England to return to India for what turned out to be his final year in office.[70] Lady Curzon did not return with him, but once feeling well enough in the spring she would come back out to India also, an event much anticipated by Kitchener – 'How splendid it is!', he wrote to her.[71] After sharing in many of her husband's early triumphs, including of course the Delhi Durbar at which she had worn the spectacular 'Peacock Dress' made of gold cloth embroidered with peacock feathers, her health had fallen into terminal decline.[72] And so by Christmas the lonely Viceroy was back in Calcutta, as too was Kitchener, freshly returned from yet another inspection tour, this one having taken him to Burma, which would remain part of British India until 1937, and a country Kitchener thought rich though as yet undeveloped.[73]

As it happened, Curzon and Kitchener spent Christmas together at Barrackpore, near Calcutta and the site of Warren Hastings' old Governor-General's residence turned Viceregal retreat.[74] Their ongoing dispute did not seem to dampen the holiday spirit, however; indeed, they genuinely enjoyed one another's company, which included together taking a tour of the nearby Plassey battlefield made famous by Clive and his East India Company troops' seminal victory over the Nawab Siraj ud-Daula in 1757.[75] Still, the relative conviviality of the holiday season did not mask the fact that the two men continued to hold diametrically opposed views on the issue of dual control, which neither one was about to compromise in order for the other's view to carry the day. 'I regard K's proposals as a positive menace to the State', Curzon wrote emphatically to his ailing wife in London. 'He proposes to set up the C-in-C as an absolute military autocrat in our administration. The scheme would collapse within a year of his leaving India. I do not see why we should revolutionize our constitution to humour him'.[76] To Kitchener, Curzon's continuing talk of 'autocracy' and 'constitutional revolution' remained fundamentally incomprehensible. He simply could not grasp why it was that Curzon insisted on turning a question of military preparedness in an era when all agreed that Russia posed a serious threat to Indian security, into a faux question of constitutional integrity. He said as much to their common correspondent, Lady Curzon, on 19 January 1905. 'Poor Army! Poor Soldiers!' he exclaimed. 'It is hard that they should be sent to fight the battles of the empire all unprepared and without leaders to guide them. It is next door to wholesale murder'.[77] To Kitchener, Curzon was a highly skilled practitioner of the art of political obfuscation and because of that in the same letter he metaphorically threw up his hands in surrender to the Viceroy's expected victory in the dispute. But so strong did Kitchener's feelings run on the matter that he doggedly fought on nonetheless over what he believed to be an issue of essential value to the health and organization of the Indian army, even if it meant that ineluctably he was making an enemy out of the Viceroy (and presumably, eventually, his wife too) and likely to sacrifice a job which he had grown to love.

Accordingly, in order to buttress his position, Kitchener began adding to his list of military voices of support beyond that of Lord Roberts, soliciting and receiving the endorsement of a range of generals, including Sir Horace Smith-Dorrien, Adjutant General (second-in-command) of India and Sir O'Moore Creagh, eventually Kitchener's successor as Commander in Chief.[78] As the early weeks of 1905 passed by it was clear that the climactic moment in the dispute was fast-approaching. In anticipation of what he assumed would be Curzon's withholding of the full brief of the prevailing local situation from the Cabinet in London, Kitchener chose to employ Lady Salisbury to circulate privately to certain members of the Cabinet a full-orbed memorandum that he had written on 1 January. She did so and in this way circumvented official channels which otherwise would have seen the memorandum cross the Viceroy's desk first. Kitchener's critics have long-held this action to have been especially dishonourable, but what is usually ignored in the case is that without his use of unofficial means – an entirely de rigeur practice in contemporary British politics – in stating his position, the debate would have been orchestrated by Curzon in such a way as to stifle the opposing view.

On 10 March the Viceroy's Council met in session at Government House in Calcutta to consider the question of dual control as a first step in what was to lead to full Cabinet consideration in London. Kitchener rode over from Treasury Gate for the meeting, as he viewed it yet another instalment in Curzon's 'long dull councils' from which he was longing to escape, as he wearily informed Conk Marker.[79] He was pessimistic about its outcome and thinking that ultimately his only chance for success lay with the Cabinet. The despised Military Member – that 'ass' Sir Edmond Elles, who personified for Kitchener all that was wrong with dual control – of course was in attendance.[80] The meeting was interminable from Kitchener's point of view. He chose to say very little, at the end dissenting from the Council's decision to reject his proposal, but agreeing naturally that the case should now be turned over to the Secretary of State for India and the whole Cabinet in London. The final word on this 'bad show' would have to come from home.[81] That, in itself, was a victory for Kitchener and if nothing else made his point that India indeed was a constituent part of the British Empire and consequently ruled ultimately by the Cabinet in Parliament, and not by what some were now suggesting was the quasi-emperor, Lord Curzon.

The Viceroy's Council meeting had clarified the dispute, at least for the time being, and with that Kitchener shortly departed Calcutta for his usual round of inspections culminating in his going into summer residency at Simla. All the while in London, the political wheels were turning, and Kitchener's allies – which now included Conk Marker, recently appointed Assistant Private Secretary to the War Secretary, St John Brodrick, and *The Times* journalist Charles a Court Repington, did what they could to influence both public and private opinion in favour of the abolition of dual control. Repington proved especially useful in this regard. As an 'enthusiastic supporter' of Lord Kitchener 'who knows a lot about the whole business' of his contest with Curzon, as Hubert Hamilton later wrote to Marker, Repington was well-placed in London to champion the 'Chief's' position.[82] Meanwhile, far away from the political machinations in London, Kitchener was enjoying 'a very pleasant tour', as he informed a still-friendly Lady Curzon: 'I got a tiger.

I hit him in the head but he got into some very thick high reeds and the elephants would not face it – so at last we had to set fire to the reeds and got a cooked tiger'.[83]

By April Kitchener had reached Simla, there to meet the likewise recently arrived Vicereine. On the fourth of the month a severe earthquake rattled North India, killing over 15,000 people and causing enormous damage to countless buildings, including to Viceregal Lodge. Kitchener felt 'thunder and quakes' at dinner that evening although upon inspection he was relieved to find that no one had been killed in Simla itself, and neither Snowdon nor Wildflower Hall had been damaged.[84] Ensconced at Snowdon, he returned to his usual round of meetings and dinners – some still 'horrid' such as those at the Masonic Lodge – interspersed with restorative rides out to Wildflower Hall.[85] Similarly, the usual social niceties were maintained by Kitchener and Curzon while the fate of their epic clash – 'K wishes to destroy our Military Dept', the latter wrote to his father, Lord Scarsdale, in growing anguish – was about to be decided in London.[86]

For Curzon, however, as vexing as the fight with Kitchener had become, another equally vexing issue had arisen out of his insistence on partitioning the province of Bengal. For Curzon, the plan to partition Bengal, first proposed in 1903, was akin to his struggle with Kitchener in that he came to it from a position of high Raj politics; that is to say, the enemy to be engaged in the partition plan was the emergent Congress party which, he believed, needed to be reined in by a confident Raj whose best hope of continued success was to ensure that its governance of India was perceived to be far-sighted and progressive. He believed that partitioning Bengal, a province of some 80 million people, was suggestive of just this sort of administrative sense and advanced local government. Moreover, and probably more important, it was also a way to check the growth of Bengal (Indian) nationalism, the home he believed of the Congress Party's 'best wire pullers and its most frothy orators'. Upon Bengal, and therefore India itself, could be stamped ever more securely the fact of British rule as an indispensable feature of their the future, since, as Curzon asserted imperiously, the British 'possess partly by heredity, partly by upbringing, and partly by education, the habits of mind and vigour of character which are essential for the task'.[87]

Criticism and denunciation of Curzon's partition plan predictably came fast and furious. A host of febrile Bengali intellectuals, most notably Rabindranath Tagore (who later in 1913 would be the first non-European to win the Nobel Prize for Literature), had long nurtured a local indigenous cultural renaissance to which the proposed partition came as an intolerable affront.[88] Bengal, they argued, was not a Raj-engineered administrative designation, but rather a developed society in its own right even if just then it found itself under the unwelcome political control of the British Raj. Tagore and likeminded others therefore pushed back as hard as they dared against the plan, and in so doing had the sympathies of some leading British administrators such as Sir Henry John Stedman Cotton, past Chief Commissioner of Assam, a district that under partition would fall under the proposed East Bengal province. Curzon would not be denied, however, and in a monumental display of executive arrogance he announced the partition in July 1905, with its enactment coming in the following October.[89]

The final months of Curzon's viceroyalty, therefore, were controversial in ways that sapped his strength and certainly that also of his now permanently fragile wife. For his part, Kitchener stayed well clear of the Bengal controversy while waiting on events in London. And he did not have long to do so because the Cabinet met and considered the issue of dual control at the end of May. Earlier that month, the Secretary of State for India Brodrick had established a committee in order to examine closely Curzon's despatch describing the proceedings of the Viceroy's Council meeting in March, to which Kitchener had appended a dissenting minute. The committee, which consisted of Brodrick, Balfour, Roberts, and Lord Lansdowne, the Foreign Secretary and formerly Viceroy of India, duly met, and then made its report to Cabinet. The Military Member, the report recommended, should be replaced by a 'Military Supply Member' who would *not* have a seat on the Viceroy's Council: 'The organisation now proposed will give the C-in-C a Staff which will make it possible for him to meet the more extended responsibilities which we propose to cast upon him'.[90] On 30 May the Cabinet then convened and made its decision based largely on the committee's report. The culminating moment in the protracted controversy had arrived at last.

First news of the Cabinet's decision reached Kitchener via a telegram from Conk Marker the next day, 1 June. In the telegram, Marker made it clear that the Cabinet had decided in favour of Kitchener and that the Military Department would indeed be abolished. Kitchener was instantly pleased with the news, a pleasure sustained privately for the following almost three weeks until the official despatch had made its way from the India Office in London to Viceregal Lodge in Simla, and then distributed. Once the full despatch had been read, however, it was clear that Marker's post-Cabinet meeting enthusiasm had gotten some elements of the decision wrong; still, in essence, the victory remained Kitchener's. The Military Department would indeed cease to exist, the former Military Member to become the Military Supply Member, as advised by Brodrick's committee, retaining some control over financial and political matters but none whatsoever over those deemed to be of a military nature. Brodrick and the Cabinet had been at pains to cobble together a 'fair compromise', as he wrote to Lord Cromer in Egypt, who had taken a keen interest in the dispute, without forcing either man to resign on a point of principle.[91] Brodrick's clarifying despatch, while it was not the triumphant document that Marker had led Kitchener to believe it would be, nevertheless still signalled a sea-change in the way the Indian Army would henceforth be commanded. Notwithstanding Kitchener's correct assumption that Curzon would still try to 'wreck it', the way forward to achieve a new iteration of command and control of the Indian Army had been reached.[92] Indeed, to Kitchener, this new system was merely a return to what had earlier prevailed for years in British India. As he had recently written to General Sir Edward Stedman, the Military Member in the India Office in London, 'From 1785 to 1853 – that is, during the whole period in which the Indian Empire was being built up by constant warfare – the C-in-C not only held the executive command of the army, but, as President of the Military Board, controlled all its departments'.[93] The view expressed to Stedman was merely a partial articulation of the long memorandum Kitchener would write in July spelling out his conviction that despite recent wrangling India's military policy must ultimately be determined by the Committee of Imperial Defence; yet another demonstration that far from attempting to arrogate to himself dictatorial powers over the Indian Army, as Curzon had always maintained, Kitchener's primary concern remained the Empire as a whole, and India's place within it.[94]

Curzon's reaction to the Cabinet's decision, on the other hand, was typically operatic. After receiving it in full he took a week to contact Kitchener, then inviting him to meet at the Retreat, the Viceroy's cottage situated along the Mall. Kitchener duly attended only to find a distraught Curzon fretting over the assumed loss of prestige that the

Cabinet's decision entailed for himself, and threatening to resign if modifications to the despatch were not undertaken immediately by Brodrick. Kitchener attempted to mollify the plainly agitated Curzon, but to no avail as the Viceroy suddenly upped the ante by bursting into tears.[95] Embarrassed by Curzon's show of emotion in this way, Kitchener reluctantly agreed to send a jointly-written telegram to Brodrick containing some suggested modifications. After an annoyed but satisfied Kitchener shortly had left to return to Wildflower Hall, Curzon then pieced together a series of five modifications to the despatch that he said were non-negotiable. One of these was saving the name of 'Military Department', and all five modifications, he stated, came together with the agreement of the Commander in Chief. Curzon then sent them off to Brodrick in London. Once received, the India Secretary could not quite believe what he was reading and when Kitchener was duly contacted for confirmation of the despatch's revised content, neither could he. There then ensued a rather ridiculous series of accusations and counter-accusations as both Curzon and Kitchener scrambled to explain and clarify their positions with respect to the Cabinet's decision. The 'discrepancy between what I write and what you write', as Curzon had earlier characterized their ongoing dispute, was at the centre of the turbulence, a roil made worse by the assumption now that each man was a liar, and that as far as Kitchener was concerned Curzon's conduct amounted to little more than a series of 'knavish tricks'.[96]

In this penultimate act of their two-year old controversy Curzon had much more to lose than Kitchener. Threats of resignation by the former had grown tiresome to the Balfour government, and indeed it had already been decided that the spring of 1906 would be the right moment for the Curzon Viceroyalty to come to an end. What would it really matter if it came a little earlier than planned? No one in politics is ever really indispensable, and that was surely true of Curzon by mid-1905. In full-flail mode now the Viceroy desperately attempted to save face by attempting to blacken Kitchener's name with charges that the Commander in Chief displayed 'indifference to truth'.[97] All through June and July the bickering and bad-blood continued. But in the midst of it Kitchener was prevailing nonetheless. Conk Marker confirmed that the King now was simply waiting for Curzon to 'yield'.[98] Ultimately, a final showdown between the Viceroy and the Commander in Chief ensued over who should be named the new Military (Supply) Member:

Curzon wanted Major General Sir Edmund Barrow, Secretary to the Military Department since 1901; Kitchener, on the other hand, plumped for Major General Sir Charles Scott, the Indian Army's Director General of Ordnance. In the event, Kitchener won the day. The Cabinet sided with him, a decision Curzon took as undercutting his fundamental ability to carry on as Viceroy. He therefore submitted his resignation on 12 August, which a relieved Balfour duly accepted a few days later. The Curzon era in India had formally come to an end. 'The end of the crisis has at last come', Kitchener wrote in evident relief to Marker.[99] Curzon would remain in office until 18 November, for him a sad, three-month-long, good-bye. On 25 October, just prior to his departing Simla, all the local great and good assembled on the expansive front lawn of Viceregal Lodge to bid Curzon farewell in a leave-taking that was teary for many in attendance except for the stoical Kitchener, who looked on bemusedly.

The three months from Curzon's resignation in August until his departure from India in November would see a campaign undertaken by the Viceregal couple to assassinate Kitchener's character to whomever might listen to a tale they regarded as being one of betrayal. In this way, Lady Curzon now turned on Kitchener ferociously, writing to her mother in October about his 'bare faced lies' and 'intrigues'; about how he had gone out on tour in order to avoid showing 'his face' in Simla; about how he was 'abhorred' and that 'the Army hate[d] him'. If that were not enough, Lady Curzon then became excruciatingly personal in her attack. In an almost unhinged way she ranted to her presumably shocked mother (Kitchener had maintained a friendly correspondence with her in the past also) 'that he has never been the same since that accident [the broken leg] – he is *purple* and his hands and feet shake like palsy. England thinks him a hero – I know him to be a liar . . .'. And then in a pathetic fillip: 'Everyone is stirred . . . to lose the Great man [Curzon] and keep the ignoble one'.[100]

Lady Curzon's plaintive wailings aside, Curzon himself was doing an effective job of likewise libeling Kitchener, though on a broader stage, by writing to the journalist Valentine Chirol of *The Times* in which he referred to the Commander in Chief as having 'not a regard for truth'.[101] Naturally, each side in what had become an epic dispute and a scarcely less epic aftermath marshalled their forces in defence of their man. But of course Curzon's resignation was a clear admission of defeat whatever his bitter recriminations might suggest about his opponent's character and veracity. To Kitchener, for the Viceroy to have resigned in the end simply over the choice of a new Military Member was a weak, incomprehensible, and foolish act, deserving of contempt.[102] Perhaps it was in the nature of a military man to play to win above all else and so Kitchener took the victory in stride. For Curzon, on the other hand, in losing all the features of the martinet in him were there to be seen, that part of his otherwise impressive character which had always been the fly in the ointment. Still, he had his champions, some even today insisting, for example, that in the dispute Kitchener had shown himself to be a 'vain, amoral self-seeker', or that Kitchener was at the centre of a vast 'conspiracy' to bring down Curzon.[103] A simpler, certainly less shrill, and arguably much more accurate summation of the dispute between the two men is that their views of the correct nature of Indian governance were sharply at odds; as a result they each pursued their stated goals, and did so within the accepted political and social conventions of the day; Kitchener's position was ultimately much more consonant with that of the British government than was Curzon's, and, ironically, he was more adept at *realpolitik* than was Curzon the professional politician; and finally, in losing Curzon made it much worse for himself by allowing his demise to become as theatrical as possible. In many ways he had been a great Viceroy: he is almost the only one remembered with respect and even affection by Indians today owing to his steady work in preserving many of the country's historic buildings and monuments such as the Red Fort in Delhi and the Mughal emperor Humayun's Tomb. But Curzon besmirched his reputation in the nasty dispute with Kitchener. While it would be an overstatement to say that Curzon returned to England a spent force, he would not hold high government office again for almost 15 years and of course never found his way to occupying No. 10 Downing Street, a life-long ambition of his which would be left unfulfilled at the time of his death in 1925.

The resignation and subsequent departure of Lord and Lady Curzon in the late-autumn of 1905 opened the way for the appointment and arrival of the 4th Earl of Minto as Viceroy. A career soldier, Minto had seen military service in most of the main theatres of the late-Victorian empire, including Afghanistan, Egypt, and South Africa. Subsequently, he was appointed Governor-General of Canada where he spent six happy years until 1904. Now, a year later, he was to succeed Curzon, in the process becoming the second Minto to hold the Viceroyalty, his great-grandfather, the 1st Earl of Minto, having occupied what amounted to the same office as Governor-General of the Presidency of Fort William (Bengal) about a century earlier, from 1807 until 1813.

If Curzon had been the Viceregal high-flyer: handsome, intellectual, confident of his destiny but with a whiff of megalomania about his person, Minto was his antithesis. Soldierly, sporting, a bit of a plodder, but supremely loyal and practical, Minto took an instant liking to Kitchener despite Curzon's attempts to warn him off. Indeed, both Minto and John Morley, Brodrick's newly-named successor as Secretary of State for India, were of a similar mind about Kitchener and rejected Curzon's continuing attempts to poison their thinking about him. Indeed, by the New Year 1906, Minto was confirming to Morley that Kitchener had been nothing if not 'perfectly straightforward with me'.[104] Morley, appointed by the new Liberal Prime Minister, Sir Henry Campbell-Bannerman, was an internationalist schooled by the late William Gladstone and his avowed follower in this regard – not to mention his official biographer – and it is revealing to note that if anyone might have come to office suspicious of Kitchener's alleged militarist designs on usurping civil authority, it would have been him. Needless to say, he found nothing of the kind.[105]

For Kitchener, now something of an Old India Hand after over three years in the country, the winter of 1906 saw him effectively move clear of the Curzon controversy. He was able, therefore, to get on with implementing the reforms of the army that he had long anticipated, but which had been held up by the resistance of the old regime. During this period the Prince and Princess of Wales – the future King George V and Queen Mary – toured India, spending considerable time with Kitchener over a span of about six months. While on tour the Prince forged a ready friendship with Kitchener and encouraged him with respect to his planned Indian reforms, which he likewise believed were 'to the great benefit of the Army and to the safety of the Empire'.[106]

Accordingly and gradually, Kitchener began to reorganize and to some extent centralize Indian Army operations. He had already established a temporary Staff College at Deolali in 1905, which in 1907 was moved to Quetta and made permanent.[107] Northern and Southern Armies were created in an attempt to make the historic presidency armies act as a complementary national force. Such thinking by

Kitchener was engendered by the constant apprehension that Russia might choose to invade across the North-West Frontier and that such a course of action could only be met properly by a 'national' response. He reaffirmed his commitment to the divisional system, which put more power into the hands of local commanders. Altogether the Campbell-Bannerman government – for which he had harboured no great hopes: 'South African Methods of Barbarism are not easily forgotten', as he had opined earlier to Marker – turned out to recognize the value of Kitchener's reforms by extending his tenure in India in 1907 for two years beyond his initial five year appointment.[108] Soon thereafter also, Kitchener's original recommendation that the position of Military Member on the Viceroy's Council be abolished was acted upon when under the Asquith government, which succeeded Campbell-Bannerman's in 1908, the compromise position of Military Supply Member ceased to exist altogether (albeit mainly in order to save money). In this regard, almost four years after Curzon had departed India in defeat, Kitchener's victory in the dispute was both complete and vindicated.

Kitchener's final years in India thus became somewhat valedictory. He presided over the implementation of his well-earned reforms. He toured relentlessly throughout the sub-continent – all told covering some 65,000 miles – including a visit to Nepal, then still a mysterious kingdom almost unknown to the outside world.[109] He kept up the usual round of dinners and balls; now that he was again a welcome guest at Government House and Viceregal Lodge he even looked forward to attending at least some of them, and certainly he enjoyed playing the host himself at his own frequently-held dinner parties. Kitchener's abiding interest in flowers and gardening had plenty of scope for fulfillment at Treasury Gate, Snowdon, and especially the magnificently situated Wildflower Hall, and he continued to enlarge his collection of ceramics and china. Altogether there was a domesticity and quiescence to Kitchener's last years in India that go some distance in belying the militarist stereotype that defined him.

The only major political issue for Kitchener that arose during his final period in India was the negotiation and enactment of the Anglo-Russian Entente signed in August of 1907. Originating under the Salisbury government in 1898, it later fell to Sir Edward Grey, Foreign Secretary beginning in 1905, to bring the Entente to pass and with it a clear definition of spheres of influence in Central Asia; in other words, it was an attempt to effectively close out the Great Game.[110] Not many people with an intimate knowledge of the history of the Anglo-Russian rivalry in Central Asia, India, and Afghanistan, however, thought that this course of action was the right one for Britain. Their number included both Kitchener and Curzon, the latter who was just beginning to re-enter public life after a period of recovery and rehabilitation from his chastening Indian experiences, and even more the death of Mary in July of the previous year. His considered position was that the Entente had given away too much in respect to 'the efforts of a century'.[111] Later, during a speech in the House of Lords in February of 1908, Curzon's critique of the Entente was closely-argued but by then his view was of no real consequence. For Grey and the government, the issue was always the security of India and they believed that limiting Russian territorial ambition in the region in the way accomplished by the Entente would provide exactly that outcome.

Kitchener, with similar misgivings to Curzon over the issue, argued that an Entente, whatever its good intentions, could never safeguard India in the way that the strongest possible and most highly unified Indian Army could do – if only the British Treasury would yield up sufficient funds for its continued creation.[112] Only through a blatant show of force, Kitchener believed, could Russia be dissuaded from any putative plan to invade British India. On this issue, however, both men were proved wrong for as far as Indian security was concerned, the Entente did take most of the heat and light out of the old Great Game and Anglo-Russian relations did in fact generally relax. And, as a bonus, in the resultant opening of the City of London to Russian investment, some of the sting was taken out of the country's surprising and ignominious defeat to Japan in 1904 and the anarchic Decembrist revolt of the following year.

The year 1908–9, Kitchener's last in India, indeed saw little for him to do other than to offer steady, reforming administration, and relentless regimental inspection. The official plan now was for him to depart India in September of the latter year and then step into a new appointment. But as yet that putative next step remained inchoate. When the time of his leave-taking duly came Kitchener was sent off with the usual round of banquets and salutes. At the Viceroy's farewell dinner, held at Viceregal Lodge on 3 September, for example, Kitchener gave an (uncharacteristically) excellent speech, part of the content of which had been drawn inadvertently from Curzon's own of four years earlier! One of Kitchener's staff had written it for him so that he was unaware of its provenance, and when he did find out about this (on his part, at least) mistaken act of plagiarism, he simply laughed it off. Reported a few days later in the London newspapers Curzon, however, could not see the humour in it. After reading coverage of it in a copy of the *Westminster Gazette* an angry Curzon had scribbled in its margins: 'What a cheat the man is! How glad I am he has been exposed'.[113] Even years later after Kitchener's death, Curzon still nursed this particular grievance, calling it 'Lord Kitchener's famous plagiarism'.[114] As pyrrhic victories go, one might say, Curzon's here was rather a textbook case.

On 6 September 1909 Kitchener left Simla for the last time and journeyed down to Bombay where he gave another farewell speech, this time without including the plagiarized content. As speech-giving was always a trial for him having to deliver another one in such a short time was hardly to be relished. But in front of a friendly audience he spoke from the heart: 'I most sincerely regret that the time has come', he opined, 'for me to leave this vast and wonderful country with all its teeming millions and its many unsolved problems'.[115] And with that the next day, 10 September, he relinquished command of the Indian Army and was immediately gazetted Field Marshal. He then steamed out of Bombay. After seven remarkable years in India he would never return to it again.

Beginning with his departure from Bombay, for the next two years until September of 1911, as it turned out, Kitchener would be at large. In leaving India he certainly planned a long holiday; but what he absolutely did not wish to do was accede to a request made a few months earlier by Richard Haldane, the Secretary of State for War, to take over the Royal Navy's Mediterranean Command. Haldane had written to Kitchener in July of 1909 asking if he would consider the appointment, explaining that it was critical to the 'defence of the forces of the Empire .... We [the King and Cabinet] think that the Mediterranean Command would be in your hands capable of being developed into an instrument of power'.[116] True, such an appointment would return him to the Middle East (Malta was the fleet's base) and in that way the appointment held some appeal. But on balance, and despite Haldane's high-flown rhetoric, Kitchener saw the post as simply a way-station for which he held no significant aspiration. Especially was this true in light of the fact that the appointment he truly did covet was that of Viceroy of India, and with Minto expected to retire in the autumn of 1910 after serving a five year term the timing seemed potentially auspicious.

Complicating the Mediterranean Command appointment and making it difficult for Kitchener to resist, however, was the fact that Haldane had enlisted the help of the King, as noted above in convincing him to take it up. Edward VII was in declining health and would die the next year, but in the summer of 1909 he had pressed Kitchener to accept, which, at length, and following his initial refusal of the appointment, he did: 'When they played the King card I was done', Kitchener wrote wryly to Lord Roberts.[117] Thus, upon leaving India Kitchener's future seemed set, although he was a reluctant participant in it.

In the meantime, as part of an open-ended leave, Kitchener had agreed to sail to Australia in order to conduct a review of its defence policy and nascent armed forces. The recent rise of Germany's concerted militarism had made British Empire defence a major topic of discussion and planning, both at home and in the various Dominion capitals. Canada, for example, was deciding whether or not to create its own navy, and if not to make a direct contribution to the strength of the Royal Navy; it would choose the former. Kitchener's review of Australian and New Zealand defence, therefore, was of a piece with the wider Imperial policy of the day.[118]

Accordingly, after touring Singapore, and various ports in Korea, China, and Japan for a few months – and taking a brief holiday in Indonesia – Kitchener arrived in Australia at the beginning of the New Year 1910. His welcome there was overwhelmingly positive (very little by way of sniping about the earlier fate of Breaker Morant was to be heard). 'Be assured', the Australian Prime Minister, Alfred Deakin, told him, 'your coming is highly appreciated by all of us'.[119] Indeed, the Australian and New Zealand newspapers were full of rapturous coverage of Kitchener's progress. 'Kitchener of Khartoum, Britain's Big Fighting Chief', blared the headline of *The Times* of Wellington, for example, upon his arrival there.[120] In the early winter of 1910 after successfully completing his tour Kitchener duly wrote up a report containing a series of recommendations, including the establishment of a military college in Australia, which the Canberra (designated as the nation's federal capital just two years earlier) government acted upon in short order by founding the Royal Military College at Duntroon the following year.

Upon leaving the Antipodes in mid-March, Kitchener sailed to the United States via Tahiti. Landing at San Francisco on 8 April he travelled cross-country by rail, arriving in New York City a week later. He visited briefly the military academy at West Point, and then on the 20th sailed for home early in keen anticipation of what was assumed to be the imminent naming of Minto's successor as Viceroy. After almost a week at sea he landed at Plymouth on the 26th, his first time back in England for nearly eight years.

But unlike some of his previous arrivals home, which had become exhibitions in 'conquering hero' fanfare, Kitchener's return to England this time was quiet, but for him much more portentous. His world tour had only heightened his desire to be named Viceroy; indeed, in cutting short his stay in America in order to be on hand for the Cabinet's deliberations concerning the appointment of a new Viceroy his hope for winning it was made clear.[121] Haldane and John Morley, who remained Secretary of State for India, expected Kitchener to plump hard for the post as the conclusion of Minto's viceroyalty was now being counted in mere months. The Mediterranean Command appointment remained, of course, but now more than ever Kitchener wished to refuse it, if possible, and when the ailing King – just weeks from death – surprisingly reversed himself on the matter and told Kitchener to throw it over, that is exactly what he did.[122] Kitchener's move enraged Haldane, naturally, but by that point he could not have cared less. His eyes remained steadfast on the much bigger prize of the Viceroyalty, which he hoped would shortly be his. But alas, in this hope Kitchener would be cruelly disappointed.

On 6 May the King died. The state funeral and the obligatory period of mourning combined to slow down the Viceregal appointment process, but the heightening tension over it broke on 9 June when Morley wrote to Kitchener, informing him that 'a decision has been reached on the Indian Viceroyalty .... We are not going to invite you to go back in a new capacity'.[123] In relaying the Cabinet's decision to Kitchener, Morley explained that 'the sole difficulty arises from misgivings as to the impression that would be likely to arise in India from a military appointment .... I do not think I ever had a more disagreeable task in my life than the writing of this letter', he concluded.[124] In adding this encomium, Morley was gilding the lily as it was he, more than anyone else directly concerned with the appointment, who did not want to see Kitchener back in India. Even though the former Commander in Chief was uniquely qualified for the job, the negative residue of the Curzon affair remained, as did Morley's antipathy toward Kitchener's insistence on the wholesale (and therefore costly) reform of the Indian Army. To be sure, also philosophically, Morley was opposed to having 'the most famous soldier you can find to be the chief agent of His Majesty'. To do so, he maintained, would be to 'hoist the signal flag of military power before India and the world'.[125] In the event, Morley's bald politics won out in the decision to bypass Kitchener over any other consideration.

Political symbolism matters, of course, but since the holding of India had been the especial job of the army ever since the Mutiny half a century earlier, it counts as passing strange that the Imperial government would shy away now from appointing the strongest man available in this regard for the job. In this particular political round Kitchener had simply lost. In an environment of increasing Indian nationalist agitation and consequent constitutional reform – the Indian Councils Act (the Morley-Minto Reforms) had been passed in 1909, which allowed for an expanded Indian role on Legislative Councils and the opportunity for them to sit on the Viceroy's Council and on the Secretary of State for India's Council – Kitchener was considered too much the military man to be made viceroy. The late King had been an ally, but without his voice at the moment of decision there were few around the Liberal government's Cabinet table who thought Kitchener to be the right choice. The Prime Minister, Asquith, in fact did think Kitchener highly suitable, but Morley's position was adamant, backed up by threats to resign should his view be overruled. Moreover, hovering in the domestic background was Margot Asquith, the Prime Minister's highly-opinionated wife, who had grown in her dislike over the years for Kitchener. 'He is a natural cad', she had written to Lord Crewe, Colonial Secretary and Leader of the House of Lords, in May, 'tho' he is remarkably clever. I know if you and Henry [the Prime Minister] . . . send him to India you will regret it all your days'. By that point she too had accepted Morley's view that the best man for the job was Sir Charles Hardinge, formerly an ambassador and now the Permanent Under-Secretary at the Foreign Office. He 'is the man to send', she concluded, 'and he is younger and straight and a great gentleman.' And then to add to her ever-present classism, she confirmed her belief in the calumnies about Kitchener spread by Curzon and his supporters: 'Never have dealings with a liar however clever'.[126]

Hardinge was duly appointed Viceroy and sailed for India, and – like his grandfather before him, Sir Henry Hardinge, who had been Governor-General in the mid-nineteenth century – he would serve out an unremarkable tenure of six years. But then perhaps that was the point of such a low-risk appointment. In any case, for Kitchener, his rejection for the post came as a sharp blow. Unsurprisingly, rather than remain in London – whatever the creature comforts he always enjoyed at Pandeli Ralli's West End townhouse, and brooding over what might have been – he took himself off to Ireland where he engaged in a kind of personal heritage tour, visiting scenes from his long-ago boyhood in Co. Kerry. Naturally, the disappointment of not being appointed Viceroy stayed with him: 'Old Morley would not have me for India at any price', he lamented to one of his favourite former staffers, Frank Maxwell, 'and the Mediterranean command was mere bunkum so I am at a loose end with nothing to do'.[127]

During much of the succeeding year, therefore, Kitchener exhibited a sustained wanderlust. Following his sojourn in Ireland he went across to Scotland where he observed the Royal Navy's manoevres alongside the First Lord of the Admiralty, Winston Churchill, having risen to high political office since Kitchener first encountered him as an irritating presence at Omdurman a dozen years earlier. This encounter, however, was much friendlier than their first had been. Later that summer, having by then returned to England, Kitchener acted on a plan of his that he had been nursing for years, which was to find a country property suitable for his approaching retirement. After an intensive search, by the end of August he had found it in the form of Broome Park. 'I have bought a house in Kent, six miles from Canterbury', he wrote to Maxwell. 'It is rather a big place and will want a lot of doing up but as I have nothing else to do it will interest me enormously to make it a nice abode'.[128] Negotiations to secure title to the property were protracted and would take until the following year to complete but Kitchener believed that the right place for his retirement had indeed been found.

Meanwhile, Kitchener decided to continue in his peripatetic sabbatical by going off to Sudan and East Africa for the winter.

He departed in November, therefore, stopping first in Cairo where he was joined by his naval officer nephew and eventual heir, Henry 'Toby' Kitchener, son of his eldest brother, Chevallier; and thence to Khartoum to re-visit the sites of past triumphs, as well as to see how the city and country were progressing. At the turn of the New Year 1911 he proceeded south to British East Africa, then just on the cusp of the arrival of a large influx of British and other European settlers.[129] He, like most of them, was instantly taken with the natural beauty of East Africa, the abundance of its game, and the plentitude of its available land, which was just beginning to be parceled out to settlers in a hurried process that would come back to haunt the British severely some half-a-century later in the savage violence of the Mau Mau Rebellion. Kitchener hoped to find a piece of land upon which to build a winter home for his future retirement, a complement to Broome. He did so at Songhor in the Nandi Hills about 40 miles east of Port Florence (today's Kisumu) and 200 hundred miles north of the then recently established ramshackle capital of Nairobi.[130]

Adding to the success of the visit was the opportunity to socialize with the Governor of the British East African Protectorate, Sir Percy Girouard, Kitchener's old Canadian railwayman from the re-conquest of the Sudan, as well as from the war in South Africa. After service in South Africa, Girouard had gone on to a pair of gubernatorial appointments, the latest having brought him to Nairobi in 1909. The reunion of the two former comrades was celebratory. 'I have had a splendid time in Africa', he wrote to his sister Millie in mid-March not long before leaving for home, 'and am sorry it is all over'.[131] Much of his enjoyment came from the endless opportunities it afforded at that time for shooting – 'I got an elephant, buffaloes and all sorts of antelope' – made even easier by the Uganda Railway, newly finished within the previous ten years and linking Lake Victoria in the interior with Mombasa on the coast.

Indeed, the entire spring of 1911 would be celebratory for Kitchener as the coronation of King George V was impending and, owing to the new King's particular regard for him, he was asked to command the troops at the elaborate ceremony that would take place in London on 22 June. Arriving back in England at the beginning of April he readied himself for this signal event, as well as the equally happy prospect of soon occupying Broome Park, the L1,400 sale having finally just gone through. 'Broome is mine' he excitedly telegraphed to family members upon his return.[132] His professional future may still have remained unclear, but for the first time in his life Kitchener was a satisfied landlord, and at just shy of his 61st birthday retirement beckoned as perhaps the clearest and best prospect of all.

8

Egypt Again, 1911–14

Following the King's coronation, Kitchener's leave-taking continued throughout mid-1911, his only official duty at that time being the seat he occupied on the Committee of Imperial Defence. But even this relatively minor assignment had been the focus of a mild contretemps with the government the previous October when Kitchener suspected that his rejection of the Mediterranean Command appointment might have been the reason for his 'removal' from the CID. In reply to Kitchener's query, the Prime Minister, H.H. Asquith, was at pains to clarify to him that he had not been removed, but rather that the Mediterranean appointment and the one to the CID were 'part and parcel of the same offer' so that when the former was rejected it meant that the seat on the CID automatically went with it. Kitchener, still sore over India, acted a little huffily in this exchange, but in the same letter Asquith now offered him a seat unconditionally, to which he promptly replied: 'I shall be glad to accept'.[1] Upon his return from Africa in time for the coronation he had duly begun to sit on the Council, an ideal vantage point from which to monitor the possibility of other (greater) appointments, especially that of Agent and Consul General in Egypt, the likelihood of which, as we shall see, was now growing.

In the meantime, the renovation of Kitchener's new country home of Broome Park was a constant pre-occupation, but as it was not yet ready for full-time habitation (he did stay over from to time in order to supervise work on it) he spent considerable time at Pandeli Ralli's in London, as well as visiting family and the country estates of various society figures, especially his old favourite, Hatfield House.

These largely domestic and social activities, however, masked the real anticipation Kitchener felt over the prospect of the Egyptian appointment. The current holder of the office was Sir Eldon Gorst, who had succeeded the inimitable Lord Cromer upon his retirement to England in 1907. A career diplomat who had been in Egypt since 1886, Gorst had fulfilled the role of British Agent competently, but the long shadow cast over the job by the singular figure of Cromer was a very difficult one to escape. Moreover, Gorst's health had broken down in 1910 and now, by mid-1911, and suffering acutely from advanced cancer of the pancreas and liver, he had returned to England in anticipation of dying.[2] He did so on 12 July and with his sad passing (he was just 50 years old) the Egyptian appointment indeed went to Kitchener.

In the weeks leading up to Gorst's expected death the Foreign Secretary, Sir Edward Grey, had requested Kitchener to come to Whitehall for a meeting, which he did on 19 June. Throughout this period Cromer had been recommending strongly to Grey that Kitchener be given the appointment, and in this the two men's views were consonant.[3] Indeed, Cromer's view on this point was the only one that carried much weight with the Foreign Secretary. Grey's interview with Kitchener went gratifyingly well, the result of which was an offer made to him to return to Egypt as the new British Agent and Consul General. The appointment was approved of heartily by the King the next day, to whom, Grey informed Kitchener, it had given 'much pleasure'.[4] A few weeks later on 16 July, following the splendours of the coronation and Kitchener's role in it, and Gorst's passing, Parliament was informed that 'K of K' would be going back to Egypt. In a deliberate gesture aimed at ameliorating past animosities, the Khedive, Abbas Hilmi II, wrote to Kitchener immediately to say that he was 'very pleased to know that you are returning to the scene of your earlier labours', and for the next two months until his departure for Cairo on 16 September the new British Agent readied himself to undertake his first major administrative task since leaving India two years earlier.[5]

In returning to Egypt Kitchener was over ten years removed from the scene of many of his former triumphs. Always one of his favourite theatres of imperial service, Egypt remained a place of administrative idiosyncrasies played out now within the context of markedly increased local nationalism, a feature of Egyptian society harking back directly to Urabi Pasha and the revolt of 1882. Over this issue, as was true of many others, Kitchener could, and did, take the long view. As would be described of Winston Churchill many years later when he became prime minister near the outset of World War II, he had been all his life in preparation for that day. By May 1940, when he succeeded his discredited predecessor Neville Chamberlain, Churchill indeed had accumulated vast experience of high government office, something which, as he declared forcefully to the House of Commons, 'has been bought, not taught'.[6] Similarly, on 28 September 1911 when Kitchener's special train pulled into Cairo station, the same thing could be said of him. He brought vast experience to the job: indeed, a lifetime's preparation for this particular proconsular position, one that would amount to his becoming the effective ruler of Egypt for most of the next three years.

Much has been written about the 40 years, 1882 to 1922, that Britain spent ruling Egypt.[7] Cromer, naturally, looms large in any re-telling of the period prior to the establishment of the Kingdom of Egypt in the latter year. Like much else in the history of the Middle East, the impact of World War I would smash the old verities of Egyptian rule. For Kitchener, his arrival on the cusp of the war was (unknowably) portentous in that he inherited a colonial state in the throes of renewed nationalism and anti-European feeling. Indeed, his deceased predecessor Gorst, had been grappling with these very things in the last years of his abbreviated service. In an attempt to begin a process of liberalization from the traditional governing autocracy embodied by Cromer, Gorst had undertaken a clutch of reforms beginning in the autumn of 1907. These changes in governing style – such as rendering 'our rule more sympathetic to the Egyptians in general, and to Muhammedans in particular'; or cultivating 'good relations with the Khedive'; or settling 'quickly and definitely various questions regarding the pay and pension of officers and officials', were carried out in line with the wishes of first, the Campbell-Bannerman, and then the Asquith, governments under the aegis of Grey as Foreign Secretary.[8]

In so doing, both the Anglo-Egyptian and British governments were engaged in a 'liberal experiment', the goal of which was to blunt disruptive nationalist thrusts. The difficulty with the experiment, however, as it proceeded in the years following its adoption, was rather than blunt nationalist feeling, such feeling became inflamed. This kind of outcome was hardly the first or the last time that it would be seen in the history of nationalist reactions to empire, but the fact that it happened under the 'self-effacing' Gorst was evidence for some that a much a stronger figure was required in order to right the listing ship of British control in Egypt.[9] Accordingly, Kitchener's endorsement and appointment came quite clearly with Grey's desire that the dangerously sharp edge of Egyptian nationalist protest, as witnessed beginning in 1908 and demonstrated especially the following year when the Egyptian Prime Minister, Boutros Ghali, had been assassinated, be dulled. Ghali, whose cooperation Gorst had cultivated along with that of the Khedive, had been shot by a member of the Nationalist Party who cited, among other reasons for his act of violence, the recent extension of Britain's Suez Canal concession (potentially running until 2008!).[10] Into this simmering mix of violent nationalism, aspirational liberalism, and residual authoritarianism, therefore, strode the invariably autocratic figure of Kitchener in the early autumn of 1911.

As if to defy the stereotype of the military autocrat, for his arrival at Cairo railway station Kitchener chose to wear civilian clothes; indeed, he wore a frock-coat and top-hat, a move self-consciously disingenuous, presumably, and one which he would not repeat. He lingered only briefly at the station, but long enough to receive a rousing cheer from the assembled onlookers and then departed immediately by carriage for the short ride to the British Agency. The central location of the British Agency in Cairo meant that every site of governmental importance, especially the Abdin Palace and various ministries, was easily reachable from it, which since 1894 had been located in an elegant neo-classical building near the Nile river. As was his wont, Kitchener settled in quickly to the Agency, immediately affording it his personal touch as seen earlier in Calcutta and Simla.

Between Kitchener and Grey in particular there was agreement that one of the first and most important tasks to be undertaken in Egypt was to restore a clear sense of authority emanating from the person of the British Agent and Consul General. Cromer, in the main, had supplied exactly that and it was understood a figure as militarily august as Kitchener would have little trouble in exercising this feature of his brief too. To do so meant initially that the two consultative bodies established by the existing Egyptian constitution following the usual British colonial pattern of Legislative Council and General Assembly be made to toe the new authoritarian line. A sharp turn of this sort was believed to be necessary in light of their having been given their relative head under Gorst's somewhat relaxed oversight, which in turn had been mediated unsuccessfully by the unfortunate Ghali. Kitchener was not a natural constitutionalist, given to re-making forms of colonial governance, but over the first two years of his tenure in Egypt, as we shall see, he delved nonetheless rather deeply into reforming the way in which Britain chose to rule its Egyptian subjects.

The other area of especial interest to Kitchener, but which fit much more closely his own predilections as a nascent civilian governor, was the Egyptian economy. The financial crisis of the period leading up to the British occupation of 1882 had never been wholly resolved in its aftermath; indeed, almost the totality of Cromer's long service as Agent and Consul General was comprised of a steady attempt to stave off national bankruptcy, and then to increase Egypt's national economic output. Cromer undertook the first task successfully beginning in the mid- to-late 1880s, with the second one a marked feature of the years 1900–4.[11]

In the early years of the twentieth century Egypt remained an almost completely pre-industrial country; a kind of primeval agricultural land gathered round the rich alluvial delta of the Nile before the gigantic imposition of the Sahara Desert swallowed up everything in its path as far south as the still-dependent Sudan. Accordingly, economic reform and industrial growth meant altering at least some of the traditional Egyptian patterns of agricultural production, and more particularly how they had long been financed. The growth and harvesting of cotton remained the overwhelming economic driver of the country – comprising 93 per cent of all Egyptian exports at the time of Kitchener's arrival – so reforming the cotton trade was clearly at the heart of any attempt at more general economic and fiscal reform.[12] Indeed, the dominance of cotton meant that Egyptian agriculture was very close to being a monoculture economy, the result of which was had been to severely marginalize the production of other crops. Limited exports in this regard were one thing, but the increasing inability of the country to grow enough basic food crops – such as rice, peas, and lentils – in order to feed itself was reaching crisis proportions. In part, therefore, Kitchener's early resolve to reform the land tenure system in Egypt sprang from the eminently practical concern of food production for the local market, a concern that he had first grappled with in Sudan back in 1899.

To this end, Kitchener got to work right away. One of the crying grievances of the tens of thousands of small peasant cultivators, the fellaheen, was that they could be readily expelled from their plots of their land, or their simple agricultural implements seized by creditors for debt. The regime then in place in Egypt was akin to that which had prevailed in Ireland before the agricultural reforms of the mid- to late-nineteenth century began to re-set the balance of land rights for Irish smallholders. Similarly, in Egypt, the 'fellah' smallholder was at the mercy of landlords and their financial backers who profited from their ability to hold in thrall a whole class of peasant producer. Kitchener, while certainly always holding conservative views on property-holding generally, as on all other social issues, nevertheless had a well-developed sense of natural justice, particularly as it pertained to the poor. Throughout 1911 and into the following year, therefore, he worked towards reforms that would benefit the peasantry in particular, the result of which was the promulgation of the 'Five Feddans Law'.[13] A 'feddan' was the equivalent of about one acre, and a typical Egyptian fellah worked a plot of some five feddans. Hence the attempt to pass a law that would empower the fellaheen – traditionally at the mercy of capricious money lenders and debt collectors and their obliging legal counsel – to avoid expropriation for debt. The social and political objective of the law, argued Kitchener, was to create a contented, conservative, even prosperous peasant class who would furnish an impermeable bar against creeping Egyptian political radicalization.[14]

As a complementary legislative move to the Five Feddans Law, Kitchener then chose to establish local or 'cantonal' courts to enforce the new system, located in close proximity to the life and work of the peasants. As a form of 'Indirect Rule', the peasant cantonal in Egypt was an early example of what would become central to the way in which the British sought to govern many parts of Africa in the very near future, and under Frederick (later Lord) Lugard in Nigeria, IR as a form of colonial governance would reach its apotheosis.[15]

Kitchener's twin legislative moves in 1912 naturally were opposed by the entrenched moneyed interests who benefited directly from Egypt's existing system. Their complaints were made loudly because under what had long been established as the 'capitulations' system of foreigner privilege their unearned increment had allowed for the creation of a class of small financiers now run to ground by the implementation of the new law. Kitchener could not have been better pleased than to go after them and their sense of entitlement which had resulted in moneylending 'at exorbitant rates of interest – 30–40 per cent, and even higher', he complained.[16] Kitchener's successes in practical administration were met with (perhaps surprising) approbation by Cromer, who followed closely events in Egypt from England and was in steady correspondence with him about his reforms. In July of that year, for example, Cromer wrote at length to Kitchener praising him for 'how thoroughly sound I think all your Egyptian views are. May you go on and prosper'. Cromer then continued, although in a somewhat maudlin tone, telling Kitchener that 'it is a real consolation to me to think that under your auspices the work of my lifetime will not be thrown away; until your advent I confess that I began to fear that such would not be the case'.[17] Given Cromer's long and rather uneven personal history with Kitchener his tone comes across as cloying in this missive; equally, however, Cromer was of the strong opinion that the Gorst regime had indeed weakened Britain's hand in Egypt and if nothing else the undoubted resolve of Kitchener to restore a fulsome British authority in the country was to him highly welcome.

Cromer's enthusiastic approbation of Kitchener's reforming plans continued as they were extended throughout 1912 and into 1913, and latterly were made to include the widespread drainage of alluvial swamp and the reclamation and creation of arable land. The drainage project was undertaken on a vast scale and put under the control of the highly biddable Lord Edward Cecil, Under-Secretary at the Egyptian Ministry of Finance, and, it will be recalled, a former aide to Kitchener during the Sudan campaign. Indeed, as had been the case in India, Kitchener worked closely in Egypt with a small coterie of trusted lieutenants, another one of which was Ronald Storrs, the British Agency's Oriental Secretary. Though barely 30 years of age upon Kitchener's arrival, Storrs had been in Cairo since 1904 and was seen properly as a high-flyer. Indeed, T.E. Lawrence, with whom Storrs and others at the Agency in Cairo would be closely associated during the First World War, later described him as 'the most brilliant Englishman in the Middle East ... always first, and the great man among us'.[18] Kitchener took an immediate liking to Storrs and they got on very well together. The feeling was mutual, as Storrs later described working under Kitchener as having brought him 'three years of such happiness, interest and responsibility as no gratitude could repay'.[19] Destined for a long career in the service of the British Empire, Storrs would go on to fulfill gubernatorial appointments in Jerusalem, Cyprus and Northern Rhodesia.

In pursuing his drainage and land reclamation scheme Kitchener became a kind of all-seeing supervisor, going out on tour regularly by train to examine the rate of progress being made and to urge continued expansion and development. In this activity Kitchener adopted much the same approach as he had taken during his military inspections in India, but with the added feature of the whistle-stop display of a large banner featuring a likeness of himself emblazoned with the words: 'Welcome to Lord Kitchener – the Friend of the Peasant'. To a later generation such self-promotion may smack of the potentate-approach to politics, and undoubtedly, amongst the traditionally downtrodden fellaheen, there were endless malleable marks to be had. But, despite the mild propagandistic theatrics, it should not be overlooked that Kitchener's personal and reforming impact was real. Storrs remembers that Kitchener 'actively liked meeting, talking and laughing with Egyptians, who in spite of the habitual sternness of his expression never said of him, as of some of his compatriots, that the Englishman's face is *mubawwiz* – sullen or overcast'.[20] And whether it was the steady rise in Egypt's export base that occurred under his administration, or the establishment of a midwifery school that would evolve into Cairo's first modern hospital, Kitchener's impact on Egypt was neither simply authoritarian nor mainly militaristic.[21] In Egypt, for the first time in his long professional life, Kitchener was neither solely the lord of war nor the negotiating diplomat of earlier iterations, but rather he had become a proconsul of significant skill and progressive impact.[22]

This proconsular evolution of Kitchener's was measured also – and perhaps most forcefully – by his understanding and treatment of the political and constitutional constructs of the Anglo-Egyptian state. In particular this meant the Khedive, Abbas Hilmi, Kitchener's old nemesis from his time as Sirdar of the Egyptian Army. The Khedive's youthful and clumsy nationalism of the late-1890s in which he had tried to take an *a priori* stance against the authority of the British Agent, gradually had given way to a more mature statesmanship. But it is clear that regardless of this change neither the new British Agent nor the former one, Cromer, had any use for him. Indeed, Cromer's view of the

Khedive remained intensely negative: he was 'an inveterate liar', Cromer wrote to Kitchener in July 1913, who needed to be brought 'to book'.[23] Just then home on his annual summer leave, Kitchener's view of the Khedive after 1911 had become fairly pragmatic in that he believed constitutional reform in Egypt could be brought about best through abolishing the General Assembly, a body full of 'political wirepullers', he argued, who had come very close to wrecking the extension of the Suez Canal concession.[24] Out of that regrettable protest – engendered by Gorst's attempt at liberalization, it was believed by Kitchener, Cromer and others – had come the assassination of Boutros Ghali. 'After I left', in a direct attack on Gorst's administration, wrote Cromer to Kitchener, 'he [the Khedive] got completely out of hand'. Therefore, to rein in what Kitchener believed was the Khedive's nefarious influence on the increasingly radical General Assembly, he decided that it should be abolished and then replaced by a new Legislative Assembly comprised of both appointed and elected members. Kitchener argued that with proper constitutional evolution this new iteration of an Egyptian assembly would in time come to provide measured good government, embodying the 'true progress' that all desired.[25]

Later, Kitchener's decision to re-make the cardinal features of Egypt's nascent representative governmental institutions was seen by some as confirming his reputation for autocracy and high-handedness. Unsurprisingly, Gorst's recent biographer, in defence of his subject's record in Egypt, continues to perpetuate the view that the 'autocratic Kitchener' reversed the achievements of his predecessor.[26] Gorst himself had an intense dislike for Kitchener from his days working under Cromer during the Sudan campaign (the feeling, it will be recalled, was mutual) and it seems that this fact more than any other is what coloured his perception of the man. In turn, so too that of his biographer. Where Gorst had tried to curry favour with the Khedive, Kitchener made no secret that he saw Abbas Hilmi as weak, unprincipled, and in thrall to Egyptian nationalists who were intent upon inciting chaos in the country. Indeed, one of their number had already tried to assassinate Kitchener outside the railway station in Cairo in April.[27] The attempt to do so was weak and easily rebuffed, but Kitchener believed that the Khedive's known succour of radical nationalists had emboldened the violent among them to take action against the British. For these reasons he believed that the best course politically was for the Khedive to abdicate, thereby leaving the door open for the installation of his much more trustworthy and cooperative uncle, Hussein Kamel. Cromer, meanwhile, while continuing to despise the Khedive, counselled Kitchener against the active 'deposition' of Abbas in order to preclude the possibility of a level of 'public sympathy' that would make of him a political martyr.[28]

Reluctantly, Kitchener took Cromer's sage advice to heart. So in place of taking executive action to depose the Khedive, Kitchener instead began to restrict his privileges in what amounted to serial humiliation. On one hand, banning the Khedive from attendance at meetings of the Council of Ministers without the permission of the British Agent, was indeed humiliating and perhaps unjustifiable. On the other, Kitchener putting a stop to the routine corruption engaged in by the Khedive and his circle of advisers in the handling of contributions to Muslim charities, by establishing a new and accountable ministry, was a reforming act of good governance. Naturally, neither the Khedive nor his henchmen agreed, but Kitchener was unmoved. Indeed, what was really at stake in these moves by the British Agent – beyond the reduction in status of someone he believed to be a pseudo-potentate – was someone he hoped would be a steady progression towards the foundation of a new British Imperial viceroyalty of Egypt and Sudan. If created, Kitchener argued, it would end both the pretense of Ottoman overrule altogether, and the privileged position of the various European investor states.

On both fronts, however, the prospect of a new British colony along the lines of India was virtually impossible to envisage, much less undertake. The unaligned historical parallels were obvious, but more to the point was the heightened symbolism of a Western power potentially usurping wholly the position of an Islamic one in an age that had begun to witness sustained *jihad* for the first time since Islam's foundational era in the seventh and eight centuries AD. Moreover, the intractable problem of the foreign 'capitulations' – the web of financial and tax privileges in Egypt accorded to invested Europeans and the states they represented – appeared to most observers with any knowledge of the complexities of Egpytian governance at least as far back as the 1870s to be an impossible knot to unravel. Cromer, for one, whose knowledge of Egypt's labyrinthine financial system was probably unequalled by anyone else, strongly advised Kitchener to drop any plan that he might be fomenting to have Egypt annexed.[29] Accordingly, Kitchener did so, but not without resistance and not before pleading his case to others, especially to Grey at the Foreign Office.

Altogether when it came to Egypt's place in the Empire, as well as to its local politics, Kitchener displayed a closely reasoned conservatism, one that was not out of step with wider informed British opinion on Egypt. Wilfred Scawen Blunt's provocative views notwithstanding, most government and journalistic voices agreed with Kitchener that radical nationalism must be restrained in Egypt, and therefore a policy of constitutional gradualism was the right way forward for the country. The Khedive was entirely untrustworthy in this regard, they believed, and so replacing him would be a worthy example of an acceptable practice – what a later age would call 'regime change' – and demonstrative to nationalist sympathizers that the British Lion as represented by Kitchener intended to carry on administering the country in the established pattern. Accordingly, attempting to blunt nationalist agitation was at the very heart of the early twentieth-century British project in Egypt, as it was just then in India also, as was seen in the previous chapter. 'I deprecate any very large expansion of what is called in Egypt primary education', advised Cromer to this end in a letter to Kitchener in the summer of 1913, 'which merely turns out a number of discontented youths of the babu description .... All this class go to swell the ranks of the discontented'.[30] There was no stronger epithet against colonial nationalism anywhere than the derogatory 'babu' of (in)famous Indian usage. And of course, such a reference resonated greatly with Kitchener given his understanding of nationalist agitation as he had seen it expressed some years earlier in India, especially in Bengal.

By 1914, Kitchener had achieved substantial economic and political reform in Egypt. He was well into his third year as British Agent and Consul General, with the anticipation of more to follow. The alluring prospect of the Indian viceroyalty remained aspirational, if likely unrealizable, in what was assumed would be the change-over year of 1915, but Kitchener was well-contented to continue in Egypt until his impending retirement. (In the end, with the outbreak of war, Hardinge remained in office as Viceroy of India until 1916.) But the tension of Kitchener's rocky relationship with the Khedive was wearing on him, and in the spring of the year he seemed almost to buckle – one of the few such times ever in his career – under the pressure of governing the restless country while at the same time holding at bay the imprecations of the perpetually dissatisfied Abbas Hilmi.[31] Indeed, one might have thought it a joint plan to escape one another when they both left the country that summer at almost the same time, Kitchener for his usual summer leave at home in England, and the Khedive to journey to a number of European capitals in what for him over the years had become a kind of annual Egyptian royal progress in an attempt to reinforce his kingly status. Naturally, one of the European capitals he was supposed to visit that summer was London, which for Kitchener of course was the very last place he wanted the Khedive to go. Kitchener got to London first, however, and insisted that the Khedive should not be received by King George. Ever-compliant when it came to a request from Kitchener, the King agreed and the Khedive was duly informed that should he indeed come to London that summer he would not be granted a royal audience. Insulted, the Khedive duly took the hint and stayed away.

Little did either Kitchener or the Khedive know in leaving Egypt during June of 1914 that neither one of them would ever again return to it. Abbas Hilmi's summertime European peregrinations eventually brought him to Constantinople, there to await events, the most portentous of which for him personally was the declaration in November of a state of war existing between Britain and the Ottomans, which in turn led Britain to declare a protectorate over Egypt. Establishing a British protectorate meant the effective deposition of the Khedive, the exigencies of war having done what Kitchener could not achieve himself. Naturally enraged by this development, the Khedive issued a virulently anti-British proclamation in which he claimed that 'the decisive hour for its [Egypt's] liberation has now arrived'.[32] In response, the Asquith government then formally deposed him. The now former Khedive – he refused to acknowledge his diminished status and did not formally abdicate until years later in 1931 – would go on to live in rather ignominious European exile for the rest of his life, dying in Geneva in 1944.

As for Kitchener, like most everyone else in England, the summer of 1914 brought increased anticipation of war with each passing day, especially during the 37 days that separated the assassination of the Austrian Archduke Franz Ferdinand on 28 June with the lapse of the British ultimatum given to Germany to withdraw from Belgium on 4 August. As of a few weeks earlier, Kitchener had been elevated to the rank of earl when the King had seen fit to create him Earl Kitchener of

Khartoum, and of Broome. Good wishes over this latest honour poured in: 'I was so pleased to see your name in the Gazette', wrote Sir Spencer Harcourt Butler, longtime Indian Civil Servant and future Governor of Burma, 'and congratulate you on the Earldom'.[33] In Kitchener's long string of royal honours the creation of an earldom marked the pinnacle. And upon reaching England on 23 June from Egypt he went straight to his country estate of Broome Park, as if to confirm in his own mind the intersection of his new title with the broad and well-treed acres – Lady Ilchester had recently added to its greenery by sending 'a lovely lot of trees' – that (at least symbolically) supported it.[34] The anticipation of war did not necessarily dampen Kitchener's spirits, however. Staying at Broome and, when in London, at Pendali Ralli's, he engaged in the usual social round. His expectation was to go back to Egypt at the beginning of August and once there to continue along the reforming path that he had begun to follow three years earlier. A long holiday, an unsurpassed royal honour, and the timely comeuppance given the Khedive, had all combined to refresh his spirits for a return to Cairo, even if the candle still burned unrequitedly for India. And so on 3 August after a rejuvenating six-weeks in England he departed Broome for Dover, just ten miles away, from which he planned to proceed to Calais and then on to Paris, Marseilles and across the Mediterranean to Alexandria. But as he waited impatiently in his cabin for the delayed steamer to cross the Channel on the first leg of the journey back to Egypt, a telephone message from the Prime Minister was brought to him by the ship's captain: Would he return immediately to London? War with Germany, as Kitchener was about to find out, was just hours away and his presence there was urgently required. At just before 1:00 p.m., therefore, he quickly disembarked from the ship and departed for the capital. 'Kitchener's War' was at hand.

9

Supreme British Warlord, 1914–16

The protracted lead-up to the outbreak of the Great, or as it would be called later, World War I, is easily one of modern history's more fully-researched and debated subjects. As I write this book, during the early stages of the marking of the centenary of the war, I have on the shelves of my library a number of such studies; many more could be added. The most recent of them, such as those by Margaret MacMillan and Christopher Clark, have once again told the general story well and hence it needs no re-telling here.[1] Suffice to say that the various interpretations of why the war came to pass, in what was an uncommonly warm and beautiful English summer of 1914, made little difference to Kitchener as he sped north by rail from Dover to London on the afternoon of Monday, 3 August 1914. Upon arrival at Pendali Ralli's always welcoming Belgravia residence, he was greeted by a waiting message from Prime Minister Asquith that was both apologetic and prospective in tone: 'I am very sorry to interrupt your journey today, and I fear caused you inconvenience ...', he wrote, 'but I was anxious that you should not get beyond the reach of personal consultation and assistance'.[2] After reading the note Kitchener spent an agitated 24 hours awaiting Asquith's expected telephone call and what was now assumed to be its likely outcome: an offer to sit in the Cabinet as Secretary of State for War.

In the last frantic days before Britain went to war against Germany at 11:00 p.m. London time on 4 August, Asquith agonized over who should be offered the vital post of War Secretary. The Prime Minister himself had been shouldering the responsibility for over a year, but 'I can't go on with this heavy work', as he told his wife Margot, and was anxious to relieve himself of the burden, most especially now with the outbreak of war imminent.[3] In addition to Kitchener, the most likely possibilities for the post were Viscount Haldane, who had held it formerly from 1905 to 1912, before becoming Lord Chancellor, a position in which he still served; and his successor at the War Office, J.E.B. (Jack) Seely, who had been forced to resign in March over the Curragh Incident in Ireland, thus necessitating Asquith's fairly recent assumption of the job.[4]

Beginning to settle on Kitchener as the right choice in the last hours before war was declared, Asquith had called him in for an interview at No. 10 Downing Street. The meeting took place without benefit of minutes so there is no record of precisely what was said during it, but Margot Asquith's diary entry based on a conversation held with her husband shortly afterwards records Kitchener as not wanting the appointment '*at all*' (her italics). 'I wondered', she continues, 'in my heart of hearts whether 'K' was waiting to be pressed'.[5] She may have been right. Indeed, in the middle of Asquith's ongoing deliberations Kitchener wrote him to ask 'if there is any objection now to my making arrangements to leave for Egypt on the P & O next Friday'.[6] Disingenuous? Perhaps. In any event, by the morning of Wednesday, 5 August, with the war less than 12 hours old, Asquith made up his mind, summoned Kitchener to Downing Street to formally offer him the position – which was accepted in a dutiful spirit – informed the King of his decision, and plunged the country into war under Kitchener's direction. News of Kitchener's appointment broke upon an expectant country – much of the press was pushing for him – almost immediately and the public's reception of him as supreme British warlord was rapturous.[7] The man himself, however, remained somewhat circumspect about the coming task: 'May God preserve me from the politicians', he commented wryly to his old Sudan and South Africa comrade Sir Percy Girouard, the next day.[8]

Kitchener, indeed, was a reluctant office-holder as the newly-named Secretary of War. Hardly the military autocrat in the offing as Curzon once thought him to be, Kitchener had received the agreement of the Prime Minister that once the war was over he would be able to return to

Egypt as British Agent and Consul General. No one could and no one did question his ability as a career practitioner of arms, and his public reputation was that of the first military man of the Empire, a genuine martial hero who stood above the vicissitudes and petty jealousies of politics and would see the British through to victory just as he had already done in Sudan and South Africa. But his experience of Cabinet government was non-existent, he disliked the leaden bureaucracy of the War Office over which he would now have to preside, and he was not naturally verbally prolix nor a nimble debater and disliked the necessity of having to explain, as opposed to issue, an order. All of these features of his make-up were entirely understandable given his almost half-century of military service and command, and therefore later when some (within the Cabinet especially) chose to see these deficiencies as debilitating defects they had only themselves (or perhaps Asquith) to blame.

Kitchener's introduction to his new politician colleagues, came late on the morning of 5 August when a hastily called and unofficial Council of War met around the Cabinet table at Downing Street. The newspapers, hitherto filled with the reportage of domestic strife – Emmeline Pankhurst and the Suffragettes' campaign for the vote, for example, had been the bane of Asquith's recent existence with their hunger strikes and poisoning of golf greens, so well-dramatized later by Ford Madox Ford in his novel of the time, *Parade's End* – now were taken up with war news; that is to say, what was the government doing to execute the war now that it come upon the country? In addition to the Prime Minister, the main participants sitting around the table that portentous morning were the long-time Foreign Secretary, Sir Edward Grey; Winston Churchill as First Lord of the Admiralty; Field Marshal Sir John French, recently named Commander in Chief of the British Expeditionary Force (BEF); and General Sir Douglas Haig, then in command at Aldershot; brought into this intimate high-level military circle too was the almost-82-year-old Lord Roberts, the grand old man of British arms, but still spry, acute and beloved by his colleagues, as well as by the general public.

Most of the Council's members were old friends and battlefield comrades of one sort of another. Generals French and Haig, of course, had been with Kitchener in South Africa, for example; Churchill had been, too, but in a different way, needless to say. But the new perilous circumstances in which they found themselves on the eve of a general

European conflagration meant that the meeting was tense with war-worry, the first of many to come. His earlier meeting with Asquith not long over, Kitchener had yet to receive the seals of office, but for all intents and purposes he was acknowledged as the Secretary of War, and accordingly he took a leading position in the two-hour-long meeting. General Cabinet agreement was achieved immediately over the alacrity with which the BEF should be sent to the Continent, but not, however, as to where it should be deployed once having arrived. Here, Kitchener disagreed sharply with French (in a foretaste of things to come) in rejecting the latter's stated position that British troops should be dispatched to Maubeuge, located five miles from the Franco-Belgian border and fortified since the end of France's disastrous war with Prussia in 1870 during which, it will be recalled, Kitchener had had his first tentative encounter with the realities of war. Now, in the summer of 1914, Kitchener thought (rightly) that German strategy would include wheeling through Belgium, which in the event of British troops congregating in Maubeuge would leave them subject to encirclement. Instead, Kitchener suggested Amiens as the optimal destination for the first wave of British troops, which was located about 70 miles southeast of Maubeuge and therefore in little danger of first-wave German investment. For the moment, Kitchener's persuasive view prevailed, but the question remained open nonetheless because of the weight of the pre-existing Anglo-French Continental war plan that hinged on Maubeuge.[9]

The other main topic of discussion on that sombre morning, and one which would carry over to the next afternoon's Council meeting, was the expected duration of the war. In the years that followed World War I's ending in 1918 it became (and remains today) a popular belief that the British generals of the day somewhat airily assumed that the war would be 'over by Christmas'. A short war was to be anticipated, they maintained, victory assured, casualties light, the *status quo ante bellum* restored, or at least a mutually agreeable alteration of the European map reached. While French held this view, indeed, as did the civilian members of the Council, Kitchener (along with Haig) was emphatic in stating that the war would be long – at least three years – and demand tens of thousands of soldiers – perhaps, staggeringly, as high as a million or more – to execute and win, if such a word could even be used for the mutual devastation that would be wrought by a modern, mechanized war.[10]

In stating his views Kitchener was typically blunt, did not elaborate on how they had been arrived at, nor did he engage in a prolonged debate about his conclusions. In short, he acted like the career military commander he was in the midst of a fast-breaking war. In so doing, he pushed hard against accepted opinion, and once informed of his Amiens idea an alarmed French High Command got involved immediately by sending a special delegation to London in order to speak directly to the new Secretary of War over what it assumed had been a set plan for British troops to join their French counterparts at Maubeuge. Over the course of an almost-three-hour-long meeting at the War Office on 12 August Kitchener parried their attempts to change his mind, but to no avail. Sir John French had come with them and he, too, found Kitchener impermeable to their combined reasoning. At a logjam over the issue, it was turned over to Asquith to decide, and quite naturally he took the safest course by agreeing with the delegation from France and with the BEF Commander in Chief that since Maubeuge had been the previously agreed point of Anglo-French troop coalescence it should remain so.[11] Kitchener thought it the wrong choice, however, which it would prove to be. But he was already so swamped with other work that he immediately had to leave the issue behind in order to focus on the bigger task at hand, which was that of raising the size of army he believed was required in order for Britain to have any hope whatsoever of waging a victorious war.

Famously, Kitchener's first day at the War Office, the seeming impregnable hulk of a building located between Whitehall and the Victoria Embankment, was marked by his comment, flung out in disgust over the comparative smallness of the British force immediately at his disposal: 'There is no Army!'[12] To help himself acclimate quickly to the War Office he brought along Herbert Creedy as his Principal Private Secretary, and Ronald Storrs in the subordinate job of Personal Private Secretary. Storrs, however, was ordered back to Cairo a couple of days later and was replaced by Sir George Arthur, known and liked by Kitchener as a society favourite and, as it would turn out, his future official biographer. Immediately, they began to plan for the raising of thousands of fresh recruits to replace those who had begun to embark for France on 9 August. Kitchener's belief in the necessity of a rapid expansion of the British Army, stated clearly in the first meeting of the War Council, was repeated again and became a kind of War Office

mantra from the moment he occupied his new office. At the beginning of
the war, the Regular Army consisted of about 230,000 men. But only
around half of them were stationed in Britain; the other half were posted
abroad, mainly in India. Divided into six infantry divisions, these home-
based soldiers comprised the core of the BEF, the kernel from which a
massive, million-man British Army – the largest volunteer force in
history to that date – would swiftly emerge. But in the early days of
August 1914, such a 70-division juggernaut existed only in prospect.
For Kitchener, the main task at hand was how to achieve its realization.

Various options in this regard presented themselves to him for
consideration. There was the Territorial Army, which numbered some
270,000 men. But it was tasked with home defence only, and its men
were trained at a much inferior level than were the regular troops.
Kitchener himself certainly believed them to be far from ideal for what a
comprehensive Continental war demanded. For this reason he insisted
that one of the standing Army divisions be kept behind for training
purposes, which, for the time being, meant that even fewer British
troops were available who could be put into the field. But off went
'Tommy Atkins' anyway, four infantry divisions and one of cavalry on 9
August, 90,000 men in their itchy woolen uniforms, puttees wrapped
around their calves, Short Magazine Lee Enfield rifles at the ready, and
folded into their Pay Book Kitchener's own words enjoining them to
perform their dutiful service with a high moral purpose.[13] Courage,
energy, discipline, and patience would be required, he reminded them;
indeed, 'individual conduct' was paramount. Be 'courteous, considerate
and kind', and 'always look upon looting as a disgraceful act'. Since they
were going to France, after all, Kitchener added a fillip that spoke
exactly of its time, as well as his personally held view of Christian
chivalry: 'wine and women' as always would be temptations, but be
careful to treat 'all women with perfect courtesy' and above all 'avoid any
intimacy'. He concluded his message by commanding them to: 'Do your
duty bravely. Fear God. Honour the King'.[14] And with that, four-plus
years of as yet unimaginably brutal warfare commenced.

As Kitchener quickly settled into both the job at hand and into the
physical surroundings of the War Office, he decided to leave his guest
living quarters at Pendali Ralli's and take up the offer to reside –
temporarily at least – at No. 2 Carlton Gardens. Located overlooking
the Mall and St James's Park, with Gentlemen's Clubland and Piccadilly

nearby also, Carlton Gardens was a short, calming walk away from the War Office. The townhouse belonged to Lady Wantage who had made the offer, initially for six-months. Kitchener came to so enjoy living there with his immediate staff that he was sorry when Lady Wantage decided to take back the lease after the allotted half-year, necessitating a move elsewhere. While living there his immediate neighbor, ironically, was Lord Curzon who lived directly east in No. 1 Carlton House Terrace. And, as shall be seen in another twist later in the war, circumstances would bring the two men back together as Cabinet colleagues, which restored to them at least some measure of the harmony lost completely in their dispute of ten years earlier.

In these early August days of the conflict Kitchener effected a whirlwind of activity at the War Office, becoming a kind of Minister of Everything.[15] He was determined to expand the army's numbers as quickly as possible, and at his bidding the government acted accordingly by immediately authorizing the expansion of the army to 500,000 men. As his working style was clearly that of the career commander, right away some around him were put off by his characteristic brusqueness. But he remained nonplussed by that all the same, whether at the Cabinet table or in the warren of rooms that comprised the War Office. If today much is made in corporate and institutional circles of the virtues of the 'consensual' leader, Kitchener's expressed habit of authority was its antithesis. Critics both then and earlier had derided Kitchener's on-the-job manner by nicknaming him 'K of Chaos', owing to his style of keeping most of his ideas and plans close to the vest and not offering much either by way of explanation or of invitation to discuss their scope.[16] A fair criticism, perhaps, but there is little doubt that without the presence of Kitchener's determined whip-hand at the War Office Britain's ability to wage war in its earliest days would have been even more hindered than it was already.

Despite his predilection to not spend much if any time explaining his reasoning for a chosen course of action in his messaging to Cabinet, Kitchener never varied from expressing himself with force. Infantrymen would win the war, he maintained, and therefore the Royal Navy, the long-accepted senior service, would almost assuredly be a sidelight during its execution. Neither of these two positions was much palatable to most of his Cabinet colleagues, but Kitchener insisted that such was the nature of this war, 'that we must be prepared to put millions of men in the field and maintain them for several years'.[17] Usually he was much more forthcoming with the Prime Minister about the range and scope of his ideas and plans, but around the Cabinet table with the 'politicians', and their wont to discuss and debate and prevaricate and compromise all in the name of collective decision making and Cabinet solidarity, Kitchener's only desire was first to inform, and then to adjourn.

By the end of his first month in office the initial recruiting effort had proved stunningly effective. In a new iteration of the eighteenth-century's practice of 'taking the King's shilling', some 300,000 men had jammed the recruiting offices, now a ubiquitous feature of the towns and cities of the realm. By November the number had reached 600,000.[18] Indeed, over the wildly popular first 16 months of the war, until Christmas 1915, almost 2.5-million men joined the British Army in a tidal wave of flag-waving 'patriotic eagerness' and prospective adventure.[19] 'Never such innocence', as Philip Larkin would write years later in his poem 'MCMXIV', an elegy for all those killed in the war, 'Never before or since ... Never such innocence again'.[20] Indeed, the War Office could not keep up with the 'unparalleled expansion' of the army and its demands, especially for rifles, boots, uniforms, and horses. If, for example, the peacetime requirement for boots was 245,000 pairs annually, the war, in a memo written for the Cabinet by Kitchener six months after it began, demanded ten-million such pairs.[21] Meanwhile, for at least the first year of the war, 5,000 horses per month were being sent to France in order to keep up with their steady wastage, which would reach the grisly total of 160,000 by the spring of 1915.[22] Indeed, an ongoing shortage of horses would force a small number of British regiments to use bicycles as substitutes.[23]

Key to telescoping the point that their country was in peril and therefore in great need of the people's armed service in its defence was the use by the War Office of recruiting posters. To this end, it has long been believed by scholar and layperson alike that the most important of these posters featuring Kitchener's image was based on a design by the graphic artist Alfred Leete for a popular London weekly magazine of the time, the *London Opinion*.[24] First published on 5 September, the design featured an illustration of Kitchener portrayed from the neck up, cap on head, eyes staring straight ahead, bushy moustache dominant and with gloved right hand pointing directly at the prospective recruit, while issuing the command that 'Your Country Needs YOU'. If the febrile male masses of England needed any additional encouragement to join up and 'do their bit' for the war, the poster put out subsequently by the War Office surely provided it. Or did it? Based on recent archival research it seems that the archetypal poster with Kitchener's caricatured visage, which later became singularly representative of the war and would have an enduring afterlife in the popular culture of Britain and beyond, in fact was never used by the War Office. Instead, a differently designed poster with some similarities to Leete's totemic illustration and displaying much more text was employed to spur recruiting efforts beginning in the autumn of 1914. 'Your King & Country Need You', it read, 'A Call to Arms – 100,000 Men'. This poster included the period of required service (three years), rates of pay (between one and ten shillings per day) and concluded with a banner across the bottom that read, 'God save the King'.[25] Alas, it would seem that Leete's famously caricatured Kitchener poster never played a role in World War I at all, but later was mistakenly catalogued by the Imperial War Museum along with some other wartime posters as having been central to the recruiting effort. Given its clean lines and direct messaging, the Leete poster probably should have been used by the War Office. But, according to James Taylor who has researched the question thoroughly, and from my own examination of the Kitchener Papers, it was not.[26]

The use of Leete's poster or no, the 'New' or 'Kitchener's Armies' exploded into being that first autumn of the war, growing from 21 August by 100,000-man tranches until eventually later in the war they reached their maximum size of some 5.7-million men.[27] Kitchener's settled position that the war would be long in duration and require soldiers on a scale never before seen in European armed conflict proved prophetic and stood in the face of the skepticism and sniping of both some members of the Cabinet, as well as others of the elite political classes. 'Lord K. has asked the country to give him a new army of 100,000 men', Margot Asquith diarized incredulously four days after Kitchener's appointment as Secretary of War, as if to emphasize the point that it was still believed by her and most others in or near the government that the puny six-division British Army (the 5th Division embarked on 23 August with the 6th shipping out on 8 September) would prevail by Christmas.[28] Her ignorance on this point, as well as that of others – such as the terminally dyspeptic Sir Henry Wilson, the BEF's Deputy Chief of Staff – who given their governmental responsibilities should have been much better informed than they were, now appears unbelievable in light of the fact that Germany had entered the war with 1.85-million men and 87 infantry divisions and of course, like everywhere else in Europe save Britain, employed a system of national compulsory military service.

Kitchener's insistence on expanding the size of the army as quickly as possible was based on a two-pronged strategy that in some ways was a natural reflection of his many years of overseas service in most of the main theatres of empire. In the first place, now that war with Germany had arrived – one which he had long thought inevitable – its most important outcome was to preserve Britain's status as a leading international power, complete with a world-girdling empire. A diminution of the country's international position could not be tolerated, he maintained, and the only way to ensure that such a development would not occur was to defeat Britain's only real enemy, Germany. Secondly, in order to do that, the country must be able to marshal its fighting men and resources in such a way as to maximize their impact when deployed at the right time. The right time, Kitchener believed, would not be reached until 1917; hence his three-year prediction for the length of the war and for subsequent victory won. What others mistook as 'chaos', or an inability to explain himself, or an exasperating reticence, as we shall see, were really none of these things per se, but rather they were reflective of his iron determination to achieve two clear goals from what was rapidly becoming a highly complicated, an uncommonly brutal, and a colossally costly war.

For Kitchener, the New Armies, called for by him on 7 August and as we have seen, inaugurated two weeks later, were the means by which both these two main war objectives could be achieved. In a sense, despite his conservative demeanor and stentorian reputation, Kitchener's approach to executing and winning the war was decidedly radical. His rejection of attempting to turn the Territorials into the basis of the New Armies was part of his general strategy of creating a wholly new kind of British force by which to win a modern, industrialized war. And based on the overwhelming response by his enthusiastic countrymen, he was right. So too in a different way, perhaps, was the hated Kaiser Wilhelm, whose status as Queen Victoria's eldest grandchild was now a highly unfortunate feature of the Anglo-German bilateral relationship. The Kaiser's description of his grandmother's fighting men as comprising a 'contemptible little army' was deeply insulting, to be sure, but at least in one way accurate.[29] The BEF indeed was tiny. Valiant, all in Britain naturally agreed, but undeniably small. Perhaps, therefore, given his expansive war strategy, Kitchener might have silently agreed with the Kaiser. After all, even the great Wellington had once called, in a not wholly dissimilar vein, the British Army he commanded the 'scum of the earth'.[30] But henceforth in building a new version of the army Kitchener was determined to swiftly change that view, and in time even the Kaiser would be forced to see the change too.

The burgeoning recruiting centres gave Kitchener his first tranche of would-be soldiers almost immediately and within a few weeks these fresh recruits were in training and under the purview of General Sir Archibald Hunter. Later called Kitchener's 'sword arm' by his biographer in reference to Hunter's status as second-in-command to the Sirdar in the Sudan campaign, in 1914 he was living in Scotland on half-pay while enduring a reluctant semi-retirement.[31] On 9 August Hunter had written to Kitchener in plaintive mode: 'I live in hopes of your giving me a command'.[32] Kitchener obliged, although not exactly in the way that Hunter might have imagined. He would not be going to the fast-developing front line, but rather to Aldershot Training Centre in order to whip the men of the New Armies into fighting shape.

And the fighting would come soon enough. With embarkation of the BEF ongoing since 9 August the entire force of 120,000 men was in France less than a month later. Indeed, on 22 August British soldiers had gotten their first taste of action when a squadron of Royal Irish Dragoons fired upon a group of German soldiers near Mons, just inside the Belgian border.[33] Battle was duly joined and in a foretaste of what was to come in this war that first day of fighting proved long and bloody, especially for the French who also saw action and in much greater numbers than did the British. By the following day the British had dug-in along the left flank of their more numerous French allies and were taking a solid artillery pounding from the attacking Germans. Indeed, over the course of that day the British barely held their stretch of the line. The job proved immediately to be a grim and losing one and already the price paid in blood was high: over 1,600 British casualties, including 330 killed. The Battle of Mons was a markedly inauspicious start to the war for the British, and just as Kitchener had feared when he argued strenuously that the BEF should be sent to Amiens rather than to the

Maubeuge region (which included Mons), potentially disastrous. Allied encirclement by the hard-charging Germans (the French were faltering, their fortress of Namur having succumbed to attack), now was a reality. Sir John French, in command of the British, saw no way out of the fast-breaking predicament other than to have his troops fall back, which they duly did, commencing late on the 23rd. By then he had sent Kitchener a telegram informing him of his decision to retreat southwards toward the French frontier, an operation that he indicated in a forbidding tone would itself be 'difficult'.[34]

In London, upon receipt of French's grim telegram, Kitchener exploded in anger at this (predicted) development, and later when speaking with the Prime Minister uncharacteristically 'had cursed and sworn' a blue streak over the folly of having sent the BEF directly into the path of the onrushing Germans at Mons.[35] A 'Black Day' all-around, as Margot Asquith recorded it, for what she still regarded as 'our fresh keen, wonderful force'.[36] Moreover, Kitchener, neither then nor later, had any faith in the French Army and their almost immediate collapse upon commencement of hostilities on the 22nd sealed his thinking on the question. Additionally, when shortly thereafter he was informed that they had also thrown 'untrained African troops' into the fray along the most vulnerable part of the line, his incredulity knew no bounds.[37] Churchill, for whom Kitchener had now developed much greater respect, shared his outrage and together they agonized over the next few hours over whether or not the BEF was about to suffer a humiliating rout at the very outset of the war. It did not come to that, of course, but the British retreat was extremely taxing as the Germans stayed in close pursuit, pushing the now-exhausted and overmatched Tommies further and further south. In the meantime, the much larger French force continued to fare no better and by the end of August the retreat had devolved into a kind of protracted death march, the late-summer heat and dust and the stench of hundreds of dead and dying horses adding to the miseries of the many wounded and psychologically shattered men. An equally beleaguered Sir John French could see no way out of the deplorable situation except to withdraw the BEF all the way to a position behind Paris and leave France to what was expected now to be its sad fate. 'It is, of course, always difficult to work with an ally,' wrote a defeated-in-spirit French to Kitchener on 25 August, 'and I am feeling this rather acutely'.[38]

Informed by Sir John of his impending 'retirement' from the front line and the implication that the Anglo-French battlefield alliance, the actualized military result of the 'Entente Cordiale' of 1904, would therefore sunder disastrously, Kitchener reacted with singular purpose. He may not have had a great deal of respect for abilities of the French soldiers or of their High Command, but he was enough of a diplomat and even a politician to understand that if the British pulled out now and indeed left France to its fate a great deal of international opprobrium would fall upon Britain's head, not to mention gravely imperiling the country by opening it up to the prospect of a cross-Channel German invasion. Equally alarmed were Asquith and the Cabinet. Accordingly, Sir John was told clearly not to do anything that would jeopardize Anglo-French cooperation. Naturally, the issue now became also one of dealing effectively with the French government as President Raymond Poincare had already begun to express great dismay at what appeared to be Britain's impending departure from the field.

On the evening of 31 August Sir John sent a long and revealing telegram to the War Office detailing the position of the BEF and what he thought constituted the right way forward. Upon having its alarming contents read to him over the phone while at home at Carlton Gardens, Kitchener resolved to go immediately to France and meet with Sir John face-to-face. The effect of his message, especially the part of it that read: 'I think you had better trust me to watch the situation, and act according to circumstances', was not the least bit reassuring to Kitchener.[39] Accordingly, he went directly to Downing Street for a midnight meeting with the Prime Minister and by 1:30 a.m. was readying himself to depart Charing Cross station for the Channel and a flying 24-hour visit to France. 'He is a real old sportsman', wrote Asquith admiringly of Kitchener to his (platonic) mistress, Venetia Stanley, 'when an emergency appears'.[40]

A short while later, on the afternoon of 1 September, Kitchener and Sir John duly met at the British Embassy in Paris. Kitchener had planned for a meeting of the two of them alone, but upon his arrival found that the embassy was rather crowded with various officials, including the French Minister of War, Alexandre Millerand. Finally, after some unfruitful general discussions, Kitchener and Sir John were able to steal away and meet privately. The result of this short, unrecorded session was that Sir John agreed to remain in the line and under the general instructions of Marshal Joseph Joffre, Chief of the French General Staff since 1911 and now commander of France's troops in the field. The alliance was preserved, Kitchener's task completed, and the still reeling Anglo-French troops given their unified head to fight another day.

A greatly relieved Kitchener was back home at Carlton Gardens by later that same day and once there was able to relax briefly and turn his attention to the much happier prospect of an invitation for him to become Rector of the University of Edinburgh, in succession to Arthur Balfour.[41] Assured by Balfour that 'there are no duties attached to the place except that of addressing the students at any period during your three years of office', Kitchener happily accepted Edinburgh's offer, although events would preclude his ever having to fulfill even the light requirement of making a single address.[42] As to the much more pressing matter of the conduct of the war, Kitchener's instinct had been right in going to France, although a petulant Sir John himself felt the visit demonstrated 'interference', as he complained immediately to Churchill.[43] Indeed, the Kitchener-Sir John French relationship would deteriorate steadily in the latter part of 1914 and by the New Year Kitchener was telling Asquith despairingly that indeed the Commander in Chief was 'not really a scientific soldier: a good and capable leader in the field; but without adequate equipment of expert knowledge for the huge task of commanding 450,000 men'.[44]

Meanwhile, on 5 September, the hitherto beaten-down Anglo-French forces began finally to push back with resistance and authority against the German onslaught with the commencement of the Battle of the Marne. Up until that point, the British had retreated some 150 miles in two weeks. Defeat and ignominy, as we have seen, seemed imminent, but fortuitously on the same evening that Kitchener had returned to London from his rapid visit to Paris, a valuable piece of intelligence concerning German troop movements had fallen into the laps of French High Command. The German First Army was not, as had been believed, heading south to Paris, but rather was beginning to angle slightly to the southeast toward the Marne river and the retreating BEF. For the men themselves the worst of the retreat now seemed finally to be over, and having survived the hellish first fortnight of the war they were intent on finally being able to take the fight to the Germans. 'The troops have quite recovered their spirits', wrote General Horace Smith-Dorrien positively, Kitchener's former Sudan and South Africa colleague whom he had appointed to lead the British Army Corps II and was proving himself to be the confident commander that Kitchener believed was lacking in French.[45] Crossing the Marne river on 3 September, the BEF blew up the bridges behind them in a last act of defiance. Two days later the Battle of the Marne began and with it would come a certain welcome vindication for the BEF, as well as the destruction of any hope the Germans had of keeping to their Schlieffen Plan timetable and its promise of an early and decisive victory in the war.

A tributary of the Seine that begins a little southeast of Paris, the Marne river flows east and then south in a long 320-mile arc all the way down to the Chaumont region located roughly in the middle of France. As a natural barrier against invasion from the east, the Marne was the last hope for the French in the Germans' rapid advance westward. For over 30 days they had moved steadily forward in fulfillment of the plan first enunciated by the former Chief of the German General Staff, Count Alfred von Schlieffen, back in 1905. Now the moment of truth had come for both countries. As World War I would make routine, the size of the opposing armies at the outset of the battle was staggering and on a scale never before seen in the history of human warfare. The Germans had massed an army of almost 1.3-million men while the French mustered about one-million, with the BEF topping up their number by some 120,000. In a cataclysm of modern battle they threw themselves at one another in what became a ferocious four-day encounter along a 125-mile front. The belching guns and rising smoke could be heard and seen easily by Parisians, who were less than 20 miles away from the raging fight. Soldiers from both sides advanced and then retreated, and then advanced again in a see-saw action that used the Marne river as a kind of watery fulcrum. At last on 9 September, and with General Ferdinand Foch of the French 9th Army leading the way – 'the honour and safety of France are in the balance. One more effort and you are sure to win' – the Germans were pushed back across the Marne. Paris was saved, western France secured, and the Germans left temporarily dumbfounded by this unexpected setback to their plans.[46]

Sir John, having been forced effectively by Kitchener to remain under Joffre's instructions, had led the BEF to take up a critical role in the middle of the fray, holding the gap against the Germans while the much larger French army fought hard on either side of it. Altogether, the first month of the war had cost the British almost 4,000 dead, many of the soldiers' bodies having been destroyed beyond recognition by the explosively disintegrating power of the modern weapons in use. The French alone suffered some 250,000 casualties at the Marne, including about 80,000 killed, while the Germans endured similar numbers. The sheer killing power of industrialized warfare had done its grim business, but after a stumbling start the Allies were now in harness. The adversaries were well-matched, after all, but as Sir John informed Kitchener mid-way through the battle: 'It will never do to oppose them [the Germans] with anything but very highly trained troops led by the best officers'.[47] As a description of exactly what Kitchener was attempting to achieve by the raising of the New Armies, Sir John's words could not have been improved upon. The Marne proved a singular defensive victory: 'They are routed', Kitchener insisted the triumphant War Office communique should read, 'in what I think will be the decisive battle of the War'. He was not wrong, although hyperbole is never a good thing in war, and in World War I especially 'decisive battle' became a rather debased term given the epic scale of a large number of the battles fought. Still, the Anglo-French forces had survived, and now had put paid (almost) to the main German plan for victory.

Exhausted but exhilarated, the defensive Battle of the Marne was duly celebrated by the British almost as an offensive victory, but there was much more fighting to come nonetheless in the days that followed. The Germans, scratching and clawing and desperate to avoid the total destruction of their vaunted Schlieffen Plan, re-engaged the Allies along the Aisne river, not far to the north and west of the Marne. For the balance of September, the resulting Battle of the Aisne evolved into the storied 'Race for the Sea', in which the opposing sides tried to outflank one another in a mad rush to the English Channel, centred on the fortified Belgian port city of Antwerp. Kitchener was absolutely firm in insisting that Antwerp must not fall to the frenzied German attack, and in concert with the French the city was reinforced with Allied divisional strength and a fresh influx of ammunition. 'Please give us any you can spare from your ships to us', wrote Kitchener to Churchill at the Admiralty at the end of August. After setting the desired figure at 'ten million rounds' Kitchener suggested sending over an officer 'to talk to your people about this'. Desperate for ammunition like everyone else

Churchill's marginalia, written in red marker at the bottom of Kitchener's letter, pointed out that such a request would reduce what he had at his disposal for the fleet to nothing: 'No! No! No! No!!! 10,000,000 rounds is all I have for the Fleet'. (In the end, 500,000 rounds were sent.)[48] Meanwhile, the embattled Belgians were fast running 'out of morale' too, wrote Asquith wearily to Venetia Stanley on the last day of September, but 'Kitchener has given them some good advice – namely not to mind the bombardment of their forts, but to entrench themselves with barbed wire etc. in the intervening spaces, and challenge the Germans to come on'.[49]

And 'come on' the Germans did, bombarding Antwerp with 17-inch shells spewed from the angry mouths of huge Howitzers.[50] After taking a pulverizing pounding for two days, on the morning of 10 October, a heartbroken King Albert finally surrendered his beleaguered nation to the German invaders, the first phase of the 'rape' of Belgium, as it would later be characterized, complete.[51] As for the BEF, the time spent by the Germans doing their worst at Antwerp had given it a small window of opportunity to move from the Marne and the Aisne to Flanders and the Channel ports. As First Lord of the Admiralty Churchill took the lead in this removal, the (rather far-fetched) spectre of a sea-borne invasion of Britain inspiring him to rush the Royal Navy into position.[52] In the event, throughout October and into November the front line – the 'Western Front' – began to congeal around the towns and villages whose names would come to be seared first into the minds of the soldiers who fought in them, and then into those of the public back home: Ypres, Passchendaele, Langemarck, Messines, Neuve Chapelle, and others. The complete formation of the Western Front was now in prospect, the war moving from its early weeks of frantic movement ineluctably towards a static battle of entrenchment. Sir John French informed Kitchener that the effort being expended by the Germans to try and dislodge the Allies from their series of hard-won positions in a bid to reach the Channel was their 'last card'.[53] If so, they played it with a grim determination uninhibited by the fact that in the Ypres salient alone it would cost them some 5,000 dead, a figure matched by an equally immovable BEF.

Loss of life on an unprecedented scale was the early defining feature of the war, and given the size of the military operations in France and Belgium the volume of ordnance required to give the BEF its sharp end was enormous. Everything pertaining to fielding a potentially vast army was necessary of course. Uniforms and boots topped the list, as we have seen, but so too was the ongoing and always pressing need for guns and ammunition. And very soon in September and October shortages of rifles, bullets, and shells became a recurring problem for Kitchener and one that would prove a protractedly knotty one to solve. 'The Chief is also very anxious to get out some mortars', wrote Lieutenant General William Robertson, Quartermaster General, to Major General Sir Stanley von Donop, Master General of the Ordnance, at the end of November, in a recurring form of communication between them.[54] The organizational and administrative pressures on Kitchener as Secretary of War in this period were unrelenting. Moreover, like thousands of his countrymen, emotional demands pressed in on him too as he had begun to lose friends and colleagues in battle, most notably his former close aides in India, Conk Marker, cut down by an exploding shell during the retreat from the Marne, and Hubert Hamilton, likewise killed a short time later at Ypres. Equally disheartening was the death (though not in battle) in mid-November of Lord Roberts. Thus far throughout the early months of the war he and Kitchener had been in close touch. 'The want of both officers and non-commissioned officers', he wrote to Kitchener from France on 17 September, 'has been evident to me at the camps I have visited'.[55] Shortly thereafter, this observation spurred Roberts to enjoin Kitchener to keep a group of Indian Army cavalry officers from following their orders and heading home: 'India is quiet, a few officers will not be any risk and we need them'. Kitchener agreed.[56]

Indeed, Roberts' special interest in Indian troops spurred him to make a visit to the line and on 13 November he encountered a group of them who had recently arrived at the Front near Messines. While there however he caught a chill, which his elderly body could not fight off, and a mere two days later he died of pneumonia.[57] Kitchener felt keenly the loss of his old colleague, addressing the House of Lords shortly after Roberts's death that 'I, more than most men, had occasion to learn and admire his qualities of head and heart . . . . To us soldiers, the record of his life will ever be a cherished possession'.[58]

For Kitchener, addressing the issue of supply shortages was thorny and never-ending and made more onerous because of the close involvement in it of both the War Council and the Cabinet. The first body's necessary interest in supply Kitchener could of course understand and (just about) abide; the second's constant querying about the issue, however, he had a growing distaste for, and he did little to disguise his ill-feeling in this regard. Kitchener worked relentlessly to increase as rapidly as possible munitions production, mobilizing national resources in an unprecedented way in the service of what was fast-becoming a 'total war'.[59] American and Canadian suppliers were tapped also, and every bit of ordnance they could produce was necessary in order to equip the million-man army that Kitchener had promised the French president and his High Command would be in France by 1 July 1915. Indeed, dependence on sources of supply from abroad would remain heavy throughout the war, epitomized by the creation of the Canadian-based Imperial Munitions Board in 1915, which was chaired by the prominent Toronto captain of industry, Joseph Flavelle.[60]

On 1 November, travelling across the Channel for the second time since the war began, Kitchener said 'non' to the query by French leaders that could not at least some of the newly recruited men be sent over sooner than July, even if they were still only half-trained? 'Before that date', he continued forcefully, 'do not count on anything'.[61] Kitchener was dogmatic on this point, in the same way that he had been staunch on a similar point in India; that is, he was loath to send under-trained and ill-equipped men into battle. He regarded doing so as being little short of morally repugnant, and certainly militarily irresponsible. His constant reprise at the outset of the war was that the lack of preparedness exhibited by the War Office and the government in general in the years leading up to 1914 had to be overcome in order for success to follow. 'Did they remember', he exploded in exasperation one evening in the privacy of Carlton Gardens, 'when they went headlong into a war like this that they were without an army, and without any preparation to equip one?'[62] The New Armies would go to France when they were ready to fight, and not a minute before, Kitchener insisted, although in the meantime in recognition of the pressing need for men he did relent partially by authorizing the sending of a small number of Territorial troops.

The Secretary of War's bulldoggish position in this regard naturally had an intensely negative impact on his high-ranking governmental colleagues. The members of both the War Council and the Cabinet found Kitchener's taciturn bearing to be little more than the demonstration of an assumed secretive nature that had no place at the ministerial table in a time of acute national crisis. While Kitchener had long been used to a degree of professional independence that none of his political colleagues had ever experienced, it is too simple, however, to ascribe to his guarded manner a mere predilection for running a 'one-man show', as has been sometimes suggested.[63] Most hard-pressed leaders in just about any walk of life when faced with great responsibility become 'one-man shows', at least for a time. Rather, for Kitchener, he recognized that for the most part trying endlessly to explain complicated military strategy and tactics, turgid supply orders, and detailed troop training and disposition plans were an unnecessary expenditure of time and energy, a further drag upon his already remarkably taxing working day. To those of his colleagues whom he believed had a right to detailed information – namely, of course, the Prime Minister – he was readily forthcoming. To others, principally, for example, David Lloyd George, Chancellor of the Exchequer, whom he felt could neither understand what he was saying nor be trusted to keep it *in camera*, he found incessant demands to be explanatory and detailed simply unjustifiable and intolerable.[64]

The autumn of 1914 presented Kitchener with a number of instances where his patience was exhausted by what he took to be the constant querying and pestering of some of his colleagues, especially that of the aforementioned Lloyd George. As far as Kitchener was concerned the future prime minister was verbose, needling, and maddeningly self-assured; indeed, the very embodiment of the career politician from whom he had hoped to be 'saved'. On top of that, Lloyd George was known to be politically indiscreet and therefore potentially compromising of Cabinet secrets, as well as an inveterate adulterer, which to a person of Kitchener's conservatively religious cast of mind, spoke of sexual immorality and weakness of character. His strong Welsh nationalism also rubbed Kitchener the wrong way. Altogether for the Secretary of War, Lloyd George was just about as objectionable a man as could be imagined for a close governmental colleague. They sparred and jousted regularly. Sometimes their disputes devolved into shouting matches, and on one occasion in late-October an exasperated Kitchener threatened to resign as a result. In the end, however, and remarkably, they always seemed to manage to find a way to patch up the worst tears in the fabric of their tense relationship. To Lloyd George, ultimately Kitchener was a 'Big Man'; and to the Secretary of War, while the 'little Welshman' might have been 'peppery', they were manifestly on the same side.[65] Such unity would be tested severely in 1915, as shall be seen. But in the meantime, as the war reached December it was clear that certainly it would not be over by Christmas. Indeed, in a remarkable show of fraternization that broke out along the by-now heavily entrenched front line near Ypres on 24 December, British and German troops engaged in their own brief unofficial truce by singing carols, playing football, and generally exchanging seasonal goodwill in what were the most bitterly ironic of circumstances imaginable.[66] Elsewhere in the forward lines, as Sir John French telegraphed Kitchener: 'There is nothing to report and Christmas Day passed quietly'.[67] Then, soon enough however, it was back to shooting one another.

Despite the best efforts of some opposing soldiers to celebrate the season, Christmas and the New Year 1915 brought no reason for celebration at the War Office, however, or indeed anywhere else in London. In light of the Race to the Sea and the serial entrenchment of the opposing lines that followed, the Western Front now had taken on a firm shape, snaking all the way from the North Sea coast, south through Belgium and northeastern France, to Alsace on the Swiss border. Altogether, the network of trenches – usually three tier deep – if laid end to end eventually would have stretched some 25,000 miles, a figure almost evenly divided between the opposing armies. The 'troglodyte world' created by the trenches has been well-described by historians, and the deprivations and horrors endured by the troops on both sides lodged in them throughout the war cannot be exaggerated.[68] The nature of the war in this regard as it developed in the autumn of 1914 in Belgium and France simply could not be reversed. 'The war we are engaged in,' as General Robertson described it to von Donop, 'is, in fact, one of a process of exhaustion and demoralization, far more than any previous war has been'.[69] But acceptance of this state of affairs was resisted fiercely. Indeed, Anglo-French High Command, far from being complicit in the growing hegemony of the stultifying trench, was desperate to somehow break out of its controlling maw: but entrenchment and the 'exhaustion and demoralization' that went along with it would prove too difficult a style of warfare to overcome. The great perplexity and ultimate tragedy of World War I on the Western Front especially was that through a combination of weaponry – particularly the machine gun – troop configuration, and topography, no one could release the trench's grip on the execution of the war. Attrition was nobody's choice, but it settled on both men and their commanders like a funeral pall that simply could not be removed. In this way, the wastage of French troops alone was reckoned to be approximately 150,000 per month by November.[70] 'I don't know what is to be done', Kitchener admitted wearily that autumn, 'this isn't war'.[71]

In this admission Kitchener was not alone, of course, and during the winter of 1915 both the War Council and Allied High Command grappled with possible courses of action that might restore movement to the war and with it a chance to break through the line and engender a victory. Indeed, the hope of 'breakout' was the leading aspiration of commanders and their political masters, ultimately becoming a kind of unachievable but constantly pursued 'holy grail' in the context of the war. And if punching a hole through the line in order to effect victory could not be achieved, then victory – or at least a modicum of movement – would have to be tried elsewhere. In the face of this great war of stultification along the Western Front it was hoped that a different kind of war could possibly be fought in other theatres, and it was this very thought that began to be expressed systematically during the latter days of 1914 and in the early ones of 1915.

Among those in the vanguard of such thinking on the War Council were Haldane, Churchill, and Lloyd George. On 28 December, for example, Haldane had sent a memo to Kitchener in which he wrote that the 'remarkable deadlock' on the Western Front 'invites consideration of the question whether some outlet can be found for the effective employment of the great forces of which we shall be able to dispose in a few months' time'[72] The anticipation of the New Armies' impact on the war can scarcely be understated, but in the meantime Haldane was quick to point out that in his view 'such deadlocks are not unique to the present war'. Instancing the Peninsular War and Wellington's creation of the 'lines of Torres Vedras' a little over 100 years before, Haldane suggested a number of ways to effect a breakthrough along the Western Front: 'heavy rollers' [a precursor of the tank]; 'bullet-proof shields or armour'; 'smoke balls' as a 'screen' for advancing troops; 'rockets with a rope and grapnel attached, which is used to haul in barbed wire'; 'spring catapults, or special pumping apparatus to throw oil or petrol into the enemy's trenches'. Indeed, Haldane was a veritable fount of ideas, and in their articulation is to be found a foretaste of some of the later technological developments in the war, as well as beyond. Lest his suggestions were thought to be 'fantastic and absurd', however, Haldane also counselled 'diversion elsewhere'.[73] And in this particular idea there was almost universal agreement amongst those on the Council.

At almost the same time that Haldane was making his views plain to Kitchener, Churchill was writing to Asquith, enjoining the Prime Minister to launch a seaborne landing on Germany's Baltic shores north of Berlin, a scheme developed initially by Admiral 'Jacky' Fisher, First Sea Lord. Better the Baltic, said Churchill, than to send more men 'to chew barbed wire in Flanders'[74] Similarly, on 1 January 1915, Lloyd George drafted a long memo for the Committee of Imperial Defence in which he chose to criticize Churchill and Fisher's German plan as being 'very hazardous', while substituting his own proposals for either an attack on Austria, which he believed would draw in Italy on the Allied side, or an attack on Ottoman Turkey. Either way, he encouraged pressing on to a 'decision without delay'.[75]

In these appeals for opening up fighting theatres elsewhere, the Turkish Dardanelles Campaign came clearly into view. From the very beginning, however, of all such non-Western Front considerations, Kitchener remained wary, and this was true of the Turkish proposal in particular. Of the various strategic ideas floated at this time the Dardanelles garnered the most support in the War Council and was loudly and consistently advocated by Churchill especially.[76] While Fisher continued to favour his own Baltic plan, his Admiralty colleague Churchill (ably supported by Lloyd George) believed strongly that a properly executed naval operation could force open the straits of the Dardanelles, the channel between the Aegean Sea and the Sea of Marmora, and the first part of the strategic waterway that links the Mediterranean with the Black Sea. As the choke point in this link the Dardanelles lay about 130 miles southwest of Constantinople. If successful in forcing their way through the Narrows, then the British could split Turkey in half, knocking it out of the war, and opening up a direct supply line to Russia, which would be a major assist to its imperiled position in the east. Altogether, the knock-on effect would lessen the pressure on the Western Front. In prospect, at least, the plan was imaginative and daring, and encouraged by a direct Russian request for help to relieve its southern flank, was debated excitedly in the War Council and Cabinet over the first two weeks of 1915.

On 15 January, after meeting almost daily, the Council accepted the Dardanelles plan, as moved by Churchill. Taking Constantinople would be its objective. The decision had come, however, after a clear cleavage had opened up in the Council between those who advocated a continued concentration on the Western Front as the surest road to victory since an enormous infusion of men into the line was soon expected courtesy of the New Armies, and those who believed that a strategic shift east must be taken in order to alter the hitherto stultifying nature of the war. In holding the former view no one was stauncher than Sir John French. 'There are no theatres, other than the ones in progress', he wrote determinedly to Kitchener, 'in which decisive results can be attained'.[77] Kitchener was inclined to agree, although, launching a naval attack on the Dardanelles would not change materially what could, and still should, be done in the West, he believed. Critically, at this point the Turkish operation was understood to be wholly naval, involving no soldiers. Therefore, Kitchener had agreed with it and strategizing for the initial bombardment of Turkish channel defences had duly commenced.

Hurried planning ensued, and barely a month later on 19 February the Royal Navy began its bombardment at the Dardanelles. By that time, however, an irreparably deep rift had been driven between Churchill and Fisher over the Expedition, one that would ultimately undermine the ability of the Asquith government to remain in office. But buoyed by the initial promising results of the operation as it continued through late- February and into mid-March, the War Council and the Cabinet believed the chances of success were high. During this period debate ensued among all the principal participants over whether or not soldiers were ultimately going to be a necessary part of the operation; and if so, which ones they would be, and where and when would they be sent once the naval bombardment had done its work. At the operation's outset, Kitchener remained of the view that troops need not be sent to the Dardanelles as the navy should be capable of forcing the Narrows without calling upon the army for assistance. As always, the number of troops available for use in France and Belgium, and therefore how many would be left for home defence, was uppermost in Kitchener's mind. Consequently, he was determined to see the Dardanelles plan succeed or fail as a solely naval operation. His reasoning was simple in that should the naval operation not succeed in its objectives, it could be called off readily without an immense investment of men and materiel. 'Much depends upon the Navy in forcing the Dardanelles', he wrote in an understated memo to the CID on 25 February, as 'we have not sufficient men at present to attack the Turkish troops on the Gallipoli Peninsula'.[78]

But during the closing days of February and then into March the pressure exerted by virtually the whole Cabinet on Kitchener to release a division for use in the Dardanelles became intense. Most of the intensity emanated from Churchill, as he was committed fully to the operation within Cabinet, while outside of it he was fast becoming the Dardanelles' public face. During these tense days Kitchener resisted every argument designed to change his mind on the question of deploying soldiers, while Asquith was in a real quandary over which way to exert his final support. As he noted in a letter to Venetia Stanley on 26 February, following another long meeting of the War Council: 'Winston was in some ways at his worst – having quite a presentable case. He was noisy, rhetorical, tactless & temperless – or full. K., I think on the whole rightly, insisted on keeping his 29th Division at home, free to either go to the Dardanelles or to France'.[79] Altogether, during the winter of 1915, Churchill's verbal clashes over the issue with Kitchener dominated Cabinet and Council meetings, with the unintended effect (for Churchill) of making him by 'far the most disliked man in my cabinet', as the Prime Minister frankly told his wife, Margot.[80]

By early March, Kitchener, clearly worn down by the persistence of Churchill's verbal dexterity and incorrigible histrionics, unleashed within Cabinet usually at the Secretary of War's expense, had begun to shift his thinking about dispatching a British division to the Dardanelles. Not an easy shift to make since, if acted upon, it would mean that there would be just one division remaining on home soil from the original army. But Kitchener did so in part because of the fresh availability of the 30,000 men of the Australian and New Zealand Army Corps (the Anzacs), recently arrived in theatre and training in Egypt. On 10 March, therefore, Kitchener made a final decision to send the British 29th Division to the Dardanelles, to be assisted by the Anzacs, and eight days later on 18 March the Royal Navy (together with its French counterpart) launched an attack in three lines in an attempt to force the Narrows. The results of the bombardment were mixed as two British and one French battleship were sunk by Turkish mines. Nevertheless, the day promised subsequent success had the naval plan been vigourously pursued. Certainly, the Turks themselves assumed that the partially damaged fleet would resume operations, for which they were manifestly unprepared. But, fatefully, it did not. The recently appointed (by Kitchener) commander of the Dardanelles Expeditionary Force, General Sir Ian Hamilton, having arrived *in situ* just one day earlier, decided that a follow-up to the day's less than impressive naval attack should wait until a combined amphibious operation was ready in order to offer a comprehensive engagement of the Turkish enemy. Churchill, for his part, was apoplectic about the delay; Asquith, always calm in disposition, thought it at least unwise, while Kitchener simply believed Hamilton when told that the fleet was not in a position to carry on the offensive immediately. What turned out to be a ponderous five-week delay, however, allowed the Turks – who as fighters were clearly underestimated by Kitchener, as well as by all the other members of British High Command – to move troops and guns into position in such numbers that by the time the combined operation entered the combat zone at the Gallipoli Peninsula beginning on 25 April their ability to resist had become fierce. And paying the initial price for that resolute fierceness fell largely to the Anzacs, who lost 900 men killed and 2,000 wounded in short order, while the rest were engulfed swiftly in trench warfare every bit as stultifying and immobile as that found on the Western Front.[81] In the immediate aftermath of being informed about the initial slaughter at Gallipoli, a vexed Kitchener brooded in the darkness of his new residence, York House, contained within St James's Palace, a short distance from No. 2 Carlton Gardens, which Lady Wantage now wished returned for her own use. Led along by the overly optimistic and hectoringly persistent Churchill, Kitchener had allowed himself to agree with the Dardanelles operation, which now had the look about it of an impending debacle. Indeed, it would be Kitchener's only serious error in judgement of the war.

If the Dardanelles disaster marked the first major setback of the war for the British since the retreat from Mons that defined its beginning, an issue of a different kind sprang forward at almost the same time and its impact hit Kitchener directly. One of the clear marks of fighting a modern, industrialized war was the exceedingly high demand for ammunition. From very early in the war's execution this demand had been felt by all the combatant armies, and shortages of shells, as we have seen, had been a recurring complaint by most commanders in the field. In attempting to explain why these shortages persisted, Hew Strachan makes the point that an unexpected but then routine over-reliance on high explosive shells and on shrapnel from the start of the war had put enormous pressure on factory production.[82] Heavy guns emerged quickly as the centerpiece of a new World War I battlefield doctrine, which was designed to pound stable trench lines in what we have seen had become a war of limited movement, or even stasis. As a result, the voracious use of shells – easily brought up to the front by an accommodating rail network – outstripped supply and an ongoing crisis over the issue ensued.

In March of 1915 this crisis burst upon the British public when complaints about shortages of shells began to be made in the press, which had the effect of severely politicizing what had hitherto been essentially an internal War Office issue. On the 10th of the month, the same day that Kitchener had decided to release the 29th Division for temporary service at the Dardanelles – a withering attack was launched by the British on the entrenched German position at Neuve Chapelle, a town located along the Western Front south of the River Lys in the Artois region. Commanded by Sir John French, the British 1st Army was led into action by General Sir Douglas Haig, and throwing it at Neuve Chappelle was the first major British offensive of the war. In planning the attack an element of surprise was retained by the British, which meant that a much-coveted breakthrough indeed was achieved on the first morning of the battle, although as usual at great human cost. In a pointed example of the war's new style of fighting, in excess of 500 heavy guns were used to devastating effect by the British over the course of the four-day battle. But the gains won on the first day were not followed up successfully on the next, and by 12 March the Germans were able to rally and launch a ferocious counter-attack which failed in its objectives but so embroiled the British that the next day they postponed the offensive, and then on the 15th called it off altogether.[83]

Some 11,000 British and Indian troops were either killed or wounded at Neuve Chapelle. In the process, the town had been captured and four lines of German trenches overrun, but to the north the important objective of the village of Aubers had not been taken. In the context of the stultifying style of warfare on the Western Front the gains were not inconsiderable: a salient 2,000 yards wide and 1,200 yards deep had been won, and the point proven that a sustained bombardment (especially if it came as a surprise) could punch through the line and bring about some degree of mobility and at least a small territorial advance with the promise of more to come. The British tactical success was incomplete, however, and even though the reasons for it were varied: telephone communications interruptions; Intelligence failures; delayed troop movements owing to the halting receipt of orders; the main message that emerged from Neuve Chapelle was that had there been a sufficient supply of shells a complete victory might have been won and a precedent set for successful operations in the future. Notwithstanding the fact that in the opening cacophonous barrage on the morning of 10 March the British had used more shellfire in just 35-minutes than had been used in the entire almost three-year long South African War – a clear example of Hew Strachan's view of 'over-reliance' – Sir John French insisted that had there been even more ordnance at his disposal over the course of the days that followed total success would have been his.

By the end of March Sir John had begun (secretly) to use various London newspapers to highlight his belief that British strategic and tactical plans were being hampered by the inability of the War Office to ensure enough shells for the army's use. Naturally, this criticism put Kitchener in the frame as Secretary of War as its main initial target, but beyond that lay the desire of the Fleet Street magnate Lord Northcliffe to engineer the removal of Asquith as Prime Minister, to be replaced by his personal favourite, Lloyd George. As proprietor of *The Times*, as well as the *Daily Mail* and the *Daily Mirror*, Northcliffe was the epitome of a self-styled tribune of the people, a view shared by Lloyd George, and used his newspapers as vehicles to foist his opinions on the British reading public in a manner still seen today, for example, in the form of Rupert Murdoch. On 27 March *The Times* gave an interview to French in which he made the call for more ammunition. This was followed shortly thereafter by Northcliffe publicly blaming Kitchener for the recent battlefield death of his nephew, Lucas King, in which he implied that a better supply of ammunition would have made a difference and therefore saved his life. A few weeks later, on 9 May, Kitchener's old journalistic scourge with whom however, as we saw earlier, he had more or less made-up over the Curzon controversy, Charles a Court Repington, telegraphed his employers at *The Times* informing them that the failure of the recent British offensive at Aubers was because of the lack of shells necessary to dislodge the Germans from their entrenched position on the ridge.

Hence, such shortages had acted as 'a fatal bar to our success'. In so doing Repington was merely acting as Sir John's cypher, but in the process exacerbating the damage already done to Kitchener's reputation. Less than a week later on 14 May the paper followed it up by running a blaring headline that read: 'Need for shells: British attacks checked: Limited supply the cause: A Lesson from France'.[84] Then came the coup de grace in Northcliffe's campaign, which headlined the front page of the *Daily Mail* on 21 May: 'The Shell Scandal: Lord Kitchener's Tragic Blunder'.[85] Altogether, the munitions 'crisis' had taken over the government's agenda and both Asquith and Kitchener scrambled madly to stay ahead of events.

Indeed, the early spring of 1915 brought with it an almost perfect storm of linked politico-military crises in Britain. For Kitchener, the attempt to blacken his name became the preamble to the call made by Lloyd George in particular (with Northcliffe as his public mouthpiece) for the government to strike a Munitions Committee with himself as chairman and Kitchener excluded from membership. But of a piece with the putative Munitions Committee was an attempt to undermine Asquith's leadership. Both of these pursuits pre-occupied Lloyd George and in order to stave off intra-Cabinet and -Party strife in the context of maintaining wartime unity, Asquith decided on 17 May to form a coalition government with the Conservatives, although choosing to retain most of the important portfolios for existing Liberal ministers. Kitchener's ongoing value was confirmed when Asquith kept him on as Secretary of War. On the other hand, Churchill's star, owing to the Dardanelles fiasco with which he was properly and inextricably linked, had waned and in conjunction with Jacky Fisher's resignation two days earlier, he was removed from the Admiralty to be replaced by Arthur Balfour. Lloyd George indeed was chosen to be the new Minister of Munitions, but to separate both person and function from Kitchener the War Office no longer would preside over munitions production. The long political play in all of these machinations would not of course come to pass until December of 1916, six months after Kitchener's death, when Lloyd George completed the campaign by forcing Asquith from high office in order to assume the mantle of Prime Minister himself, which he would hold until 1922.

Throughout this period of exceptionally fierce politics, Kitchener somehow had managed to retain his equanimity. Furious at Sir John French for what he rightly saw as his personal betrayal, he did not nonetheless wish to weaken the government further by demanding that Asquith relieve Sir John of his command. Churchill, ever mercurially unpredictable and now throwing his weight behind a surging Lloyd George, got his just reward by being sacked and then given the ignominiously minor Cabinet post of Chancellor of the Duchy of Lancaster. 'Winston was pretty bad, but he is impulsive and borne along on the flood of his too copious tongue', as the still-generous Asquith had recorded of a particularly fierce Cabinet fight over munitions during which Kitchener had started to walk towards the door in a gesture that suggested he was about to leave the room and resign.[86] At home, Margot Asquith's reaction to the relentless political drama was typically pointed. 'Winston is always gassing about a coalition Gov. – so disloyal to his PM', she wrote two weeks before it came to pass. 'Winston has no sort of political heart or 'sentiment".[87]

By the end of May and with the formation of the coalition government the acute political crisis of 1915 had passed. Kitchener himself had moved into calmer waters, while the nascent Ministry of Munitions was able to expand the labour pool under the auspices of the new Munitions Act – which he had helped to draft – by making it illegal for munitions workers to resign without their employer's consent.[88] An enormous munitions factory was built at Gretna in Scotland beginning in November 1915 which soon was producing 800 tons of cordite per week, the smokeless propellant used in explosive shells. That the country needed a greater supply of munitions to effectively fight and potentially win the war was never in doubt. But to have blamed Kitchener for shortages in the first eight months of the war was an exercise in blame-shifting and the worst kind of Machiavellian politics. After all, when Kitchener handed munitions over to the new ministry in May he was in charge of an industry that since August of 1914 had increased British munitions production to the point that what had previously taken an entire year to produce was then being supplied in a mere three days.[89]

On 24 June 1915 Kitchener turned 65 years of age. For his era he had already outlived by a decade the average life expectancy of the British male. He remained lean and vigorous, with no diminution of his intellectual faculties and no chronic physical complaints apart from the leg which he had fractured long ago in India. At one time a few years earlier he had told his sister Millie that, 'I shall very probably go to Germany and have my leg broken again and reset. They say they can make a good job of it'.[90] But organizing a visit for this purpose never happened, so he remained slightly hobbled by the leg for the rest of his life. During that summer he made regular visits to Broome, still under renovation but approaching the point where full-time occupancy could be made. War Office issues continued to crowd in relentlessly. Recruiting remained a lively topic for debate, of course, especially when it included the possibility of compulsory service.[91] To this end, he examined British casualty figures constantly. 'Wastage' reports sent to Kitchener showed, for example, that 186,074 casualties had occurred during the first six months of the war, with 18,724 killed in action and a further 4,693 having died of wounds.[92] After close consideration of the figures he came to the conclusion that compulsory service – conscription – was almost certainly going to be necessary in order to maintain frontline strength. For the autumn of 1915 he put the required recruiting figure at 65,000 per month.[93] Since Kitchener now believed that Britain would have to put a force of at least 3-million men into the field, and volunteering was just beginning to dip – even the promise of joining a 'Pals battalion' comprised of friends and neighbours, alas, was losing its appeal – Cabinet discussions about compulsion began to take place in earnest that summer.[94]

Apart from building up morale both at home and at the Front – 'The Secretary of State for War ...', as a Special Routine Order informed British soldiers in July, 'wishes the troops to understand that ... their daily deeds are closely and earnestly watched, and very warmly appreciated, by all those in authority at home' – and the move to restructure munitions production, Kitchener also was obliged to give attention to the impact of the seminal Defence of the Realm Act (DORA).[95] Legislated during the first week of the war, it was subsequently amended a number of times over the course of the years that followed. As the Act's powers were sweeping, touching upon a variety of social and political features of British life, its impact on wartime society became pervasive. Press censorship was central to its provisions, of course, as too would become the buying and selling of alcohol. On this latter point the government's concern about factory productivity – tied closely as it was to meeting the demand for shells and ammunition at the front – meant that any impediment to a worker's ability to produce maximally for the war effort had to be addressed. Most of the other combatant countries were wrestling with the same sort of problem and, within the context of the munitions debate and the wider social movement of temperance, drunkenness and absenteeism were identified as key inhibitors to the ability of the British factory worker to put their best foot forward.

David Lloyd George, earnest and well-versed in the tee-totaling traditions of the Welsh dissenting chapel (although he did not adhere to them himself), had initiated public discussion about the issue of the (over-)consumption of alcohol's impact on factory production in January of 1915 when he addressed the Shipbuilding Employers' Federation in London, telling the assembled union members with characteristic hyperbole that Britain was 'fighting Germans, Austrians, and Drink, and as far as I can see the deadliest of these foes is Drink'.[96] In Russia, Tsar Nicholas II had outlawed the production and sale of vodka as soon as the war started, although as a piece of social policy doing so had proven to be a disaster as illegal stills became rampant and government tax revenue plummeted. Nonetheless, Lloyd George was determined to engender British government intervention on this score as he argued that drinking had 'seriously retarded' munitions supplies, as workers were 'throwing up their tools about the third day in every week to drink the rest of their time'.[97] Despite the typical Lloyd George rhetoric, once he had plumped for and then taken the 'pledge' himself against consuming alcohol for the duration of the war, he began to encourage other leading national figures to do likewise, and the movement gathered a great deal of momentum during the spring and summer of that year.

In April, on Easter Monday, King George himself took up the challenge and indeed pledged that the entire Royal household would remain dry until the war was over. Consequently, public pressure became intense for prominent figures in government to do likewise. As one of their number, Kitchener felt the hot breath of the moralizing Lloyd George on his back and, after hesitating briefly, took the pledge. Not many others did likewise, however. Haldane was one of those who pledged; Churchill was not, the thought of life without Pol Roger champagne, his favourite tipple, presumably being too much to bear. Asquith vacillated, but finally refused to take the pledge, which hurt him politically. In the main and unsurprisingly, Margot thought the whole pledging business amusing, especially when told by the Prime Minister that the pledge had caused Kitchener to become 'depressed'.

Indeed, 'neither the retreat at [the] beginning of War or Neuve Chapelle affected his spirits as badly as 3 days on lemonade', she jested.[98] To be sure, there's little doubt that Kitchener missed his regular glass of wine, but it was an absence made that much harder to accept when he learned that the crusading Lloyd George himself had been unable to live up to the pledge and had taken to imbibing occasionally.[99] In any event, the DORA was amended that same month to give the government close control over the liquor trade, and in May Lloyd George delivered his last budget as Chancellor of the Exchequer which contained substantial tax increases on the production, sale, and consumption of alcohol.[100] His spasm of temperance would have a long reach, however, with many of the main provisions – afternoon closing hours, for example – of the new Licensing Act of wartime passage remaining on the books in Britain until 1988.

During all the upheavals of the first half of 1915 Kitchener and Asquith had managed to maintain a good and forthright relationship. For both men equanimity in the face of crisis was always the goal, and in its pursuit they had been able to forge a mostly respectful, even cheerful, partnership in the challenging execution of the war. Indeed, Asquith's skillful handling of both his relationship with Kitchener, and of the war altogether during this period has been pointed out persuasively in a recent article by Roland Quinault.[101] His conclusion in this regard is that contrary to the way in which Asquith was later portrayed, during the years 1914 to 1916 he was not 'lethargic and 'disinterested', but instead was 'a successful and effective war premier'. As such, therefore, he was anything but an unfortunate predecessor of the dynamic Lloyd George. Certainly, Asquith knew exactly how to achieve the best results from Kitchener as Secretary of War, which included giving him proper public reward. Accordingly, in recognition of 'these many months of association in times of stress and trial', Asquith wrote to Kitchener at the end of May, he had with 'great pleasure' advised the King to make him a Knight in the Order of the Garter in the upcoming birthday honours.[102] Kitchener, naturally, was delighted since the honour, outside of royalty, is limited to just 24 living members at a time. As it turned out the Garter would be his last royal reward in a string that now numbered ten in total, and as a mark of appreciation for the enormous challenge he had shouldered of directing the country's war effort thus far, none other could have been higher.

Just a few days prior to this happy exchange, on 27 May, the Cabinet of the new coalition government had met for the first time. On the way to Downing Street for it Kitchener had called at Curzon's home, No. 1 Carlton House Terrace, very near his old abode and not far from his new one, and together the two former enemies had enjoyed an eirenic walk to the Prime Minister's residence. As a leading Conservative Curzon had been brought into the Cabinet by Asquith and given the post of Lord Privy Seal, a sinecure to be sure, but also a mark of respect for its holder. Meantime, the main Cabinet portfolios remained unchanged except for the forced departure of Churchill and his replacement at the Admiralty, by Arthur Balfour. As an issue of pressing importance for the Cabinet munitions had receded, only now to be replaced in earnest by the disposition of the New Armies in the field, as well as the concomitant probable need for conscription. Debate over conscription had now become lively and earnest and, as a first step in its incremental adoption, a National Registration bill was proposed and agreed to the Cabinet.

By this point in time both Asquith and Kitchener saw conscription as virtually inevitable given the nature of the war. To maintain the Western Front in the face of steady German attacks required an unrelenting infusion of men by the hundreds of thousands. They acknowledged the sad reality that the modern war machine had to be fed in order to carry out the strategic plan, but sadness and regret in this regard could not be allowed to change the government's course. And so as Cabinet allies they moved their colleagues – especially those such as Lloyd George, Curzon, and, for the time being, Churchill – along a path that would end with legislation to enact compulsory military service in Britain. The challenge for both Kitchener and Asquith in this regard was to control the process by which compulsion would be made government policy. As Margot made clear to Kitchener that summer, as far as she was concerned, 'I know *for a fact* what is happening. Northcliffe, George Curzon & co. are running this campaign for conscription to put you in a hole. You must show pluck and beat them. It is for *you* to say to the Prime Minister *when* you want conscription'.[103]

In June, Kitchener made plans to go over to France in order to meet once again with Allied High Command. Accordingly, on 6 July in Calais he huddled with Marshal Joffre and Sir John French. The two Allied commanders had agreed that a new offensive to commence that summer would make excellent use of the New Armies, just then starting to enter the line in high numbers. Kitchener resisted the plan, however, thinking that delaying their deployment until full strength could be reached was the wiser course of action. But Joffre in particular was insistent that it should happen immediately and for the following few weeks upon his return to London Kitchener ruminated over the best course of action to take. Late in August he met again with Joffre and Sir John. They implored him that an offensive should be attempted, bolstered by fresh British troops. He rejected their reasoning, but believed that without his endorsement of the plan the Anglo-French alliance faced potential rupture, unfortunately now a recurring feature of the war. On 20 August, therefore, Kitchener reported to the Cabinet that despite some misgivings as to its military utility he was of the opinion that an offensive along the western part of the Front Line should shortly be undertaken. Questions were raised immediately by some of his colleagues: 'the drawbacks and even dangers of the proposed operation were pointed out with great force by Mr Churchill and other members of the Cabinet', Asquith reported to the King, 'but after much consideration the Cabinet adopted Lord Kitchener's view and the necessary steps will be taken'.[104] Some five weeks later the offensive began. For the British the ensuing Battle of Loos, as the offensive was called, brought very little by way of territorial gains or mobility, as Kitchener had predicted. Meanwhile, for the French at nearby Champagne, the story was much the same. Similar too was the exceedingly high cost in soldiers lost during the offensive. The British suffered about 60,000 casualties, while the French staggered under the weight of almost 150,000.[105] Altogether, the offensive achieved next to nothing and merely put a rueful exclamation point beside the escalating human cost of the war while deepening the gathering crisis over the potential move to full conscription.

If the outcome at Loos was not bad enough, the Dardanelles-Gallipoli Expedition had been renewed unsuccessfully on 6 August with a second landing, this time at Suvla Bay. Kitchener was keen to try and overcome the failed naval bombardment of April and in a long memo written for the Committee of Imperial Defence sent on 28 May he had concluded that the right course of action now was 'to continue to push on and make such progress as is possible'.[106] Ultimately, this recommendation, along with Churchill's assessment from a visit to the region in July, was followed.[107] Under the continuing command of General Hamilton and of Lieutenant General William Birdwood ('Birdie' to Kitchener, another of his old India and South Africa comrades), the mostly Anzac force stormed the heights of Suvla Bay in an attempt to take the Sari Bair ridge and scatter its Turkish defenders. But once again a vigorous attempt by the Anzacs was beaten off by the equally-determined Turks at an extremely high cost. Over the two weeks that the offensive lasted Anzac and British casualties together reached some 20,000. Again, stalemate ensued and an ultimate decision to reinforce and continue the expedition now lay in wait. To Asquith, the futility of this latest attempt at Gallipoli to change the whole course of the war was a disappointment unequalled in the conflict's duration thus far.[108] To Kitchener, similarly disappointed, the 'Dardanelles incubus' now had become almost a lost cause, as he wrote to Asquith on 17 August, because 'to send such reinforcements as those asked for would be a very serious step to take at the present moment when an offensive in France is necessary to relieve pressure on Russia and keep the French Army and people steady'.[109]

As Kitchener's words quoted above would suggest, his map of World War I – to borrow from Bismarck's famous dictum on Germany's (nineteenth-century) interests in Africa – lay always in Europe. Kitchener remained a 'Westerner' throughout the war, in the sense that he believed success along the Western Front was paramount in ensuring Britain's safety and as such fulfilled one of his two key strategies for the war. But, as has been suggested elsewhere, vital to ensuring Britain's safety too was the place of Russia and the Eastern Front in the war. To Kitchener, therefore, whatever assistance could be accorded her both through provision of materiel and by success in the Dardanelles, meant a necessary widening of the war effort. Equally, routing the Ottoman Turks in the Middle East through a sponsored rising of the Arabs, and driving the Germans out of their recently acquired colonies in Africa as well, were all of a piece for Kitchener in safeguarding Britain's empire of rule, bound up as it was in the even broader international trading and balance of power interests that comprised Britain's prevailing 'world system'.[110]

This broader imperial and international strategy also contained of course the stellar contributions made by the Dominions and India, all of whom supplied manpower at very high levels proportionate to their population (India being the obvious exception in this particular calculus), and some of whom did likewise in terms of equipment, foodstuffs, and munitions. The enthusiasm that had greeted the outbreak of war back in August 1914 in Toronto, Sydney, Wellington, Cape Town, and Delhi was matched by the almost immediate raising, equipping, and sending of tens of thousands of soldiers. The 30,000 Anzac troops at Gallipoli, by British standards an unruly band at the beginning, but whose physique 'could not be improved upon', had become soldiers that 'understand now that an order is something more than a mild suggestion to be acted upon or not as they think proper', wrote Hamilton to Kitchener in March 1915, was a celebrated case in point.[111] But, so too the Canadians, who had begun to arrive in Britain in the autumn of 1914, where unsurprisingly there had been 'practically immune from the 'chilled feet' trouble' of the first winter at the Front. They had duly entered the line at Ypres in April 1915, in the face of the inaugural use of chlorine gas by the Germans, had acquitted themselves exceedingly well, in the report to Kitchener saying that they had 'held intact' while the 'Belgians and French fell back'.[112] Indeed, the Canadians had done much more than that; they had, in fact, overrun the Germans, which marked the first time a British colonial force had defeated a European one in conventional warfare.[113]

But the advent of the use of 'asphyxiating gas' by the Germans under General Erich von Falkenhayn on the Western Front in blatant contravention of the Hague Conventions of 1907 had changed the nature of the war significantly. In a memo written just after the devastating and terrifying Second Battle of Ypres – the gas cloud was reported to have risen to over 40 feet high – by Lord Dundonald, another veteran of Sudan and South Africa then serving as Chairman of the Admiralty Committee on Smoke Screens, suggested, 'if we are not to suffer grave disadvantages, we must give equal or more thought to the preparation of our plans for retaliation by the same effective means'.[114] Regretfully, and partially to ward off the possibility of a 'gas scandal' that would 'eclipse the munitions scandal', Kitchener agreed.[115] But, as he subsequently wrote to Sir John French, 'before ... we fall to the level of the degraded Germans I must submit the matter to the government'.[116] He did, approval was duly granted, and the British used chlorine gas for the first time against the Germans at the Battle of Loos in the following September. The grim calculus of death by poison gas had now been made mutual and by later that autumn War Office suppliers had shipped to France over a million respirators and almost 200,000 gas helmets.[117]

In the Middle East and Africa, much of the climactic military activity would take place after Kitchener's death in 1916. But throughout the first two years of the war he was kept steadily informed of British actions taken in each theatre and in the case of the Middle East especially his voice was a prominent one in setting and executing British policy.[118] German Southwest Africa (today's Namibia), German East Africa (modern Tanzania), and the Cameroons were all ultimately to fall under British control. But in 'German East' the serial success of Lieutenant Colonel Paul von Lettow Vorbeck kept the British on the defensive for the entire length of the war.[119] Indeed, recalling the hard-driving enemy in the South African War prompted Kitchener to opine to Balfour at the Admiralty in the summer of 1915, that 'I hope we shall have some Boers at work in East Africa before long but it requires careful handling'.[120] By the next year, after just such 'careful handling' ensued, Boer soldiers indeed had arrived, although they and others would not succeed in defeating Vorbeck. Indeed, he did not surrender until two weeks after the war in Europe had ended in November of 1918.

In the Middle East, on the other hand, and under the command of General Edmund Allenby, British military operations allied with the Arab rising succeeded in pushing out the Turks, symbolized by his capture of and triumphant entrance into Jerusalem in December 1917.[121] By that time, T.E. Lawrence's signal role in helping to inspire and lead the Arab Revolt had succeeded, only to be undercut later by the secret Sykes-Picot Note of early 1916, the outcome of which would effectively divide up the former Ottoman-controlled Middle East between Britain and France. As we shall see, Kitchener was privy to both the Note's planning and its drafting.

In early October 1915, in the aftermath of the failure of the Battle of Loos and another long butcher's bill of casualties, Kitchener was at a low ebb over the state of the war. Compounding the grim news from the Western Front was the fact that having stalled again, the Gallipoli Expedition now, as suggested earlier, required a decision as to its future. Moreover, conscription continued to vex as an issue that likewise would soon demand resolution. While ever 'the hero of the man in the street', as the Archbishop of Canterbury, Randall Davidson, had said of Kitchener in reference to his public standing, the War Council and Cabinet battles had taken their toll, both on Kitchener and on the man charged with the duty of somehow engendering executive consensus, Prime Minister

Asquith.[122] The Secretary of War still had powerful champions, none more so than the King himself who, while taking tea at Buckingham Palace on 6 October, had enjoined Kitchener to put any thoughts of resigning out of his mind because 'I had every confidence in him'.[123]

Kingly confidence was one thing; that of the Cabinet, however, was another. This commodity now was distinctly lacking among many of Kitchener's colleagues. The Secretary of War had taken a number of hits over the preceding few months, none harder than the Lloyd George-Northcliffe campaign to discredit him over munitions production, and together with the challenging news from all war fronts, Asquith was seeking to reinvigorate his Cabinet's execution of the war within its new coalition iteration. Kitchener was tired, yes, but despite Lloyd George's petulant demands that as long as he remained at the War Office nothing would work – exactly the kind of exaggerated claim that his long-suffering colleagues had come to expect from the 'Welsh Wizard' – the system nevertheless continued to work, but of course could stand to be improved. One such improvement that Asquith envisaged was a new, smaller War Council (the original had expanded into the 'Dardanelles Committee' with a 12-person membership). Initially, the Cabinet as a whole balked at this suggestion, but certain members of it who believed that they might potentially be part of a smaller group of chosen men pressed for its creation nonetheless. On 11 November therefore a new War Council was duly struck with a membership of just five ministers. Chaired by Asquith, it included Lloyd George and three others, none of whom was Kitchener (nor, unsurprisingly, Churchill, who took this pointed exclusion from it as an opportunity to resign from his lowly Cabinet post as Chancellor of the Duchy of Lancaster and go off to the Western Front near Ploegsteert, south of Ypres, in January 1916 for a bracing two-month stint as an infantry lieutenant colonel).

The Cabinet's deliberations in this regard had been undertaken while Kitchener was out of the country. Earlier, he had agreed with Asquith that he should travel to the Dardanelles and see firsthand the nature of the prevailing situation preparatory to making a final decision about the Gallipoli Expedition's future. Kitchener's absence – he departed London on 4 November – brought with it the whiff of an impending coup inasmuch as Lloyd George had written an 'odious' letter to Asquith just four days earlier, as Margot described it, 'threatening all kinds of things if K. remained' at the War Office.[124] Perhaps, as one of Asquith's biographers suggests, the Prime Minister himself 'was determined to get his hands on the War Office for at least a period'.[125] More likely, however, is that Asquith needed time to keep the hard-charging Lloyd George at bay in order to conjure a softer way of reducing Kitchener's control of the War Office, which, of course, had already been demonstrated by having hived off munitions from his purview and creating it as a new and separate ministry.

Kitchener was hardly in the dark about these machinations, and of course Asquith was well aware that another public crisis over the popular and heroic Secretary of War's status in Cabinet could well bring his government to its knees. Roy Jenkins suggests bluntly – in strong and dated language in reference to Kitchener's Irish birthplace – that he left for the Dardanelles 'taking with him, with a suspicious peasant's misplaced sense of cunning, his seals of office'.[126] The unfortunate prejudice of such a remark is obvious, but more to the point there is no evidence that a 'cunning' Kitchener packed his seals of office along for the trip. In any event, after passing through Paris Kitchener arrived in-theatre on 10 November and for the next week he was able to take a close look at the military situation at Gallipoli and what he believed should be the correct course of action to be taken there by the British in the immediate future. Upon embarking for the Dardanelles, Kitchener's view of Gallipoli had been that the campaign should continue to be waged, despite its miserable results thus far and the regrettable prospect of ongoing 'frightful loss', as he informed Balfour at the Admiralty.[127] Initially, on site, General Birdwood agreed nominally with Kitchener, telling him that 'I consider evacuation would be considered by Turks as complete victory'.[128] Birdwood's colleague, General Sir Charles Monro, however, having just succeeded the ever-loyal Hamilton as Commander in Chief, was firm in advising that evacuation indeed should be undertaken.[129] 'The Turks', he had pointed out to Kitchener in a letter of 2 November, just prior to the latter's leaving London, '[are] in very formidable entrenchments, with all the advantages of position and power of observation of our movements . . . . I am therefore of opinion that another attempt to carry the Turkish lines would not offer any hope of success. Hence I think loss of prestige caused by withdrawal would be compensated for in a few months by increased efficiency'.[130]

Kitchener's main rationale for maintaining the Anzac and British forces in position at the Dardanelles was that if they were withdrawn, it would, as he pointed out to Asquith, release 'the Turkish army now held up to act elsewhere'.[131] For Kitchener, however, loss of prestige was of no account. What really mattered to him was where, when, and how the freed-up Turks might assist the Germans. But the more he travelled throughout the region, especially his visit to Anzac Cove, site of some of the campaign's worst defeats, the more he could see that hanging on against the entrenched and strong Turkish resistance – which had proven itself impervious to what earlier had been at least the 'moral' value of the 'guns of the navy', as Hamilton had written – was futile.[132] 'Here, at present, Gallipoli looks a much tougher nut to crack than it did on the map in my office'. Though they were Hamilton's words to describe what he had seen upon first entering the forward zone in March, they might just as well have been Kitchener's in November.[133]

In light of what he was able to see while visiting Gallipoli, Kitchener made the final decision to evacuate. Given his initial reluctance to wage the campaign, it caused him little distress.[134] He wrote his report to this end for the Cabinet and telegraphed it to London on 22 November.[135] Kitchener's recommendation for a two-stage withdrawal: Suvla and Anzac, and then (eventually) Cape Helles, was debated on the 23rd by the War Council, endorsed, and then brought to Cabinet the next day. Some around the table, notably Curzon, objected to withdrawal, fearful of the ignominy that would accrue to Britain should it be seen to be fleeing (especially by Indians) from anywhere in the East. Nursing still, it would seem, his anger over having been bested by Kitchener in India, Curzon wrote a long and occasionally purple memo in defence of his position, that should Gallipoli be given up it would be followed by 'the crowding into the boats of thousands of half-crazy men, the swamping of craft, the nocturnal panic, the agony of the wounded, the hecatombs of the slain'.[136] One wonders at what must have been Curzon's great surprise that when evacuation duly came first in December, and then secondarily in January of 1916, not a single Anzac or British life was lost in the process.

Having arrived back in London on 30 November, the last month of the year brought with it for Kitchener a pair of substantial changes in the conduct of the war, one with which he agreed, and the other about which initially, at least, he was highly suspicious. The first was the decision taken by Asquith during Kitchener's almost month-long absence, to replace Sir John French as Commander in Chief of the BEF in

France with General Haig, Commander of the 1st Army. Margot, always a revealing source about her husband's political decisions, could not see the reason for the change, although to her it had nothing to do with professional competence. As she complained after entertaining Haig and his wife to lunch at Downing Street: he was 'handsome and Scotch' and 'a very fine soldier', but he was 'a remarkably stupid man to talk to'.[137] As usual the Prime Minister's settled views in a case of this sort were not swayed by the fluttering criticism of his wife and on 8 December Haig was formally offered command, taking over at British headquarters at St Omer ten days later. Sir John, who had remained stolidly unperturbed throughout the change, returned to Britain as Commander in Chief of the Home Forces. In some respects a long time in coming given his protracted inability to work well with French Marshals Foch and Joffre, not to mention Kitchener, relieving Sir John of command became inevitable after the disaster at Loos. (Contributing to it perhaps also was his complicity in the Lloyd-George and Northcliffe campaign to unseat Kitchener.) In any case, Kitchener took the change in command in stride, relieved that he would no longer have to deal with Sir John in the manner that had characterized the preceding 17 months.[138]

The second significant change that came at the end of 1915 had a more direct, but ultimately no less positive, impact on Kitchener than did Sir John's demotion. As part of Asquith's intention to exert greater control over the War Office he resurrected the old idea of establishing an Imperial General Staff with a chief of his own choosing. The Prime Minister had two possible candidates in mind for the job of chief. The first was Sir Henry Wilson, who, given their mutual animosity, would never have been agreed to by Kitchener. The other possible choice, Major General Sir William Robertson, however, was much more amenable and, arguably, able than the crusty Wilson. A decade younger than Kitchener, the two men knew one another from South Africa where Robertson had been deputy assistant adjutant general to Lord Roberts. Before that, Robertson had spent considerable time in India, including being present at the Siege of Malakand in 1897 along with Churchill, who, it may be recalled, made the siege the subject of his first book.[139] Most recently, Robertson had been serving as Sir John's Chief of Staff in France. He was a strong supporter of the Western Front school of thinking, going so far as to say that the Dardanelles campaign had been a sad and 'ridiculous farce'.[140] Most important, however, was the fact that Kitchener liked and respected Robertson and was willing to work with him in what quickly became a marked devolution of power and control away from the War Secretary and toward the new Chief of the Imperial General Staff.

Asquith's plan for Robertson's appointment was presented to Kitchener immediately upon his arrival back in London from Gallipoli. Initially and naturally, given the chronic disquiet in Cabinet epitomized by that 'little beast' Lloyd George, as Kitchener had called him to Margot, about his remaining as War Secretary, he was suspicious that Asquith's proposal was merely a sleight of hand to undercut his position and force him to resign.[141] Indeed, when first presented with the plan by Asquith, Kitchener promptly offered him his resignation on the spot. But having the heroic 'symbol of the nation's will to victory' out of office was never the Prime Minister's intention.[142] Rather, bringing in Robertson as CIGS was to Asquith the best means by which to inject fresh vigour and administrative expertise into the vast and complicated machinery that comprised the War Office, while at the same time retaining the prestige and inspiration that Kitchener as the nation's first soldier brought to the execution of the war. By this point Kitchener may not have been any longer the largely unalloyed hero of victorious Imperial wars, but he still represented winning, and that is what Asquith wished to emphasize in realigning command.

Explained to him in this way, Kitchener's agreement in principle was then won almost immediately. Indeed, Kitchener had Robertson to dine with him that same evening at York House where they began discussions about the proposed change, and then a short time later in Paris while staying at the Hotel de Crillon, negotiations, over the precise nature of the devolution of power away from the Secretary of War. These talks were cordial: 'I am not the K they think I am', said Kitchener at their outset and over the next ten days on both sides of the Channel the two men worked out their 'bargain'.[143] The centerpiece of their agreement – about which Asquith insisted – was that Robertson should have control over strategy, the content of which he alone would present to the Cabinet. Meanwhile, Kitchener would retain control over recruiting and supply. Mutual agreement was duly reached on 10 December and on the 23rd it was formalized, with Robertson assuming the position of CIGS. Both men were highly pleased, even relieved, that this unexpected but welcome partnership had come to pass.[144] 'For myself', Robertson later wrote, 'I never had occasion to give it another thought, and I shall always regret that the unfounded gossip [about Kitchener] ... caused me to misjudge him, even though temporarily'.[145] Thus for the weary and hitherto embattled Secretary of War a long and brutal year had come to an end on an optimistic note, with the festivities of Christmas 1915 at Broome adding a moment's levity to the unrelenting pressures of what had been the first full year of the conflict.

The New Year 1916 opened with Kitchener feeling considerable relief at having passed on much of the burden of guiding Britain's war effort to the obliging Robertson. They worked well together, which came as a surprise – even a disappointment – to some of Kitchener's old enemies in Cabinet who hoped that the appointment of the new CIGS would mark the effective removal of what they considered to be Kitchener's baleful influence on the conduct of the war.[146] He made another visit to France in February, spending time with Haig at his St Omer headquarters and mingling with the troops going up the line. Haig, as the new British Commander in Chief, was strategizing with his French counterparts about the prospect of an enormous summertime offensive taking place at the River Somme, located south of Arras. Kitchener, however, thought such an offensive was probably premature as he believed 1917 would be the war's critical year, both from the standpoint of the projected size by then of the New Armies, and from that of the relative weakening of the field strength of the Central powers.

Linked to Kitchener's initial reluctance to endorse an imminent big offensive in 1916 was his resistance to compulsory service in order to bolster British troop strength. On the issue of conscription he had always been a gradualist, whereas Robertson, conversely, had not. 'Don't try to hurry things so', was Kitchener's usual stance when discussing conscription with the CIGS[147] But in taking this position Kitchener was increasingly out of step with his colleagues, especially Robertson. Asquith had long resisted conscription too, but on 5 January he had relented and introduced a conscription bill in the House of Commons, which, as the National Service Act, would go fully into force in May. All able-bodied British males aged 18 to 41, thereafter, were liable for service in the armed forces.

Meanwhile, in early February, Kitchener attended a demonstration of the potential usefulness of the so-called 'tank' to alter the static nature of the Western Front when 'Big Willie' was put through its paces in the mud and barbed wire of a battlefield simulation at Hatfield Park in

Hertfordshire. Unlike a year earlier when a modified tractor had been unsuccessfully tested, the latest iteration of the tank by its Royal Engineer creator, Colonel Ernest Swinton, impressed everyone – especially its persistent sponsor, Churchill – and 100 of them were ordered. Tank training for the men in 'Heavy Section, Machine-Gun Corps' began soon thereafter.[148]

Both the prospective Somme offensive that Haig and his French counterparts were considering, and the possibility of British conscripts being called up, were put into even sharper relief on 21 February when unexpectedly the Germans unleashed a ferocious attack on the ancient French fortress city of Verdun. Initially, the assault on Verdun was intended by the Germans under their commander, von Falkenhayn, who was now well into the job having had replaced Helmuth von Moltke as Chief of the German General Staff after the Marne, 'to bleed the French white' in a prolonged battle of attrition. Accordingly, Fort Douaumont fell swiftly to the Germans four days later, a prelude to what fast developed into a battle not so much of attrition as of mutual slaughter. By 1 March the British Military Attaché in France, Colonel Henry Yarde-Buller, was reporting to Kitchener that 'Verdun has been evacuated since the early days of the fighting and has suffered considerably'.[149]

Meanwhile, General Philippe Petain, in command of the city, issued the order that 'They shall not pass', and the galvanized French threw themselves into ensuring that under no account would Verdun fall, which it did not.[150] Inspired in this way, into the breach were flung 1.1-million French troops, while the Germans offered up in excess of 1.2-million of their own. The battle would go on until December, by which time some 300,000 men from both sides had been killed. Altogether French casualties would number some 400,000 at Verdun, a devastatingly high figure to those shepherding the Anglo-French alliance, and one that provided clinching logic to the need for British conscription.

For Kitchener, meanwhile, the German attack at Verdun changed his calculation for the prospective Somme offensive. France's dire situation there made it clear that should the Somme offensive be undertaken it would have to be primarily a British enterprise since more and more French troops were being poured into saving Verdun and, perhaps, France altogether. If the Somme was going to have to become an essentially British operation, therefore Kitchener was less than keen.

The ongoing mutual annihilation at Verdun had only one potentially positive outcome for him, which was that it might so weaken the Germans that in response to their crippling a concerted, but limited-in-scope, British attack on them in its aftermath, might actually achieve a signal breakthrough and finally put paid to the most overused field report of World War I: 'The situation on our front remains unchanged'.[151] In this way, as a deliberate but measured attack, Kitchener came to agree with the planned Somme offensive, which of course he would not live to see. Had he lived there is no doubt that he would have been rightly appalled that Haig – who in March had written to him, blaming the failure of the French at Verdun on mere 'carelessness' – had decided to turn the Somme into a massive undertaking, the name of which became the supreme byword for the futile slaughter characteristic of the Western Front during World War I.[152] Indeed, for some, the 1st of July 1916, the day battle was joined, came to be 'understood as a holocaust moment'.[153]

Kitchener's February visit to France was followed in late March by his attendance at the Allied war conference in Paris. In addition to the Western Front, the other theatres of action were discussed, especially the crisis that had developed in Mesopotamia (today's Iraq) where the British garrison at Kut lay under siege by the Turks. Beginning in December 1915, the siege had intensified quickly. By the end of January 1916, Major General Charles Townshend's 6th (Poona) Division of the Indian Army was significantly understrength, trapped, and desperately short of supplies. Attempts at relief had failed in January and then did so again in March, and in April the new Royal Flying Corps would drop food and ammunition to the defenders of Kut, the first such aerial operation in history. All to no avail. After a rejected attempt at ransom undertaken by Kitchener by using the Arab Bureau's T.E. Lawrence as conduit – the British offered the Turks L2-million – the garrison surrendered on 29 April. Some scholars, such as Eugene Rogan, have criticized this attempt by Kitchener to purchase the liberation of the garrison with cash, commenting on its apparent crudity and assuming therefore that he held to the view 'of the inherent corruption of Turkish officialdom'.[154] But in criticizing Kitchener for what Rogan regards as a ham-fisted action that traded upon racial stereotype, he displays a somewhat patronizing attitude toward the Turks themselves. Were they not perfectly capable of negotiating their own deals in wartime? In Egypt and Sudan, as well as much earlier during his diplomatic stint in the Turkish town of Kastamonu, or even before that in Palestine, Kitchener had had ample opportunity to engage in (financial) negotiations with the Turks. Why not again? In offering to ransom the garrison in the midst of a tension-wracked wartime siege he did so as a studied last resort and therefore as a reasonable and conventional course of action given the desperate circumstances that prevailed at Kut.

During the war conference in Paris which Kitchener was attending, the last part of these events was underway. Since February the Indian Army's Iraq operations had come under War Office direction, which meant that Kitchener was closely involved in their execution. For the British, the Kut situation had become irredeemably bad, with 30,000 troops killed or wounded and 13,000 taken prisoner at the time of surrender – some of whom would end up later convalescing at the wartime 'Kitchener Indian Hospital' in Brighton.[155] In the aftermath of Kut's fall, which came as a shock to the British public, unused to defeats at the hands of non-European foes, Kitchener gave a speech in the House of Lords which reinforced Asquith's own comment that the British people 'were sore and depressed at a deplorable incident, though not one of serious military significance, like the surrender last week of the heroic garrison of Kut'.[156] Both men, in fact, underplayed Kut's ignominious symbolism, although they were right in stating that militarily it was not of the first importance. Indeed, within 11 months of Kut's surrender Baghdad would be taken by the British in a preliminary act in the ensuing reconstruction of Iraq to which much of the credit would go to Sir Percy Cox, Chief Political Officer to the governor, and posthumously in a celebrated though not uncontroversial way, to the British Oriental Secretary, Gertrude Bell.[157]

The Gallipoli Expedition and the Siege of Kut had worked to draw Kitchener ever more closely into wartime Middle Eastern affairs; one more event would complete a troika, that of the Sykes-Picot Note negotiated secretly in 1915–16 between the British and the French with Russian concurrence to divide up the region between themselves come the successful defeat of the Ottomans and the conclusion of the war. Today, the supposed ramifications of Sykes-Picot are bitterly contested by many as having sown the seeds of ongoing regional strife, even though the map of the contemporary Middle East bears almost no resemblance to what Sykes and Picot negotiated. Yet, the Sykes-Picot myth continues to offer a powerful motivation to the jihadists of the current Islamic State to re-draw what they argue is the deeply-flawed European- and Zionist-designed map of the Middle East. At the time of its negotiation, attempts by the Anglo-French alliance to configure prospective spheres of influence in the post-war Middle East were seen entirely as natural extensions of the longstanding Eastern Question in British affairs, one part of which was France's historic link with Egypt, as well as elsewhere in the region, originally stemming from Napoleon's invasion of 1798. In addition, strong pressure had been put on the British government by insistent Zionists such as Chaim Weizmann that it use the occasion of the war and the potential dismemberment of the Ottoman Empire as an opportunity to bring about a long-desired Jewish homeland in Palestine. In Lloyd George especially they had found a readily sympathetic ear for the previous decade, and he remained keenly committed to the Zionist cause throughout the war years.[158]

Sir Mark Sykes, a seasoned traveler, and patrician diplomat, had also served briefly in an infantry regiment during the war in South Africa. He was elected as a Conservative MP in 1911 and with his social connections and traveler's expertise soon became known at Westminster as a figure of depth on Middle Eastern affairs, so much so that when war broke out in 1914 he was duly placed on the Parliamentary de Bunsen Committee charged with advising the Cabinet in this regard. Kitchener came to know Sykes as a member of the committee, and upon the latter's recommendation the creation of the Arab Bureau was agreed to by the Asquith government in January of 1916. Once established, the Bureau's mandate was to advise the government on policy making in the Middle East, with, as we have seen both in this chapter and earlier in the book, the active participation of Ronald Storrs and Lawrence. In the meantime, Sykes had undertaken earnest discussions with his French counterpart, Georges Picot, over the future of the region in light of the anticipated fall of the Ottoman Empire, whose existence had been the fulcrum of prevailing Anglo-French policy since at least the mid-Victorian era and the epic debates it had engendered between Gladstone and Disraeli especially.[159] But now, an early twentieth-century policy vacuum loomed in the Middle East and Sykes was determined to fill it.[160]

The path to final negotiations in January 1916 had been uneven, however, with the first attempt at an Anglo-French agreement foundering under the tepid leadership of Sir Arthur Nicolson, Permanent Under-

Secretary at the Foreign Office. The well-placed Sykes – with his 'ebullient orientalism', a comment, when made later by the colourless colonial administrator of Mesopotamia, Sir Arnold Wilson, was not intended as a compliment – was then asked to step in as Nicolson's replacement, which meant that Kitchener was similarly a close participant in the weeks leading up to the final agreement.[161] Sykes was charged with day to day negotiations, while Kitchener remained in the background offering advice and superintendence. 'He inspired' is the way Sykes described Kitchener's part in the month-long talks.[162] Essential to Kitchener's 'inspiration' was his strongly-held view that the Middle East was an integral part of Britain's general strategic plan; that is, as always, at the centre of such a plan was India, with spokes shooting out from it in various directions, the most vulnerable of which, he believed, towards the northeast and Russia. If France could have its regional aspirations fulfilled by a sphere of influence that would come to include northern Mesopotamia (containing the oil-rich area centred on the city of Mosul), south-eastern Turkey, Syria, and Lebanon, then, it was believed by the British, Russia could be held at bay. Throughout the talks the Russians were an assenting partner and therefore they were granted their own concessions of Istanbul and the Dardanelles, so that when the negotiations were concluded and the draft agreement approved by the Foreign Office on 4 February 1916, the Sykes-Picot Note – known officially as the Asia Minor Agreement – was effectively a tripartite pact. For Britain, Sykes's work had yielded much of Palestine, Jordan, and southern Mesopotamia. Although the lines were drawn in secret they would later be exposed in the glare of revolutionary light in the autumn of 1917 when the new Bolshevik government in Russia first discovered, and then published the agreement as a way to embarrass the Western powers who were unified in their opposition to its Marxist-inspired success. In conjunction with the Balfour Declaration of 2 November 1917, which announced the British government's support of the establishment of a Jewish national homeland in Palestine, Sykes-Picot was seen by the Arabs as a betrayal of their cooperation – engendered in considerable measure by the inspiring words and actions of Lawrence – in battling the Turks. The Turks themselves, meanwhile, used it as a provocation which stiffened their waning resistance against the Anglo-French enemy, if only for a short time.[163]

Kitchener's death in June of 1916 of course precluded his witnessing either the immediate outcome of Sykes-Picot, or any of its longer-term implications. As for 'betraying' the nationalist aspirations of the Arabs by privileging Anglo-French war aims, Kitchener – had he lived – doubtless would have seen British regional security as of preeminent importance to any such agreement. Accordingly, promises made to Arab leaders, principally Sharif Hussein of Mecca, about the potential for post-war statehood would have been conditional upon both events and further negotiations.[164] As for the principal author of the agreement, Sykes himself, he did not survive long enough to see the impact of his controversial diplomatic handiwork, succumbing to the Spanish Flu in February 1919 while in Paris attending the peace conference. He was just 39 years of age at the time of his death.

More important to Kitchener, of course, even than the destruction of the Ottoman Empire and its implications for the post-war map of the Middle East, however, was Britain's wartime relationship with Imperial Russia. By the middle of 1915 the Eastern Front had become a fast-collapsing house of cards with the Russians in full, if not panicked, retreat in the face of the relentless onslaught of the Austro-Germans. Their desperation was symbolized on 5 September of that year when Tsar Nicholas took command of the Russian Army by relieving the incumbent, his uncle, the Grand Duke Nicholas, of his position at its head, an event not welcomed by Kitchener among many others.[165] Fortunately for the Russians the approaching winter proved once again to be their ally and early that autumn the German commander, General Falkenhayn, called a halt to the season's campaign. The immediate result was a fair degree of stability along the over 500-mile- long Eastern Front, and for the Germans, no chance of an impending Napoleon-like debacle in the face of the hard Russian winter.

All through this period Kitchener, as he had always done, kept a close eye on events in Russia. As the eastern counterweight to the Western Front, Russian success in the war continued as a key strategic plank for him and that meant helping to ensure that all manner of available war materiel was sent there. British, American, and Canadian factories were at almost full capacity producing for British needs alone, however, and this meant that Russia could only ever expect marginal assistance from Britain itself.[166] Still, by the spring of 1916 the British had been able to extend war credits to Russia of just over L100-million, with little hope of re-payment.[167] Fears of a rejuvenated German campaign along the Eastern Front arrived with the new fighting season, and along with

Russia's perpetual shortage of munitions, its ongoing financial crisis, and the unclear strategic aims of its High Command, the *Stavka*, the War Council discussed the idea that a special mission to Russia should be undertaken as a means to more closely discern the prevailing situation of its embattled ally. At the beginning of May, therefore, Reginald McKenna, Lloyd George's successor as Chancellor of the Exchequer, nominated Kitchener for the task. McKenna, long in sympathy with Lloyd George, despised Kitchener every bit as much as the voluble Welshman and his action in this regard may have carried with it yet another attempt to remove Kitchener from the heart of the conduct of the war. Still, the prospect of the mission and being able to speak directly to the *Stavka* about all aspects of the Russian war effort was highly enticing to Kitchener, and thus regardless of the prevailing circumstances he was keen to go. Within two weeks of the War Council's consideration of the mission the Russians – having easily discovered the Cabinet's deliberations in this regard from their network of London informants – made plain that they were equally keen to have him visit. Indeed, on 14 May Kitchener duly received a formal invitation from the Tsar to visit Russia, via the King's Private Secretary, Lord Stamfordham.[168] Effectively, the mission was on.

Events now moved very quickly. The Cabinet met quickly to consider the Tsar's invitation, the refusal of which was never really an option. For a time it was thought that Lloyd George might accompany Kitchener in order to deal directly with Russia's requests for munitions. But just then the Easter Rising in Dublin and the subsequent (short-lived) Irish rebellion were preoccupying the government, and Asquith had tapped Lloyd George to work as his Chief Secretary for Ireland in order to resolve the crisis.[169] 'It is a *unique* opportunity', the Prime Minister wrote flatteringly to Lloyd George, 'and there is no-one else who could do so much to bring about a permanent solution'.[170] On 26 May, therefore, the Cabinet duly approved of what would now be Kitchener's solo mission to Russia.[171] Naturally, Kitchener was happy to be going alone and without the otherwise occupied Lloyd George, and immediately requested that the Admiralty arrange his journey, which was to commence within two weeks. What would prove shortly to be Kitchener's last days of life, were now at hand.

10

A Watery Grave and a Contested Reputation: 1916 and Beyond

As May 1916 came to an end Kitchener anticipated keenly his rapidly approaching secret mission to Russia. 'Nothing would give me greater pleasure', he had written to the Russian Foreign Minister, Sergei Sazanov – who was shortly to be deposed through the machinations of an increasingly desperate Tsarina Alexandra – two weeks earlier.[1] For some in Parliament, Kitchener could not go to Russia soon enough, however. The criticisms and general dyspepsia concerning his handling of the war continued unabated amongst the usual cabal of ministers and MPs. On 31 May, one of the latter, Sir Ivor Herbert, a career soldier who had been General Officer Commanding of the Militia of Canada and would be raised to the peerage as Baron Treowen in the following year, rose in the Commons to move that Kitchener's salary be reduced by L100. Though a political non-entity himself, Herbert's symbolically-weighted motion signalled an attempt by his more powerful allies, such as Lloyd George, to have Kitchener formally censured for his conduct of the war. As their cypher Herbert duly uttered the usual calumnies about the Secretary of War having acted the martinet by holding the direction of the war in an 'iron grasp', and that he had conducted the British effort as if he were both blind and stupid, particularly over the issue of compulsory service.[2] But if Herbert's feeble moment of occupying the attentions of the House amounted to what a later generation would call his '15 minutes of fame', then it was overshadowed quickly by the Prime Minister's powerful and eloquent defence of his terminally embattled minister.

Asquith had been aware that an attempt to censure Kitchener in Parliament was coming. 'He's going to be abused in the House tomorrow', he told Lady Kathleen Scott, wife of the late Antarctic explorer and one of his regular female conversation partners, on the evening of 30 May. 'I suppose I must defend him', she records him as remarking wearily.[3] But Asquith was anything but resigned and weary when he rose from his place on the government's front bench the following day and struck back hard at those who would not rest in their campaign to destroy the reputation of his Secretary of War and, by extension, his own government. 'The army', he declared, 'the country and the Empire are under a debt which cannot be measured in words for the services Lord Kitchener has rendered since the beginning of the war'.[4] Asquith carried on in the same vein for a few minutes, and then was ably assisted by the similar words of Sir Mark Sykes and others. Having effectively quashed the verbal uprising in this way, it then fell to the diminutive H.J. (Jack) Tennant, Kitchener's long-time friend, Under-Secretary, and Margot Asquith's younger brother, to offer up a surprise to the House by informing it that Kitchener would be happy to discuss his conduct of the war, in-person, with any MPs who cared to come to the War Office two days hence.[5]

Just before noon on the morning of 2 June, therefore, a confident-looking Kitchener strode into a Parliamentary committee room – the event had to be changed from the War Office because over 200 MPs were keen to attend – adjusted his spectacles, and with unusual eloquence declaimed on his own record and that of the War Office generally over the course of the previous two years of unprecedented-in-scope European armed conflict. The session proved an overwhelming triumph for him. Sitting beside Kitchener throughout the meeting was General Robertson, in confirmation of their genuine partnership. Like Gladstone, who was known to be humourless (in public), Kitchener pricked the balloon of his own reputation for over-seriousness by commenting wryly on his lack of ability as a 'ready debater', and on his weak facility with the 'various twists and turns of argument'.[6] But none of that need preclude, he maintained, an honest assessment of the 'colossal task' of a war that continued to be marked by 'great and terrible' battle casualties. Despite Lloyd George's serial disloyalty that would extend of course to the writing of his highly critical war memoirs in the 1930s, Kitchener complimented him on his 'loyal co-operation' as Minister of Munitions.[7] He then went on to parry one of Herbert's pointed criticisms of two days earlier that the manpower crisis in the soldiers' ranks could have been staved off by initiating compulsory service at the outset of the war, by stating sensibly that 'the question of a social change involving the whole country, and running counter to most ancient traditions of the British people', was best left for the Cabinet to decide and not to a mere department of government. And in due course when the Cabinet did decide, the decision to implement conscription 'came at the right time and in the right way as a military necessity and for no other reason'.[8] Altogether, Kitchener gave a bravura performance to the assembled MPs that afternoon. Invariably, not all of those present were impressed, however. The Canadian-born Andrew Bonar Law, then Colonial Secretary but who would later serve briefly as prime minister, had earlier remarked churlishly to Asquith that his chief's rousing speech defending Kitchener in the House would 'make it harder than ever to get rid of him'.[9] The Secretary of War's polished remarks and ready handling of the MPs' questions that followed confirmed Law in his opinion, especially when the two-hour long meeting in the packed committee room ended with loud cheers and sustained applause. As Kitchener's unbeknownst last Parliamentary moment the 2 June meeting was a personal high-water mark for him as a member of Asquith's government, and after all the long months of harsh and mostly unfounded criticism from both within and without Westminster, and the concomitant attempts to unseat him, he returned home to York House later that afternoon 'under an unmistakable glow of satisfaction'.[10]

A little later that day at 5:45 p.m. Kitchener had an audience of the King at Buckingham Palace, during which he said his good-byes in anticipation of the imminent Russian trip, and then afterwards proceeded on to Downing Street to do the same thing with the Prime Minister.[11] Asquith later remembered that evening's long conversation with Kitchener as being marked by 'high spirits' and humour about the successful 'passages of arms' earlier that day with hitherto hostile MPs.[12] Margot Asquith remembered her last encounter with Kitchener in much the same way too, later recording (somewhat melodramatically) that while on his way out 'I looked at his tall, distinguished figure and vigorous face, and taking both hands in mine, bade him God-speed'.[13]

The following morning, Saturday, 3 June, Kitchener went for a penultimate few hours to the War Office and then in the afternoon accompanied by his nephew and heir, Toby, and by his longtime aide, Colonel Oswald FitzGerald, with both of whom he had shared the memorable African tour of 1911, drove down to Broome Park for a hasty weekend visit in anticipation now of departing for Russia the next day. Broome was just about ready for permanent occupancy and Kitchener planned on moving into it on at least a part-time basis soon after his return from Russia, three weeks hence, and then permanently at war's end, whenever that would be. The next day attendance at the early service of Holy Communion at Barham church was followed by a return to London and a brief stop at the War Office. That evening he and his party of some ten others went to King's Cross station to board a special carriage attached to the night train to Scotland. By late the next morning, Monday, 5 June, the Kitchener party had arrived at Thurso via Edinburgh, there to board HMS *Oak* for the short journey across Pentland Firth to the Royal Navy base at Scapa Flow.[14]

Met at Scapa by Admiral Sir John Jellicoe, Commander in Chief of the Grand Fleet – who just a few days earlier had conducted the protractedly victorious Battle of Jutland against the German Navy in the North Sea – Kitchener went aboard his flagship, HMS *Iron Duke*, where lunch was served and a tour of the vast dreadnought battleship was undertaken. By mid-afternoon, final preparations were complete for Kitchener's departure for Archangel and at 4 o'clock he boarded the nearly 11,000-ton cruiser HMS *Hampshire*, which had been designated for the purpose. Heavy weather prevailed, however, which was encountered directly upon departure at 4:45. An hour later and fighting gale-force winds, two destroyers, HMS *Unity* and HMS *Victor*, converged to accompany the *Hampshire*, but a short time later in worsening weather and unable to keep up with the much faster cruiser (it was capable of making 22 knots) they were sent back to base, leaving the larger ship alone as it journeyed northwards along the west side of Orkney's Mainland Island. Unbeknownst to Jellicoe, or to the captain of the *Hampshire*, H.J. Savill, a German U-Boat submarine, *U-75*, had been active in the area laying mines just a week earlier. After three hours of hard sailing the U-Boat's field of 22 mines was entered and at 7:45 the *Hampshire* tripped one of them, blowing an enormous hole in the hull of the ship between the bow and the bridge and causing it to heel sharply to starboard. The explosion cut the ship's electrical power immediately, plunging its interior into an inky darkness. Desperate men poured immediately from their stations and out of the mess and congregated on the main deck. Kitchener, who had been given Captain Savill's cabin to use, emerged quickly from it to stand and survey the harrowing scene from the quarterdeck. There was also a report of him having been seen in the Gunroom right after the explosion, possibly on his way from the cabin.[15]

Recognizing immediately that the *Hampshire* was going down, Captain Savill gave the order to abandon ship. However, in the gale-force winds and crashing waves the lifeboats could not be properly deployed, bouncing around like so many corks and smashing up against the sides of the nearly 500-foot-long ship. Savill urged Kitchener to try to get into one of them nonetheless, but his directive seems to have gone unheard amidst the noise of the storm and that of the creaking ship; or perhaps it was ignored. Either way, Kitchener remained on the quarterdeck until the end. About 8:00 p.m. the rapidly sinking ship pitched forward, nearly somersaulting, and sank swiftly out of sight in some 200 feet of water before coming to rest upside down on the seabed, where it lies still, just one and a half miles from shore and near to the promontory of Marwick Head. The loss of men was almost complete: there were only 12 survivors out of a crew of about 650. Kitchener (and all members of his party, including the faithful FitzGerald) went down with the ship, his body disappearing into the depths from which attempts at recovery were fruitless.[16] He died just a few weeks short of his 66th birthday.[17]

News of the sinking of the *Hampshire*, and the assumed death by drowning of Kitchener, was made public around 12 noon on the following day, 6 June. The country was stunned by the report, no less than the government. Having just seen his Secretary of War a few days earlier at Downing Street Asquith especially shared the shock, but found it to be poignant, as he told Margot, that Kitchener 'had died at the height of his fame, and at the happiest moment of his life'.[18] Later, a retrospective Asquith would write that he believed that if Kitchener's secret journey to Russia had succeeded it just 'might have deflected the subsequent course of history'.[19] His claim is much too great here, however, and strays firmly into the terrain of counter-factual history, especially as it pertains to the Bolshevik Revolution of 1917; what is certain, though, is that Kitchener's wholly unexpected death presented

Asquith with the significant problem of who should replace him at the War Office, as well as how to reassure both the country and its allies that the British prosecution of the war would not suffer without the commanding figure of the great warrior Kitchener at the helm.

From 6 June until a memorial service was held nine days later on the 15th at St Paul's Cathedral in London public outpourings of grief over the fact and manner of Kitchener's death were acute and country wide. 'HE IS DEAD', shouted the *Daily Graphic* in London on 7 June, in a cryptically powerful headline that mirrored that of many others.[20] His closest senior military colleagues, Generals Robertson and Haig, expressed similar shock and grief. 'How shall we get on without him?' the former asked.[21] Churchill melodramatically quoted Tacitus: 'Fortunate was he in the hour of his death', but nevertheless was clearly shaken by the news first heard when shouted by a newsboy in the street outside his home in Kensington.[22] Curzon, conversely and true to form, could summon no grace in the hour of his old colleague's passing. 'The papers and the public have got hold of the wrong end of the stick about K,' he wrote to his Cabinet ally, Lord Lansdowne. 'Genius for organisation', 'wonderful foresight' – alas, as we know only too well, the very things he had not got. His death came in a most fortunate hour for his reputation. For he will now always be a national hero'.[23]

Curzon's ungracious tone would be matched by that of others. Raymond Asquith, for example, then fighting on the Western Front, wrote to his wife on 9 June complaining that 'an intolerable thing has happened' recently, 'much more deeply felt by the troops than Kitchener's death – leave has been reduced to 6 days or some say to 5'. Again in the same vein a few days later, he criticized his sister Violet ('Visey') and step-mother Margot for making such 'a fuss about Lord K. As if it mattered these old men being killed'. And then to complete the rather heartless triptych of missives, although with a smile at the end, he wrote on 13 June that 'I share your feelings about the badness of being drowned as compared with being shot, but can't help still suspecting that Kitchener will stroll into the House of Lords combing the seaweed out of his hair as strong and silent as ever'.[24]

The memorial service at St Paul's for Kitchener which took place two days later was small by national standards, although perhaps the fact that other such services were held at various locations along the Western Front at exactly the same time made its impact widely felt all the same. The King and Queen, along with the Prime Minister and Cabinet were in attendance. Various military worthies were there also, of course, although understandably their number did not include Haig, who remained on operational duty in France, and Robertson, likewise then at St Omer. Toby, raised now to the peerage as Viscount Broome, headed the Kitchener family delegation. 'Abide with Me' was sung – as it had been so emotionally in Gordon's honour at his belated memorial service in Khartoum in 1898 – and the Book of Common Prayer's funeral sentences were read. Handel's baroquely solemn 'Dead March in Saul' was played (as it would be at Churchill's state funeral almost half-a-century later).[25] Kitchener had passed from the scene less than a month before the Somme Offensive would commence, no bad thing in light of its unprecedented charnel house impact on the war. Swiftly, in little more than a week, Kitchener had become a part of history, dying in Arthur Balfour's eulogizing words: 'as he lived, in work which he was doing for his country'.[26]

But if Kitchener's physical presence had been removed from the heart of Britain's wartime trials his career-long impact and reputation would prove to be a source of much debate and partisanship both then and for years to come; indeed, even now a century later, Kitchener's life and work – especially that as Secretary of War – can stir not just many historians and biographers to fierce disagreement, but also leading journalists too – most notably recently, for example, Jeremy Paxman.[27] The 'fight for Kitchener', as it were, commenced almost as soon as his memorial service came to an end, sparked by the Dardanelles Commission, which the government announced in July 1916 and would report three years later. Wrapped up in such considerations, as well as much else as we shall see, was a struggle for reputation, for either blame or exculpation, for the meaning of 'hero'; indeed, for the nature and impact of the legacy not only of Kitchener himself but of Britain as the world's leading imperial power of the day and what that meant then, and what it continues to mean now, for those parts of the globe over which the 'Lion Rampant' once held sway.

In the days and weeks following Kitchener's death encomiums and memorials were published regularly. 'In that waste of seas', wrote G.K. Chesterton soaringly, 'beyond the last northern islets where his ship went down, one might fancy his spirit standing, a figure frustrated yet prophetic and pointing to the East; whence is the light of the world and the reunion of Christian men'.[28] A thick volume of remembrance was published quickly, *The Lord Kitchener Memorial Book*, which contained numerous testimonials, photographs, and illustrations, all in praise of the fallen warrior, though none so theologically fulsome as that offered by Chesterton.[29] In addition to the memorial services in London and at the Front, services of remembrance were held in the capitals of empire – 12,000 people gathered in front of the recently completed Union Buildings in Pretoria, for example, to honour Kitchener's memory – and letters and cards of condolence poured into the War and Colonial Offices. 'Truly Canada's admiration, appreciation and love for Kitchener', gushed a woman from Toronto, 'has been a wonderful revelation to me. If ever a man died heroic and glorious to thousands, nay I might say millions of human beings, it was Kitchener'.[30]

The timing and manner of Kitchener's death, together with his long military and proconsular record, had admitted him immediately to the pantheon of British heroes, about which few in wartime Britain dared then dispute (at least publicly). Indeed, the normative understanding of Kitchener as a hero prevailed for the first decade after his death until the so-called 'Kitchener Hoax' broke in 1926 in which a muck-raking journalist who went by the name of Frank Power (his real name was Arthur Freeman) scandalized the country by claiming (falsely) that he had found Kitchener's body buried in an unmarked grave in Norway. In retrospect, this tawdry episode can be pointed to as initiating a long period of contestation and conspiracy (unfounded and ridiculous) over whether or not Kitchener had in fact died when the *Hampshire* went down, and if not, was he now living secretly abroad somewhere, particularly in the USSR.[31]

The only thing that can be said in praise of the debate that Power began so shoddily is that the 'Kitchener Hoax' led gradually to a reappraisal of Kitchener's reputation, and therefore later to a close examination and evaluation of the meaning of hero, at least as the term had been attached to him personally. Prototypically in modern English letters, hero and heroism had been defined by Thomas Carlyle in 1840 in *On Heroes, Hero-Worship and the Heroic In History*.[32] Essentially, Carlyle offered a 'Great Man' thesis into which a later heroic figure such as Kitchener fit well, if not seamlessly. Certainly, for someone such as Chesterton, as suggested above, Kitchener's heroism lay in his being an agent of the 'divine will'. In offering this interpretation Chesterton was clearly following closely Carlyle's own prescription for what constituted the hero and heroic behaviour. For most, (although not all) in post-modern society, employing the divine in such a prescription for the heroic of course no longer holds sway; nonetheless, what does remain strongly today is a public desire for identifying and aggrandizing heroes. In this respect our digitized and atomized Western society of 2016 is no different than that of a century ago. Where the two societies do differ in this regard, however, is in the definition and content given to heroes and the heroic, and here the recent work of Max Jones is illuminating. Jones proposes that in seeking to assess heroes of past eras contemporarily, neither aggrandizement nor derision should prevail, but instead what must guide today's scholars (and others) in this pursuit is 'locating heroic reputations in historical context, and analyzing heroes as sites within which we can find evidence of the cultural beliefs, social practices, political structures and economic systems of the past'.[33] Apart from Jones's oversight in neglecting to include the impact of religious beliefs on a given society as an important feature of this prescription, he is surely right. Indeed, in the example of Kitchener such had been tried already (in part) a few years prior to the publication of Jones's work by Keith Surridge.[34]

Taking his cue from the cutting remark misattributed to Margot Asquith (in fact, it was uttered by her daughter, Elizabeth Bibesco) that Kitchener 'was not a great man, but at least he was a great poster', Surridge probes Kitchener as the embodiment of the British military hero, but uniquely so for the age in which he lived.[35] Borrowing from the work of John Mackenzie, Surridge suggests that it was as an 'imperial hero' in a new, highly internationally competitive (especially with Germany) and therefore uncertain era that Kitchener resonated deeply with the British public, as Charles Gordon, the hero of Khartoum, had done before him, and as Henry Havelock, of Indian Mutiny fame, had done earlier still.[36] In a carefully reasoned and explicated argument Surridge (rightly) concludes that in the late-Victorian and Edwardian age Kitchener was able to fuse together the older traditions of British (Nelsonian) military heroism with the newer strain of chivalrous imperialism – the Victorian moral uplift idea in action – to create a heroic persona. Indeed, as far as Surridge is concerned, in this way Kitchener became 'the last of the heroic titans'.[37] Or did he?

None of this is to say that in his day Kitchener was roundly venerated by all of his contemporaries. Of course, as we have seen earlier, he had many critics and even enemies who viewed his ascension to the pantheon of the heroic as little more than the predictable expression of the low and vulgar tastes inherent in an increasingly mass society. Some of Kitchener's peers had long spoken in critical terms of his Irish birth, his eccentrically severe father, and his own taciturn nature. Later it was his 'Orientalism', acquired by having lived for so many years in the East and used pejoratively to suggest that his 'habits of thought and methods of action ... astonished and baffled both his colleagues and subordinates'; or his personal 'cruelty'; or his 'mechanistic' battlefield ways that blotted the Kitchener ledger, all of which evidently fatally hindered a man who might otherwise have attained true greatness and real heroism.[38] Most of these latter criticisms especially, however, can be put over to the petty jealousies and score-settling of Kitchener's contemporaries (namely Lloyd George and Churchill) who, with him long in his watery grave, believed themselves free to contrast their own apparent moral and political rectitude with what they argued was lacking in their erstwhile nemesis.

Today however, a century after Kitchener's death, his long career record can be looked at much more dispassionately. If, as Colin Matthew observes, the Victorian era is near to our own chronologically but is not close to ours in just about every other way: 'We live with its consequences, but we do not live with it itself', then we need not expend too much psychic energy on categorizing Kitchener as the last of the era's 'heroic titans'.[39] Is he therefore something else? Is he an anti-hero, a typology developed most clearly during the Western cultural ferment of the 1960s? Is he, as has been suggested recently, an 'anachronistic' hero, belonging to a Victorian and Edwardian age that celebrated empire, (racial) domination, and militarism in ways that now are at least officially condemned by the West?[40] Or can Kitchener be seen properly in some other perspective now at the beginning of the twenty-first century that does not consign him merely to the margins as a type representative of an all-too-unfortunate age from which the West has at long-last graduated?

Given that empire-building, the desire to conquer and control, to spread what are considered to be the gifts of light and learning and commerce and good government (or even democracy) are as prevalent today in the world as they have ever been, it seems to me a highly restrictive exercise to attempt to limit Kitchener to simply having been a tribune of his age. He was surely that, yes, but he was not only that. Nor, as this biography has attempted to elaborate, was he an unfathomable enigma, as has sometimes been maintained.[41]

The particularities of Kitchener's persona, the age in which he lived, and the nature of the tasks that the British government called upon him to undertake were all understood by society at the time, and the tools of the historian's trade have made such things even clearer since. But the essence of what Kitchener stood for speaks most persuasively to that which has long been archetypically heroic; that is, saving the nation (and, in his case, the Empire) from peril. Whether that meant in Sudan; in South Africa; in India; or in terrestrial Britain itself, the task that fell regularly to Kitchener for the final 20 years of his life was this one, which helps to explain why he generated such immense popularity amongst ordinary Britons, as well as around the Empire, and why especially when World War I rapidly became an unprecedented cataclysm he was seen by his fellow countrymen and –women as their best (and indeed only) hope for victory.

Far from being simply 'the last of the heroic titans', as was suggested earlier, Kitchener rather in many ways became the model for the modern (British) national hero, a type that would be embodied again by Churchill a generation later during the even darker days that came with the Battle of Britain in 1940. In both cases neither man ever expressed any doubts or misgivings about the task at hand. For Kitchener, he was singularly untroubled by the arguments of early twentieth-century critics of empire, especially, as suggested elsewhere, those of J.A. Hobson. His critique of the war in South Africa formed a significant part of the conflict's intellectual backdrop but, as we saw, it made no discernible impact on Kitchener's thinking. For Churchill, much more famously of course, it meant his rejection of the British government's prevailing policy of appeasement throughout the 1930s. In this way Kitchener indeed was not anti-heroic – at least not until the post-colonial era – nor simply anachronistically heroic, but rather, it may be argued, he remained traditionally heroic until after World War II. In Kitchener, the British had found a hero who gave corporeal form to what was most required at a given historical moment, regardless of those features of his character, or indeed some of his actions, which might otherwise have repelled them. Just as Nelson's well-known adultery and cruel treatment of his first wife Fanny scandalized many of his contemporaries, his (posthumous) claim as the saving hero – he of the Immortal Memory – whose virtues extended beyond time-bound circumstance became virtually incontestable in Britain. So likewise, to some extent at least, Kitchener. If he had lived and had continued in office as Secretary of War he would have found himself standing over a weary, traumatized, but ultimately victorious Britain in 1918 and therefore it is almost certain that his status as a national hero would not have come under the severe scrutiny that it later did, if only because he would have been physically present to parry the attacks of those who wished to blame him (alone) for the conduct of an exceptionally brutal war fought unavoidably and mainly in the trenches.

The reality of the last years of Kitchener's life was that he – as well as everyone else in both high military command and prominent political office in Britain – was in thrall to a new kind of warfare from which neither he nor they could break free, and over which they had little control. 'The belief,' observes Keith Neilson rightly, 'that Britain was somehow capable of making military moves which would prove decisive simply was not true'.[42] And here was the rub. In the midst of this cruel wartime conundrum stood the commanding figure of Kitchener, the victor over all the other major British (imperial) military challenges of the preceding 20 years but faced now with the biggest problem yet in military history and – like everyone else – unable to see with clarity through the darkness to its solution, if one even existed. The accretions of heroism accorded him through long imperial service had made him the obvious choice to marshal Britain's war effort from the start. Kitchener wisely, if unpopularly, told the Cabinet and the country in 1914 that the war would be a long one and that Britain would not be fully ready to fight it successfully for three years. In the meantime, he maintained the integrity of the Entente with France, as well as with a habitually shaky and ultimately disastrous Russia for the first two years of the war. He tried to keep the focus of the struggle on the Western Front and away from 'sideshows' such as the Dardanelles; he incorporated rather smoothly the substantial contributions of manpower and materiel from the Dominions and India; and gradually built up the men and munitions of the British Army until it was in a position to take on and finally defeat the Germans and their allies, together which constituted the greatest land-based armed force the world had ever seen.

Endorsements of Kitchener's historical record such as the one offered by Harold Temperley, Professor of Modern History at Cambridge in the 1930s, that during World War I Kitchener was 'the whole Empire's shield in Armageddon' now come across as badly dated in tone and overly effusive in reach. Chesterton's words of praise, as noted above, now read as similarly anachronistic. Still, as we have seen, the pivotal role Kitchener played both during World War I and for years earlier in maintaining Britain's world position cannot be gainsaid either easily or persuasively.[43] Perhaps therefore, now a century after his death, it is finally time to agree that Kitchener's achievements over the course of his long service to the British imperial state and culminating in World War I do indeed constitute a form of enduring heroism. However redefined or deconstructed the term hero has become today, Kitchener's version of it lived out over almost four decades from the 1880s until his death in 1916 is recognizable in its own time and place. Acknowledging this fact helps therefore to point the way to a fuller and more nuanced understanding of the man both then – as a hero in a world dominated by empire – and now, as an anti-hero in a world defined by empire's anathema.

Chronology

1850	Horatio Herbert Kitchener, born 24 June, County Kerry, Ireland
1863	Moves to Switzerland
1868	Enters Royal Military Academy Woolwich
1871	Commissioned Lieutenant, Royal Engineers
1874	Seconded to Palestine Exploration Fund
1878	Seconded to Foreign Office and sent on survey to Cyprus
1879	Appointed Military Vice-Consul, Kastamonu, Turkey
1882	Viewed British naval bombardment of Alexandria, Egypt; onshore intelligence work
1883	Promoted Captain; appointed to Egyptian cavalry
1884	Promoted brevet Major; on Gordon Relief Expedition
1885	Promoted brevet Lieutenant Colonel; appointed Zanzibar Boundary Commission
1886	Appointed Governor General, Eastern Sudan and the Red Sea Littoral
1888	Promoted brevet Colonel; appointed Adjutant General of the Egyptian army
1890	Appointed Inspector General of the Egyptian police
1892	Appointed Sirdar of the Egyptian army
1896	Promoted brevet Major General
1898	Battle of Omdurman
1898	Created Baron Kitchener of Khartoum and Aspall in the County of Suffolk

1899	Appointed Governor General of Sudan; promoted Lieutenant General
1900	Appointed Commander in Chief, South Africa
1902	Promoted brevet General; created Viscount Kitchener of Khartoum; appointed Commander in Chief, India
1909	Promoted Field Marshal
1911	Appointed British Agent and Consul General, Egypt
1914	Created Earl Kitchener of Khartoum and of Broome; appointed Secretary of State for War
1916	Died; drowned at sea, 5 June, Orkney Islands, Scotland

Notes

1 An Irish and Continental Childhood and Youth, 1850–67

1. Quoted in John Pollock, *Kitchener: Architect of Victory, Artisan of Peace* (New York, Carroll & Graf, 2001), p. 9.
2. Harold F. B. Wheeler, *The Story of Lord Kitchener* (London, George G. Harrap & Co., 1916), p. 14.
3. See, for example, Robert Blake, *Disraeli* (New York, St Martin's Press, 1967); and H.C.G. Matthew, *Gladstone 1809–1898* (Oxford, Clarendon Press, 1997). Also, Roland Quinault, Roger Swift and Ruth Clayton Windscheffel, eds, *William Gladstone: New Studies and Perspectives* (Farnham, Ashgate, 2012).
4. See John Darwin, *The Empire Project: The Rise and Fall of the British World System, 1830–1970* (Cambridge, Cambridge University Press, 2009).
5. Horatio Herbert Kitchener, *Oxford Dictionary of National Biography*.
6. Philip Magnus, *Kitchener: Portrait of an Imperialist* (London, John Murray, 1958), p. 4.
7. Quoted in Roy Jenkins, *Gladstone* (London, Macmillan, 1995), p. 3. First recorded by Walter Bagehot in 'Mr Gladstone', *National Review* (July 1860).
8. George H. Cassar, *Kitchener: Architect of Victory* (London, William Kimber, 1977), p. 19.
9. The sentiment is given one of its most famous expressions in Coventry Patmore's poem, 'The Angel in the House', published in 1854.
10. Christopher Hibbert, *The Great Mutiny: India 1857* (London, Penguin, 1980), pp. 188–97; Lawrence James, *Raj: The Making and Unmaking of British India* (London, Little, Brown, 1997), pp. 278–98.
11. KP, PRO 30/57/93.
12. Ibid.
13. Ibid.

14. C. Brad Faught, *The Oxford Movement: A Thematic History of the Tractarians and Their Times* (University Park, PA, Pennsylvania State University Press, 2003), p. 87.
15. Pollock, *Kitchener*, p. 16. One of the cardinal works in shaping modern thinking on this subject remains that by Elizabeth Kubler-Ross, *On Death and Dying* (New York, Simon & Schuster, 1969).

2 The Making of a Surveyor-Soldier, 1868–82

1. Harold Begbie, *Kitchener: Organizer of Victory* (Boston, Houghton Mifflin, 1915), p. 15.
2. Trevor Royle, *The Kitchener Enigma* (London, Michael Joseph, 1985), p. 19.
3. Sir George Arthur, *Life of Lord Kitchener*, vol. I (London, Macmillan, 1920), p. 6.
4. See, for example, A.N. Wilson, *The Victorians* (London, Hutchinson, 2002), pp. 278–9.
5. See John Pollock, *Kitchener: Architect of Victory, Artisan of Peace* (New York, Carroll & Graf, 2001), pp. 19–23.
6. See Fenton Bresler, *Napoleon III: A Life* (New York, Carroll & Graf, 1999).
7. Pollock, for example, thinks not, *Kitchener*, p. 24.
8. See David Wetzel, *A Duel of Nations: Germany, France, and the Diplomacy of the War of 1870–1871* (Madison, WI, University of Wisconsin Press, 2012).
9. Quoted in Reginald Viscount Esher, *The Tragedy of Lord Kitchener* (London, John Murray, 1921), p. 192. Other versions of the story, such as George Arthur's, have the content of the Duke's encomium reading this way: 'I am bound to say that in your place I should have done the same thing'. Arthur, *Life of Lord Kitchener*, vol. I, p. 11.
10. KP, PRO 57/30/91.
11. Linda Colley, *Britons: Forging the Nation, 1707–1837* (New Haven, CT, Yale University Press, 1992). See, among many works on the subject, C. Brad Faught, *The Oxford Movement: A Thematic History of the Tractarians and Their Times* (University Park, PA: Pennsylvania State University Press, 2003).
12. KP, PRO 57/30/91.
13. See Alan Lloyd, *The Drums of Kumasi: The Story of the Ashanti Wars* (London, Longmans, 1964).
14. Quoted in Pollock, *Kitchener*, p. 29.
15. See John Witheridge, *Excellent Dr Stanley: the Life of Dean Stanley of Westminster* (Norwich, Michael Russell, 2013).
16. Still in existence in London, in good order, and name unchanged, the PEF celebrated its 150th anniversary in 2015.
17. Quoted in Arthur, *Life of Lord Kitchener*, vol. I, p. 16.
18. Quoted in Pollock, *Kitchener*, p. 32.
19. Conder would continue in association with the PEF until 1882, at which time he would join Gen. Wolseley's intelligence staff in Egypt.
20. Quoted in Pollock, *Kitchener*, p. 33.

21. See C. Brad Faught, *Gordon: Victorian Hero* (Washington, DC, Potomac, 2008), pp. 72–3.

22. C.R. Conder, *Tent-Work in Palestine*, vol. II (London, Richard Bentley, 1879), p. 164.

23. Quoted in Palestine Exploration Fund, *Quarterly Statement* (1875), p. 198.

24. 'Kitchener's Working Papers Relating to Palestine Survey', BL, Add. 69848, ff. 128

25. See Arthur, *Life of Kitchener*, vol. I, pp. 19–21.

26. Royle, *The Kitchener Enigma*, p. 33.

27. Quoted in Pollock, *Kitchener*, p. 37.

28. See H.C.G. Matthew, *Gladstone 1809–1898* (Oxford, Clarendon Press, 1997), pp. 267–92.

29. Quoted in Royle, *The Kitchener Enigma*, p. 35.

30. Brian Thompson, *Imperial Vanities: The Adventures of the Baker Brothers and Gordon of Khartoum* (London, HarperCollins, 2002), pp. 160–7.

31. Mrs Kitchener would continue to live in Dinan until her death in 1918.

32. Quoted in Robert Blake, *Disraeli* (New York, St Martin's Press, 1967), p. 637.

33. See Andrew Roberts, *Salisbury: Victorian Titan* (London, Phoenix, 2000), pp. 191–2.

34. Ibid., p. 649.

35. See Robert Holland and Diana Markides, *The British and the Hellenes: The Struggle for Mastery in the Eastern Mediterranean 1850–1960* (Oxford, Clarendon Press, 2006). See, also, C. Brad Faught, 'Gladstone and the Ionian Islands', in Roland Quinault, Roger Swift and Ruth Clayton Windscheffel, eds, *William Gladstone: New Studies and Perspectives* (Farnham, Ashgate, 2012), pp. 219–31.

36. See Tabitha Morgan, *Sweet and Bitter Island: A History of the British in Cyprus* (London, I.B.Tauris, 2010). Also, Gail Ruth Hook, *Protectorate Cyprus: British Imperial Power Before World War I* (London, I.B.Tauris, 2013).

37. Quoted in Philip Magnus, *Kitchener: Portrait of an Imperialist* (London, John Murray, 1958), p. 23.

38. Gilbert and Sullivan's highly popular comic opera, *The Pirates of Penzance*, would premiere in 1879 with Wolseley acting as the model for their 'Major-General Stanley'.

39. KP, PRO 30/57/1.

40. Quoted in Pollock, *Kitchener*, p. 42.

41. See Ian Knight, *Zulu Rising: The Epic Story of Isandlwana and Rorke's Drift* (London, Pan Books, 2011), pp. 676, 684–8.

42. See Faught, *Gordon*, pp. 91–2.

43. Quoted in Royle, *The Kitchener Enigma*, p. 45.

44. The career choice proved a good one for in April 1880 the Liberals under Gladstone won the general election over Disraeli's Conservatives and shortly thereafter the new government made the decision to withdraw all British vice-consuls from Anatolia.

3   In Egypt and Sudan, 1882–92

1. Alfred Viscount Milner, *England in Egypt* (New York, Howard Fertig, 1970), pp. 180–2.
2. See Roger Owen, *Lord Cromer: Victorian Imperialist Edwardian Proconsul* (Oxford, Oxford University Press, 2004), pp. 117–40.
3. C. Brad Faught, *Gordon: Victorian Hero* (Washington, DC, Potomac, 2008), p. 59.
4. See H.C.G. Matthew, *Gladstone 1809–1898* (Oxford, Clarendon Press, 1997), pp. 374–94.
5. Ibid., p. 389.
6. Ibid.
7. KP, PRO 30/57/1.
8. Wood was the elder brother of Katharine O'Shea. Dubbed 'Kitty' by the American press, she was at the centre of the Charles Parnell politico-marital scandal in 1890 that delayed, and then nearly derailed, the second attempt by the Gladstone government to achieve Home Rule for Ireland. See Robert Kee, *The Laurel and the Ivy: The Story of Charles Stewart Parnell and Irish Nationalism* (London, Penguin, 1994).
9. KP, PRO 30/57/1.
10. Ibid.
11. Ibid.
12. Quoted in John Pollock, *Kitchener: Architect of Victory, Artisan of Peace* (New York, Carroll & Graf, 2001), p. 53.
13. See Wendy R. Katz, *Rider Haggard and the Fiction of Empire* (Cambridge, Cambridge University Press, 1987).
14. Andrew Haggard, *Under Crescent and Star* (Edinburgh, William Blackwood, 1895), p. 49.
15. Ibid., p. 24.
16. Kitchener stayed at Shepheard's regularly, taking advantage of the services of 'servant, beer, and bath' – according to his bills – whenever he was in residence. KP, PRO 30/57/5.
17. GP, Add. 51305, f. 52.
18. KP, PRO 30/57/102.
19. Quoted in P.M. Holt, *The Mahdist State in Sudan* (Oxford, Clarendon Press, 1958), p. 51.
20. See Fergus Nicoll, *The Mahdi of Sudan and the Death of General Gordon* (Stroud, Sutton, 2005), ch. 13.
21. Brian Thompson, *Imperial Vanities: The Adventures of the Baker Brothers and Gordon of Khartoum* (London, HarperCollins, 2002), pp. 209–11.
22. The Cabinet confirmed the decision on 3 January 1884. Matthew, *Gladstone*, p. 395.
23. *Parliamentary Debates*, 12 May 1884.
24. GP, Add. 52388, f. 135.
25. Quoted in the *Pall Mall Gazette*, 9 January 1884.
26. Quoted in Matthew, *Gladstone*, p. 396.

27. See Owen, *Lord Cromer*, pp. 191–3.

28. See, for a recent example, Michael Asher, *Khartoum: The Ultimate Imperial Adventure* (London, Penguin, 2006). Also, Faught, *Gordon*, ch. 7.

29. See M.W. Daly, *Sirdar: Sir Reginald Wingate and the British Empire in the Middle East* (Philadelphia, American Philosophical Society, 1997). Also, R.J.M. Pugh, *Wingate Pasha: The Life of General Sir Francis Reginald Wingate 1861–1953* (Barnsley, Pen & Sword, 2011).

30. KP, PRO 30/57/3, 'Notes from Berber'.

31. Quoted in Trevor Royle, *The Kitchener Enigma* (London, Michael Joseph, 1985), p. 60.

32. GP, Add. 51298, f. 195.

33. Ibid., Add. 56451, f. 87.

34. Ibid., Add. 51298, f. 195.

35. KP, PRO 30/57/3, 'Report on the Arab Tribes from Dongola to Khartum, by Major H.H. Kitchener'.

36. Ibid., PRO 30/57/4.

37. Quoted in A. Egmont Hake, ed., *The Journals of Major-General C.G. Gordon, C.B at Kartoum* (London, Kegan Paul, Trench, 1885), p. 92.

38. KP, PRO 30/57/4.

39. GP, Add. 52388, f. 154b.

40. KP, PRO 30/57/4.

41. Ibid.

42. Quoted in Faught, *Gordon*, p. 91.

43. Quoted in Royle, *The Kitchener Enigma*, p. 65.

44. KP, PRO 30/57/6.

45. Based on a report given to Kitchener he telegraphed the War Office that 'General Gordon had light coloured clothes on when killed'. This message would give rise to the belief that Gordon had died fighting in his Governor General's white uniform. GP, Add. 52408, f. 71.

46. Christopher Hibbert, ed., *Queen Victoria in her Letters and Journals* (Markham, ON, Penguin, 1985), pp. 284, 289.

47. KP, PRO 30/57/5.

48. Quoted in Sir George Arthur, *Life of Lord Kitchener*, vol. I (London, Macmillan, 1920), pp. 104–5.

49. See Edward Berenson, *Heroes of Empire: Five Charismatic Men and the Conquest of Africa* (Berkeley, University of California Press, 2011), ch. 3, 'Charles Gordon, Imperial Saint'.

50. Quoted in Arthur, *Life of Lord Kitchener*, vol. I, p. 105.

51. See, for example, *The Times* edition of 7 October 1884.

52. KP, PRO 57/30/6.

53. Quoted in Arthur, *Life of Lord Kitchener*, vol. I, p. 128.

54. KP, PRO/30/57/8.

55. The historiography on the partition question is long and deep. See, especially, Ronald Robinson and John Gallagher with Alice Denny, *Africa and the*

Victorians: The Official Mind of Imperialism 2nd edn (London, Macmillan, 1985); a new edition is due to be brought out shortly by I.B.Tauris; and Thomas Pakenham, *The Scramble for Africa: White Man's Conquest of the Dark Continent from 1876 to 1912* (New York, Avon Books, 1991).

56. KP, PRO 57/30/8.

57. Ibid.

58. Quoted in Pollock, *Kitchener*, p. 77.

59. The Zanzibar episode, however, did bring Kitchener his first honour or 'gong', the CMG (Companion of the Most Distinguished Order of St Michael and St George), bestowed on him by the Queen later in 1886.

60. KP, PRO 30/57/5.

61. Quoted in Pollock, *Kitchener*, p. 78.

62. 'Fuzzy-Wuzzy' was published by Kipling in *Barrack Room Ballads and Other Verses* in 1892. See Daniel Karlin, ed., *Rudyard Kipling: A Critical Edition of the Major Works* (Oxford, Oxford University Press, 1999), p. 437.

63. Winston S. Churchill, *The River War: An Account of the Reconquest of the Sudan* (New York, Carroll & Graf, 2000), p. 47.

64. *The Times*, 18 January 1888.

65. KP, PRO 30/57/5.

66. Quoted in Andrew Roberts, *Salisbury: Victorian Titan* (London, Phoenix, 2000), p. 108.

67. Owen, *Lord Cromer*, p. 239.

68. Quoted in Pollock, *Kitchener*, p. 84.

69. Quoted in Philip Magnus, *Kitchener: Portrait of an Imperialist* (London, John Murray, 1958), p. 80.

4   Sirdar of the Egyptian Army, 1892–8

1. Evelyn Baring Earl of Cromer, *Modern Egypt*, vol. II (London, Macmillan, 1908), p. 87.

2. F.R. Wingate, *Mahdiism and the Egyptian Sudan* (London, Macmillan, 1891).

3. See Roy Pugh, *Wingate Pasha: The Life of Sir Reginald Wingate 1861–1953* (Barnsley, Pen & Sword, 2011), chs 2–4.

4. John Tosh, *Manliness and Masculinities in Nineteenth-Century Britain* (Harlow, Pearson, 2005), p. 206. Also, David A.J. Richards, *The Rise of Gay Rights and the Fall of the British Empire: Liberal Resistance and the Bloomsbury Group* (Cambridge, Cambridge University Press, 2013).

5. See, for example, Rictor Norton, *The Myth of the Modern Homosexual: Queer History and the Search for Cultural Unity* (London, Cassell, 1997), and Adam Green 'Gay But Not Queer: Toward a Post-Queer Study of Sexuality', *Theory and Society* (August 2002), vol. 31(4), pp. 521–45.

6. John Pollock, *Kitchener: Architect of Victory, Artisan of Peace* (New York, Carroll & Graf, 2001), pp. 225–7.

7. Jad Adams, 'Was 'K' Gay?' *History Today*, Vol. 49, Issue 11 (November 1999). A.N. Wilson, *The Victorians* (London, Hutchinson, 2002), p. 598. Ronald Hyam, *Empire and Sexuality: The British Experience* (Manchester, Manchester University Press, 1990), pp. 38–9. Denis Judd, *Empire: The British Imperial Experience from 1765 to the Present* (London, I.B.Tauris, 2012), pp. 172–6.

8. Lord Edward Cecil, *The Leisure of an Egyptian Official* (London, Hodder and Stoughton, 1921), p. 184.

9. Ibid.

10. Ibid.

11. Margot Asquith, *More Memories* (London, Cassell, 1933), p. 121.

12. Roger Owen, *Lord Cromer: Victorian Imperialist Edwardian Proconsul* (Oxford, Oxford University Press, 2004), p. 289.

13. See Gordon Martel, *Imperial Diplomacy: Rosebery and the Failure of Foreign Policy* (Montreal and Kingston, McGill-Queen's University Press, 1986).

14. Quoted in the Earl of Cromer, *Abbas II* (London, Macmillan, 1915), p. 27.

15. Blunt's full critique of the British occupation was later summed up in his book, *Atrocities of Justice under the English Rule in Egypt* (London, T. Fisher Unwin, 1906).

16. Viscount Alfred Milner, *England in Egypt* (New York, Howard Fertig, 1970). Milner served as undersecretary of finance in the Egyptian government from 1890 until 1892.

17. Owen, *Lord Cromer*, p. 271.

18. Pugh, *Wingate Pasha*, p. 38.

19. Quoted in Pollock, *Kitchener*, pp. 87–8.

20. See, for example, Pollock, *Kitchener*, pp. 87–8; Philip Magnus, *Kitchener: Portrait of an Imperialist* (London, John Murray, 1958), pp. 83–8; Owen, *Lord Cromer*, pp. 271–2.

21. Owen, ibid., p. 272.

22. G.W. Steevens, *Egypt in 1898* (Edinburgh, William Blackwood, 1898), p. 64.

23. See C. Brad Faught, '"The Uganda Business": Gladstone and Africa Revisited', Peter Francis, ed., *The Gladstone Umbrella* (Hawarden, St Deiniol's Library, 2001), pp. 156–74.

24. Andrew Roberts, *Salisbury: Victorian Titan* (London, Phoenix, 2000), p. 640.

25. Quoted in Pollock, *Kitchener*, p. 89.

26. See Wm. Roger Louis, *Ends of British Imperialism* (London: I.B.Tauris, 2006), pp. 35–48.

27. John Gallagher and Ronald Robinson, 'The Imperialism of Free Trade', *Economic History Review*, vol. VI, no. 1 (1953), p. 15.

28. See R.A. Jonas, *The Battle of Adwa: African Victory in the Age of Empire* (Cambridge, MA, Belknap Press of Harvard University, 2011).

29. Frank Scudamore, *A Sheaf of Memories* (London, T. Fisher Unwin, 1925), p. 99.

30. KP, PRO 30/57/9.

31. Philip Warner, *Kitchener: The Man Behind the Legend* (New York, Athenaeum, 1986), p. 75.

32. Quoted in Pollock, *Kitchener*, p. 93.
33. He was appointed governor of Bermuda in 1908 and served until his death there in 1912.
34. Pugh, *Wingate Pasha*, p. 51
35. Ibid.
36. Quoted in Pollock, *Kitchener*, p. 96.
37. See Archie Hunter, *Kitchener's Sword Arm: The Life and Campaigns of General Sir Archibald Hunter* (Staplehurst, Spellmount, 1996).
38. Ronald Robinson and John Gallagher with Alice Denny, *Africa and the Victorians* 2nd edn (London, Macmillan, 1985), pp. 350–4.
39. Dominic Green, *Three Empires on the Nile: The Victorian Jihad, 1869–1899* (Toronto, Free Press, 2007), p. 249.
40. Quoted in Magnus, *Kitchener*, p. 102.
41. Owen, *Lord Cromer*, p. 290.
42. Robinson and Gallagher, *Africa and the Victorians*, p. 358.
43. *Queen Victoria's Journals*, 16 November 1896, The Royal Archives and the Bodleian Library, Oxford, online.
44. Quoted in Duncan H. Doolittle, *A Soldier's Hero: The Life of General Sir Archibald Hunter* (Narragansett, RI, Anawan, 1991), p. 80.
45. See Clarence B. Davis, Kenneth E. Wilburn, and Ronald E. Robinson, eds, *Railway Imperialism* (Westport, CT, Praeger, 1991).
46. Quoted in Sir George Arthur, *Life of Lord Kitchener*, vol. I (London, Macmillan, 1920), p. 208.
47. Girouard's lifelong imperial service is covered comprehensively in A.H.M. Kirk-Greene's, 'Canada in Africa: Sir Percy Girouard, Neglected Colonial Governor', *African Affairs*, vol. 83, no. 331 (April 1984), pp. 207–39. See also, Roy MacLaren, *Canadians on the Nile* (Vancouver, University of British Columbia Press, 1978), pp. 142–60.
48. Quoted in Magnus, *Kitchener*, p. 105.
49. Winston S. Churchill, *The River War: An Account of the Reconquest of the Sudan* (New York, Carroll & Graf, 2000), pp. 170–1.
50. Ibid., p. 173.
51. Quoted in Arthur, *Life of Lord Kitchener*, p. 217.
52. KP, PRO 37/57/11.
53. Ibid.
54. Robinson and Gallagher, *Africa and the Victorians*, pp. 364–5.
55. *Parliamentary Debates*, 29 November 1897.
56. Green, *Three Empires on the Nile*, p. 253.
57. Owen, *Lord Cromer*, p. 295.
58. KP, PRO 30/57/9.
59. Quoted in Charles a Court Repington, *Vestigia: Reminiscences of Peace and War* (Boston, Houghton Mifflin, 1919), p. 116.
60. Ibid., p. 117.
61. See Pierre Berton, *Vimy* (Toronto, McClelland & Stewart, 1986).

62. Pollock, *Kitchener*, p. 121.
63. G.W. Steevens, *With Kitchener to Khartoum* (Edinburgh, Blackwood, 1898).
64. Ibid., p. 166.
65. KP, PRO 30/57/10.
66. 'Too late', the poignant words from Gordon's penultimate journal entry on 13 December 1884, a few weeks before the fall of Khartoum and his death. A Egmont Hake, ed., *The Journals of Major-General C.G. Gordon, C.B. at Kartoum* (London, Kegan Paul, Trench, 1885), p. 394.

5   Omdurman, Fashoda, and Khartoum, 1898–9

1. Roy Pugh, *Wingate Pasha: The Life of General Sir Francis Reginald Wingate 1861–1953* (Barnsley, Pen & Sword, 2011), p. 62.
2. Martin Gilbert, *A History of the Twentieth Century: Volume One, 1900–1933* (New York, William Morrow, 1997), p. 11. Hilaire Belloc, *The Modern Traveller* (London, Edward Arnold, 1898).
3. George Alfred Henty, the prolific writer of 122 books of historical fiction, most of it celebrating the glories of the British Empire and aimed at school children. He would die just four years later in 1902. The following year his fictional account of the campaign was published posthumously as *With Kitchener in the Soudan* (London, Blackie & Son, 1903).
4. Winston L. Spencer Churchill, *The Story of the Malakand Field Force: An Episode in Frontier War* (London, Dover, 1898).
5. Quoted in Martin Gilbert, *Churchill: A Life* (London, Heinemann, 1991), p. 92.
6. Ibid., p. 90.
7. Ibid., p. 92.
8. Winston S. Churchill, *The River War: An Account of the Reconquest of the Sudan* (New York, Carroll & Graf, 2000), pp. 251–2.
9. Quoted in John Pollock, *Kitchener: Architect of Victory, Artisan of Peace* (New York, Carroll & Graf, 2001), p. 127.
10. Churchill, *The River War*, p. 255.
11. Quoted in Michael Asher, *Khartoum: The Ultimate Imperial Adventure* (London, Penguin, 2006), p. 370.
12. Philip Ziegler, *Omdurman* (London, Collins, 1973), p. 93.
13. Asher, *Khartoum*, p. 377.
14. Churchill, *The River War*, p. 271.
15. Charles a Court Repington, *Vestigia: Reminiscences of Peace and War* (Boston, Houghton Mifflin, 1919), p. 147.
16. Quoted in John Meredith, ed., *Omdurman Diaries 1898* (Barnsley, Pen & Sword, 1998), p. 170.
17. Quoted in Ziegler, *Omdurman*, p. 127.
18. Quoted in E.W.C. Sandes, *The Royal Engineers in Egypt & the Sudan* (Chatham, Institute of Royal Engineers, 1937), p. 264.
19. Ziegler, *Omdurman*, p. 136.

20. Ibid., p. 140.
21. Andrew A. Wiest, *Haig: The Evolution of a Commander* (Washington, DC, Potomac, 2005), p. 5. Captain (later General Sir) Henry Rawlinson was another participant at Omdurman who would become a prominent British commander in World War I.
22. Asher, *Khartoum*, p. 385.
23. Churchill, *The River War*, pp. 283–9.
24. Ibid., p. 283.
25. Ibid., p. 285.
26. The VC was awarded to: Private Thomas Byrne, Lieutenant Raymond de Montmorency, and Captain Paul Kenna. See Terry Brighton, *The Last Charge: the 21st Lancers and the Battle of Omdurman* (Marlborough, Crowood, 1998).
27. Pugh, *Wingate Pasha*, p. 50. Also, Ziegler, *Omdurman*, p. 180.
28. Churchill, *The River War*, p. 300. See, also, Henry Keown-Boyd, *A Good Dusting: The Sudan Campaigns, 1883–1899* (London, Leo Cooper, 1986).
29. Robin Neillands, *The Dervish Wars: Gordon and Kitchener in the Sudan 1880–1898* (London, John Murray, 1996), p. 211.
30. G.W. Steevens, *With Kitchener to Khartoum* (Edinburgh, William Blackwood, 1898), p. 201.
31. C. Brad Faught, *Gordon: Victorian Hero* (Washington, DC, Potomac, 2008), p. 91.
32. Fergus Nicoll, *The Mahdi of Sudan and the Death of General Gordon* (Stroud, Sutton, 2005).
33. Pollock, *Kitchener*, p. 136.
34. Quoted in Ziegler, *Omdurman*, p. 204.
35. Churchill, *The River War*, p. 306.
36. Rudolf von Slatin, *Fire and Sword in the Sudan: A Personal Narrative of Fighting and Serving the Dervishes 1879–1895* (London, Edward Arnold, 1930), p. 206.
37. Pugh, *Wingate Pasha*, pp. 42–3.
38. Quoted in Ziegler, *Omdurman*, pp. 206–7.
39. Quoted in Pollock, *Kitchener*, p. 150.
40. Gilbert, *Churchill*, p. 98.
41. The second edition, published in 1902 as an abridged one-volume account of the re-conquest, omitted these pointed criticisms. But the damage was done nonetheless. At this point in their relationship Kitchener loathed Churchill, and the feeling was mutual, though the intensity of their dislike would moderate over time to become nearly-collegial during World War I.
42. KP, PRO 30/57/14.
43. Quoted in Roger Owen, *Lord Cromer: Victorian Imperialist, Edwardian Proconsul* (Oxford, Oxford University Press, 2004), p. 302.
44. Ernest Bennett, 'After Omdurman', *Contemporary Review*, no. 75 (January 1899), pp. 18–33.
45. KP, PRO 30/57/14.
46. Magnus, *Kitchener*, p. 132.
47. Repington, *Vestigia*, p. 195.

48. James Morris, *Pax Britannica: The Climax of Empire* (Harmondsworth, Penguin, 1987), p. 240.

49. *Queen Victoria's Journals*, 5 September 1898. The Royal Archives and the Bodleian Library, Oxford, online.

50. There is much historical writing on the subject. See, for example, Lewis Levering, *The Race to Fashoda: Colonialism and African Resistance* (New York, Weidenfeld & Nicolson, 1987). Also, Darrell Bates, *The Fashoda Incident of 1898: Encounter on the Nile* (Oxford, Oxford University Press, 1984).

51. Ronald Robinson and John Gallagher with Alice Denny, *Africa and the Victorians: The Official Mind of Imperialism* 2nd edn (London, Macmillan, 1985), p. 369.

52. Patricia Wright, *Conflict on the Nile: The Fashoda Incident of 1898* (London, Heinemann, 1972), p. 173.

53. Ibid., p. 111.

54. Ibid., p. 176.

55. J.B. Rye and Horace G. Groser, eds, *Kitchener in His Own Words* (London, T. Fisher Unwin, 1917), p. 139.

56. Wright, *Conflict on the Nile*, p. 180.

57. Quoted in Robinson and Gallagher, *Africa and the Victorians*, p. 371.

58. Quoted in Andrew Roberts, *Salisbury: Victorian Titan* (London, Phoenix, 2000), p. 710.

59. Robinson and Gallagher, *Africa and the Victorians*, p. 378.

60. KP, PRO 30/57/10.

61. *The Times*, 28 October 1898.

62. Steevens, *With Kitchener to Khartoum*, p. 2.

63. *The Times*, 30 November 1898.

64. KP, PRO 30/57/10.

65. Quoted in Clara Boyle, *Boyle of Cairo: A Diplomatist's Adventures in the Middle East* (Kendal, Titus, 1965), p. 103.

66. KP, PRO 30/57/11.

67. Ibid., PRO 30/57/12.

68. Ibid., PRO 30/57/10.

69. Quoted in Pugh, *Wingate Pasha*, p. 83.

70. Quoted in Magnus, *Kitchener*, p. 151.

71. Quoted in Pollock, *Kitchener*, p. 166.

72. See A.H.M. Kirk-Greene, 'The Sudan Political Service: A Preliminary Profile', (Oxford, Parchment, 1982).

73. KP, PRO 30/57/12.

74. Asher, *Khartoum*, p. 405.

75. *The New Penny Magazine*, 26 November 1898. KP, PRO 30/57/16.

6   The South African War, 1900–2

1. HHP, Add. 51370, ff. 165–6.

2. Rodney Atwood, *The Life of Field Marshal Lord Roberts* (London, Bloomsbury, 2015), pp. 189–90. Also by Atwood, see *Roberts and Kitchener in South Africa, 1900–1902* (Barnsley, Pen & Sword, 2012).

3. Ibid., p. 190. For which the younger Roberts would be posthumously awarded the Victoria Cross. Martin Gilbert, *Churchill: A Life* (London, Heinemann, 1991), p. 107.

4. See Donald Harman Akenson, *God's Peoples: Covenant and Land in South Africa, Israel and Ulster* (Montreal and Kingston, McGill-Queen's University Press, 1992).

5. John Darwin, *The Empire Project: The Rise and Fall of the British World-System, 1830–1970* (Cambridge, Cambridge University Press, 2009), p. 220.

6. Leonard M. Thompson, *The Political Mythology of Apartheid* (New Haven, CT, Yale University Press, 1985), pp. 144–88.

7. See Ian Knight, *Zulu Rising: The Epic Story of Isandlwana and Rorke's Drift* (London, Pan Books, 2010).

8. Thomas Pakenham, *The Boer War* (New York, Perennial, 2001), p. 11.

9. Darwin, *The Empire Project*, p. 225.

10. See Martin Meredith, *Diamonds, Gold, and War: The British, the Boers, and the Making of South Africa* (New York, Public Affairs, 2007).

11. Quoted in Antony Thomas, *Rhodes: The Race for South Africa* (New York, St Martin's Press, 1997), p. 284.

12. Quoted in Denis Judd and Keith Surridge, *The Boer War* (London, Palgrave Macmillan, 2002), p. 40.

13. Robert I. Rotberg, *The Founder: Cecil Rhodes and the Pursuit of Power* (Oxford, Oxford University Press, 1988), p. 374.

14. Pakenham, *The Boer War*, p. 87.

15. Quoted in Mark Weber, 'The Boer War Remembered', *The Journal of Historical Review*, Vol. 18, No. 3 (May–June 1999), p. 15.

16. Ibid.

17. Quoted in Robin W. Winks, ed., *British Imperialism* (New York, Holt, Rinehart and Winston, 1967), p. 80. See, also, John Marlowe, *Milner: Apostle of Empire* (London, Hamish Hamilton, 1976).

18. Andrew Roberts, *Salisbury: Victorian Titan* (London, Phoenix, 2000), pp. 742–4.

19. Quoted in Pakenham, *The Boer War*, p. 110.

20. KP, PRO 30/57/17.

21. Quoted in Atwood, *Lord Roberts*, p. 190. *Globe*, 10 October 1899.

22. Pakenham, *The Boer War*, pp. 301–22.

23. John Pollock, *Kitchener: Architect of Victory, Artisan of Peace* (New York, Carroll & Graf, 2001), p. 176.

24. *Diamond Fields Advertiser*, 10 February 1900.

25. Quoted in Judd and Surridge, *The Boer War*, p. 150.

26. Ibid., p. 164.

27. Quoted in Leo Amery, ed., *The Times History of the War in South Africa*, vol. III (London, Sampson Low, Marston, 1902), p. 425.

28. See Carman Miller, *Painting the Map Red: Canada and the South African War, 1899–1902* (Montreal and Kingston, McGill-Queen's University Press, 1998).

29. In addition to the military histories of the Canadians in South Africa, recently a highly-lauded novel was published by Fred Stenson entitled, *The Great Karoo* (Toronto, Doubleday Canada, 2008). In the book, Kitchener is not regarded favourably either by its author or by any of his fictional characters.

30. Quoted in Pakenham, *The Boer War*, p. 354.

31. Ibid., p. 356.

32. Thomas Hardy, 'The Dead Drummer' or 'Drummer Hodge' (1899).

33. KP, PRO 30/57/21.

34. 'They've caught De Wet, an' now we shan't be long'. Rudyard Kipling, 'Ubique' (1903).

35. Quoted in Pakenham, *The Boer War*, p. 357.

36. *The Globe*, 2 March 1900.

37. See Tim Jeal, *Baden-Powell* (London, Hutchinson, 1989).

38. Quoted in Pollock, *Kitchener*, p. 181.

39. Pakenham, *The Boer War*, p. 463.

40. KP, PRO 30/57/22(1).

41. Quoted in Pollock, *Kitchener*, p. 186.

42. Milner's 'Credo' was published posthumously, first in *The Times*, 25 July 1925.

43. Cecil Headlam, ed., *The Milner Papers, Vol. II: South Africa, 1899–1905* (London, Cassell, 1933), p. 179.

44. Rudyard Kipling, 'Bridge-Guard in the Karroo', first published in *The Times*, 5 June 1901.

45. Pakenham, *The Boer War*, p. 516.

46. For example, ibid., pp. 511–17.

47. Quoted in Pollock, *Kitchener*, p. 189.

48. Christiaan Rudolf De Wet, *Three Years' War: October 1899-June 1902* (Westminster, Archibald Constable, 1902), p. 321.

49. Quoted in Pollock, *Kitchener*, p. 192.

50. L. March Phillips, *With Rimington* (London, Edward Arnold, 1901), p. 187.

51. KP, PRO 30/57/22(2).

52. See J.C. de Villiers, 'The Medical Aspect of the Anglo-Boer War, Part II', *Military History Journal*, Vol. 6, No. 3 (June 1984), pp. 74–93.

53. See Emily Hobhouse, *The Brunt of War and Where it Fell* (London, Methuen, 1902).

54. Birgit S. Seibold, *Emily Hobhouse and the Reports on the Concentration Camps during the Boer War, 1899–1902* (Stuttgart, Ibidem, 2011), p. 112.

55. Quoted in Niall Ferguson, *Empire: The Rise and Demise of the British World Order and the Lessons for Global Power* (New York, Basic Books, 2003), p. 280.

56. Pakenham, *The Boer War*, p. 548.

57. Quoted in Weber, 'The Boer War Remembered', p. 4.

58. Quoted in Philip Magnus, *Kitchener: Portrait of an Imperialist* (London, John Murray, 1958), p. 180.

59. Pakenham, *The Boer War*, p. 524.

60. Quoted in Ferguson, *Empire*, p. 279.
61. Quoted in Pollock, *Kitchener*, p. 195.
62. Quoted in Roberts, *Salisbury*, pp. 798–9.
63. KP, PRO 30/57/22(2).
64. Ibid.
65. Johannes Meintjes, *General Louis Botha: A Biography* (London, Cassell, 1970).
66. KP, PRO 30/57/22(2).
67. See John Marlowe, *Milner: Apostle of Empire* (London, Hamish Hamilton, 1976). See also, Deborah Lavin, *From Empire to International Commonwealth: A Biography of Lionel Curtis* (Oxford, Oxford University Press, 1995); and Andrew Lownie, *John Buchan: The Presbyterian Cavalier* (Toronto, McArthur & Co., 2004).
68. KP, PRO 30/57/22(2).
69. Quoted in Pollock, *Kitchener*, p. 191.
70. Quoted in Rayne Kruger, *Goodbye Dolly Gray: The Story of the Boer War* (London, Pimlico, 1996), p. 413.
71. HHP, Add. 51370, f. 167.
72. William Woolmore, *The Bushveldt Carbineers and the Pietersburg Light Horse* (Sydney, Slouch Hat Publications, 2002).
73. Owing especially to the Australian New Wave feature film, *Breaker Morant*, released in 1980.
74. Most of the biographical material pertaining to Morant is taken from his entry in the *Australian Dictionary of Biography*.
75. KP, PRO 30/57/22(3).
76. Quoted in Fred R. Shapiro, ed., *The Yale Book of Quotations* (New Haven & London, Yale University Press, 2006), p. 536.
77. Quoted in Weber, 'The Boer War Remembered', p. 4.
78. Quoted in Judd and Surridge, *The Boer War*, p. 230.
79. Quoted in Weber, 'The Boer War Remembered', p. 4.
80. For example, in *The Argus*, 7 April 1902. The headline reads: 'The Court-Martialled Australians'.
81. Jim Unkles, lawyer, quoted in *The Daily Telegraph*, 25 July 2013.
82. The director of 'Breaker Morant', Bruce Beresford, has Morant utter this line in the film to suggest his way of rationalizing the killing of Boer prisoners of war.
83. George Witton, *Scapegoats of the Empire: The True Story of Breaker Morant's Bushveldt Carbineers*, new edn (Sydney, Angus & Robertson, 1982).
84. Quoted in Pakenham, *The Boer War*, p. 574.
85. Ibid., p. 583.
86. KP, PRO 30/57/22(3).
87. A.C.M. Tyrrell, 'Melrose House', *Military History Journal* [South Africa], Vol. 1, No. 2 (June 1968), p. 3.
88. Quoted in J.D. Kestell and D.E. van Velden, *The Peace Negotiations Between Boer and Briton in South Africa* (London, Richard Clay, 1912), p. 77.
89. Pollock, *Kitchener*, p. 210.
90. Quoted in ibid., 210.

91. Kestell and van Velden, *The Peace Negotiations*, p. 45.
92. Quoted in Judd and Surridge, *The Boer War*, p. 285.
93. Ibid., p. 290.
94. Quoted in Sir George Arthur, *Not Worth Reading* (London, Longmans, 1938), p. 98.
95. KP, PRO 30/57/22(3).
96. Quoted in Judd and Surridge, *The Boer War*, pp. 291–2.
97. Ibid., p. 296.
98. Kestell and van Velden, *The Peace Negotiations*, p. 339.
99. Quoted in ibid., pp. 343–5. Also, Pollock, *Kitchener*, p. 212, and Judd and Surridge, *The Boer War*, p. 296.
100. Pakenham, *The Boer War*, p. 607.
101. Of course, there is much historiography on these points. A useful place to start is T.R.H. Davenport, *South Africa: A Modern History*, 3rd edn (Toronto, University of Toronto Press, 1987).
102. Rudyard Kipling, 'The Lesson' (1901).
103. See Spencer Jones, *From Boer War to World War: Tactical Reform of the British Army, 1902–1914* (Norman, OK, University of Oklahoma Press, 2012).
104. J.A. Hobson, *The War in South Africa: Its Causes and Effects* (London, James Nisbet & Co., 1900).
105. Ibid. *Imperialism: A Study* (London, Constable, 1902).
106. Pollock, *Kitchener*, p. 216.

7   India and Afterwards, 1902–11

1. NAM, *Diary of Major Sir William Rawlinson, Bt., afterwards General Lord Rawlinson of Trent.*
2. CP, MSS Eur F 111/405, f. 2.
3. 'He remains a man of remarkable ability,' wrote Sir Rennell Rodd from the British Agency in Cairo to Curzon in December 1899, 'of a caliber of which I believe we have few in our army [...] here is a big man who runs a chance of being wasted'. Ibid., ff. 4–9. Also, see David Gilmour, *Curzon* 3rd edn (London, John Murray, 2003), p. 249.
4. Gilmour, *Curzon*, p. 248.
5. KP, PRO 30/57/36.
6. *New York Times*, 23 November 1902.
7. MP, Add. 52276B, f. 18.
8. CP, MSS Eur F 111/162, f. 4.
9. Ibid., MSS Eur F 111/405, f. 3.
10. LCP, MSS Eur F 306/36A, f. 95.
11. Rodney Atwood, *The Life of Field Marshal Lord Roberts* (London, Bloomsbury, 2015), p. 150.
12. See Harold Lee, *Brothers in the Raj: The Lives of John and Henry Lawrence* (Oxford, Oxford University Press, 2002).

13. Charles Allen, *Kipling Sahib: India and the Making of Rudyard Kipling* (London, Little, Brown, 2007), pp. 134–47.

14. The building that Kipling knew as the Tendrils is now incorporated into the Oberoi Cecil, a luxury hotel with breathtaking views southwards from the Mall.

15. Years later, after Indian independence, Snowdon became a hospital (prior to Lord Roberts's occupancy it had functioned as a dispensary), and later still was incorporated into the Indira Gandhi Medical College of today.

16. Wildflower Hall survived in much the same form that Kitchener had left it until 1994 when it was sold by the Himachal Pradesh state government to Oberoi Hotels & Resorts. In 2001, a luxury hotel of the same name was opened on the 22-acre site. The setting is spectacular, with unobstructed views of the Himalayas – Tibet is located just some 70-kilometres to the northeast. As a nod to the property's founder, a portrait of Kitchener hangs above the fireplace in the main lobby.

17. 'My name is George Nathaniel Curzon, I am a most superior person, my cheek is pink, my hair is sleek, I dine at Blenheim once a week'.

18. See Robert Johnson, *Spying for Empire: The Great Game in Central and South Asia* (London, Greenhill, 2006).

19. See Anthony Verrier, *Francis Younghusband and the Great Game* (London, Jonathan Cape, 1991).

20. See, for example, George Nathaniel Curzon, *On the Indian Frontier*, Dhara Anjaria, ed. (Oxford, Oxford University Press, 2011).

21. Jayanta Sengupta, ed., *Charles D'Oyly's Calcutta: Early Nineteenth Century* (Kolkata, Victoria Memorial Hall, 2014).

22. All of these buildings remain, the core of modern Kolkata (Calcutta) still remarkably suggestive of the Raj of a century ago. The Black Hole memorial – which Curzon had raised in honour of those East India Company servants who died in 1756 while imprisoned by Suraj ud-Daula in the 'Black Hole' within the captured Fort William – was moved from Dalhousie Square (today's B.B. D. Bagh) in 1940 to the nearby yard of St John's Church. It remains there today standing sentinel over the memory of what, to the British of the Eighteenth- and Nineteenth- Centuries especially, was an epic of the race and evidence of 'Oriental' cruelty. See C. Brad Faught, *Clive: Founder of British India* (Washington, DC, Potomac, 2013), pp. 48–9.

23. LCP, MSS Eur F 306/36A, f. 3.

24. Ibid., f. 96.

25. Ibid., f. 103.

26. Ibid., f. 104.

27. F.A. Steel and G. Gardiner, *The Complete Indian Housekeeper and Cook* (Oxford, Oxford University Press, 2011), p. 43.

28. Rudyard Kipling, *Plain Tales from the Hills* (Calcutta, Thacker, Spink & Co., 1888).

29. Thomas Pinney, ed., *The Letters of Rudyard Kipling*, vol. I (London, Palgrave Macmillan, 1990), p. 101.

30. Thomas Pinney, ed., *'Something of Myself' and other Autobiographical Writings* (Cambridge, Cambridge University Press, 1990), p. 77.

31. LCP, MSS Eur F 306/36A, f. 112.

32. Ibid.

33. The church remains a prominent part of modern Shimla (as the city was renamed in independent India), and as a parish in the contemporary Church of North India holds regular services in both Hindi and English, although the respective congregations are very small. The brass nameplate denoting the Commander in Chief's reserved place is still affixed to the original pew, a talisman of a bygone age.

34. Recently, the Gaiety has been fully restored and is about to be named a UNESCO World Heritage Site. Modern Shimla makes use of it in various ways, although its Gilbert & Sullivanesque past is quite gone. The theatre's curators maintain an extensive photographic collection, especially of the various casts of long-ago productions. Staring out from a number of these photos can be seen the unmistakable face of Conk Marker.

35. Quoted in John Pollock, *Kitchener: Architect of Victory, Artisan of Peace* (New York, Carroll & Graf, 2001), p. 255.

36. LCP, MSS Eur F 306/36B, f. 146.

37. Ibid., 306/36A, f. 108.

38. Ibid., f. 115.

39. Ibid., 306/36B, f. 172.

40. British Online Archives, 'Indian Papers of the 4th Earl of Minto, Military Department, including Lord Kitchener's administration of the Army in India, 1902–1909', MS 12599–12603.

41. Field Marshal Lord Roberts, *Forty-one Years in India: From Subaltern to Commander-in-Chief* (London, Richard Bentley & Son, 1898).

42. See Richard Holmes, *Sahib: The British Soldier in India* (London, HarperCollins, 2005), pp. 181–97.

43. See Stephen P. Cohen, 'Issue, Role, and Personality: The Kitchener-Curzon Dispute', *Comparative Studies in Society and History*, vol. 10, issue 03, (April 1968), pp. 337–55.

44. Quoted in Pollock, *Kitchener*, p. 256.

45. CP, MSS Eur D 686/18.

46. Ibid.

47. Cohen, 'Issue, Role, and Personality', p. 341.

48. CP, MSS Eur D 686/18.

49. Ibid.

50. Ibid.

51. Ibid.

52. KP, PRO 30/57/28.

53. LCP, MSS Eur F 306/36A, f. 131.

54. Now called the Dhalli Tunnel, it remains essentially as Kitchener would have known it, although enlarged, well lit, and supported by concrete.

55. LCP, MSS Eur F 306/36A, ff. 138–9.
56. BP, Add. 49726, f. 8.
57. LCP, MSS Eur F 306/36A, ff. 141–2.
58. Ibid., f. 143.
59. Quoted in C. Brad Faught, 'An Imperial Prime Minister? W.E. Gladstone and India, 1880–1885', *The Journal of the Historical Society*, VI: 4 (December 2006), pp. 555–78.
60. The view held by Corelli Barnett, for example, in *The Collapse of British Power* 2nd edn (Stroud, Sutton, 1997), pp. 77–80.
61. Quoted in David Dilks, *Curzon in India, Volume II: Frustration* (London, Rupert Hart-Davis, 1970), pp. 183.
62. LCP, MSS Eur F 306/36B, f. 151.
63. Ibid., f. 160. For the domestic life of Lord and Lady Curzon and their children, see Anne de Courcy, *The Viceroy's Daughters: The Lives of the Curzon Sisters* (London, Phoenix, 2001).
64. LCP, MSS Eur F 306/36B, f. 169.
65. Ibid., f. 178.
66. Ibid., f. 171.
67. CP, MSS Eur F 111/405, ff. 23–3.
68. Gilmour, *Curzon*, chs 17–22.
69. Dilks, *Curzon in India, Vol. II*, chs. 7–9.
70. LCP, MSS Eur F 306/36B, f. 181.
71. Ibid., f. 196.
72. Today the dress can be seen on display, along with a number of other Indian and Asian artifacts collected both prior to and during Curzon's years as Viceroy, in the Eastern Museum located in his Derbyshire ancestral home, Kedleston Hall.
73. LCP, MSS Eur F 306/36B, f. 188.
74. Most of the early East India Company senior officials lived outside Calcutta, so pestilential was the city considered to be. Clive, for example, lived at Dum Dum and commuted into Calcutta daily. His house, now in a decrepit state but still standing, is located not far from modern Kolkata's Netaji Subhash Chandra Bose International Airport.
75. See Faught, *Clive*, ch. 4.
76. Quoted in Nigel Nicolson, *Mary Curzon* (New York, Harper & Row, 1977), p. 199.
77. LCP, MSS Eur F 306/36B, f. 192.
78. CP, MSS Eur F 111/405, f. 63.
79. MP, Add. 52276 A, f. 23.
80. Quoted in Pollock, *Kitchener*, p. 306.
81. Ibid.
82. MP, Add. 52277 A, f. 4.
83. LCP, MSS Eur F 306/36B, ff. 205–6.
84. Ibid., f. 208.

85. Ibid., f. 209. The local Masonic Lodge, of which Kitchener had become a member shortly after arriving in Simla two years earlier, met in a hall contained within the same building as the Gaiety Theatre. The hall remains today, but is unused, rather forlorn, and not (yet) deemed worthy of restoration.
86. CP, MSS Eur F 111/405, f. 14.
87. Ibid., f. 27. Quoted in Daniel Argov, *Moderates and Exiles in the Indian Nationalist Movement, 1883–1920, with special reference to Surendranath Banerjea and Lajpat Rai* (London, Asia Publishing House, 1967), p. 105.
88. See Krishna Dutta and Andrew Robinson, *Rabindranath Tagore: The Myriad-Minded Man* (London, Bloomsbury, 1995).
89. Later, in 1911 under Lord Hardinge as Viceroy, the partition was annulled and the divided province of Bengal was reunited.
90. CP, MSS Eur F 111/405, Command Paper on the 'Administration of the Army in India', May 1905, ff. 68–79.
91. CrP, FO, PRO 633/7, f. 289.
92. MP, Add. 52276 A, f. 91.
93. CP, MSS Eur F 111/405, f. 47.
94. General Lord Kitchener, 'A Note on the Military Policy of India', PRO 30/57/30.
95. Sir Philip Magnus, *Kitchener: Portrait of an Imperialist* (London, John Murray, 1958), p. 220.
96. CP, MSS Eur D 686/13, f. 42. Also, MP, Add. 52278, f. 96.
97. Ibid., MSS Eur F 111/211, f. 27.
98. MP, Add. 52278, f. 9.
99. Ibid., Add. 52276 A, f. 107.
100. LCP, MSS Eur F 306/13A, ff. 1–2; ff. 143–6.
101. CP, MSS Eur F 111/183, f. 17.
102. Pollock, *Kitchener*, p. 322.
103. Lawrence James: *Raj: The Making and Unmaking of British India* (London, Little, Brown, 1997), p. 362. Gilmour, *Curzon*, p. 296.
104. Quoted in Sir George Arthur, *Life of Lord Kitchener*, vol. II, (London, Macmillan, 1920), p. 219n.
105. For a detailed study of Morley as Secretary of State for India, see Stanley Wolpert, *Morley and India* (Berkeley, University of California Press, 1967).
106. Quoted in Pollock, *Kitchener*, p. 331.
107. Now known as Command and Staff College, it is one of modern Pakistan's most prestigious military institutions and is a constituent college of the National Defence University at Islamabad.
108. MP, Add. 52276 A, f. 34.
109. Ibid., Add. 52278, f. 96.
110. See Jennifer Siegel, *Endgame: Britain, Russia and the Final Struggle for Central Asia* (London, I.B.Tauris, 2002).
111. Quoted in Gilmour, *Curzon*, p. 377.
112. See Herbert Horatio Kitchener, *Oxford Dictionary of National Biography*.

113. CP, MSS Eur F 111/405, f. 20.

114. Ibid., f. 18.

115. KP, PRO 30/57/31.

116. Ibid., PRO 30/57/38.

117. KP, PRO 30/57/38. Quoted in Pollock, *Kitchener*, p. 343.

118. See Avner Offer, 'Costs and Benefits, Prosperity and Security, 1870–1914', Andrew Porter ed., *The Oxford History of the British Empire: The Nineteenth Century* (Oxford, Oxford University Press, 1999), pp. 690–711.

119. KP, PRO 30/57/39.

120. Ibid., PRO 30/57/40.

121. Magnus, *Kitchener*, p. 246.

122. Ibid., 30/57/31.

123. Ibid.

124. Ibid.

125. Quoted in Pollock, *Kitchener*, p. 348.

126. Quoted in Roy Jenkins, *Asquith* (London, Collins, 1964), p. 343.

127. National Army Museum, 7807.25.44.

128. Ibid.

129. Denys Finch Hatton, the aristocratic big game hunter, for example, had come out two years earlier. Karen Blixen, later to be his lover and eventually the famous novelist Isak Dinesen, arrived at the beginning of 1914. See Errol Trzebinski, *Silence Will Speak: A Study of the Life of Denys Finch Hatton and His Relationship with Karen Blixen* (Chicago, University of Chicago Press, 1985). Also, Isak Dinesen, *Letters from Africa, 1914–1931*, Trans. Anne Born, (Chicago, University of Chicago Press, 1981).

130. KP, PRO 30/57/98.

131. Ibid., PRO 30/57/110.

132. Ibid., PRO 30/57/97.

8   Egypt Again, 1911–14

1. KP, PRO 30/57/41.

2. Archie Hunter, *Power and Passion in Egypt: A Life of Sir Eldon Gorst* (London, I.B.Tauris, 2007), pp. 239–41.

3. Roger Owen, *Lord Cromer: Victorian Imperialist Edwardian Proconsul* (Oxford, Oxford University Press, 2004), p. 380.

4. Quoted in Sir Philip Magnus, *Kitchener: Portrait of an Imperialist* (London, John Murray, 1958), p. 259.

5. KP, PRO 30/57/36.

6. Quoted in Martin Gilbert, *Continue to Pester, Nag and Bite: Churchill's War Leadership* (Toronto, Vintage Canada, 2004), p. 3.

7. See, for example, Robert L. Tignor, *Modernization and British Colonial Rule in Egypt, 1882–1914* (Princeton, Princeton University Press, 1966), and Peter Mansfield, *The British in Egypt* (London, Weidenfeld & Nicolson, 1971).

8. Quoted in Hunter, *Gorst*, p. 176.
9. As John Pollock too-critically describes him. *Kitchener: Architect of Victory, Artisan of Peace* (New York, Carroll & Graf, 2001), p. 355.
10. Ibid., p. 218.
11. See Owen, *Lord Cromer*, pp. 215–35 and 304–24.
12. See Afaf Lutfi Al-Sayyid-Marsot, 'The British Occupation of Egypt from 1882', Andrew Porter, ed., *The Oxford History of the British Empire: The Nineteenth Century* (Oxford, Oxford University Press, 1999), pp. 651–64. Also, E.R.J. Owen, *Cotton and the Egyptian Economy, 1820–1914: A Study in Trade and Development* (Oxford, Clarendon Press, 1969).
13. KP, PRO 30/57/42.
14. Ibid.
15. See Lord Lugard, *The Dual Mandate in British Tropical Africa* (London, Frank Cass, 1965).
16. KP, PRO 30/57/42.
17. Ibid.
18. T.E. Lawrence, *Seven Pillars of Wisdom* (London, Penguin, 2000), pp. 56–7.
19. Sir Ronald Storrs, *Orientations* (London, Nicholson & Watson, 1943), p. 122. See, also, *The Memoirs of Sir Ronald Storrs* (New York, G.P. Putnam's Sons, 1937).
20. Ibid., *Orientations*, p. 136.
21. Owen, *The Middle East in the World Economy, 1800–1914* (London, I.B.Tauris, 1993), p. 241.
22. As reported to British readers of *The Fortnightly Review* in 'Lord Kitchener in Egypt' (July 1912) by his future official biographer, Sir George Arthur. KP, PRO 30/57/42.
23. Ibid., PRO 30/57/44.
24. Ibid., PRO 30/57/45.
25. Ibid.
26. Hunter, *Gorst*, p. 242.
27. KP, PRO 30/57/36.
28. Ibid., PRO 30/57/44.
29. Ibid.
30. Ibid.
31. Pollock, *Kitchener*, p. 366.
32. KP, PRO 30/57/47.
33. Ibid., PRO 30/57/70.
34. HHP, Add. 51370, f. 197.

9 Supreme British Warlord, 1914–16

1. Margaret MacMillan, *The War that Ended Peace: The Road to 1914* (London, Allen Lane, 2013); Christopher Clark, *The Sleepwalkers: How Europe Went to War in 1914* (London, Allen Lane, 2012).

2. KP, PRO 30/57/76.

3. Quoted in Michael and Eleanor Brock, eds, *Margot Asquith's Great War Diary 1914–1916: The View from Downing Street* (Oxford, Oxford University Press, 2014), p. 14.

4. The approach of the implementation of Home Rule in Ireland in the spring of 1914 caused a number of British officers stationed at Curragh Camp near Dublin to choose dismissal over being forced to fire upon their Protestant co-religionists in Ulster who were opposed to the measure. Ultimately, the British government backed down by assuring such officers that Home Rule would not be forced upon Ulster and therefore they would not be put in a position where their resignation was necessary. But part of the price to be paid politically for the decision was that Asquith demanded Seely's resignation as War Secretary. Of course, the outbreak of war would scuttle the implementation of Home Rule itself. See Ian F.W. Beckett, *The Army and the Curragh Incident 1914* (London, Bodley Head, 1986).

5. Brock and Brock, eds, *Margot Asquith's Great War Diary*, pp. 14–15.

6. KP, PRO 30/57/76.

7. George H. Cassar, *Kitchener: Architect of Victory* (London, William Kimber, 1977), p. 177.

8. Quoted in ibid.

9. See Spencer Jones, *From Boer War to World War: Tactical Reform of the British Army, 1902–1914* (Norman, OK, University of Oklahoma Press, 2012), pp. 58–70.

10. KP, WO 159/3.

11. Sir Philip Magnus, *Kitchener: Portrait of an Imperialist* (London, John Murray, 1958), p. 281.

12. Quoted in Sir George Arthur, *Life of Lord Kitchener*, vol. III (London, Macmillan, 1920), p. 7.

13. Peter Doyle and Chris Foster, *What Tommy Took To War 1914–1918* (Oxford, Shire Publications, 2014).

14. 'Lord Kitchener's Guidance to British Troops, August 1914', Primary Documents Online, firstworldwar.com.

15. Virtually everything war-related crossed Kitchener's desk; to wit: 'Would it be possible', wrote Lord Halifax, future Viceroy of India and Foreign Secretary, and the so-called 'Holy Fox' because of his seriously-held Anglo-Catholic beliefs, which were shared by the Secretary of War, 'for you to say a word to the Chaplain-General about the selection of chaplains he makes for the Army [. . .]. I do earnestly desire that they [the soldiers] should all have that help and comfort, so far as is possible, upon which so much depends in this world and the next'. KP, PRO 30/57/73.

16. Such, for example, was the view of Raymond Asquith, the Prime Minister's eldest son by his deceased first wife, Helen Melland. Brilliant and a highly successful barrister, he would become part of Britain's World War I lost generation when he fell at the Somme in September of 1916. 'K of Chaos, as

they call him', he wrote to a friend in August 1914, 'seems to be a sad mixture of gloom, ignorance and loquacity: says the war will last three years [...].' Brilliant Raymond Asquith was, but perhaps not much of a judge of character, nor, it would seem, of the length of the war. John Joliffe, ed., *Raymond Asquith: Life and Letters* (London, Century, 1987), p. 182.

17. Quoted in Winston S. Churchill, *The World Crisis*, vol. I (New York, Charles Scribner's Sons, 1951), p. 253.

18. KP, WO 159/19.

19. Ibid., WO 159/18.

20. Quoted in David Reynolds, *The Long Shadow: The Legacies of the Great War in the Twentieth Century* (New York, W.W. Norton & Co., 2014), p. 353.

21. KP, WO 159/21.

22. Ibid., WO 159/7. The place of the horse in World War I has received much attention recently, both scholarly and otherwise. Notable in this regard is the novel by Michael Morpurgo, *War Horse* (London, Kaye & Ward, 1982), which was made into a highly popular West End play in 2007, as well as a successful Hollywood film four years later.

23. KP, WO 159/8.

24. The *London Opinion* sold for a penny and had a circulation of about 300,000, very wide for the time. KP, PRO 30/57/123.

25. Many years after its publication in 1914 the Leete-designed Kitchener poster – and not the very much lesser known and wordier War Office one – was voted by a (mainly) British electorate to be the most influential of the twentieth century. See Maurice Rickards, ed., *Posters of the First World War* (London, Evelyn Adams & MacKay, 1968), pp. 10–12.

26. James Taylor, *Your Country Needs You: The Secret History of the Propaganda Poster* (Glasgow, Saraband, 2013).

27. KP, WO 159/21. See Peter Simkins, *Kitchener's Army* (Manchester, Manchester University Press, 1988).

28. Brock and Brock, eds, *Margot Asquith's Great War Diary*, p. 20.

29. 'Kaiser Wilhelm II and the Contemptible Little Army, 19 August 1914', Primary Documents Online, firstworldwar.com.

30. Famously, written by Wellington to Lord Bathurst, Secretary of War, in 1813 during the Peninsular Campaign.

31. Archie Hunter, *Kitchener's Sword Arm: The Life and Campaigns of General Sir Archibald Hunter* (Staplehurst, Spellmount, 1996).

32. KP, PRO 30/57/80.

33. Martin Gilbert, *First World War* (Toronto, Stoddart, 1994), p. 55.

34. KP, PRO 30/57/49.

35. Brock and Brock, eds, *Margot Asquith's Great War Diary*, p. 23.

36. Ibid.

37. KP, WO 159/2.

38. KP, PRO 30/57/49.

39. Quoted in Arthur, *Life of Lord Kitchener*, vol. III, p. 53.

40. Michael Brock and Eleanor Brock, eds, *H.H. Asquith: Letters to Venetia Stanley* (Oxford, Oxford University Press, 1982), p. 213.
41. BP, Add. 49726, f. 14.
42. KP, PRO 30/57/78.
43. Quoted in Martin Gilbert, *Winston S. Churchill, vol. III: The Challenge of War, 1914–1916* (Boston, Houghton Mifflin, 1971), p. 61.
44. Quoted in Roy Jenkins, *Asquith* (London, Collins, 1964), p. 343.
45. General Sir Horace Smith-Dorrien, *Memories of Forty-Eight Years' Service* (London, John Murray, 1925), p. 201.
46. Quoted in Gilbert, *First World War*, p. 75.
47. KP, PRO 30/57/49.
48. Ibid., WO 159/23.
49. Brock and Brock, eds, *Letters to Venetia Stanley*, p. 224.
50. KP, WO 159/6.
51. See Larry Zuckerman, *The Rape of Belgium: The Untold Story of World War I* (New York, New York University Press, 2004).
52. KP, WO 159/2.
53. Ibid., PRO 30/57/49.
54. Ibid., WO 159/15.
55. Ibid., PRO 30/57/73.
56. Ibid., PRO 30/57/52.
57. Rodney Atwood, *The Life of Field Marshal Lord Roberts* (London, Bloomsbury, 2015), p. 263.
58. Ibid., p. 267.
59. Simkins, *Kitchener's Army*, p. 39.
60. See Michael Bliss, *A Canadian Millionaire: The Life and Business Times of Sir Joseph Flavelle, Bart., 1858–1939* (Toronto, Macmillan, 1978).
61. Quoted in Ferdinand Foch, *The Memoirs of Marshal Foch*, Trans. T. Bentley Mott, (London, Heinemann, 1931), p. 162.
62. Quoted in John Pollock, *Kitchener: Architect of Victory, Artisan of Peace* (New York, Carroll & Graf, 2001), p. 415.
63. Horatio Herbert Kitchener, *Oxford Dictionary of National Biography*.
64. George H. Cassar, *Kitchener's War: British Strategy from 1914 to 1916* (Washington, DC, Potomac, 2004), p. 117. Unbeknownst to Kitchener, as later discovered, Asquith was similarly inclined to divulge information pertaining to some of the issues discussed in Cabinet to both his wife and his mistress.
65. Quoted in Pollock, *Kitchener*, p. 419.
66. See Malcolm Brown, ed., *No Man's Land: Christmas 1914 and Fraternization in the Great War* (London, Constable, 2007).
67. KP, WO 159/13.
68. See Paul Fussell, *The Great War and Modern Memory* (Oxford, Oxford University Press, 1977), ch. 2. Also, Modris Eksteins, *Rites of Spring: The Great War and the Birth of the Modern World* (Toronto, Lester & Orpen Dennys, 1989), ch. 3.

69. KP, WO 159/15.

70. Ibid., WO 159/10.

71. Quoted in Cassar, *Kitchener's War*, p. 119.

72. KP, WO 159/2.

73. Ibid.

74. Quoted in Jenkins, *Asquith*, p. 349.

75. KP, WO 159/3.

76. In the end, Churchill paid the price for the Dardanelles disaster and indeed had earned his sacking from Cabinet as he had 'owned' the campaign from the outset. Still, however, there are those who continue to put the blame for the Dardanelles on Kitchener. See, for example, Eugene Rogan, *The Fall of the Ottomans: The Great War in the Middle East* (New York, Basic Books, 2015), p. 189.

77. KP, PRO 30/57/50. See, also, Richard Holmes, *The Little Field Marshal: A Life of Sir John French* (London, Cassell, 2007), pp. 265, 277, 280.

78. KP, WO 159/3.

79. Quoted in Jenkins, *Asquith*, p. 353.

80. Brock and Brock, eds, *Margot Asquith's Great War Diary*, p. 84.

81. See Peter Hart, *Gallipoli* (Oxford, Oxford University Press, 2011).

82. See Hew Strachan, *The First World War: Volume I: To Arms* (Oxford, Oxford University Press, 2001), ch. 11. One of the British soldiers killed at Loos was John Kipling, the 18-year-old only son of Rudyard and his wife Carrie. His death sparked enormous remorse by Kipling, who had strongly encouraged his son to join up and fight. Despite a number of attempts by his parents, John Kipling's grave was not found in their lifetimes. Indeed, only in 1992 was it finally located, although since then its authenticity has been disputed. See David Gilmour, *The Long Recessional: The Imperial Life of Rudyard Kipling* (London, Farrar, Straus and Giroux, 2002), p. 250.

83. Gilbert, *First World War*, pp. 132–3.

84. *The Times*, 14 May 1915.

85. *Daily Mail*, 21 May 1915.

86. Quoted in Jenkins, *Asquith*, p. 357.

87. Brock and Brock, eds, *Margot Asquith's Great War Diary*, p. 105.

88. KP, PRO 30/57/82.

89. Cassar, *Kitchener's War*, p. 182.

90. KP, PRO 30/57/110.

91. Ibid., PRO 30/57/73.

92. KP, WO 159/3.

93. Ibid.

94. Ibid.

95. KP, PRO 30/57/53.

96. Quoted in Martin Pugh, *Lloyd George* (Abingdon, Routledge, 2013), p. 89.

97. Quoted in Travis L. Crosby, *The Unknown David Lloyd George: A Statesman in Conflict* (London, I.B.Tauris, 2014), p. 183.

98. Brock and Brock, eds, *Margot Asquith's Great War Diary*, p. 92.

99. Pugh, *Lloyd George*, p. 89.

100. Crosby, *The Unknown David Lloyd George*, p. 184.

101. Roland Quinault, 'Asquith: A Prime Minister at War', *History Today*, Vol. 64, Issue 5 (May 2014).

102. AP, MSS. Asquith 14:52; KP, PRO 30/57/111.

103. KP, PRO 30/57/106.

104. Quoted in Jenkins, *Asquith*, p. 372.

105. Ibid.

106. KP, WO 159/3.

107. AP, MSS. Asquith, 14:117.

108. Jenkins, *Asquith*, p. 372.

109. KP, WO 159/3; WO 159/7.

110. See John Darwin, *The Empire Project: The Rise and Fall of the British World System, 1830–1970* (Cambridge, Cambridge University Press, 2009), ch. 8, 'The War for Empire, 1914–1919'. Also, Cassar, *Kitchener's War*, chs 3, 8, and 12.

111. KP, PRO 30/57/61.

112. Ibid., WO 159/16; PRO 30/57/56.

113. The Second Battle of Ypres also inspired one of its Canadian participants, Lieutenant John McCrae, a physician, to pen an ode to a comrade killed there, which he called 'In Flanders Fields'. Once published in *Punch* later that year, McCrae's simple three-stanza poem would fast become one of the best-known of World War I.

114. KP, WO 159/3.

115. Ibid., WO 159/7.

116. Ibid., WO 159/5; WO 159/13.

117. Ibid., WO 159/7.

118. Cassar, *Kitchener's War*, pp. 44–7.

119. See Hew Strachan, *The First World War in Africa* (Oxford, Oxford University Press, 2004). Also, Edward Paice, *Tip and Run: The Untold Tragedy of the Great War in Africa* (London, Phoenix, 2008).

120. BP, Add. 49726, f. 19.

121. See Matthew Hughes, *Allenby and British Strategy in the Middle East, 1917–1919* (London, Frank Cass, 1999).

122. Quoted in Pollock, *Kitchener*, p. 446.

123. Ibid., p. 452.

124. Brock and Brock, eds, *Margot Asquith's Great War Diary*, p. 209.

125. Jenkins, *Asquith*, p. 380.

126. Ibid., p. 381.

127. BP, Add. 49726, f. 35.

128. AP, MSS. Asquith, 121:17.

129. KP, PRO 30/57/62.

130. AP, MSS. Asquith, 121:14.

131. Ibid., 121:12.
132. Much like the sepia-tinged treatment accorded the life of *Breaker Morant* (1980) in the eponymously named film, the role of the Anzacs at Gallipoli was given a powerful (though somewhat sentimental and inaccurate) retelling in the film *Gallipoli* (1981). The two films were similarly anti-British in tone, an unsurprising stance given that one of the latter's executive producers is the now-disgraced Australian expatriate newspaper magnate and fierce republican, Rupert Murdoch. Recently, in 2014, a superbly-made television serial, *ANZAC Girls*, which concentrates on the Australian and New Zealand nurses who served in Egypt, at Gallipoli, and in France was broadcast to wide acclaim in both countries. Also, BP, Add. 49726, f. 17.
133. KP, PRO 30/57/61.
134. Ibid., PRO 30/57/92.
135. Ibid., PRO 30/57/66.
136. Quoted in David Gilmour, *Curzon* (London, John Murray, 2003), p. 442.
137. Brock and Brock, eds, *Margot Asquith's Great War Diary*, p. 218.
138. Arthur, *Life of Lord Kitchener*, vol. III, pp. 293–5.
139. Winston S. Churchill, *The Story of the Malakand Field Force: An Episode of Frontier War* (1898).
140. Quoted in David R. Woodward, *Field Marshal Sir William Robertson* (Westport, CT, Praeger, 1998), p. 11.
141. Brock and Brock, eds, *Margot Asquith's Great War Diaries*, p. 227.
142. Quoted in Jenkins, *Asquith*, p. 384.
143. Quoted in Sir William Robertson, *From Private to Field Marshal* (London, Constable, 1921), p. 237.
144. KP, PRO 30/57/67.
145. Robertson, *From Private to Field Marshal*, p. 243.
146. Reginald Viscount Esher, *The Tragedy of Lord Kitchener* (London, John Murray, 1921), p. 189.
147. Quoted in Robertson, *From Private to Field Marshal*, p. 264.
148. Cassar, *Kitchener: Architect of Victory*, pp. 460–1.
149. KP, WO 159/12.
150. Quoted in Gilbert, *First World War*, p. 232.
151. Cassar, *Kitchener's War*, p. 269. Such was the essential message contained in the frequent telegrams sent by Sir John French to Kitchener during the first year-and-a-half of the war. KP, WO, 159/13.
152. Ibid., PRO 30/57/53. See also, J.P. Harris, *Douglas Haig and the First World War* (Cambridge, Cambridge University Press, 2008), pp. 210–13.
153. Reynolds, *The Long Shadow*, p. 353.
154. Rogan, *The Fall of the Ottomans*, p. 260.
155. See Paul K. Davis, *Ends and Means: The British Mesopotamian Campaign and Commission* (London, Associated University Presses, 1994). For the Kitchener Hospital, see Suzanne Bardgett, 'A Mutual Fascination: Indians in Brighton',

History Today, Vol. 65, Issue 3 (March 2015). See also, KP, WO 159/17: 'Care of the Sick and Wounded Indian Troops in France'.

156. Quoted in Brock and Brock, eds, *Margot Asquith's Great War Diaries*, p. 262.

157. See John Townsend, *Proconsul to the Middle East: Sir Percy Cox and the End of Empire* (London, I.B.Tauris, 2010), and Georgina Howell, *Daughter of the Desert: The Remarkable Life of Gertrude Bell* (London, Macmillan, 2006).

158. Elizabeth Munroe, *Britain's Moment in the Middle East, 1914–1971* 2nd edn (Baltimore, Johns Hopkins University Press, 1981), p. 26.

159. See, for example, H.C.G. Matthew, *Gladstone 1809–1898* (Oxford, Clarendon Press, 1997), pp. 267–71.

160. See Karl E. Meyer and Shareen Blair Brysac, *Kingmakers: The Invention of the Modern Middle East* (New York, W.W. Norton, 2008). Also, Roger D. Adelson, *Mark Sykes: Portrait of an Amateur* (London, Jonathan Cape, 1975).

161. Quoted in Rogan, *The Fall of the Ottomans*, p. 325.

162. KP, PRO 30/57/91.

163. Jeremy Wilson, *Lawrence of Arabia: The Authorized Biography of T.E. Lawrence* (New York, Atheneum, 1990), chs 13–15.

164. Cassar, *Kitchener's War*, pp. 276–7.

165. BP, Add. 49726, f. 21.

166. Keith Neilson, *Strategy and Supply: The Anglo-Russian Alliance, 1914–1917* (London, Allen and Unwin, 1984), p. 172.

167. Cassar, *Kitchener's War*, p. 282.

168. KP, PRO 30/57/67.

169. Ibid, PRO 30/57/60.

170. Quoted in Jenkins, *Asquith*, p. 399.

171. KP, PRO 30/57/85.

10 A Watery Grave and a Contested Reputation: 1916 and Beyond

1. KP, PRO 30/57/85.

2. *Parliamentary Debates*, 31 May 1916.

3. Quoted in Roy Jenkins, *Asquith* (London, Collins, 1964), p. 405.

4. *Parliamentary Debates*, 31 May 1916.

5. Sir George Arthur, *Life of Lord Kitchener*, vol. III (London, Macmillan, 1920), p. 326.

6. Quoted in ibid., p. 327.

7. Ibid., p. 334.

8. Ibid., p. 335.

9. Quoted in Duff Cooper, *Old Men Forget: The Autobiography of Duff Cooper* (New York, E.P. Dutton, 1954), p. 56.

10. Quoted in John Pollock, *Kitchener: Architect of Victory, Artisan of Peace* (New York, Carroll & Graf, 2001), p. 475.

11. KP, PRO 30/57/85.

12. Earl of Oxford and Asquith, *Memories and Reflections 1852–1927*, vol. II (Boston, Little, Brown, 1928), p. 84.

13. Margot Asquith, *More Memories* (London, Cassell, 1933), p. 141.

14. George H. Cassar, *Kitchener's War: British Strategy from 1914 to 1916* (Washington, D.C., Potomac, 2004), pp. 286–88.

15. KP, PRO 30/57/85.

16. Ibid.

17. Norman Friedman, *British Cruisers of the Victorian Era* (Barnsley, Seaforth, 2012). See, also, 'The Loss of HMS *Hampshire*', n.a., Royal Naval Museum Library, 2000.

18. Michael Brock and Eleanor Brock, eds, *Margot Asquith's Great War Diary 1914–1916: The View from Downing Street* (Oxford, Oxford University Press, 2014), p. 266.

19. Oxford and Asquith, *Memories and Reflections*, vol. II, p. 84.

20. KP, PRO 30/57/119.

21. Quoted in Pollock, *Kitchener*, p. 486.

22. Martin Gilbert, *Churchill: A Life* (London, Heinemann, 1991), p. 363.

23. Quoted in David Gilmour, *Curzon* (London, John Murray, 1994), p. 447.

24. John Joliffe, ed., *Raymond Asquith: Life and Letters* (London, Century, 1987), pp. 267–8.

25. KP, PRO 30/57/118.

26. Ibid., PRO 30/57/94.

27. An overly critical and sensationalist stance towards Kitchener is held by Paxman, both in his earlier book, *Empire: What Ruling the World Did to the British* (London, Viking, 2011), especially pp. 184–6 – which was followed by a five-part BBC television series broadcast in 2012 – and in his latest, *Great Britain's Great War* (London, Viking, 2013), pp. 173–9. See also, Paxman's essay on the death of Kitchener published in the *Daily Mail* on 15 November 2014, pp. 64–5.

28. KP, PRO 30/57/115.

29. Sir Hedley Le Bas, ed., *The Lord Kitchener Memorial Book* (London, Hodder and Stoughton, 1917).

30. KP, PRO 30/57/113.

31. See Stephen Heathorn, *Haig and Kitchener in Twentieth-Century Britain: Remembrance, Representation and Appropriation* (Farnham, Ashgate, 2013), ch. 3.

32. Thomas Carlyle, *On Heroes, Hero-Worship and the Heroic In History* (London, Chapman & Hall, 1840).

33. Max Jones, 'What Should Historians Do With Heroes? Reflections on Nineteenth- and Twentieth-Century Britain', *History Compass* 5/2 (2007), pp. 439–40.

34. Keith Surridge, 'More than a Great Poster: Lord Kitchener and the Image of the Military Hero', *Historical Research*, Vol. 74, No. 185 (August 2001), pp. 298–313.

35. Asquith, *More Memories*, p. 135.

36. See John M. MacKenzie, ed., *Popular Imperialism and the Military 1850–1950* (Manchester, Manchester University Press, 1992), pp. 1–24.

37. Surridge, 'More than a Great Poster', p. 313.
38. *Hawera & Normanby Star*, 22 August 1916.
39. H.C.G. Matthew, *Gladstone 1809–1898* (Oxford, Clarendon Press, 1997), p. vii.
40. Heathorn, *Haig and Kitchener*, p. 234.
41. Surridge, 'More than a Great Poster', p. 313.
42. Keith Neilson, 'Kitchener: A Reputation Refurbished', *Canadian Journal of History*, Vol. 15, Issue 2 (August 1980), p. 226.
43. Harold Temperley, *The Listener*, Vol. 15, No. 386 (3 June 1936), p. 1049. KP, PRO 30/57/94.

Bibliography

Archival Sources

Asquith Papers (AP), Bodleian Library, Oxford
Balfour Papers (BP), British Library, London
Cromer Papers, (CrP) The National Archives, London
Curzon Papers (CP), British Library, London
firstworldwar.com, Primary Documents Online
Gordon Papers (GP), British Library, London
Holland House Papers (HHP), British Library, London
Kitchener Papers (KP), The National Archives, London
Lady Curzon Papers (LCP), British Library, London
Marker Papers (MP), British Library, London
4th Earl of Minto, Indian Papers, British Online Archives
National Army Museum, London
Queen Victoria's Journals, The Royal Archives and the Bodleian Library, Oxford
(online)

Secondary Sources (Books)

Adelson, Roger D. *Mark Sykes: Portrait of an Amateur* (London, Jonathan Cape, 1975).

Akenson, Donald Harman. *God's Peoples: Covenant and Land in South Africa, Israel and Ulster* (Montreal and Kingston, McGill-Queen's University Press, 1991).

Allen, Charles. *Kipling Sahib: India and the Making of Rudyard Kipling* (London, Little, Brown, 2007).

Amery, Leo, ed. *The Times History of the War in South Africa*, Vol. III (London, Sampson Low, Marston, 1902).

Argov, Daniel. *Moderates and Exiles in the Indian Nationalist Movement, 1883–1920, with special reference to Surendranath Banerjea and Lajput Rai* (London, Asia Publishing House, 1967).

Arthur, Sir George. *Life of Lord Kitchener*, Vol. III (London, Macmillan, 1920).

———. *Not Worth Reading* (London, Longmans, 1938).

Asher, Michael. *Khartoum: The Ultimate Imperial Adventure* (London, Penguin, 2006).

Asquith, Margot. *More Memories* (London, Cassell, 1933).

Atwood, Rodney. *The Life of Field Marshal Lord Roberts* (London, Bloomsbury, 2015).

———. *Roberts and Kitchener in South Africa, 1900–1902* (Barnsley, Pen & Sword, 2012).

Barnett, Corelli. *The Collapse of British Power*, 2nd edn (Stroud, Sutton, 1997).

Bates, Darell. *The Fashoda Incident of 1898: Encounter on the Nile* (Oxford, Oxford University Press, 1984).

Beckett, Ian F.W. *The Army and the Curragh Incident 1914* (London, Bodley Head, 1986).

Begbie, Harold. *Kitchener: Organizer of Victory* (Boston, Houghton Mifflin, 1915).

Belloc, Hilaire. *The Modern Traveller* (London, Edward Arnold, 1898).

Berenson, Edward. *Heroes of Empire: Five Charismatic Men and the Conquest of Africa* (Berkeley, University of California Press, 2011).

Berton, Pierre. *Vimy* (Toronto, McClelland & Stewart, 1986).

Blake, Robert. *Disraeli* (New York, St Martin's Press, 1967).

Bliss, Michael. *A Canadian Millionaire: The Life and Business Times of Sir Joseph Flavelle, Bart., 1858–1939* (Toronto, Macmillan, 1978).

Blunt, Wilfrid Scawen. *Atrocities of Justice under the English Rule in Egypt* (London, T. Fisher Unwin, 1906).

Boyle, Clara. *Boyle of Cairo: A Diplomatist's Adventures in the Middle East* (Kendal, Titus, 1965).

Bresler, Fenton. *Napoleon III: A Life* (New York, Carroll & Graf, 1999).

Brighton, Terry. *The Last Charge: The 21st Lancers and the Battle of Omdurman* (Marlborough, Crowood, 1998).

Brock, Michael and Eleanor Brock, eds. *H.H. Asquith: Letters to Venetia Stanley* (Oxford, Oxford University Press, 1982).

———. *Margot Asquith's Great War Diary 1914–1916: The View from Downing Street* (Oxford, Oxford University Press, 2014).

Brown, Malcolm, ed. *No Man's Land: Christmas 1914 and Fraternization in the Great War* (London, Constable, 2007).

Carlyle, Thomas. *On Heroes, Hero-Worship and the Heroic In History* (London, Chapman & Hall, 1840).

Cassar, George H. *Kitchener: Architect of Victory* (London, William Kimber, 1977).

———. *Kitchener's War: British Strategy from 1914 to 1916* (Washington, DC, Potomac, 2004).

Cecil, Lord Edward. *The Leisure of an Egyptian Official* (London, Hodder & Stoughton, 1921).

Churchill, Winston S. *The River War: An Account of the Reconquest of the Sudan* (New York, Carroll & Graf, 2000).

———. *The World Crisis,* Vol. I (New York, Charles Scribner's Sons).

Clark, Christopher. *The Sleepwalkers: How Europe Went to War in 1914* (London, Allen Lane, 2012).

Colley, Linda. *Britons: Forging the Nation, 1707–1837* (New Haven, CT, Yale University Press, 1992).

Conder, C.R. *Tent-Work in Palestine*, Vol. II (London, Richard Bentley, 1879).

Cooper, Duff. *Old Men Forget: The Autobiography of Duff Cooper* (New York, E.P. Dutton, 1954).

Crosby, Travis L. *The Unknown David Lloyd George: A Statesman in Conflict* (London, I.B.Tauris, 2014).

Cromer, Earl of (Evelyn Baring). *Modern Egypt*, Vol. II (London, Macmillan, 1908).
———. *Abbas II* (London, Macmillan, 1915).

Curzon, George Nathaniel. *On the Indian Frontier*, Dhara Anjaria, ed. (Oxford, Oxford University Press, 2011).

Daly, M.W. *Sirdar: Sir Reginald Wingate and the British Empire in the Middle East* (Philadelphia, American Philosophical Society, 1997).

Darwin, John. *The Empire Project: The Rise and Fall of the British World System, 1830-1970* (Cambridge, Cambridge University Press, 2009).

Davenport, T.R.H. *South Africa: A Modern History*, 3rd edn (Toronto, University of Toronto Press, 1987).

Davis, Clarence B., Kenneth E. Wilburn, and Ronald E. Robinson, eds, *Railway Imperialism* (Westport, CT, Praeger, 1991).

Davis, Paul K. *Ends and Means: The British Mesopotamian Campaign and Commission* (London, Associated University Presses, 1994).

De Courcy, Anne. *The Viceroy's Daughters: The Lives of the Curzon Sisters* (London, Phoenix, 2001).

De Wet, Christiaan Rudolf. *Three Years' War: October 1899-June 1902* (Westminster, Archibald Constable, 1902).

Dilks, David. *Curzon in India, Volume II: Frustration* (London, Rupert Hart-Davis, 1970).

Dinesen, Isak. *Letters from Africa, 1814–1931*, Trans. Anne Born. (Chicago, University of Chicago Press, 1981).

Doolittle, Duncan H. *A Soldier's Hero: The Life of General Sir Archibald Hunter* (Narragansett, RI, Anawan, 1991).

Doyle, Peter and Chris Foster. *What Tommy Took To War 1914–1918* (Oxford, Shire Publications, 2014).

Dutta, Krishna and Andrew Robinson. *Rabindranath Tagore: The Myriad-Minded Man* (London, Bloomsbury, 1995).

Eksteins, Modris. *Rites of Spring: The Great War and the Birth of the Modern World* (Toronto, Lester & Orpen Dennys, 1989).

Esher, Reginald Viscount. *The Tragedy of Lord Kitchener* (London, John Murray, 1921).

Faught, C. Brad. *The Oxford Movement: A Thematic History of the Tractarians and Their Times* (University Park, PA, Pennsylvania State University Press, 2003).
———. *Gordon: Victorian Hero* (Washington, DC, Potomac, 2008).
———. *The New A-Z of Empire: A Concise Handbook of British Imperial History* (London, I.B.Tauris, 2011).
———. *Clive: Founder of British India* (Washington, DC, Potomac, 2013).

Ferguson, Niall. *Empire: The Rise and Demise of the British World Order and the Lessons for Global Power* (New York, Basic Books, 2003).

Foch, Ferdinand. *The Memoirs of Marshal Foch*, Trans. T. Bentley Mott, (London, Heinemann, 1931).

Friedman, Norman. *British Cruisers of the Victorian Era* (Barnsley, Seaforth, 2012).

Fussell, Paul. *The Great War and Modern Memory* (Oxford, Oxford University Press, 1977).

Gilbert, Martin. *Winston S. Churchill, Volume III: The Challenge of War, 1914–1916* (Boston, Houghton Mifflin, 1971).

————. *Churchill: A Life* (London, Heinemann, 1991).

————. *First World War* (Toronto, Stoddart, 1994).

————. *A History of the Twentieth Century: Volume One, 1900–1933* (New York, William Morrow, 1997).

————. *Continue to Pester, Nag and Bite: Churchill's War Leadership* (Toronto, Vintage Canada, 2004).

Gilmour, David. *The Long Recessional: The Imperial Life of Rudyard Kipling* (London, Farrar, Straus & Giroux, 2002).

————. *Curzon* 3rd edn (London, John Murray, 2003).

Green, Dominic. *Three Empires on the Nile: The Victorian Jihad, 1869–1899* (Toronto, Free Press, 2007).

Haggard, Andrew. *Under Crescent and Star* (Edinburgh, William Blackwood, 1895).

Hake, A. Egmont, ed. *The Journals of Major-General C.G. Gordon, C.B. at Kartoum* (London, Kegan Paul, Trench, 1885).

Hart, Peter. *Gallipoli* (Oxford, Oxford University Press, 2011).

Headlam, Cecil, ed. *The Milner Papers, Volume II: South Africa, 1899–1905* (London, Cassell, 1933).

Heathorn, Stephen. *Haig and Kitchener in Twentieth-Century Britain: Remembrance, Representation and Appropriation* (Farnham, Ashgate, 2013).

Henty, G.A. *With Kitchener in the Soudan* (London, Blackie & Son, 1903).

Hibbert, Christopher. *The Great Mutiny: India 1857* (London, Penguin, 1980).

————, ed. *Queen Victoria in her Letters and Journals* (Markham, ON, Penguin, 1985).

Hobhouse, Emily. *The Brunt of War and Where it Fell* (London, Methuen, 1902).

Hobson, J.A. *The War in South Africa: Its Causes and Effects* (London, James Nisbet & Co., 1900).

————. *Imperialism: A Study* (London, Constable, 1902).

Holland, Robert and Diana Markides. *The British and the Hellenes: The Struggle for Mastery in the Eastern Mediterranean 1850–1960* (Oxford, Clarendon Press, 2006).

Holmes, Richard. *Sahib: The British Soldier in India* (London, HarperCollins, 2005).

————. *The Little Field Marshal: A Life of Sir John French* (London, Cassell, 2007).

Holt, P.M. *The Mahdist State in Sudan* (Oxford, Clarendon Press, 1958).

Hook, Gail Ruth. *Protectorate Cyprus: British Imperial Power Before World War I* (London, I.B.Tauris, 2013).

Howell, Georgina. *Daughter of the Desert: The Remarkable Life of Gertrude Bell* (London, Macmillan, 2006).

Hughes, Matthew. *Allenby and British Strategy in the Middle East, 1917–1919* (London, Frank Cass, 1999).

Hunter, Archie. *Kitchener's Sword Arm: The Life and Campaigns of General Sir Archibald Hunter* (Staplehurst, Spellmount, 1996).

————. *Power and Passion in Egypt: A Life of Sir Eldon Gorst* (London, I.B.Tauris, 2007).

Hyam, Ronald. *Empire and Sexuality: The British Experience* (Manchester, Manchester University Press, 1990).

James, Lawrence. *Raj: The Making and Unmaking of British India* (London, Little, Brown, 1997).

Jeal, Tim. *Baden-Powell* (London, Hutchinson, 1989).

Jenkins, Roy. *Asquith* (London, Collins, 1964).

————. *Gladstone* (London, Macmillan, 1995).

Johnson, Robert. *Spying for Empire: The Great Game in Central and South Asia* (London, Greenhill, 2006).

Joliffe, John, ed. *Raymond Asquith: Life and Letters* (London, Century, 1987).

Jonas, R.A. *The Battle of Adwa: African Victory in the Age of Empire* (Cambridge, MA, Belknap Press of Harvard University, 2011).

Jones, Spencer. *From Boer War to World War: Tactical Reform of the British Army, 1902–1914* (Norman, OK, University of Oklahoma Press, 2012).

Judd, Denis. *Empire: The British Imperial Experience from 1765 to the Present* (London, I.B.Tauris, 2012).

────── and Keith Surridge. *The Boer War* (London, Palgrave Macmillan, 2002).

Katz, Wendy R. *Rider Haggard and the Fiction of Empire* (Cambridge, Cambridge University Press, 1987).

Kee, Robert. *The Laurel and the Ivy: The Story of Charles Stewart Parnell and Irish Nationalism* (London, Penguin, 1994).

Kestell, J.D. and D.E. van Velden, *The Peace Negotiations Between Boer and Briton in South Africa* (London, Richard Clay, 1912).

Kipling, Rudyard. *Plain Tales from the Hills* (Calcutta, Thacker, Spink & Co., 1888).

Knight, Ian. *Zulu Rising: The Epic Story of Isandlwana and Rorke's Drift* (London, Pan Books, 2011).

Kruger, Rayne. *Goodbye Dolly Gray: The Story of the Boer War* (London, Pimlico, 1996).

Kubler-Ross, Elizabeth. *On Death and Dying* (New York, Simon & Schuster, 1969).

Lavin, Deborah. *From Empire to International Commonwealth: A Biography of Lionel Curtis* (Oxford, Oxford University Press, 1995).

Lawrence, T.E. *Seven Pillars of Wisdom* (London, Penguin, 2000).

Le Bas, Sir Hedley, ed. *The Lord Kitchener Memorial Book* (London, Hodder & Stoughton, 1917).

Lee, Harold. *Brothers in the Raj: The Lives of John and Henry Lawrence* (Oxford, Oxford University Press, 2002).

Levering, Lewis. *The Race to Fashoda: Colonialism and African Resistance* (New York, Weidenfeld & Nicolson, 1987).

Lloyd, Alan. *The Drums of Kumasi: The Story of the Ashanti Wars* (London, Longmans, 1964).

Lloyd George, David. *War Memoirs*, Vol. VI (London, I. Nicholson & Watson, 1933–6).

Louis, Wm. Roger. *Ends of British Imperialism* (London, I.B.Tauris, 2006).

Lownie, Andrew. *John Buchan: The Presbyterian Cavalier* (Toronto, McArthur & Co., 2004).

Lugard, Lord. *The Dual Mandate in British Tropical Africa* (London, Frank Cass, 1965).

MacKenzie, John M., ed. *Popular Imperialism and the Military 1850–1950* (Manchester, Manchester University Press, 1992).

MacLaren, Roy. *Canadians on the Nile* (Vancouver, University of British Columbia Press, 1978).

MacMillan, Margaret. *The War that Ended Peace: The Road to 1914* (London, Allen Lane, 2013).

Magnus, Sir Philip. *Kitchener: Portrait of an Imperialist* (London, John Murray, 1958).

Mansfield, Peter. *The British in Egypt* (London, Weidenfeld & Nicolson, 1971).

Marlowe, John. *Milner: Apostle of Empire* (London, Hamish Hamilton, 1976).

Martel, Gordon. *Imperial Diplomacy: Rosebery and the Failure of Foreign Policy* (Montreal & Kingston, McGill-Queen's University Press, 1986).

Matthew, H.C.G. *Gladstone 1809–1898* (Oxford, Clarendon Press, 1997).

Meredith, John, ed. *Omdurman Diaries 1898* (Barnsley, Pen & Sword, 1998).

Meredith, Martin. *Diamonds, Gold and War: The British, the Boers, and the Making of South Africa* (New York, Public Affairs, 2007).

Meintjes, Johannes. *General Louis Botha: A Biography* (London, Cassell, 1970).

Meyer, Karl E. and Shareen Blair Brysac. *Kingmakers: The Invention of the Modern Middle East* (New York, W.W. Norton, 2008).

Miller, Carman. *Painting the Map Red: Canada and the South African War, 1899–1902* (Montreal & Kingston, McGill-Queen's University Press, 1998).

Milner, Viscount Alfred. *England in Egypt* (New York, Howard Fertig, 1970).

Morgan, Tabitha. *Sweet and Bitter Island: A History of the British in Cyprus* (London, I.B.Tauris, 2010).

Morris, James. *Pax Britannica: The Climax of Empire* (Harmondsworth, Penguin, 1987).

Munroe, Elizabeth. *Britain's Moment in the Middle East, 1914–1971* 2nd edn (Baltimore, John Hopkins University Press, 1981).

Neilson, Keith. *Strategy and Supply: The Anglo-Russian Alliance, 1914–1917* (London, Allen & Unwin, 1984).

Nicoll, Fergus. *The Mahdi of Sudan and the Death of General Gordon* (Stroud, Sutton, 2005).

Nicolson, Nigel. *Mary Curzon* (New York, Harper & Row, 1977).

Niellands, Robin. *The Dervish Wars: Gordon and Kitchener in the Sudan 1880–1898* (London, John Murray, 1996).

Norton, Rictor. *The Myth of the Modern Homosexual: Queer History and the Search for Cultural Unity* (London, Cassell, 1997).

Oxford and Asquith, Earl of. *Memories and Reflections 1852–1927*, Vol. II (Boston, Little, Brown, 1928).

Owen, Roger. *Cotton and the Egyptian Economy, 1820–1914: A Study in Trade and Development* (Oxford, Clarendon Press, 1969).

———. *The Middle East in the World Economy, 1800–1914* (London, I.B.Tauris, 1993).

———. *Lord Cromer: Victorian Imperialist Edwardian Proconsul* (Oxford, Oxford University Press, 2004).

Paice, Edward. *Tip and Run: The Untold Tragedy of the Great War in Africa* (London, Phoenix, 2008).

Pakenham, Thomas. *The Scramble for Africa: White Man's Conquest of the Dark Continent from 1876 to 1912* (New York, Avon Books, 1991).

———. *The Boer War* (New York, Perennial, 2001).

Paxman, Jeremy. *Empire: What Ruling the World Did to the British* (London, Viking, 2011).

———. *Great Britain's Great War* (London, Viking, 2013).

Phillips, L. March. *With Rimington* (London, Edward Arnold, 1901).

Pinney, Thomas, ed. *The Letters of Rudyard Kipling*, Vol. I (London, Palgrave Macmillan, 1990).

———. *Rudyard Kipling, 'Something of Myself' and other Autobiographical Writings* (Cambridge, Cambridge University Press, 1990).

Pollock, John. *Kitchener: Architect of Victory, Artisan of Peace* (New York, Carroll & Graf, 2001).

Porter, Andrew, ed. *The Oxford History of the British Empire: The Nineteenth Century* (Oxford, Oxford University Press, 1999).

Pugh, Martin. *Lloyd George* (Abingdon, Routledge, 2013).

Pugh, Roy. *Wingate Pasha: The Life General Sir Francis Reginald Wingate 1861–1953* (Barnsley, Pen & Sword, 2011).

Quinault, Roland, Roger Swift, and Ruth Clayton Windscheffel, eds. *William Gladstone: New Studies and Perspectives* (Farnham, Ashgate, 2012).

Repington, Charles a Court. *Vestigia: Reminiscences of Peace and War* (Boston, Houghton Mifflin, 1919).

Reynolds, David. *The Long Shadow: The Legacies of the Great War in the Twentieth Century* (New York, W.W. Norton & Co, 2014).

Richards, David A.J. *The Rise of Gay Rights and the Fall of the British Empire: Liberal Resistance and the Bloomsbury Group* (Cambridge, Cambridge University Press, 2013).

Rickards, Maurice, ed. *Posters of the First World War* (London, Evelyne Adams & MacKay, 1968).

Roberts, Andrew. *Salisbury: Victorian Titan* (London, Phoenix, 2000).

Roberts, Field Marshal Lord. *Forty-One Years in India: From Subaltern to Commander-in-Chief* (London, Richard Bentley & Son, 1898).

Robertson, Sir William. *From Private to Field Marshal* (London, Constable, 1921).

Robinson, Ronald and John Gallagher with Alice Denny. *Africa and the Victorians: The Official Mind of Imperialism* 2nd edn (London, Macmillan, 1985).

Rogan, Eugene. *The Fall of the Ottomans: The Great War in the Middle East* (New York, Basic Books, 2015).

Rotberg, Robert I. *The Founder: Cecil Rhodes and the Pursuit of Power* (Oxford, Oxford University Press, 1988).

Royle, Trevor. *The Kitchener Enigma* (London, Michael Joseph, 1985).

Rye, J.B. and Horace G. Groser, eds. *Kitchener in His Own Words* (London, T. Fisher Unwin, 1917).

Sandes, E.W.C. *The Royal Engineers in Egypt & the Sudan* (Chatham, Institute of Royal Engineers, 1937).

Scudamore, Frank. *A Sheaf of Memories* (London, T. Fisher Unwin, 1925).

Seibold, Brigit S. *Emily Hobhouse and the Reports on the Concentration Camps during the Boer War, 1899–1902* (Stuttgart, Ibidem, 2011.)

Sengupta, Jayanta, ed. *Charles D'Oyly's Calcutta: Early Nineteenth Century* (Kolkata, Victoria Memorial Hall, 2014).

Siegel, Jennifer. *Endgame: Britain, Russia and the Final Struggle for Central Asia* (London, I.B.Tauris).

Simkins, Peter. *Kitchener's Army* (Manchester, Manchester University Press, 1988).

Smith-Dorrien, General Sir Horace. *Memories of Forty-Eight Years' Service* (London, John Murray, 1925).

Steel, F.A. and G. Gardiner. *The Complete Indian Housekeeper and Cook* (Oxford, Oxford University Press, 2011).

Storrs, Sir Ronald. *The Memoirs of Sir Ronald Storrs* (New York, G.P. Putnam's Sons, 1937).

———. *Orientations* (London, Nicholson & Watson, 1943).

Strachan, Hew. *The First World War: Volume I: To Arms* (Oxford, Oxford University Press, 2001).

———. *The First World War in Africa* (Oxford, Oxford University Press, 2004).

Taylor, James. *Your Country Needs You: The Secret History of the Propaganda Poster* (Glasgow, Saraband, 2013).

Thomas, Antony. *Rhodes: The Race for South Africa* (New York, St Martin's Press, 1997).

Thompson, Brian. *Imperial Vanities: The Adventures of the Baker Brothers and Gordon of Khartoum* (London, HarperCollins, 2002).

Thompson, Leonard M. *The Political Mythology of Apartheid* (New Haven, CT, Yale University Press, 1985).

Tignor, Robert L. *Modernization and British Colonial Rule in Egypt, 1882–1914* (Princeton, Princeton University Press, 1996).

Townsend, John. *Proconsul to the Middle East: Sir Percy Cox and the End of Empire* (London, I.B.Tauris, 2010).

Steevens, G.W. *Egypt in 1898* (Edinburgh, William Blackwood, 1898).

———. *With Kitchener to Khartoum* (Edinburgh, William Blackwood, 1898).

Tosh, John. *Manliness and Masculinities in Nineteenth-Century Britain* (Harlow, Pearson, 2005).

Trzebinski, Errol. *Silence Will Speak: A Study of the Life of Denys Finch Hatton and His Relationship with Karen Blixen* (Chicago, University of Chicago Press, 1985).

Verrier, Anthony. *Francis Younghusband and the Great Game* (London, Jonathan Cape, 1991).

Von Slatin, Rudolf. *Fire and Sword in the Sudan: A Personal Narrative of Fighting and Serving the Dervishes 1879–1895* (London, Edward Arnold, 1930).

Warner, Philip. *Kitchener: The Man Behind the Legend* (New York, Athenaeum, 1986).

Wetzel, David. *A Duel of Nations: Germany, France, and the Diplomacy of the War of 1870-1871* (Madison, WI, University of Wisconsin Press, 2012).

Wheeler, Harold F.B. *The Story of Lord Kitchener* (London, George G. Harrap & Co., 1916).

Wiest, Andrew A. *Haig: The Evolution of a Commander* (Washington, DC, Potomac).

Wilson, A.N. *The Victorians* (London, Hutchinson, 2002).

Wilson, Jeremy. *Lawrence of Arabia: The Authorized Biography of T.E. Lawrence* (New York, Atheneum, 1990).

Wingate, F.R. *Mahdiism and the Egyptian Sudan* (London, Macmillan, 1908).

Winks, Robin W., ed. *British Imperialism* (New York, Holt, Rinehart & Winston, 1967).

Witheridge, John. *Excellent Dr Stanley: The Life of Dean Stanley of Westminster* (Norwich, Michael Russell, 2013).

Witton, George. *Scapegoats of the Empire: The True Story of Breaker Morant's Bushveldt Carbineers*, new edn (Sydney, Angus & Robertson, 1982).

Wolpert, Stanley. *Morley and India* (Berkeley, University of California Press, 1967).

Woodward, David R. *Field Marshal Sir William Robertson* (Westport, CT, Praeger, 1998).

Woolmore, William. *The Bushveldt Carbineers and the Pietersburg Light Horse* (Sydney, Slouch Hat Publications, 2002).

Wright, Patricia. *Conflict on the Nile: The Fashoda Incident of 1898* (London, Heinemann, 1972).

Ziegler, Philip. *Omdurman* (London, Collins, 1973).

Zuckerman, Larry. *The Rape of Belgium: The Untold Story of World War I* (New York, New York University Press, 2004).

Secondary Sources (Journal and Periodical Articles/Chapters in Books)

Adams, Jad. 'Was K Gay?' *History Today*, Vol. 49, Issue 11 (November 1999).

Bagehot, Walter. 'Mr. Gladstone', *National Review* (July 1860).

Bardgett, Suzanne. 'A Mutual Fascination: Indians in Brighton', *History Today*, Vol. 65, Issue 3 (March 2015).

Bennett, Ernest. 'After Omdurman', *Contemporary Review*, No. 75 (January 1899), pp. 18–33.

Cohen, Stephen P. 'Issue, Role, and Personality: The Kitchener-Curzon Dispute', *Comparative Studies in Society and History*, Vol. 10, Issue 03, (April 1968), pp. 337–55.

de Villiers, J.C. 'The Medical Aspect of the Anglo-Boer War, Part II', *Military History Journal*, Vol. 6, No. 3 (June 1984), pp. 74–93.

Faught, C. Brad. '"The Uganda Business": Gladstone and Africa Revisited', Peter Francis, ed. *The Gladstone Umbrella* (Hawarden, St Deiniol's Library, 2001), pp. 156–74.

_____. 'An Imperial Prime Minister? W.E. Gladstone and India, 1880-1885', *The Journal of the Historical Society*, VI:4 (December 2006), pp. 555–78.

Gallagher, John and Ronald Robinson, 'The Imperialism of Free Trade', *Economic History Review*, Vol. VI, No. 1 (1953), pp. 1–15.

Green, Adam, 'Gay But Not Queer: Toward a Post-Queer Study of Sexuality', *Theory and Society* (August 2002), Vol. 31(4), pp. 521–45.

Jones, Max. 'What Should Historians Do With Heroes? Reflections on Nineteenth- and Twentieth-Century Britain', *History Compass* 5/2 (2007), pp. 439–54.

Kirk-Greene, A.H.M. 'Canada in Africa: Sir Percy Girouard, Neglected Colonial Governor', *African Affairs*, Vol. 83, No. 331 (April 1984), pp. 207–39.

———. 'The Sudan Political Service: A Preliminary Profile', (Oxford, Parchment, 1982).

Offer, Avner, 'Costs and Benefits, Prosperity, and Security, 1870–1914', Andrew Porter, ed. *The Oxford History of the British Empire: The Nineteenth Century* (Oxford, Oxford University Press, 1999), pp. 690–711.

Neilson, Keith. 'Kitchener: A Reputation Refurbished', *Canadian Journal of History*, Vol. 15, Issue 2 (August 1980), pp. 207–27.

Royal Naval Museum Library, 'The Loss of HMS *Hampshire*' (2000).

Surridge, Keith. 'More than a Great Poster: Lord Kitchener and the Image of the Military Hero', *Historical Research*, Vol. 74, No. 185 (August 2001), pp. 298–313.

Tyrell, A.C.M. 'Melrose House', *Military History Journal* [South Africa], Vol. 1, No. 2 (June 1968), pp. 1–4.

Quinault, Roland. 'Asquith: A Prime Minister at War', *History Today*, Vol. 64, Issue 5 (May 2014).

Weber, Mark. 'The Boer War Remembered', *The Journal of Historical Review*, Vol. 18, No. 3 (May-June 1999), pp. 14–27.

Reference

Australian Dictionary of Biography
Oxford Dictionary of National Biography
Parliamentary Debates
The Yale Book of Quotations

Novels

Stenson, Fred. *The Great Karoo* (Toronto, Doubleday Canada, 2008).

Newspapers

The Argus (Melbourne)
Daily Mail (London)
The Daily Telegraph (London)
Diamond Fields Advertiser (Kimberley)
Globe (London)
The Globe (Toronto)
Hawera & Normanby Star (New Zealand)
New York Times
Pall Mall Gazette (London)
The Times (London)

Feature Films, Television Serials, and Documentaries

ANZAC Girls (2014)
Breaker Morant (1980)
Empire (BBC 1, 2012)
Gallipoli (1981)
Khartoum (1966)
Reputations: Kitchener: The Empire's Flawed Hero (BBC 2, 1998)

Index